Integrating Young Children with Disabilities into Community Programs

W9-BEP-362

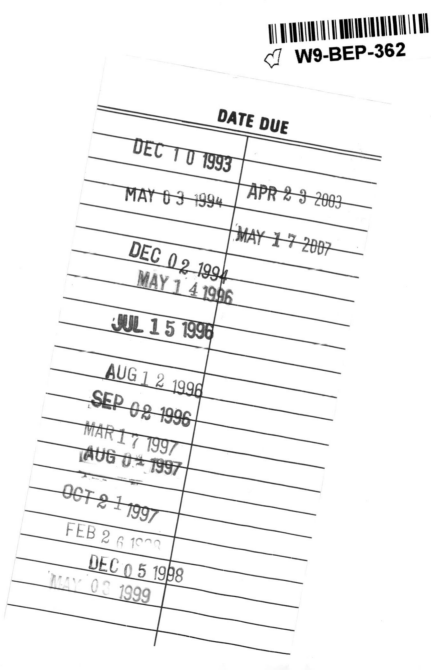

INTEGRATING YOUNG CHILDREN WITH DISABILITIES INTO COMMUNITY PROGRAMS

Ecological Perspectives on Research and Implementation

edited by

Charles A. Peck, Ph.D.

Washington State University–Vancouver
Vancouver, Washington

Samuel L. Odom, Ph.D.

Vanderbilt University
Nashville, Tennessee

and

Diane D. Bricker, Ph.D.

University of Oregon
Eugene, Oregon

·P A U L·H·
BROOKES
PUBLISHING C°

Baltimore • London • Toronto • Sydney

Paul H. Brookes Publishing Co.
P.O. Box 10624
Baltimore, Maryland 21285-0624

Typeset by Brushwood Graphics, Inc., Baltimore, Maryland.
Manufactured in the United States of America by
The Maple Press Company, York, Pennsylvania.

Library of Congress Cataloging-in-Publication Data
Integrating young children with disabilities into community programs :
   ecological perspectives on research and implementation / edited by
   Charles A. Peck, Samuel L. Odom, Diane D. Bricker.
      p.   cm.
   Includes bibliographical references and index.
   ISBN 1-55766-108-1
   1. Handicapped children—Education—United States.   2. Early childhood education—
United States.   3. Mainstreaming in education—United States.   4. Education and state—
United States.   I. Peck, Charles A.   II. Odom, Samuel L.   III. Bricker, Diane D.
[DNLM: 1. Child, Exceptional—education—United States.   2. Mainstreaming (Education).
3. Public Policy—United States.   LC 4031 I605]
LC4031I575   1993
371.9'046—dc 20
DNLM/DLC
for Library of Congress   92-17404
                                                                                 CIP

British Library Cataloguing-in-Publication data are available from the British Library.

CONTENTS

CONTRIBUTORS

Diane D. Bricker, Ph.D.
Center on Human Development
University of Oregon
901 East 18th Street
Eugene, Oregon 97403-1211

William H. Brown, Ph.D.
John F. Kennedy Center for Research on
   Education and Human Development
Box 40, Peabody College
Vanderbilt University
Nashville, Tennessee 37203

Kevin Cole, Ph.D.
Experimental Education Unit
Child Development and Mental Retardation
   Center, WJ-10
University of Washington
Seattle, Washington 98195

Nancy File, Ph.D.
Department of Family Studies
University of New Hampshire
Durham, New Hampshire 03824

Lucy A. Fleming, Ed.D.
Early Childhood Intervention Program
Allegheny-Singer Research Institute
320 East North Avenue
Pittsburgh, Pennsylvania 15212

Gail Chase Furman, Ph.D.
Department of Educational Administration
   and Supervision
Washington State University Tri-Cities
100 Sprout Road
Richland, Washington 99352

Michael J. Guralnick, Ph.D.
University of Washington
Child Development and Mental Retardation
   Center, WJ-10
Seattle, Washington 98195

Mary Frances Hanline, Ph.D.
Department of Special Education
Florida State University
Tallahassee, Florida 32306

Marci J. Hanson, Ph.D.
Early Childhood Special Education
San Francisco State University
4 Tapia Drive
San Francisco, California 94132

Edwin Helmstetter, Ph.D.
Department of Counseling Psychology
Washington State University
Pullman, Washington 99164-2131

Susan Kontos, Ph.D.
Department of Child Development and Family
   Studies
Purdue University
West Lafayette, Indiana 47907

Suzanne Lamorey, Ph.D.
Department of Special Education
University of Missouri
Columbus, Missouri 65211

Angela Notari, Ph.D.
Experimental Education Unit
Child Development and Mental Retardation
   Center, WJ-10
University of Washington
Seattle, Washington 98195

Samuel L. Odom, Ph.D.
Department of Special Education
Box 328, Peabody College
Vanderbilt University
Nashville, Tennessee 37203

Charles A. Peck, Ph.D.
Department of Special Education
Washington State University–Vancouver
1812 East McLoughlin Boulevard
Vancouver, Washington 98663

Sherrill Richarz, Ed.D.
Child, Consumer, and Family Studies
Washington State University
Pullman, Washington 99164

Barbara J. Smith, Ph.D.
Early Childhood Intervention Program
Allegheny-Singer Research Institute
320 East North Avenue
Pittsburgh, Pennsylvania 15212

Zolinda Stoneman, Ph.D.
Georgia University Affiliated Program for
    Persons with Developmental Disabilities
University of Georgia
Athens, Georgia 30602

Phillip S. Strain, Ph.D.
Early Childhood Intervention Program
Allegheny-Singer Research Institute
320 East North Avenue
Pittsburgh, Pennsylvania 15212

Anne H. Widerstrom, Ph.D.
Early Childhood Special Education
San Francisco State University
4 Tapia Drive
San Francisco, California 94132

Pamela J. Winton, Ph.D.
Frank Porter Graham Child Development
    Center
C.B. 8180
University of North Carolina
Chapel Hill, North Carolina 27599

Mark Wolery, Ph.D.
Early Childhood Intervention Program
Allegheny-Singer Research Institute
320 East North Avenue
Pittsburgh, Pennsylvania 15212

FOREWORD

The integration of young children with disabilities and nondisabled children in the same educational setting has emerged as one of the most important, complex, and controversial practices in the field of early childhood education. In part, this state of affairs is a result of the fact that the process of integration affects and is affected by so many factors at so many different levels. The developmental growth and educational achievements of children, the satisfaction of families, the degree of concordance with legislative intent, the classroom management and educational practices of teachers, and the organizational control of programs by administrators are only a few of the factors that are involved. The fact that these factors are embedded within a value system that strongly encourages integration into community life for all children with disabilities poses an additional challenge in a thoughtful analysis of the concept and practice of integration at the early childhood level.

This book is important for many reasons. It comes at a time in our history during which major changes in preschool education are taking place. Recent legislation (PL 99-457/102-119) requires that educational systems provide comprehensive and individualized services to all preschool-age children with disabilities. As a result, the least restrictive environment provisions of PL 94-142 (now known as IDEA) must now be applied to young children as well as to those of school age. By summarizing the state of our knowledge in the field of early childhood integration and making specific recommendations for practice based on that information, this book performs an important service for community programs. In essence, educational systems and communities will now be in a better position to make sensible decisions and to design more effective programs that integrate children with and without disabilities.

But most importantly, this book represents a recognition of the many factors that interact with one another when integration is being considered. In fact, the editors have had the vision to structure the book around these mutually interacting groups of issues. In this way, the reader gains an understanding of the complexities involved, as well as a sense of how the various elements fit together. From this perspective, we see immediately that the willingness of educational systems to accept the fundamental principle that all children and their families belong in the educational mainstream creates challenges to curriculum design and implementation, to teaching practices, to belief systems, and to powerful, historically rooted forces intended to both protect and separate those children whose patterns of development do not conform to some pre-established criteria. As chronicled in this book, the response of the field to these challenges in the past 15 years has been quite remarkable. A large number of demonstration programs and research projects, employing different developmental and educational models and offered to children with disabilities of varying severity and type, have revealed that integration is unequivocally a feasible process. Furthermore, these efforts have revealed that integration into high-quality programs has many potential benefits for children with disabilities, and that refinements of curricula or other adjustments throughout all levels of the educational and community system can minimize problems.

This book also constitutes a milestone in our thinking about integration at the early child-hood level. As the chapters reveal, less of our energy is currently devoted to defending or justifying this practice. Rather, efforts are focused on moving ahead to create innovative curricula, to develop new models for providing staff and services, and to discover techniques that best foster organizational and administrative changes. As a consequence of the work of so many people in the field over the years, we now have confidence that even within the context of different approaches to integration, the general practice is consistent with a philosophy that encourages maximum integration. Moreover, we are equally confident that integration is compatible with current theories and practices in child development, and that it makes sense from an educational perspective. This book takes an important step in ensuring that integration as best practice will become standard practice.

Michael J. Guralnick, Ph.D.
Child Development and
Mental Retardation Center
University of Washington

ACKNOWLEDGMENTS

During the development of this book, two of us (Peck and Odom) enjoyed the support of post-doctoral fellowships in the Special Education Program at University of California, Santa Barbara. We would like to express our appreciation to Melvyn I. Semmel for his support of our work while we were at UCSB, and for the many insights we have gained through lively argument and discussion with him.

Our deepest appreciation is extended, as always, to the children, parents, and professionals who have taught us so much about the values and challenges involved in building effective integrated programs for young children with and without disabilities.

This too, for Robert

Integrating Young Children with Disabilities into Community Programs

SECTION I

BUILDING POSITIVE INTERACTIONS AND RELATIONSHIPS AMONG CHILDREN, TEACHERS, AND FAMILIES

The adaptation and development of children in integrated settings is influenced most directly by the nature and extent of the social and communicative interactions taking place in those settings on a daily basis. Recognizing this, researchers have generated a substantial body of work over the last decade that identifies some important characteristics of integrated social environments. While it is clear that there are a number of potentially important benefits of integration for young children and their families, it is equally clear that these benefits do not always occur without planned intervention. In this section, Notari and Cole (Chapter 2) and Odom and Brown (Chapter 3) summarize research that describes a range of interventions for ensuring that integrated early childhood settings do give rise to beneficial social and communicative interactions. In addition, Winton (Chapter 4) takes up the problem of ensuring that families have opportunities for full participation in integrated programs, and describes strategies for implementing family-focused services within an array of integrated community-based programs.

Chapter 1

ECOLOGICAL PERSPECTIVES ON THE IMPLEMENTATION OF INTEGRATED EARLY CHILDHOOD PROGRAMS

Charles A. Peck

The movement to integrate children with disabilities into "mainstream" community programs may be one of the most profound challenges to traditional assumptions about the appropriate organization and function of special education and early intervention in many decades. The substance of this challenge is the implicit recognition that the segregation of a child with disabilities is in itself a powerful social act that may negatively affect the child's social and educational future. Policies and practices related to attempts to desegregate children with disabilities have consequently been the focus of intense interest, research, and advocacy (Sarason & Doris, 1979; Skrtic, 1991). The broad purpose of this volume is to summarize the substantial gains in knowledge derived from extensive research and demonstration work completed during the 1980s on the integration of young children with disabilities into programs serving nondisabled children. The work in this volume is intended to provide a platform for moving forward in implementing integrated community-based programs.

The narrower purpose of this chapter is to argue for the value of approaching the implementation of integrated programs from an *ecological* perspective (Bronfenbrenner, 1979; Gaylord-Ross & Peck, 1985; Guralnick, 1982). This approach assumes that effective implementation of change can best be achieved by considering the social ecology within which policy and practice are necessarily embedded. My arguments begin with a critical appraisal of the notion of "implementation" as it has been used in traditional discussions of the relationship between policy and practice. A more dynamic and multilevel considera-

Appreciation is expressed to Diane D. Bricker and Sam Odom for their useful comments on early drafts of this chapter.

tion of these issues is then outlined, drawing on Bronfenbrenner's (1979) ecological theory of human development. Bronfenbrenner's framework is used to clarify a number of contextual issues surrounding integration, and it also suggests some strategies for approaching the problems of implementation. The chapter concludes with a reconsideration of some traditional relationships between research and practice, and between researcher and practitioner. Changes in these relationships are suggested as necessary steps toward building stronger linkages between research and implementation.

POLICY ABOVE, IMPLEMENTATION BELOW?: RECONSIDERING THE CONCEPT OF IMPLEMENTATION FROM THE "STREET LEVEL"

Traditional views of the implementation of policy have reflected what has been termed a "rational-technical" or mechanistic notion of the relationship between policy and practice (Berman & McLaughlin, 1978; Weatherley, 1979; Weick, 1976). A central assumption of this approach to implementation is that knowledge and influence flow unidirectionally from policy generating sectors of a bureaucracy to policy implementing sectors. This perspective is reflected in the language of federal policy enactments in which the implementation process is defined operationally in terms of promulgation of federal regulations and requirements for compliance monitoring (e.g., PL 94-142 and PL 99-457). Similar notions about the implementation of changes in practice are implicit in the structures of many training and dissemination efforts in university research and demonstration projects.

In the traditional mechanistic view,

knowledge and technology are developed in response to problems identified in the field. Products of research and development efforts are then offered to the field for implementation as solutions to the identified problems. The process of implementation is thus implicitly theorized to be distinct from that of knowledge development, and consists primarily of: 1) transferring effective technological solutions to the field (typically through training), and 2) creating motivational conditions sufficiently powerful to ensure adoption (typically through regulation and monitoring).

This approach to implementing innovations in policy and practice has clearly changed some aspects of special education service delivery in important and useful ways. However, there is considerable evidence that, in many cases, changes have been perfunctory, superficial, or even counterproductive to the ostensible goals of policymakers (Fulcher, 1989; Mehan, Hertweck, & Meihls, 1986; Smith, 1982; Weatherley, 1979). Moreover, with regard specifically to the least restrictive environment (LRE) provisions of federal legislation, the extent of even the most rudimentary aspects of policy implementation is in question. For example, two recent multistate surveys suggest that children with significant disabilities continue to be served primarily in separate classes or segregated schools more than 15 years after the passage of LRE legislation (Danielson & Bellamy, 1989; Haring et al., in press). Similar data for preschool-age children are not yet available, but Lamorey and Bricker (chap. 12, this volume) estimate that as few as 30% of preschool-age children with disabilities attend programs with their nondisabled peers.

Whether process-oriented descriptions of what happens in local programs (e.g.,

Mehan et al., 1986; Weatherley, 1979), or more global data on the prevalence of integrated programs (e.g., Danielson & Bellamy, 1989) are used, the available evidence suggests that the success of traditional "top-down," mechanistic, and regulatory approaches to implementing change has been limited in many areas.

Concerns about the adequacy of traditional "top-down" approaches to policy implementation are not unique to special education. Similar concerns have emerged from large-scale efforts to change school policy and practice (Berman & McLaughlin, 1978; Huberman & Miles, 1984). The limited achievements of such efforts have led to broader investigations of the policy development and implementation process. An important feature of more recent work has been its analysis of the implementation process from the perspective of individuals involved at the "street level" (e.g., Ballard-Campbell & Semmel, 1981; Cohen & Ball, 1990; Peterson, 1990; Weatherley & Lipsky, 1977). Current views of the implementation process emphasize the active role of individuals traditionally considered relatively powerless (e.g., teachers, local administrators) in determining when and how changes in policy and practice will be implemented. Rather than being viewed simply as passive recipients of policy initiatives imposed by outside authorities, individuals involved in implementation at the local level are presently recognized as being actively engaged in shaping policy-as-implemented in a fashion that is responsive to local constraints, needs, and interests.

Change initiatives, such as those promoted by government agencies and university research and demonstration efforts, thus intrude upon active local contexts rich with belief systems, political interests, and practices that have devel-oped over time. Viewed from this perspective, local responses that were once seen as "resistance to change" or "noncompliance" must be reinterpreted to illuminate the *sense* of such responses as adaptations to the local situation. Nonimplementation is thus viewed not simply as a lack of knowledge or motivation to change, but as the active expression of competing interests, values, and knowledge (Peterson, 1990). Consistent with this view, Fulcher (1989) has described policymaking as an ongoing struggle for control over social conditions that is enacted at all decision levels, ranging from central government agencies and legislatures to local schools. The clear implication of this perspective on the policy implementation process is that the sources of practice (i.e., what actually happens to children and families) can only be fully understood by studying the multiple contexts in which decisions about practice are negotiated.

This ecological perspective on the implementation process carries implications for interpreting existing research data on integrated programs. As Guralnick (1982, 1990) has noted, the focus of this research to date has been primarily on the questions of whether integrated programs are feasible and effective. These have been important research goals, and considerable progress has been made in addressing them in the context of research and model demonstration efforts. There have been, however, relatively few questions about how communities may move from model demonstrations to more widespread implementation of integrated programs (Peck, Richarz, et al., 1989; Salisbury, 1991). Addressing these questions will require more careful analysis of the social ecologies of which integrated programs are a part.

This is clearly a most difficult and complex task. However, Bronfenbrenner (1979) has developed a rich and comprehensive framework for considering contextual or ecological factors that affect human development. The work of Guralnick (1982) illustrates the value of this framework for elucidating factors affecting early childhood mainstreaming programs. The following discussion outlines the assumptions of the Bronfenbrenner model, and uses the model to generate questions relevant to the implementation of early childhood mainstreaming programs.

AN ECOLOGICAL FRAMEWORK FOR CONSIDERING THE IMPLEMENTATION OF INTEGRATED PROGRAMS

Several central assumptions of Bronfenbrenner's (1979) conceptualization of the "ecology of human development" are of immediate help in clarifying issues surrounding the implementation of integrated programs. First, Bronfenbrenner characterizes the relationships between individuals and their environments as *transactional*. A transactional perspective highlights the reciprocal and co-evolutionary qualities of change occurring in both individuals and their environments over time (Peck, 1989). This assumption suggests that we should look carefully at both the effects of the integrated environment on the child, and how the inclusion of children with disabilities affects the environment itself, including possible changes in instructional practices, teacher behavior, and social relationships among children (Guralnick, 1981, 1990). Concerns about how integration may affect the programmatic environment have often focused on the possibility of negative impacts such as reduction in teacher attention to non-disabled children or deceleration of curriculum coverage (Peck, Hayden, Wand-

schneider, Peterson, & Richarz, 1989). However, recent studies conducted with preschool-age children (Peck, Carlson, & Helmstetter, 1992) and older children (e.g., Biklen, Corrigan, & Quick, 1989; Murray-Seegert, 1989) suggest that including children with disabilities may actually affect mainstream programs positively. Unfortunately, we have only limited empirical knowledge at present about the nature and prevalence of specific child, teacher, and program characteristics that may mediate the programmatic impact of integration.

Another implication of the transactional feature of Bronfenbrenner's model is that the social processes and outcomes of integrated programs are likely to change over time, as both individuals and systems develop. While there have been some descriptions of changes in social exchanges between children (e.g., Sinson & Wetherick, 1981) and between adults (e.g., Peck, Hayden, et al., 1989) in integrated programs over time, there has been little analysis of the significance of these changes as developmental processes themselves. For example, it is reasonable to expect that relationships between both children and adults in integrated programs may evolve over time in either positive or negative directions. We know little about such changes at present, and even less about their long-term effects on program implementation and maintenance.

A second basic assumption that Bronfenbrenner makes is that properties of the environment *as it is experienced by the individual* affect development. This emphasis on a phenomenological definition of the environment clarifies the importance of understanding how individuals interpret situations, events, and relationships in integrated settings. For example, some evidence suggests that parents of children with disabilities may experience their involvement in integrated programs in different ways, which in turn exacerbate or reduce their feelings of alienation and isolation from other families (Winton, 1986). Other research suggests that efforts to develop integrated programs may be perceived by some parents and professionals as threats to the lines of control they have negotiated in their local communities (Peck, Hayden, et al., 1989). Although the properties of integration-as-experienced by preschool-age children are difficult to ascertain, evidence from studies of older children suggests that some integration experiences may be interpreted by children in ways that are remarkably discrepant from adult interpretations. For example, Schnorr (1990) described the perceptions of elementary-age children who had experienced the part-time integration of a child with moderate mental retardation into their class. While the adults involved in the integration process viewed the process as being largely successful, the children interpreted many of the adult practices as indicating that the child was not really "one of the class." A more accurate knowledge of integration-as-experienced by these nondisabled children might have led the adults to undertake the integration process differently.

Perhaps the most salient feature of the Bronfenbrenner model lies in its assumption that ecological variables affecting human development operate at multiple levels. A range of ecological variables is identified, from those directly affecting the individual in daily interactions to those that operate more indirectly through the functions of social institutions, and through cultural values and beliefs. Bronfenbrenner proposes four specific levels of ecological analysis: the microsystem, meso-system, exosystem, and macrosystem.

These are conceptualized as being nested within each other like Russian dolls, and influences across levels are assumed to operate transactionally. Figure 1 represents the conceptual structure of the Bronfenbrenner model.

This framework is useful in identifying sources of environmental influence on development, and in understanding relationships between influences that operate at various levels. Bronfenbrenner's (1979) work reviews evidence of the developmental impact of factors at the four levels of ecological analysis. The following are brief definitions and descriptions of each of these levels. Each level of analysis is considered in terms of its implications for understanding issues surrounding the implementation of integrated early childhood programs. I begin with the broadest levels of analysis, since these are most foreign to our contemporary considerations of mainstreaming issues.

Macrosystem Influences

Bronfenbrenner (1979) defines the macrosystem as "consistencies in the form and content of lower-order systems (micro-, meso-, exo-) that exist, or could exist at the level of the subculture or the culture as a whole, along with any belief systems or ideology underlying such consistencies" (p. 26). The macrosystem perspective suggests that cultural values and ideology shape human relationships at every level of social organization, from social institutions such as the schools to social exchanges taking place between children and caregivers. With respect to integration issues, this level of analysis is useful in identifying some of the cultural beliefs and values that underlie organizational structures, professional practices, and daily interactions that affect the lives of children with disabilities. For example,

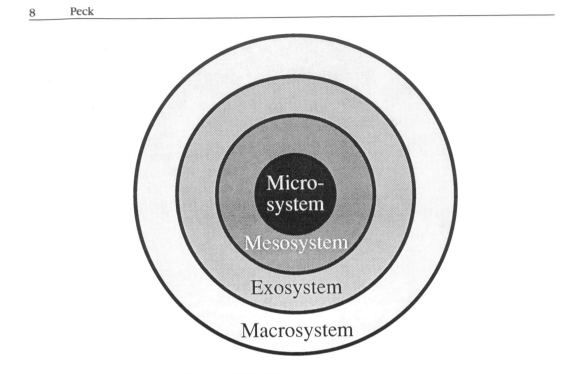

Figure 1. Bronfenbrenner's four levels of ecological analysis.

Peck, Furman, Helmstetter, and Reed (in preparation) interviewed special education teachers who explained a number of their professional practices, with both colleagues and children, in terms of several fundamental beliefs, assumptions, and values. Together, these comprised an ideology in which children were seen as having troubles primarily because they were deficient in specific skills. Child "deficits" were viewed as requiring direct and intensive remediation efforts, without which the children could not be expected to succeed. This ideology led special education teachers to reduce play interactions between children in their programs in favor of teacher-directed instruction (Mahoney, O'Sullivan, & Fors, 1989). In some cases special education teachers insisted that curricular priorities for children with disabilities should take priority over those for other children, since those children would "be all right, anyhow." While the prevalence of this view is unknown, this example illustrates the potential impact ideological perspectives may have on the development of integrated programs.

Bronfenbrenner (1979) is explicit in stating that macrosystem variables should not be viewed as immutable, but should be considered as targets for change. Indeed, research that assists us in understanding and changing basic social values and beliefs may be one of the most powerful avenues for moving forward with the development of integrated programs. Recent increases in the number of positive images of people with disabilities appearing in the popular media may also contribute to changes at the macrosystem level. In other cases, changes in macrosystem variables may be generated by changes occurring in lower-order systems, including those based on individual learning, as well as changes in social organizations resulting from experiences with integration.

Exosystem Influences

An exosystem is defined as "one or more settings that do not involve the developing person as an active participant, but in which events occur that affect, or are affected by, what happens in the setting containing the developing person" (Bronfenbrenner, 1979, p. 25). Examples affecting integration include legislative settings, school board meetings, and individualized education program/individualized family service plan (IEP/IFSP) meetings. Events occurring in these settings are strongly influenced by macrosystem variables, and directly affect events taking place in the child's daily life. For example, an exosystem variable of obvious relevance to the present discussion is the organization of the school agency. Traditional beliefs and values concerning differences among children are reflected in the creation of separate structures (sometimes physical, always organizational) for serving children with and without disabilities. These organizational structures dramatically affect the nature and extent of contact between children with disabilities and their non-disabled peers.

Occasionally, changes in macrosystem variables may lead to changes in exosystems, and of course, in lower-order systems as well. For example, Salisbury (1991) described changes in school district organizational structure (where children with disabilities were served) and process (who assumed primary responsibility for the education of these students), which re-sulted from reconsideration and clarification of core social values and beliefs about children and schooling.

Unfortunately, there have been few examinations of variables at the exosystem level that may affect the implementation of integrated programs (Guralnick, 1990; Peck, Richarz, et al., 1989). This is particularly disturbing given the fundamental importance of decisions made in these organizational contexts.

Mesosystem Influences

A mesosystem consists of "the interrelations of two or more settings in which the developing person actively participates (such as, for a child, the relations between home, school and neighborhood peer groups; for an adult, among family, work, and social life)" (Bronfenbrenner, 1979, p. 25). Influences at this level that are particularly relevant to integration include the nature and extent of relationships among children with disabilities and their peer groups, relationships among parents and teachers, and relationships among families. Each of these constitute supportive links across settings that affect the development of the child.

Bronfenbrenner's focus on the strength of social relationships across settings raises important questions about the extent to which participation in local programs with neighborhood peers, as opposed to centralized "special" programs, may contribute to the child's development and subsequent success in the community. Other important issues for research and intervention include the extent to which professionals in mainstream programs actively mediate the experiences of children and families in a fashion that creates supportive links between settings, and thus contributes to positive outcomes (see Winton, chap. 4, this volume). The quality of relationships among professionals is also identified as an important mesosystem variable, particularly as these relationships may affect transitions from one setting to another (see Hanline, chap. 7, this volume).

Research on mesosystem variables affecting the implementation of integrated programs has been more extensive than work at either the exo- or macrosystem levels. In particular, empirical evidence supports many of Bronfenbrenner's hypotheses regarding the contribution of mesosystem factors to the quality of the child's (and family's) experiences in integrated settings (see Hanline, chap. 7, and Hanson & Widerstrom, chap. 8, this volume). However, while it is relatively clear that relationships among peers, families, and professionals are extremely important, it is much less clear how they can be changed. The implementation of integrated programs will be aided considerably by intervention-oriented research that yields viable and effective strategies for improving the quality of relationships among people in the many settings in which the child participates.

Microsystem Influences

Bronfenbrenner defines a microsystem as "a pattern of activities, roles, and interpersonal relations experienced by the developing person in a given setting with particular physical and material characteristics" (1979, p. 22). The predominance of research on integrated early childhood programs has been focused on this level. In particular, there is now a relative wealth of research describing social interactions among children with disabilities and their nondisabled peers in integrated settings (see reviews by Guralnick, 1990; Odom &

McEvoy, 1988; Odom & Brown, chap. 3, this volume), as well as a growing research base on teacher–child interactions and activity patterns in preschool settings (Carta, Sainato, & Greenwood, 1988). Intervention-oriented research at the microsystem level has yielded valuable technical knowledge regarding curriculum strategies (Bricker & Woods Cripe, 1992; Odom et al., 1988; Wolery & Fleming, chap. 6, this volume) and social skills training strategies (Odom & Brown, chap. 3, this volume) for integrated settings.

A limitation of many studies conducted at the microsystem level is the relative inattention of researchers to potentially important interactions among microsystem variables and ecological variables operating within higher-order systems (e.g., exo- and macrosystem factors). These interactions between levels are of particular relevance to the problem of implementation, because ecological contexts are likely to vary in ways that strongly influence outcomes of interventions focused on aspects of the microsystem, such as social exchanges among children.

For example, some years ago several colleagues and I reported the results of an experimental evaluation of a peer imitation training strategy used in two integrated preschool settings (Peck, Apolloni, Cooke, & Raver, 1978). Our report described the general settings for the study, experimental conditions during all phases of the investigation, and procedures for direct and detailed measurement of independent and dependent variables. In short, we reported on all aspects of the (microsystem) context that appeared to us to be relevant to replication of the study.

However, Bronfenbrenner's ecological model suggests several meso-, exo- and macrosystem factors affecting implementation of this experimental intervention that we overlooked in our analysis and report. For example, our intervention required direct, active, and consistent involvement by an adult over the course of several weeks. We were able to maintain that level of intervention in part because we had high levels of administrative control over the setting (an exosystem variable), since both preschools operated as "laboratory" schools affiliated with institutions of higher education, and were thus under minimal school district supervision. Moreover, the intervention was implemented by two adults who had close social relationships, outside of the setting of the study, with members of the larger research team (a mesosystem variable).

In addition to the time-intensive nature of the intervention, the experimental procedures entailed routine intrusion on the children's play during the relatively short freeplay time they had each morning. This procedure was implemented without question from parents or teachers, in part because of the strong ideological emphasis in these preschool settings on the need for direct and intensive intervention as a means of remediating deficiencies in child behavior (a macrosystem variable).

The types of questions regarding external validity that arise from considering this study in terms of its meso-, exo-, and macrosystem contexts are relevant to evaluating much of the microsystem level research that has been conducted to date. More direct consideration of these types of contextual variables will likely improve the interpretability of research with respect to its significance for integrated programs in community settings. Additional strategies for improving the contributions of research to addressing problems of implementation are suggested below.

ADVANCING IMPLEMENTATION-ORIENTED RESEARCH

Ecological perspectives on integration suggest some research strategies that may improve our understanding of the substantive problems of implementing these programs.

First, a more holistic approach to the study of integrated programs would be useful. Holistic description and analysis is fundamental to understanding the problems of implementation, since these problems always come as a package. Thus, an *essential* quality of the situation faced by professionals, administrators, and parents involved with implementation is that multiple problems and dilemmas simultaneously demand attention and resolution. Investigations that take up a single dimension of integration, such as peer relations, effects on the family, or political negotiation of local policy, certainly have value, but these studies will inevitably fail to address the problems of implementation adequately.

Second, research that describes integration-as-experienced by the individuals involved would contribute to our understanding of the problems of implementation. The work of Winton (1986) and her colleagues on family responses to mainstreaming programs is a useful example of the kinds of information needed. In addition, studies that describe the experiences of teachers, administrators, and other early intervention professionals involved in integrated programs will be of great value in clarifying the challenges these individuals face in implementing integrated programs. This type of research entails a more phenomenological orientation in understanding the integration process than has been typical of most studies to date.

Third, detailed field studies of the implementation process itself are needed. Longitudinal, follow-along descriptions of programs as they are developed and maintained over time would yièld extremely valuable data on the kinds of problems that are encountered, how these change over time, and how resolutions or adaptations are achieved. Retrospective accounts from integrated early childhood programs that have not survived suggest that the kinds of problems these programs encountered are *not* those that have received the bulk of attention in the research literature (Peck et al., in preparation).

In addition to the general research strategies above, some changes in the ways we conceptualize and enact relationships between research and practice may contribute to addressing the problem of implementation.

CHANGING RELATIONSHIPS BETWEEN RESEARCH AND PRACTICE

The question of how research should contribute to practice often raises contentious opinions and emotions among researchers and practitioners. It has often been noted that research has been of limited value to individuals doing direct work with children and families, although the reasons given for this vary (Bolster, 1983; Odom, 1989; Peck, 1991). What follows here is *not* an attack on the validity of research conducted in laboratory schools, nor on the value of research conducted by university academicians. The relevance of such work to practice clearly depends on what research questions are addressed and how the data are interpreted. Instead, the focus of my arguments is on the need for some changes in the nature of the relationships between practitioners and re-

searchers. The goal of these changes would be to produce a different type of dialogue, and a different research agenda, related to issues of implementation.

One dimension of this change involves broadening participation in the actual design and practice of research on implementation. The kind of dialectic between research and practice that is essential to the development of a useful knowledge base concerning implementation is more likely to take place when the people who actually do the work of implementation become more active participants in research. This is not only because these individuals are the proprietors of knowledge that is essential to our common understanding of what is occurring in integrated programs, but because their political participation in the research process is likely to drive the field toward those issues of most pressing concern to the people directly charged with implementation. The goal is not simply to increase "ownership" of research results by practitioners, but to stimulate substantive communication between individuals operating primarily within the contexts of practice and those operating primarily within the contexts of research.

Setting the occasion for this kind of exchange will require more active support of collaboration among university researchers, field-based professionals, and families. For example, while it is common for research and demonstration projects to include practitioners on advisory boards and to extend footnote acknowledgments in publications, these practices seldom include substantive dialogue about the research itself. Key indicators of substantial collaborative research and demonstration endeavors may include the extent to which practitioners are supported in the research budget, actively contribute to idea-generating phases of the research, and share authorship of publications emerging from the research activity.

A number of examples of productive collaboration between university researchers and teachers have been described in the literature (Florio-Ruane, 1991; Goswami & Stillman, 1987; Jacullo-Noto, 1986; Sagor, 1991). While these projects have taken a variety of forms, many describe the difficulties involved in developing new roles and dialogues required for substantive intellectual collaboration between university-based and field-based professionals. Implicit in many of these difficulties is the need to re-examine assumptions about what kinds of knowledge are likely to be valuable in collaborative research on practice. Many of the concepts and examples of knowledge that have been produced in collaborative contexts depart in important respects from the traditional emphasis on replicability and generalizability (e.g., Florio-Ruane, 1991; Goswami & Stillman, 1987). Collaborative relationships often produce the kind of knowledge that is a "process" of constructing interpretations and responses to the research problem in context, rather than a "thing" to be created in one context and then transferred to another. It is not necessary to reject the possibility and value of formal and objective knowledge in order to recognize that a process view of knowledge is highly relevant to the problems of implementation. Individuals engaged in implementation will always be constructing new interpretations and strategies in order to respond to the demands of new situations as these continually evolve.

This is no less the situation of the university researcher when research is viewed as a tool for achieving the implementation of high-quality integrated programs. Thus construed, the *practical* activity in which both researchers and practitioners are engaged is that of learning how we may effectively act to expand opportunities for young children with and without disabilities to grow up together.

SUMMARY

The field of early intervention has clearly accomplished the task of demonstrating the value and feasibility of integrating young children with disabilities into programs with their nondisabled peers (Guralnick, 1990; Strain, 1990). However, the goal of achieving widespread *implementation* of policies and practices that support the integration of young children with disabilities into community early childhood programs raises important new challenges. As Sarason and Doris (1979) pointed out, the nature of these challenges extends considerably beyond our traditional focus on the child and the family, and involves creating changes in social organizations, human service policies, and cultural values. The ecological perspectives advanced in this chapter are intended to clarify some of the issues involved in the implementation of integrated programs. The chapters that follow document some of the progress the field has made in addressing these and other challenges involved in making opportunities for participation in integrated programs a reality for all young children with disabilities.

REFERENCES

Ballard-Campbell, M., & Semmel, M.I. (1981). Policy research and special education: Research issues affecting policy formation and implementation. *Exceptional Education Quarterly, 2*(2), 59–68.

Berman, P., & McLaughlin, M.W. (1978). *Fed-

eral programs supporting educational change: Vol. VIII. Implementing and sustaining innovations. Santa Monica, CA: Rand Corporation.

Biklen, D., Corrigan, C., & Quick, D. (1989). Beyond obligation: Students' relations with each other in integrated classes. In D.K. Lipsky & A. Gartner (Eds.), *Beyond separate education: Quality education for all* (pp. 207–221). Baltimore: Paul H. Brookes Publishing Co.

Bolster, A.A. (1983). Toward a more effective model of research on teaching. *Harvard Educational Review, 53,* 294–308.

Bricker, D.D., & Woods Cripe, J.J. (1992). *An activity-based approach to early intervention.* Baltimore: Paul H. Brookes Publishing Co.

Bronfenbrenner, U. (1979). *The ecology of human development.* Cambridge, MA: Harvard University Press.

Carta, J.J., Sainato, D.M., & Greenwood, C.R. (1988). Advances in the ecological assessment of classroom instruction for young children with handicaps. In S.L. Odom & M.B. Karnes (Eds.), *Early intervention for infants and children with handicaps: An empirical base* (pp. 217–239). Baltimore: Paul H. Brookes Publishing Co.

Cohen, D.K., & Ball, D.L. (1990). Policy and practice: An overview. *Educational Evaluation and Policy Analysis, 12*(3), 347–353.

Danielson, L.C., & Bellamy, G.T. (1989). State variation in placement of children with handicaps in segregated environments. *Exceptional Children, 55,* 448–455.

Education of the Handicapped Act Amendments of 1986, PL 99-457. (October 8, 1986). Title 20, U.S.C. 1400 et seq: *U.S. Statutes at Large, 100,* 1145–1177.

Education for all Handicapped Children Act of 1975, PL 94-142. (August 23, 1977). Title 20, U.S.C. 1401 et seq: *U.S. Statutes at Large, 89,* 773–796.

Florio-Ruane, S. (1991). Conversation and narrative in collaborative research: An ethnography of the written literacy forum. In C.W. Witherell & N. Noddings (Eds.), *Stories lives tell: Narrative and dialogue in education* (pp. 234–256). New York: Teacher's College Press.

Fulcher, G. (1989). *Disabling policies? A comparative approach to education policy and disability.* New York: Falmer Press.

Gaylord-Ross, R., & Peck, C.A. (1985). Social in-tegration of students with severe mental retardation. In D. Bricker & J. Filler (Eds.), *Serving students with severe retardation: From research to practice* (185–207). Reston, VA: Council for Exceptional Children.

Goswami, D., & Stillman, P.R. (1987). *Reclaiming the classroom: Teacher research as an agency for change.* Portsmouth, NH: Heinemann Educational Books Inc.

Guralnick, M.J. (1981). Programmatic factors affecting child-child social interactions in mainstreamed preschool programs. *Exceptional Education Quarterly, 1*(4), 71–91.

Guralnick, M.J. (1982). Mainstreaming young handicapped children: A public policy and ecological system analysis. In B. Spodek (Ed.), *Handbook of research in early childhood education* (pp. 456–500). New York: Free Press.

Guralnick, M.J. (1990). Major accomplishments and future directions in early childhood mainstreaming. *Topics in Early Childhood Special Education, 10*(2), 1–17.

Haring, K., Farron-Davis, F., Goetz, L., Zeph, L., Kara-Soff, P., & Sailor, W. (in press). Least restrictive environment and the placement of students with severe disabilities. *Journal of The Association for Persons with Severe Handicaps.*

Huberman, A.M., & Miles, M.B. (1984). *Innovation up close: How school improvement works.* New York: Plenum.

Jacullo-Noto, J. (1986). Interactive research and development—partners in craft. In A. Lieberman (Ed.), *Rethinking school improvement: Research, craft, and concept* (176–190). New York: Teachers College Press.

Mahoney, G., O'Sullivan, P., & Fors, S. (1989). Special education practices with young handicapped children. *Journal of Early Intervention, 13,* 261–268.

Mehan, H., Hertweck, A., & Meihls, J.L. (1986). *Handicapping the handicapped: Decision making in students' educational careers.* Stanford, CA: Stanford University Press.

Murray-Seegert, C. (1989). *Nasty girls, thugs, and humans like us: Social relations between severely disabled and nondisabled students in high school.* Baltimore: Paul H. Brookes Publishing Co.

Odom, S.L. (1989, May). *Translative research and social interventions: Closing the gap between research and practice.* Paper presented at the annual conference of the Association for Behavior Analysis. Milwaukee, WI.

Odom, S.L., Bender, M.K., Stein, M.L., Doran, L.P., Houden, P.M., McInnes, M., Gilbert, M.M., DeKlyen, M., Speltz, M.L., & Jenkins, J.R. (1988). *The integrated preschool curriculum: Procedures for socially integrating handicapped and nonhandicapped children.* Seattle: University of Washington Press.

Odom, S.L., & McEvoy, M.A. (1988). Integration of young children with handicaps and normally developing children. In S.L. Odom & M.B. Karnes (Eds.), *Early intervention for infants and children with handicaps: An empirical base* (pp. 241–267). Baltimore: Paul H. Brookes Publishing Co.

Peck, C.A. (1989). Assessment of social/communicative competence: Evaluating effects of environments. *Seminars in Speech and Language, 10,* 1–15.

Peck, C.A. (1991). Linking values and science in social policy decisions affecting citizens with severe handicaps. In L. Meyer, C. Peck, & L. Brown (Eds.), *Critical issues in the lives of people with severe disabilities* (pp. 1–15). Baltimore: Paul H. Brookes Publishing Co.

Peck, C.A., Apolloni, T., Cooke, T., & Raver, S. (1978). Teaching retarded preschool children to imitate nonhandicapped peers: Training and generalization effects. *Journal of Special Education, 12,* 195–207.

Peck, C.A., Carlson, P., & Helmstetter, E. (1992). Parent and teacher perceptions of outcomes for nonhandicapped children enrolled in integrated early childhood programs: A statewide study. *Journal of Early Intervention, 16,* 53–63.

Peck, C.A., Furman, G.C., Helmstetter, E., & Reed, D.B. (in preparation). *Factors affecting the survival of early childhood mainstreaming programs: A qualitative study of ten programs.* Washington State University, Vancouver.

Peck, C.A., Hayden, L., Wandschneider, M., Peterson, K., & Richarz, S.A. (1989). Development of integrated preschools: A qualitative inquiry into sources of concern by parents, teachers, and administrators. *Journal of Early Intervention, 13,* 353–364.

Peck, C.A., Richarz, S.A., Peterson, K., Hayden, L., Mineur, L., & Wandschneider, M. (1989). An ecological process model for implementing the Least Restrictive Environment Mandate. In R. Gaylord-Ross (Ed.), *Integration strategies for students with handicaps* (pp. 281–298). Baltimore: Paul H. Brookes Publishing Co.

Peterson, P.L. (1990). Doing more in the same amount of time: Cathy Swift. *Educational Evaluation and Policy Analysis, 12,* 277–296.

Sagor, R. (1991). What Project LEARN reveals about collaborative action research. *Educational Leadership, 48*(6), 6–10.

Salisbury, C.L. (1991). Mainstreaming during the early childhood years. *Exceptional Children, 58,* 146–155.

Sarason, S.B., & Doris, J. (1979). *Educational handicap, public policy, and social history.* New York: Free Press.

Schnorr, R. (1990). Peter? He comes, he goes. *Journal of The Association for Persons with Severe Handicaps, 15,* 231–240.

Sinson, J.C., & Wetherick, N.E. (1981). The behavior of children with Down's syndrome in normal playgroups. *Journal of Mental Deficiency Research, 25,* 113–120.

Skrtic, T. (1991). The special education paradox: Equity as the way to excellence. *Harvard Education Review, 61,* 148–206.

Smith, M.L. (1982). *How educators decide who is learning disabled.* Springfield, IL: Charles C Thomas.

Strain, P.S. (1990). LRE for preschool children with handicaps: What we know, what we should be doing. *Journal of Early Intervention, 14,* 291–296.

Weatherley, R.A. (1979). *Reforming special education: Policy implementation from state-level to street-level.* Cambridge, MA: The MIT Press.

Weatherley, R., & Lipsky, M. (1977). Street-level bureaucrats and institutional innovation: Implementing special education reform. *Harvard Educational Review, 47,* 171–197.

Weick, K. (1976). Educational organizations as loosely coupled systems. *Administrative Science Quarterly, 21,* 1–19.

Winton, P.J. (1986). The consequences of mainstreaming for families of young handicapped children. In C.J. Meisel (Ed.), *Mainstreaming handicapped children: Outcomes, controversies and new directions* (129–148). Hillsdale, NJ: Lawrence Erlbaum Associates Inc.

Chapter 2

LANGUAGE INTERVENTION
Research and Implications for Service Delivery

Angela Notari
and Kevin Cole

The philosophy of normalization (Bank-Mikkelsen, 1980; Nirje, 1980; Wolfensberger, 1980) is one of the foundations of the concept of integration. More recently, the term *normalization* has been modified to stress the importance of social role valorization (the term was anglicized by Wolfensberger [1983] from the French *valorisation*), defined as the conferring of social value to a person (Wolfensberger, 1983). For people with disabilities to be truly integrated, society must perceive their roles as being socially valuable and must provide them with services and educational opportunities that are highly valued by the society in which they live. Equality of educational opportunity is essential, because education plays a major role in transmitting attitudes, knowledge, and skills that are regarded by society as being very important for all children (Tomlinson, 1982). Language is one such skill. In addition to its role in providing access to a culture (Bruner, 1983), language also influences the development of cognitive (Vygotsky, 1978), academic (Aram, Ekelman, & Na-

tion, 1984), self-regulatory (Kopp, 1982), social (Guralnick, 1990), and other highly regarded skills.

IMPORTANCE OF LANGUAGE FOR INTEGRATION

With the full implementation of PL 99-457 in 1991–1992, a significant number of young children will be entitled to early intervention services. To ensure optimal opportunities for children with disabilities, specialized educational strategies that will foster skills regarded as critical for functioning in mainstreamed preschool and daycare environments need to be developed. Language, communication, and social skills have been identified by daycare teachers (Murphy & Vincent, 1989) and regular preschool and kindergarten teachers (Sainato & Lyon, 1989) as elements critical to the successful integration of preschool children with disabilities. Guidelines developed by the National Association for the Education of Young Children (NAEYC) for developmentally

17

appropriate practice (Bredekamp, 1990) emphasize appropriate communicative interactions between children and adults and the provision of language and early literacy experiences.

LANGUAGE ACQUISITION: THEORIES, RESEARCH, AND IMPLICATIONS FOR PRACTICE

Definitions

Language is part of a broad communication system. In its narrow sense, language is defined as a code of verbal symbols used to represent ideas through a conventional system of arbitrary signals for the purpose of communication (Bloom & Lahey, 1978). Language consists of three major dimensions. *Semantics,* or content, refers to the meaning of language, or the linguistic representation of knowledge about the world. *Structure,* or linguistic form, refers to the means of connecting sounds to produce meaning. This system includes a set of linguistic units (i.e., phonemes, morphemes) and rules for their combination (i.e., grammar or syntax). *Pragmatics,* or linguistic use, refers to the different communicative functions of language (Halliday, 1975) and the social context in which it is used. Knowledge of language requires the integration of content, form, and use, and is the product of complex mental processes involving both linguistic and nonlinguistic abilities (Johnston, 1985).

The development of language begins long before the child's acquisition of his or her first words. There is ample literature on the development of language during the first years of life that points to evidence of speech perception in the first 6 months: the development from cooing to babbling, vocal and gestural communication prior to speech, the emergence of first words, the passage into multiword speech, and the onset of grammaticization (Bates, O'Connell, & Shore, 1987).

Theories of Language Acquisition and Implications for Early Language Intervention

Theories of language development have been systematically interpreted in terms of their implications for language intervention (Harris, 1986). In the past, two opposing explanations were offered for the acquisition of language. The *behavioristic approach* (Skinner, 1957) argued that language was strictly a behavior that children learned from adults according to the principles of classical and operant conditioning. The behaviorist model served as a basis for a language intervention technology characterized by a didactic, adult-controlled, massed trial approach. Although this approach has been used successfully for direct instruction in specific language skills, it has not consistently resulted in generalized improvements in children's use of language (Warren & Kaiser, 1988).

The *psycholinguistic approach* (Chomsky, 1957) assumes that the capacity to learn language is innate, and that language acquisition consists of a process of deducing or discovering rules and grammatical structures from the complex speech of adults. This perspective has not proven to be of particular use for language intervention (McCormick & Schiefelbusch, 1984).

A third approach, the *interactionist perspective,* is of the most interest to those currently involved in language intervention (Warren & Kaiser, 1988). The interactionist approach assumes that many factors (e.g., social, cognitive, linguistic, maturational-biological) affect development, and that these factors interact with, modify, and are dependent upon one another (Bohannon & Warren-Leubecker, 1985). Two interactionist approaches in particular have spawned useful programs for early language intervention practices: the cognitive-interactionist approach and the social-interactionist approach.

The *cognitive-interactionist approach,* which draws heavily on Piaget's theory of cognitive development, considers language as one aspect of a more general set of cognitive abilities. Language structures emerge as a result of the continual interaction between the child's cognitive abilities and the linguistic and nonlinguistic environment. The assumption that the acquisition of cognitive concepts should precede the acquisition of linguistic expression led to the development of early language intervention programs that included training in early sensorimotor behaviors (e.g., object permanence, play, imitation, means –ends) as precursors to the teaching of verbal skills (e.g., Bricker & Bricker, 1974; Dunst, 1981).

Studies have shown associations between *specific,* rather than general, aspects of cognition (e.g., symbolic play) and early language development of both non-disabled children (Bates, Benigni, Bretherton, Camaioni, & Volterra, 1979; Kelly & Dale, 1989; McCune-Nicolich & Bruskin, 1982; Shore, 1986) and children with disabilities (e.g., Beeghly & Cicchetti, 1987; Hill & McCune-Nicolich, 1981; Ogura, Notari, & Fewell, 1991). Associations between cognitive concepts and language have also been found in older children. Johnston (1985), for example, reviewed evidence for temporal priority of nonverbal spatial concepts (e.g., notions of topological, projective, and Euclidean space) over corresponding verbal spatial locatives (e.g., in, under, next to, in back of, in front of). Rather than a unidirectional causal influence of cognition on language, current evidence, consisting mostly of correlational and temporal associations, points to reciprocal, bidirectional influences.

The *social-interactionist perspective,* based upon the work of Vygotsky (1978), stresses the social and communicative aspects of language that originate in early infant–caregiver interaction routines and games (Bruner, 1983; Snow, Perlmann, & Nathan, 1987). Infant and caregiver are seen as conversational partners, with the adult assuming responsibility for keeping the conversation going and compensating for the child's conversational inadequacies (Snow, 1989).

Research conducted within the framework of the social-interactionist perspective has produced useful materials for language intervention programs (e.g., Bricker & Schiefelbusch, 1984; Mac-Donald, 1985; Mahoney & Powell, 1988). In particular, it has identified specific features of social interaction and adult speech that appear to facilitate language acquisition. Such features include fine-tuning, joint attention, feedback, and recasts (Snow, 1989). Fine-tuning refers to the adjustment of the level of complexity of the adult's speech in relation to the level of complexity of the child's language. There is evidence of the facilitative effects of simplified maternal speech (i.e., motherese) on children's language development (Furrow, Nelson, & Benedict, 1979), but the correlational nature of the evidence precludes causal inferences. Also, other studies have been reported that have failed to confirm the relationship between motherese and children's language gains (Gleitman, Newport, & Gleitman, 1984).

Joint attention refers to the mother's contingent response to the child's shift of attentional focus. The response consists of her efforts to follow the child's gaze and talk about the jointly established topic (Snow et al., 1987). Joint attention has been linked to vocabulary growth (Tomasello & Farrar, 1986). Maternal utterances that continued the child's topic of conversation were more likely than topic initiations to elicit child responses in both typically developing children (Hoff-Ginsberg, 1987) and children with disabilities (Yoder & Davies, 1990).

The most reliable findings of the facilitative effects of adult speech on children's language have concerned the use of expansions (i.e., a correct version of an incorrect child utterance that adds no new semantic information) and recasts (i.e., a reply that structurally changes one or more major components of the child's utterance, but repeats the rest) of a correct child utterance (e.g., Barnes, Gutfreund, Satterly, & Wells, 1983; Cross, 1978; Nelson, 1977). Confirmation requests and requests for clarification and unknown information have also been positively associated with language gains (Hoff-Ginsberg, 1986; Yoder & Kaiser, 1989).

Studies of the effects of maternal directives on children's language acquisition, which is an issue of relevance for language intervention practice, have yielded inconsistent findings. Negative correlations have been found between maternal directiveness and language development in typical preschool children of various ages (Della Corte, Benedict, & Klein, 1983; Hubbell, 1977; Nelson, 1977; Olsen-Fulero, 1982; Yoder & Kaiser, 1989) and in young children with disabilities (Mahoney, 1988). When, however, directives were used within the context of joint attention, positive correlations with expressive language measures in typically developing children were found (Akhtar, Dunham, & Dunham, 1991; Barnes et al., 1983). Maternal directives to young children with disabilities were not found to be inconsistent with maternal responsivity;

rather, they appeared to serve as a supportive strategy that enabled the child to participate more fully in the interaction (Davis, Stroud, & Green, 1988; Tannock, 1988).

Although most research has sought to highlight the direct effects of maternal speech on children's language, a model of indirect and reciprocal influences between child and maternal speech appears to be more accurate (Barnes et al., 1983; Yoder & Kaiser, 1989), as it takes into account the likely influence that the child's language might have on the mother's speech, as well as the possible role of factors (e.g., the child's level of comprehension, the child's actions) that might affect the relationship between maternal and child speech.

Emergent Literacy

An increasingly important influence on early childhood curricula (Bredekamp, 1990; Strickland & Morrow, 1989), emergent literacy is concerned with the phases of literacy development occurring before children learn to read and write conventionally (Sulzby & Teale, 1991). Early literacy is directly related to early oral language and social interactions. Children are learning about literacy when they engage in such activities as listening to stories, helping an adult follow a cooking recipe, memorizing logograms, scribbling, and drawing pictures.

Several aspects of language development have been linked to early exposure to literary activities. Storybook reading in particular has been shown to facilitate vocabulary growth (Ninio & Bruner, 1978), syntactic knowledge (Snow & Goldfield, 1983), and understanding and use of story structure and narrative form (Heath, Branscombe, & Thomas, 1986; Snow, 1983; Sulzby, 1985). Participation in storybook readings with parents resulted in language gains for both typically developing preschool children (Whitehurst et al., 1988) and young children with disabilities (Swinson & Ellis, 1988). Preschool children with disabilities also gained early reading and writing skills after participating in a variety of preliteracy and literacy experiences at school (Katims, 1991).

Defining Language Delay

Defining delays in language development seems, initially, to be a fairly straightforward task. Researchers have a clear idea of the basic components of a language system (e.g., form, content, and use), and a wide variety of norm-referenced language assessment tools (McCauley & Demetras, 1990). They are also becoming more sophisticated at evaluating language use in context (e.g., Lund & Duchan, 1983), and gathering interview data from parents that accurately portray their child's language functioning (e.g., Dale, 1991). Language delay has been defined in the past as a substantial discrepancy between a child's performance and the performance of typically developing children of comparable age (Darley & Spriesterbach, 1978). Delays may include the areas of content, form, or use separately; a general delay in all areas; or a distorted or separated interaction of form, content, or use wherein children use forms to communicate in an unconventional manner, or use forms without meaning or purpose (McCormick & Schiefelbusch, 1984).

Although defining language delay in terms of a discrepancy among chronological-age peers has face validity, an alternative method of identifying children as being delayed in language development, Cognitive Referencing, has been implemented in school districts and other settings (e.g., Lyngaas, Nyberg, Hoekenga, & Gruenewald, 1983). Under the Cognitive Referencing model, children are considered to be language delayed only if they have developed cognitive skills to a greater degree than their language ability. A child with substantial delays in both language and cognitive development would *not* be considered language delayed under the Cognitive Referencing model even though he or she was performing significantly below expectations for language development for his or her chronological age. The basis for the Cognitive Referencing model is the belief that cognition sets the upper limit for language development (Cromer, 1976; Miller, 1981).

A number of criticisms have been raised regarding the theoretical bases of this model (Kemp, 1983; Lahey, 1990; Notari, Cole, & Mills, 1992), and empirical examinations of children's responses to language intervention have indicated that children with equivalent delays in language and cognition benefit from language intervention to virtually the same degree as children whose cognitive skills developed to a greater degree than language ability (Cole, Dale, & Mills, 1990; Notari et al., 1992). Responding to both theoretical challenges and empirical examination of the practice of Cognitive Referencing, Lahey (1990) and the American Speech-Language-Hearing Association Subcommittee on Language and Cognition Disorders (1987, June) have concluded that Cognitive Referencing should not be used as a means of allocating service to children. The authors agree with this position, and suggest that the allocation of particular amounts and types of services to students should be based on the degree of language delay relative to chronological age; the needs of the child in his or her particular environment; the judgment of the multidisciplinary team, including parents; and dynamic assessment of progress during trial intervention.

RESEARCH ON LANGUAGE INTERVENTION

Language Intervention Studies with Preschool Children with Disabilities

A great deal of research has documented the effectiveness of direct instruction techniques for teaching specific aspects of language content and form to children with disabilities (for a review, see Fey, 1986). The implementation of these techniques requires the careful planning of sequences of training objectives, and precise definitions of stimuli, child responses, and reinforcements. Teaching procedures make use of prompts to help the child respond correctly. Initially, reinforcement of a child's partial or approximate completion of the response may also be used to shape correct responses (see Wolery & Fleming, chap. 6, this volume). Essentially adult-directed, when these techniques are applied to language intervention and implemented in the highly structured context of the therapy, the skills learned generalized poorly to classroom and home settings (Jeffree, Wheldall, & Mittler, 1973; Mulac & Tomlinson, 1977).

To respond to this limitation, "hybrid" language interventions were developed that incorporate operant principles of learning (e.g., prompting and cuing) in a naturalistic manner into the child's everyday life activities and use natural outcomes of communicative situations as reinforcement (Fey, 1986). Grouped under the generic term *milieu teaching,* these techniques include incidental teaching (Hart & Risley, 1980), mand-model (an adapted version of incidental teaching) (Rogers-Warren & Warren, 1980), focused stimulation (Leonard, 1981), activity-based instruction (Bricker & Cripe, 1989; Losardo & Bricker, 1992), transactional teaching (McLean & Snyder-McLean, 1978), and conversational teaching (MacDonald, 1985).

Empirical evaluations of the effectiveness of incidental teaching and the mand-model technique across a wide range of populations, including preschool at-risk children (Hart & Risley, 1980) and young children with language delays (Rogers-Warren & Warren, 1980), have produced evidence of the acquisition of specific targeted language responses and of generalizations of responses across settings (see Warren & Kaiser, 1988).

Comparison Studies

The current approach to evaluating the effectiveness of language intervention is to identify strategies that might work best for particular children or for the teaching of specific types of skills. Relatively little comparative research on language intervention techniques has been conducted with preschool children with disabilities. Losardo and Bricker (1992) compared the effectiveness of direct instruction and activity-based intervention in the acquisition of object labels by preschool children who were at risk or who had developmental delays. They found that children acquired vocabulary more rapidly with direct instruction, but that activity-based intervention was more effective in facilitating generalization and maintenance.

A series of studies conducted by researchers at the University of Washington examined effects on more general measures of language skills. Cole and Dale (1986) found little difference between direct instruction and interactive instruction in language assessment measures. A second study (Dale & Cole, 1988), which compared direct instruction with mediated learning, found differential effects that were consistent with program goals: children in the direct instruction program, for example, made greater gains in tests of specific language skills, while children in the mediated learning program showed greater improvement in measures of more general language skills. These differential treatment effects continued to be observed at least 1 year after intervention (Cole, Mills, & Dale, 1989).

Two recent studies (Cole, Dale, & Mills, 1991; Yoder, Kaiser, & Alpert, 1991) examined the effectiveness of two contrasting preschool curricula as predicted by pretreatment subject characteristics. In both studies, contrary to common opinion, higher-functioning children made greater gains if they participated in the more didactic, academic program, while lower-functioning children made greater gains in the more child-directed, communicative program.

Further research is needed to examine specific aspects and components of diverse language intervention approaches, as well as their effects on pragmatic, conversational, discourse, and other language skills (Snow, 1989). In an integrated setting, the diversity of language abilities among children may call for the use of a comprehensive approach that includes characteristics of didactic, milieu, and child-directed interventions to allow for maximum flexibility and adaptation to the individual child's language level and learning style, as well as to the characteristics and uses of the skills being taught (Cole & Dale, 1986; Warren & Kaiser, 1988).

Current Research on the Relationship Between Language Development and Mainstreaming

Empirical examinations of mainstreaming as a means of facilitating communication skills have generally involved two types of outcome measures. The first is measurement of variables that are considered *likely* to facilitate language development in children with delays in communication, such as increased opportunities for peer interaction, peer language input modified to the appropriate level of complexity for children with delays, or modifications in social or play behaviors of children with disabilities during the intervention. These outcome measures provide indirect evidence that mainstreaming should be beneficial for young children with disabilities. They also provide information regarding the mechanisms by which integration may facilitate language development. A second approach is to examine changes in the language and communication performance of children with disabilities. This approach provides more direct evidence of the effects of mainstreaming, but may contribute less to our knowledge of the behaviors that led to the changes.

Examples of indirect evidence supporting the potential benefits of mainstreaming for communication development include studies by Guralnick and Groom (1988), Guralnick and Paul-Brown (1984), and Ispa (1981). These studies found, respectively, that typically developing children modify their requests appropriately to children with disabilities, that children with disabilities engaged in longer interactions with typically developing children, and that children with disabilities engaged in a higher rate of social interaction and an improved quality of cognitive play in integrated settings. While studies of this type suggest that there may be developmental benefits from preschool integration, studies that have directly examined changes in language and communication performance in young children with disabilities as a result of integration have shown less conclusive results.

Several direct evaluations of the effects of integration on language development have placed typically developing children and children with disabilities together in classes, without any accompanying program designed to arrange or modify integrated interactions. Fenrick, Pearson, and Pepelnjak (1984), for example, found no differences in language performance between settings for a group of children who attended integrated programs in the morning and segregated programs in the afternoon. Similar findings with autistic children have led Harris, Handleman, Kristoff, Bass, and Gordon (1990) to conclude that integration may need to be manipulated more systematically to increase its effectiveness.

Several studies that systematically structured the interactions of typically developing preschool children and children with disabilities did find positive results. Goldstein, Wickstrom, Hoyson, Jamieson, and Odom (1988) taught sociodramatic scripts to integrated groups of children, then encouraged the children to continue the sociodramatic play in freeplay settings. The quality of communicative interactions was increased using this structured approach. Similarly, training peer-confederates in specific techniques for initiating and maintaining communication with classmates with disabilities (establishing eye contact, suggesting joint play, appropriate responding, self-talk, etc.) resulted in increased interactions with the children with disabilities (Goldstein & Ferrell, 1987). Jenkins, Odom, and Speltz (1989) also found significant gains in language development when a specific social interaction curriculum was implemented.

While significant benefits within integrated settings were found in conjunction with various forms of structure, it should be recognized that several studies (Goldstein et al., 1988; Jenkins et al., 1989; Pearson, Pearson, Fenrick, & Greene, 1988) found that the structuring of interactions was generally as effective in segregated settings as in integrated settings. These findings suggest that integration, with either unstructured or specifically structured interactions between young children with disabilities and typically developing peers, may not influence language development to a greater degree than a segregated setting. A study by Cole, Mills, Dale, and Jenkins (1991), however, offers a different perspective regarding the possibility of different benefits resulting from integrated and segregated preschool settings. Results of this study indicated that a child's initial level of development differentially affected gains made in integrated and segregated settings. No main effect differences were found when comparing the effects of integration and segregation, which was consistent with the majority of previous findings. However, it was determined that relatively higher-functioning children made more gains in language and general cognitive development from integrated classes, and relatively lower-functioning children made greater gains from segregated settings.

These results may help explain the fact that studies designed to detect main effect differences between integrated and segregated conditions found none. The average gains for the two groups are approximately the same, but subgroups of children can be predicted to perform *slightly* better in either segregated or integrated settings depending on their level of functioning prior to intervention. Possible causes for these differences include the interaction between children's initial ability and the different levels of linguistic complexity used by teachers in the two settings. If teachers' linguistic complexity is higher in integrated settings, the language delayed children with relatively higher functioning may benefit from the increased stimulation, while it may prove too complex for the lower-functioning children. The linguistic complexity may be outside of their zone of proximal development. Similarly, there may be a differential ability on the part of children with disabilities to benefit from the higher level of linguistic input provided by typically developing peers. More information is needed to determine the mechanisms that account for these individual differences. It is important to note that these differences were consistent enough to be statistically significant, but were not large enough to be educationally earthshaking. The finding should not be interpreted to suggest that relatively lower-functioning children should be segregated, and higher-functioning children integrated. Rather, they indicate that lower-functioning children in integrated classes should have their performance monitored closely to ensure appropriate linguistic and social stimulation.

RECOMMENDATIONS FOR IMPLEMENTING LANGUAGE INTERVENTIONS IN INTEGRATED PROGRAMS

Recommendations for language interventions have been drawn from research on typical language development and from the literature on empirically based language interventions for preschool children with disabilities. While research on typical development can provide useful guidelines for interventions with children with disabilities (Guralnick, 1986), direct applications should be implemented only with caution for two reasons. First, more research is needed on the developmental processes of children with disabilities. Most available research has been conducted on white middle-class American families and on typically developing children (Snow, 1989). Second, teachers and developmental researchers are concerned with fundamentally different problems (Harris, 1986). Applications from developmental research need to be empirically tested through actual classroom practices and educational results (Harris, 1986; Piaget, 1973).

Community-based educational programs should be expected to accommodate children with disabilities within their usual programmatic and curricular structure (Guralnick, 1986). Through the collaborative teaming of regular education teachers and early childhood interventionists, inclusive programs should be developed in which the diverse needs of all children are accommodated, rather than mainstreamed programs where children with disabilities are simply allowed to participate in mainstreamed environments (Salisbury, 1991). However, the research literature suggests that, by itself, integration does not necessarily result in positive outcomes for children with disabilities (Odom & McEvoy, 1988). Specific adaptations must be carefully planned by teachers (Guralnick, 1986; Strain, 1990). "Naturalistic" environmentally based interventions appear to be best suited for teaching preschool children with disabilities in an integrated setting, since their instructional strategies were specifically devised to be used within the context of everyday routines. Research suggests that these interventions are particularly effective in facilitating language gains in lower-functioning children (Cole et al., 1991; Yoder et al., 1991), and that they foster generalization of skills across settings (Losardo & Bricker, 1992). Some children, though, may fare better with more didactic approaches, especially in situations where rapid acquisition of new skills is required (Giumento & Bricker, 1991; Warren & Kaiser, 1988). Ultimately, it is the teacher who can best make decisions as to which strategies are best suited to individual children (Brinker, 1985).

In addition to the very broad consideration of general theoratical models (e.g., direct didactic approaches, naturalistic environmentally based approaches, hybrid approaches), the teacher must consider a variety of very specific factors that influence the child's ability to develop language skills. These include classroom organization, types of materials, activities, and specific types of teacher–child interaction. The following section provides specific suggestions that have been demonstrated to be effective with young children.

Classroom Organization

The Classroom Environment The classroom environment should be organized in a way that maximizes the children's opportunities to use language and to be exposed to early literacy experiences. Small, quiet places for two or three children tend to facilitate peer conversations in normally developing preschoolers (Sylva, Roy, & Painter, 1980). A quiet, well-lighted area with easy access to books and magazines provides opportunities for social reading. Another area equipped with bulletin or marker boards, magnetic letters, photos, pictures, tape recorders, typewriters, and computers can serve as a communication center. A listening center with a tape recorder and headsets provides opportunities to listen to music and the sounds of language (Greenman, 1988). Katims (1991) found that preschool children with disabilities improved their pre-literacy skills when they had easy access to a library and a writing center.

Materials Selection of materials should be based on the child's interest in the material, and the degree to which it fosters the child's engagement and active learning through direct actions and manipulations. A child's interest in an object offers the teacher opportunities to elicit naming and requesting of desired objects. Materials should be age-appropriate, regardless of developmental level (McDonnell & Hardman, 1988).

Play with blocks or vehicles, dramatic play, water play, and games that require cooperation are more likely to facilitate peer interactions among typically developing preschoolers (Quilitch & Risley, 1973; Shure, 1963; Stoneman, Cantrell, & Hoover-Dempsey, 1983). Peterson and Haralick (1977) found that children with disabilities interacted more with their peers during block play and manipulative floor play than during table activities.

Activities There is evidence that the frequency, complexity, and functions of speech may vary according to the context. Engagement in play activities and group discussion appears to elicit more frequent and complex speech in typically developing preschoolers than does engagement in regular daily caregiving routines (Cazden, 1970; Wells, 1985). More statements and requests tend to occur during play without an adult, while more responses to questions occur during play with an adult. Situations with visual stimuli elicit labeling and name questions. Group talk may be characterized by questions, responses, and requests for explanations. The "want" function occurs more often during routine activities, such as meals and caregiving (Wells, 1985). For children with language delays, the presence of an adult appears to increase the frequency of verbalization. Interactions with peers, however, occur more often during informal activities without an adult present (Rogers-Warren, 1982).

Teacher Mediation Strategies

General Facilitative Strategies Language can generally be facilitated by creating a highly accepting and responsive environment in which the child is motivated to communicate spontaneously with social partners. Fey (1986) outlines specific procedures for the teacher to use within a child-oriented facilitative play context. *Following the child's lead* requires the teacher to wait for the child to initiate some behavior, to interpret that behavior as meaningful and communicative, and to respond to the behavior in some communicative manner. With children who are reluctant to interact, the teacher may use *self-talk* and *parallel talk*. These techniques consist of the teacher commenting verbally on objects, actions, and relations on which the child's attention is focused. *Expansions* are semantically contingent responses that repeat the child's prior utterance while adding relevant grammatical and semantic details. For example, "The baby is sleeping" is an expansion of "Baby sleep." *Recast sentences* are forms of expansion that extend or change some aspect of the child's meaning by adding new information (e.g., following the child's utterance "Baby sleep," the teacher might say "He is tired"), or by changing the original

sentence modality (e.g., the teacher might recast the child's affirmative sentence "The baby is sleeping" as the interrogative "Is the baby sleeping?"). Expansions have been used to facilitate the acquisition of multiword utterances (e.g., agent-action; agent-action-object; agent-action-location) in normally developing preschoolers (Scherer & Olswang, 1984), children with language delays (Wilcox, 1984), and young children with other disabilities (Branston, 1979).

Specific Facilitation Strategies The use of specific strategies is likely to be more effective for children with disabilities. This section provides guidelines designed to facilitate early verbal language. Language interventions for children who are not yet talking should focus on the teaching of precursor sensorimotor skills (see Bricker & Bricker, 1974; Dunst, 1981), and prelinguistic vocal and pragmatic conversational skills (see Bricker & Schiefelbusch, 1984; Mahoney & Powell, 1988).

Facilitating Spontaneous Language Teachers can arrange the environment in a number of ways to elicit spontaneous language, particularly in children in early language stages. Strategies include: withholding objects and hiding objects to elicit requests; violations of routine events, object functions, and manipulations to elicit comments and questions; and introduction of novel objects or actions following repetition of a sequence of events (e.g., handing the child a doll after having given the child blocks to place in a box) to elicit one-word naming (Fey, 1986).

Focused Stimulation The teacher can plan specific activities requiring the use of the child's individual language goal (e.g., a hiding game for the use of "gone-[noun]"). The teacher then provides frequent models of the target form in comments about the game. Focused stimulation has been used successfully to facilitate the acquisition and mastery of lexical, early relational, and more complex forms in typically developing preschoolers (e.g., Nelson, 1977), children with language delays (Leonard et al., 1982), and young children with disabilities (McConkey, Jeffree, & Hewson, 1979).

Modeling   The teacher models the targeted language form and then specifically provides an opportunity, through a general verbal prompt, for example, for the child to produce the targeted utterance (e.g., "Tell me about what is happening"). Modeling has been used most often with preschool children with language delays to teach syntactic aspects of language (Courtright & Courtright, 1979; Ellis-Weismer & Murray-Branch, 1989).

Incidental Teaching   Incidental teaching consists of four major steps: 1) the teacher arranges the environment to increase the likelihood that the child will initiate speech to the adult (e.g., places desirable objects out of reach); 2) the teacher waits for the child to select the topic stimulus and initiate the interaction verbally or nonverbally (e.g., the child gestures toward the teacher to get the object); 3) the teacher decides which language response to elicit from the child (e.g., verb-noun); and 4) the teacher uses cues to obtain a response (e.g., physical approach, eye contact, questioning look, or general questions, such as "What do you want?"). The effectiveness of incidental teaching has been demonstrated across a wide range of linguistic skills for children of various ages and abilities, including preschool children who are environmentally at risk (Hart & Risley, 1980).

Mand-Model Technique   This technique was adapted from the incidental teaching model for use with children who are developmentally delayed. The child is not required to initiate. The teacher observes the child and mands a verbal response (e.g.., "Tell me what you want."). The mand should relate to the topic of the child's attention (Akhtar et al., 1991). If the child does not respond, the teacher uses prompts such as modeling the correct response and asking the child to imitate it. This model has been used successfully with preschool children with disabilities and social delays (Rogers-Warren & Warren, 1980). A model combining features of incidental teaching and mand-modeling has been effective in enhancing the acquisition and generalization of lexical and relational semantic language forms in preschool children with disabilities (Warren & Bambara, 1989; Warren & Gazdag, 1990).

Story Reading   Story reading is an interactive activity in which children who are functioning at different levels can easily participate. Teachers can adapt their questions and comments to the individual child's interests, developmental level, and targeted language goals. Story reading provides teachers with opportunities to elicit labeling ("What's this a picture of?"), syntactic knowledge ("What happened?"), alternative ways of expressing ideas ("What does that mean?"), and aspects of narrative form and story structure ("Why did the girl do that?"; "Is this a real story or a make-believe story?"). It should be noted that story "reading," especially for children with language skills below a 3-year-old level, should generally consist of a minimum of actual reading of text. Rather, the book should be a medium for conversation, with the adult following the child's interest in the pictures, modeling, labeling, asking open-ended questions, and expanding on the child's responses. Picture books with little narrative text are generally best for this type of interaction, while books with large blocks of text, or rhyming books, may be less effective.

Sociodramatic Play   A common activity in regular daycare and preschool settings, sociodramatic play appears to have facilitative effects on language development in preschoolers who are environmentally at risk (Graul & Davey Zeece, 1990; Smilansky, 1968; Udwin, 1983). Goldstein et al. (1988) have found that children with disabilities increase their social communication interactions with typically developing peers when taught sociodramatic play through teacher modeling and role prompting procedures.

Peer Interactions   A major benefit of integrated classrooms for preschool children with disabilities is the enhancement of interactive play and language skills (Jenkins et al., 1989). Although typically developing preschoolers are capable of adjusting their communicative interactions to children who are mildly delayed (Guralnick & Paul-Brown, 1989), advanced interactions do not occur spontaneously without programming, especially for children with moderate and severe disabilities (Odom & McEvoy, 1988). Teachers can facilitate interactions between typically developing peers and children with disabilities by providing the typically developing children with information about their peers, by training them to use specific interaction techniques, by prompting them to interact during play and classroom routines, and by providing social toys that require cooperation (Odom & Brown, chap. 3, this volume).

Implementation of Special Education Procedures in Integrated Settings

Important features of early childhood special education services are the development of an individualized education program (IEP) or individualized family service plan (IFSP), multidisciplinary assessment of the child, ongoing monitoring of child progress, program evaluation, and the involvement of the family in all of these procedures. A major concern in providing appropriate services to children with disabilities in integrated programs is to find ways to successfully implement these services within regular education settings (Guralnick, 1990).

Language outcomes selected for inclusion in the IEP/IFSP should be behaviors that are valued in the child's environment and are likely to occur in regular classroom and home settings (Notari & Bricker, 1990; Price & Bochner, 1990; Vincent, Salisbury, Strain, McCormick, & Tessier, 1990). Language goals should represent functional skills and generic concepts (e.g., "Uses two-word utterances to express location," or "Uses adjectives to make comparisons"), rather than isolated specific forms (e.g., "Correctly uses 'in box' and 'on box' to identify the location of an object in relationship to a box," or "Correctly uses 'more' and 'bigger' in sentences"), so that teachers can easily elicit targeted skills during a variety of routine activities.

Teachers need to be provided with time to carefully plan activities into which individual child goals and teaching strategies can be easily incorporated. An activity such as "following a recipe to make Play-Doh" presents opportunities for eliciting skills at different levels. Vocabulary knowledge and symbolic representation can be taught by having the lower-functioning child label objects and ingredients and identify pictures on the written recipe and on ingredient containers. Syntactic knowledge and awareness of print can be facilitated by asking the higher-functioning child to verbally describe actions and to identify written words on the recipe. Children with appropriate language abilities will have opportunities to learn print conventions, practice narrative skills and discourse patterns by being asked to reconstruct sequences of actions, and follow the written instructions on the recipe.

Systematic monitoring of the child's progress with respect to language goals is essential for making appropriate data-based decisions regarding the effectiveness of individual intervention strategies. Data collection systems that are easy to use within integrated settings need to be developed. Adaptations of models such as the Individualized Curriculum Sequencing model (Mulligan & Guess, 1984) or Activity-Based Instruction model (Bricker & Cripe, 1989) might prove useful.

Assessment and evaluation procedures should be expanded to include nonintrusive methods, such as naturalistic observation (as opposed to direct testing), parent interviews, informal language samples (Vincent et al., 1990), and measures of pragmatic and conversational skills (Snow, 1989; Warren & Kaiser, 1988).

The involvement of the family in the child's educational program is of utmost importance (Winton, chap. 4, this volume). Language and communication are naturally occurring events, and many opportunities can be used by parents to facilitate their child's language acquisition (see Bricker & Schiefelbusch, 1984; MacDonald, Blott, Gordon, Spiegel, & Hartmann, 1974; Mahoney & Powell, 1988). Teaching parents to use environmental arrangement language intervention techniques (Hemmeter & Kaiser, 1990) and storybook reading, for example (Whitehurst et al., 1988), has resulted in language gains for their children.

Role of the Speech-Language Pathologist

The most appropriate role for the speech-language pathologist (SLP) in developing children's language skills in the context of regular classroom activities appears to be as a consultant and a model to teachers and parents (Warren & Rogers-Warren,

1985). Cipriani (1989) sees the SLP as the provider of information to professionals directly involved with children, particularly during four major phases of service delivery: 1) the development of language intervention objectives, 2) the selection of specific intervention strategies, 3) the implementation of the intervention program, and 4) the provision of follow-up consultation after the child's acquisition of the targeted language goal. In this role, the SLP works in the classroom and in the home, rather than in an isolated clinical setting. This allows the SLP the opportunity to observe the child's use of language in a generalized context, and to model language facilitation techniques for parents and other staff members. Occasionally, services may be more appropriately provided in an isolated clinical setting; a child may be especially distractible, or the classroom may provide too much background noise for the SLP or child to hear critical aspects of language input. Also, for some speech disorders (i.e., voice disorders, stuttering, or articulation or phonological disorders) intervention may be more effectively *initiated* in an isolated setting, then moved to the home or classroom. For most language interventions, however, service delivery will be more effective if provided within the setting where functional communication needs to occur, and will have the added benefit of eliminating any stigma associated with being "pulled out" for special services.

Training Personnel

Both regular early childhood and early childhood special education personnel need to develop the knowledge and the skills required to successfully integrate children with disabilities into regular daycare and preschool programs (Klein & Campbell, 1990; Odom & McEvoy, 1990).

With regard to the facilitation of language skills, collaboration among speech-language pathologists, regular early childhood education professionals, and early childhood special education professionals in preservice training programs would provide opportunities for the sharing and exchange of knowledge and skills in both coursework and practicum experiences.

For qualified professionals already working in the field, inservice training should be provided for teachers to acquire knowledge on normal language development and to implement effective language intervention strategies in their classrooms. Mudd and Wolery (1987), for example, successfully used an inservice model to train Head Start personnel in the use of incidental teaching strategies. Multimedia training models that combine coursework, written materials, videotapes, and on-site consultation in the application of skills seem to be most effective (Klein & Campbell, 1990; Tough, 1982).

SUMMARY

In support of philosophical, ethical, and legal arguments, current research has provided direct and indirect evidence that the education of young children with disabilities in integrated programs has been beneficial to their language development. Also encouraging is the documented effectiveness of naturalistic language intervention techniques for young children with disabilities. Designed to be used within daily settings, these techniques appear to lend themselves easily to implementation in integrated programs.

Providing teachers with professional expertise in the planning and use of facilitative language interventions, within a school setting that has adequate resources, administrative support, and a staff with positive attitudes toward integration, is important for developing quality integrated programs (Odom & McEvoy, 1990; Salisbury, 1991). Perhaps, though, the most decisive factor lies beyond the individual teacher and the immediate school community. As pointed out by Strain (1990) in reference to the universal service delivery model in Italy, it is ultimately the priorities and the commitment of society to its children and families that make a difference, as well as the recognition that all people, whether they have a disability or not, should be acknowledged as having a socially valuable role to play in the society in which they live.

REFERENCES

Akhtar, N., Dunham, F., & Dunham, P. (1991). Directive interactions and early vocabulary development: The role of joint attentional focus. *Journal of Child Language, 18,* 41–49.

American Speech-Language-Hearing Association Subcommittee on Language and Cognition. (1987). The role of speech-language pathologists in the habilitation and rehabilitation of cognitively impaired individuals. *Asha, 29,* 53–55.

Aram, D., Ekelman, B., & Nation, J. (1984). Preschoolers with language disorders: 10 years later. *Journal of Speech and Hearing Research, 18,* 229–241.

Bank-Mikkelsen, N.E. (1980). Denmark. In R.J. Flynn & K.E. Nitsch (Eds.), *Normalization, social integration, and community services* (pp. 51–70). Baltimore: University Park Press.

Barnes, S., Gutfreund, M., Satterly, D., & Wells, G. (1983). Characteristics of adult speech which predict children's language development. *Journal of Child Language, 10,* 65–84.

Bates, E., Benigni, L., Bretherton, I., Camaioni, L., & Volterra, V. (1979). *The emergence of symbols: Cognition and communication in infancy.* New York: Academic Press.

Bates, E., O'Connell, B., & Shore, C. (1987). Language and communication in infancy. In J. Osofsky (Ed.), *Handbook of infant development* (2nd ed.) (pp. 149–202). New York: John Wiley & Sons.

Beeghly, M., & Cicchetti, D. (1987). An organizational approach to symbolic development in children with Down syndrome. *New Directions for Child Development, 36,* 5–29.

Bloom, L., & Lahey, M. (1978). *Language development and language disorders.* New York: John Wiley & Sons.

Bohannon, J.N., & Warren-Leubecker, A. (1985). Theoretical approaches to language acquisition. In J.B. Gleason (Ed.), *The development of language* (pp. 173–226). Columbus, OH: Charles E. Merrill.

Branston, M. (1979). *The effect of increased expansions on the acquisition of semantic structures in young developmentally delayed children: A training study.* Unpublished doctoral dissertation, University of Wisconsin, Madison.

Bredekamp, S. (Ed.). (1990). *Developmentally appropriate practice in early childhood programs serving children from birth through age 8* (Expanded edition). Washington, DC: National Association for the Education of Young Children.

Bricker, D., & Cripe, J. (1989). Activity-based intervention. In D.D. Bricker (Ed.), *Early intervention for at-risk and handicapped infants, toddlers, and preschool children* (2nd ed.) (pp. 251–275). Palo Alto, CA: VORT.

Bricker, D., & Schiefelbusch, R. (1984). Infants at-risk. In L. McCormick & R. Schiefelbusch (Eds.), *Early language intervention* (pp. 243–265). Columbus, OH: Charles E. Merrill.

Bricker, W., & Bricker, D. (1974). An early language training strategy. In R.L. Schiefelbusch & L.L. Lloyd (Eds.), *Language perspectives: Acquisition, retardation and intervention* (pp. 431–468). Baltimore: University Park Press.

Brinker, R.P. (1985). Curricula without recipes: A challenge to teachers and a promise to severely mentally retarded students. In D. Bricker & J. Filler (Eds.), *Severe mental retardation: From theory to practice* (pp. 208–229). Reston, VA: Council for Exceptional Children.

Bruner, J. (1983). *Child's talk: Learning to use language.* New York: Norton.

Cazden, C. (1970). The neglected situation in child language research and education. In F. Williams (Ed.), *Language and poverty* (pp. 81–101). Chicago, IL: Markham.

Chomsky, N. (1957). *Syntactic structures.* The Hague, Netherlands: Mouton.

Cipriani, E. (1989). Providing language consultation in the natural context: A model for the delivery of services. *Mental Retardation, 27,* 317–324.

Cole, K., & Dale, P. (1986). Direct language instruction and interactive language instruction with language delayed preschool children: A comparison study. *Journal of Speech and Hearing Research, 28,* 205–217.

Cole, K., Dale, P., & Mills, P. (1990). Defining language delay in young children by cognitive referencing: Are we saying more than we know? *Applied Psycholinguistics, 11,* 291–302.

Cole, K., Dale, P., & Mills, P. (1991). Individual differences in language delayed children's responses to direct and interactive preschool instruction. *Topics in Early Childhood Special Education, 11*(1), 99–124.

Cole, K., Mills, P., & Dale, P. (1989). Comparison of effects of academic and cognitive curricula for young handicapped children one and two years post-program. *Topics in Early Childhood Special Education, 9*(3), 110–127.

Cole, K., Mills, P., Dale, P., & Jenkins, J.R. (1991). Effects of preschool integration for children with disabilities. *Exceptional Children, 58,* 36–45.

Committee on Language Learning Disorders. (1989, March). Issues in determining eligibility for language intervention. *Asha, 31,* 113.

Courtright, J., & Courtright, I. (1979). Imitative modeling as a language intervention strategy: The effects of two mediating varibles. *Journal of Speech and Hearing Research, 22,* 389–402.

Cromer, R. (1976). The cognitive hypothesis of language acquisition and its implications for child language deficiency. In D. Morehead & A. Morehead (Eds.), *Normal and deficient child language* (pp. 283–333). Baltimore: University Park Press.

Cross, T. (1978). Motherese: Its association with the rate of syntactic acquisition in young children. In N. Waterson & C. Snow (Eds.), *The development of communication* (pp. 199–216). New York: John Wiley & Sons.

Dale, P.S. (1991). The validity of a parent report measure of vocabulary and syntax at 24 months. *Journal of Speech and Hearing Research, 34,* 565–571.

Dale, P.S., & Cole, K. (1988). Comparison of academic and cognitive programs for young handicapped children. *Exceptional Children, 54,* 439–447.

Darley, F., & Spriesterbach, D. (1978). *Diagnostic methods in speech pathology* (2nd ed.). New York: Harper & Row.

Davis, H., Stroud, A., & Green, L. (1988). Maternal language environment of children with mental retardation. *American Journal on Mental Retardation, 93,* 144–153.

Della Corte, M., Benedict, H., & Klein, D. (1983). The relationship of pragmatic dimensions of mothers' speech to the referential-expressive distinction. *Journal of Child Language, 10,* 35–43.

Dunst, C.J. (1981). *Infant learning: A cognitive-linguistic intervention strategy.* Allen, TX: DLM Teaching Resources.

Education of the Handicapped Act Amendments of 1986, PL 99-457. (October 8, 1986). Title 20, U.S.C. 1400, et seq: *U.S. Statutes at Large, 100,* 1145–1177.

Ellis-Weismer, S., & Murray-Branch, J. (1989). Modeling versus modeling plus evoked production training: A comparison of two language intervention methods. *Journal of Speech and Hearing Disorders, 54,* 269–281.

Fenrick, N., Pearson, M., & Pepelnjak, J. (1984). The play, attending and language of young handicapped children in integrated and segregated settings. *Journal of the Division for Early Childhood, 8,* 57–67.

Fey, M.E. (1986). *Language intervention with young children.* San Diego, CA: College-Hill.

Furrow, D., Nelson, K., & Benedict, H. (1979). Mothers' speech to children and syntactic development: Some simple relationships. *Journal of Child Language, 6,* 423–442.

Gleitman, L., Newport, E., & Gleitman, H. (1984). The current state of the motherese hypothesis. *Journal of Child Language, 11,* 43–79.

Goldstein, H., & Ferrell, D. (1987). Augmenting communicative interaction between handicapped and nonhandicapped preschool children. *Journal of Speech and Hearing Disorders, 52,* 200–211.

Goldstein, H., Wickstrom, S., Hoyson, M., Jamieson, B., & Odom, S. (1988). Effects of sociodramatic script training on social and communicative interaction. *Education and Treatment of Children, 11*(2), 97–117.

Graul, S.K., & Davey Zeece, P. (1990). Effects of play training of adults on the cognitive and play behavior of preschool children. *Early Child Development and Care, 57,* 15–22.

Greenman, J. (1988). *Caring spaces, learning places: Children's environments that work.* Redmond, WA: Exchange Press.

Guralnick, M. (1986). The application of child development principles and research to preschool mainstreaming. In C.J. Meisel (Ed.), *Mainstreaming handicapped children: outcomes, controversies, and new directions* (pp. 21–41). Hillsdale, NJ: Lawrence Erlbaum Associates.

Guralnick, M. (1990). Major accomplishments and future directions in early childhood mainstreaming. *Topics in Early Childhood Special Education, 10*(2), 1–17.

Guralnick, M., & Groom, J. (1988). Peer interaction in mainstreamed and specialized classrooms. *Exceptional Children, 54,* 415–425.

Guralnick, M., & Paul-Brown, D. (1984). Communicative adjustments during behavior-request episodes among children at different development levels. *Child Development, 55,* 911–919.

Guralnick, M., & Paul-Brown, D. (1989). Peer related communicative competence of preschool children: Developmental and adaptive characteristics. *Journal of Speech and Hearing Research, 32,* 930–943.

Halliday, M. (1975). *Learning how to mean: Explorations in the development of language.* New York: Elsevier North Holland.

Harris, J. (1986). The contribution of developmental psychology to the education of mentally handicapped children in special schools. In J. Harris (Ed.), *Child psychology in action: Linking research and practice* (pp. 143–170). Beckenham, England: Croom Helm.

Harris, S., Handleman, J., Kristoff, B., Bass, L., & Gordon, R. (1990). Changes in language development among autistic and peer children in segregated and integrated preschool settings. *Journal of Autism and Developmental Disorders, 1,* 23–31.

Hart, B., & Risley, T. (1975). Incidental teaching of language in the preschool. *Journal of Applied Behavior Analysis, 8,* 411–420.

Hart, B., & Risley, T. (1980). In vivo language training: Unanticipated and general effects. *Journal of Applied Behavior Analysis, 12,* 407–432.

Heath, S., Branscombe, A., & Thomas, C. (1986). The book as narrative prop in language acquisition. In B. Schieffelin & P. Gilmore (Eds.), *The acquisition of literacy: Ethnographic perspectives* (pp. 16–34). Norwood, NJ: Ablex.

Hemmeter, M.L., & Kaiser, A.P. (1990). Environmental influences on children's language: A model and case study. *Education and Treatment of Children, 13,* 331–346.

Hill, P., & McCune-Nicolich, L. (1981). Pretend play and patterns of cognition in Down's syndrome children. *Child Development, 52,* 611–617.

Hoff-Ginsberg, E. (1986). Function and structure in maternal speech: The relation to the child's development of syntax. *Developmental Psychology, 22,* 155–163.

Hoff-Ginsberg, E. (1987). Topic relations in mother–child conversations. *First Language, 7,* 145–158.

Hubbell, R. (1977). On facilitating spontaneous talking in young children. *Journal of Speech and Hearing Disorders, 42,* 216–232.

Ispa, J. (1981). Social interactions among teachers, handicapped children, and nonhandicapped children in a mainstreamed preschool. *Journal of Applied Developmental Psychology, 1,* 231–250.

Jeffree, D., Wheldall, K., & Mittler, P. (1973). Facilitating two-word utterances in two Down's syndrome boys. *American Journal of Mental Deficiency, 78,* 117–122.

Jenkins, J.R., Odom, S., & Speltz, M. (1989). Effects of social integration on preschool children with handicaps. *Exceptional Children, 55,* 420–428.

Johnston, J. (1985). Cognitive prerequisites: The evidence from children learning English. In D.I. Slobin (Ed.), *The crosslinguistic study of language acquisition* (Vol. 2, pp. 961–1004). Hillsdale, NJ: Erlbaum.

Katims, D. (1991). Emergent literacy in early childhood special education: Curriculum and instruction. *Topics in Early Childhood Special Education, 11*(1), 69–84.

Kelly, C., & Dale, P. (1989). Cognitive skills associated with the onset of multiword utterances. *Journal of Speech and Hearing Research, 32,* 645–656.

Kemp, J. (1983). The timing of language for the pediatric population. In J. Miller, D. Yoder, & R. Schiefelbusch (Eds.), *Contemporary issues in language intervention* (pp. 183–195). ASHA Reports 12.

Klein, N., & Campbell, P. (1990). Preparing personnel to serve at-risk and disabled infants, toddlers, and preschoolers. In S.J. Meisels & J.P. Shonkoff (Eds.), *Handbook of early childhood intervention* (pp. 679–699). Cambridge, England: Cambridge University Press.

Kopp, C. (1982). Antecedents of self-regulation. *Developmental Psychology, 18,* 199–214.

Lahey, M. (1990). Who shall be called language disordered? Some reflections and one perspective. *Journal of Speech and Hearing Disorders, 55,* 612–620.

Leonard, L. (1981). Facilitating linguistic skills in children with specific language impairment. *Applied Psycholinguistics, 2,* 89–118.

Leonard, L., Schwartz, R., Chapman, K., Rowan, L., Prelock, P., Terrell, B., Weiss, A., & Messick, C. (1982). Early lexical acquisition in children with specific language impairment. *Journal of Speech and Hearing Research, 25,* 554–559.

Losardo, A., & Bricker, D. (1992). *Activity-based intervention and direct instruction: A comparison study.* Manuscript submitted for publication.

Lund, N., & Duchan, J. (1983). *Assessing children's language in naturalistic contexts.* Englewood Cliffs, NJ: Prentice Hall.

Lyngaas, K., Nyberg, B., Hoekenga, R., & Gruenewald, L. (1983). Language intervention in the multiple contexts of the public school setting. In J. Miller, D. Yoder, & R. Schiefelbusch (Eds.), *Contemporary issues in language intervention* (pp. 239–258) (ASHA Reports 12). Rockville, MD: Aspen Publishers, Inc.

MacDonald, J.D. (1985). Language through conversation: A model for intervention with language delayed persons. In S.F. Warren & A.K. Rogers-Warren (Eds.), *Teaching functional language* (pp. 89–122). Austin, TX: PRO-ED.

MacDonald, J., Blott, U., Gordon, K., Spiegel, B., & Hartmann, M. (1974). An experimental parent-assisted treatment program for preschool language delayed persons. *Journal of Speech and Hearing Disorders, 39,* 395–414.

Mahoney, G. (1988). Maternal communication style with mentally retarded children. *American Journal on Mental Retardation, 92,* 352–359.

Mahoney, G., & Powell, A. (1988). Modifying parent-child interaction: Enhancing the development of handicapped children. *Journal of Special Education, 22,* 82–96.

McCauley, R., & Demetras, M. (1990). The identification of language impairment in the selection of specifically language-impaired subjects. *Journal of Speech and Hearing Disorders, 55,* 468–475.

McConkey, R., Jeffree, D., & Hewson, S. (1979). Involving parents in extending the language development of their young mentally handicapped children. *British Journal of Disorders of Communication, 14,* 203–218.

McCormick, L., & Schiefelbusch, R. (1984). *Early language intervention.* Columbus, OH: Charles E. Merrill.

McCune-Nicolich, L., & Bruskin, C. (1982). Combinatorial competency in symbolic play and language. In D. Pepler & K. Rubin (Eds.), *The play of children: Current theory and research* (pp. 30–45). Basel, Switzerland: Karger.

McDonnell, A., & Hardman, M. (1988). A synthesis of "best practice" guidelines for early childhood services. *Journal of the Division for Early Childhood, 12,* 328–341.

McLean, J.E., & Snyder-McLean, L. (1978). *A transactional approach to early language training.* Columbus, OH: Charles E. Merrill.

Miller, J. (1981). *Assessing language production in children: Experimental procedures.* Baltimore: University Park Press.

Mudd, J., & Wolery, M. (1987). Training Head Start teachers to use incidental teaching. *Journal of the Division for Early Childhood, 11,* 124–134.

Mulac, A., & Tomlinson, C. (1977). Generalization of an operant remediation program for syntax with language–delayed children. *Journal of Communication Disorders, 10,* 231–244.

Mulligan, M., & Guess, D. (1984). Using an individualized curriculum sequencing model. In L. McCormick & R. Schiefelbusch (Eds.),

Early language intervention (pp. 299–323). Columbus, OH: Charles E. Merrill.

Murphy, M., & Vincent, E. (1989). Identification of critical skills for success in daycare. *Journal of Early Intervention, 13,* 221–229.

Nelson, K.E. (1977). Faciltating children's syntax acquisition. *Developmental Psychology, 13,* 101–107.

Ninio, A., & Bruner, J. (1978). The achievement and antecedents of labelling. *Journal of Child Language, 7,* 565–573.

Nirje, B. (1980). The normalization principle. In R.J. Flynn & K.E. Nitsch (Eds.), *Normalization, social integration, and community services* (pp. 31–49). Baltimore: University Park Press.

Notari, A., & Bricker, D. (1990). The utility of a criterion-referenced instrument in the development of individualized education plans for infants and young children. *Journal of Early Intervention, 14,* 117–132.

Notari, A., Cole, K., & Mills, P. (1992). Cognitive referencing: The (non)relationship between theory and application. *Topics in Early Childhood Special Education, 11*(4), 22–38.

Odom, S., & McEvoy, M. (1988). Integration of young children with handicaps and normally developing children. In S.L. Odom & M.B. Karnes (Eds.), *Early intervention for infants and children with handicaps: An empirical base* (pp. 241–267). Baltimore: Paul H. Brookes Publishing Co.

Odom, S., & McEvoy, M. (1990). Mainstreaming at the preschool level: Potential barriers and tasks for the field. *Topics in Early Childhood Special Education, 10*(2), 48–61.

Ogura, T., Notari, A., & Fewell, R. (1991). The relationship between play and language in young children with Down syndrome. *The Japanese Journal of Developmental Psychology, 2*(1), 18–24.

Olsen-Fulero, L. (1982). Style and stability in mother conversational behavior: A study of individual differences. *Journal of Child Language, 9,* 543–564.

Pearson, M., Pearson, A., Fenrick, N., & Greene, D. (1988). The implementation of sample, mand, and delay techniques to enhance the language of delayed children in group settings. *Journal of the Division for Early Intervention, 12,* 342–348.

Peterson, N.L., & Haralick, J.G. (1977). Integration of handicapped and nonhandicapped preschoolers: An analysis of play and social interaction. *Education and Training of the Mentally Retarded, 12,* 235–265.

Piaget, J. (1973). Foreword. In M. Schwebel & J. Raph (Eds.), *Piaget in the classroom* (pp. ix–x). New York: Basic Books.

Price, P., & Bochner, S. (1990). Mother–child interaction and early language development. In D. Mitchell & R.I. Brown (Eds.), *Early intervention studies for young children with special needs* (pp. 226–258). London, England: Chapman & Hall.

Quilitch, H.R., & Risley, T.R. (1973). The effects of play materials on social play. *Journal of Applied Behavior Analysis, 6,* 575–578.

Rogers-Warren, A. (1982). Behavioral ecology in classrooms for young handicapped children. *Topics in Early Childhood Special Education, 2*(1), 21–32.

Rogers-Warren, A., & Warren, S. (1980). Mands for verbalization: Facilitating the generalization of newly trained language in children. *Behavior Modification, 4,* 230–245.

Sainato, D., & Lyon, S. (1989). Promoting successful mainstreaming transitions for handicapped preschool children. *Journal of Early Intervention, 13,* 305–314.

Salisbury, C. (1991). Mainstreaming during the early childhood years. *Exceptional Children, 58,* 146–155.

Scherer, N., & Olswang, L. (1984). Role of mothers' expansions in stimulating children's language production. *Journal of Speech and Hearing Research, 27,* 387–396.

Shore, C. (1986). Combinatorial play, conceptual development, and early multiword speech. *Developmental Psychology, 20,* 872–880.

Shure, M. (1963). Psychological ecology of a nursery school. *Child Development, 34,* 979–992.

Skinner, B.F. (1957). *Verbal behavior.* New York: Appleton-Century-Crofts.

Smilansky, S. (1968). *The effects of socio-dramatic play on disadvantaged preschool children.* New York: John Wiley & Sons.

Snow, C. (1983). Literacy and language: Relationships during the preschool years. *Harvard Educational Review, 53,* 165–189.

Snow, C.E. (1989). Social interaction and language acquisition. In M. Bornstein & J. Bruner (Eds.), *Interaction in human development* (pp. 83–103). Hillsdale, NJ: Erlbaum.

Snow, C.E., & Goldfield, B.A. (1983). Turn the page please: Situation-specific language acquisition. *Journal of Child Language, 10,* 551–569.

Snow, C.E., Perlmann, R., & Nathan, D. (1987). Why routines are different: Toward a multiple-factors model of the relation between input and language acquisition. In K.E. Nelson & A. Van Kleck (Eds.), *Children's language:* (Vol. 6, pp. 65–97). Hillsdale, NJ: Erlbaum.

Stoneman, Z., Cantrell, M., & Hoover-Dempsey, K. (1983). The association between play materials and social behavior in a mainstreamed preschool: A naturalistic investigation. *Journal of Applied Developmental Psychology, 4,* 163–174.

Strain, P. (1990). LRE for preschool children with handicaps: What we know, what we should be doing. *Journal of Early Intervention, 14,* 291–296.

Strickland, D.S., & Morrow, L.M. (1989). *Emerging literacy: Young children learn to read and write.* Newark, DE: International Reading Association.

Sulzby, E. (1985). Children's emergent reading of favorite storybooks: A developmental study. *Reading Research Quarterly, 20,* 458–481.

Sulzby, E., & Teale, W. (1991). Emergent literacy. In R. Barr, M. Kamil, P. Mosenthal, & P.D. Pearson (Eds.), *Handbook of reading research:* (Vol. II, pp. 727–756). New York: Longman.

Swinson, J., & Ellis, C. (1988). Telling stories to encourage language. *British Journal of Special Education, 15*(4), 169–171.

Sylva, K., Roy, C., & Painter, M. (1980). *Childwatching at playgroup and nursery school.* Ypsilanti, MI: The High/Scope Press.

Tannock, R. (1988). Mothers' directiveness in their interactions with their children with and without Down syndrome. *American Journal on Mental Retardation, 93,* 154–165.

Tomasello, M., & Farrar, M. (1986). Joint attention and early language. *Child Development, 57,* 1454–1463.

Tomlinson, S. (1982). *A sociology of special education.* London, England: Routledge & Kegan Paul.

Tough, J. (1982). Language, poverty, and disadvantage in school. In L. Feagans & D.C. Farran (Eds.), *The language of children reared in poverty: Implications for evaluation and intervention* (pp. 3–18). New York: Academic Press.

Udwin, O. (1983). Imaginative play training as an intervention method with institutionalized preschool children. *British Journal of Educational Psychology, 53,* 32–39.

Vincent, L.J., Salisbury, C.L., Strain, P., McCormick, C., & Tessier, A. (1990). A behavioral-ecological approach to early intervention: Focus on cultural diversity. In S.J. Meisels & J.P. Shonkoff (Eds.), *Handbook of early intervention* (pp. 173–195). England: Cambridge University Press.

Vygotsky, L.S. (1978). *Mind in society: The development of higher psychological processes.* Cambridge, MA: Harvard University Press.

Warren, S.F., & Bambara, L.M. (1989). An experimental analysis of milieu language intervention: Teaching the action-object form. *Journal of Speech and Hearing Disorders, 54,* 448–461.

Warren, S.F., & Gazdag, G. (1990). Facilitating early language development with milieu intervention procedures. *Journal of Early Intervention, 14,* 62–86.

Warren, S.F., & Kaiser, A.P. (1988). Research in early language intervention. In S.L. Odom & M.B. Karnes (Eds.), *Early intervention for infants and children with handicaps: An empirical base* (pp. 75–89). Baltimore: Paul H. Brookes Publishing Co.

Warren, S.F., & Rogers-Warren, A.K. (1985). Teaching functional language: An introduction. In S.F. Warren & A.K. Rogers-Warren (Eds.), *Teaching functional language: Generalization and maintenance of language skills* (pp. 3–23). Baltimore: University Park Press.

Wells, G. (1985). *Language development in the preschool years.* Cambridge, England: Cambridge University Press.

Whitehurst, G.H., Falco, F.L., Lonigan, C.J., Fischel, J.E., Debaryshe, B.D., Valdez-Menchaca, M.C., & Caufield, M. (1988). Accelerating language development through picture book reading. *Developmental Psychology, 24,* 552–559.

Wilcox, M. (1984). Developmental language disorders: Preschoolers. In A. Holland (Ed.), *Language disorders in children* (pp. 101–128). San Diego, CA: College-Hill Press.

Wolfensberger, W. (1980). The definition of normalization. In R.J. Flynn & K.E. Nitsch (Eds.), *Normalization, social integration, and community services* (pp. 71–115). Baltimore, MD: University Park Press.

Wolfensberger, W. (1983). Social role valorization: A proposed new term for the principle of normalization. *Mental Retardation, 21*(6), 234–239.

Yoder, P.J., & Davies, B. (1990). Do parental questions and topic continuations elicit replies from developmentally delayed children? A sequential analysis. *Journal of Speech and Hearing Research, 23* 563–573.

Yoder, P.J., & Kaiser, A.P. (1989). Alternative explanations for the relationship between maternal verbal interaction styles and child language development. *Journal of Child Language, 16,* 141–161.

Yoder, P.J., Kaiser, A.P., & Alpert, C.L. (1991). An exploratory study of the interaction between language teaching methods and child characteristics. *Journal of Speech and Hearing Research, 34,* 155–167.

Chapter 3

SOCIAL INTERACTION SKILLS INTERVENTIONS FOR YOUNG CHILDREN WITH DISABILITIES IN INTEGRATED SETTINGS

*Samuel L. Odom
and William H. Brown*

For a typical child, a day spent in a preschool classroom will be filled with social events. With peers in the class, children talk, laugh, request and share toys and materials, suggest ideas, play, fight, and work. Most of these social interactions are positive in nature (Howes, 1988). Experts generally agree that while such interactions serve as the basis for the acquisition of a range of important developmental skills (Hartup, 1983), participation in such socially active environments affects children's acquisition of peer social interaction skills most directly. The acquisition of such interactional skills is important because they underlie the development of positive social relationships within the peer group. Failure to develop positive peer relationships, at least by the middle-childhood years, has been associated with a range of negative outcomes in adolescence and adulthood (see McConnell & Odom, 1986; Parker & Asher, 1987, for reviews).

Many young children with disabilities exhibit delays in the acquisition of peer social interaction skills. In their study of the development of peer relationships in young children with developmental delays, Guralnick and Weinhouse (1984) found that these children lagged behind peers without disabilities who were matched for mental age. That is, their delays were greater than would have been predicted from their cognitive development alone. Similarly, Spicuzza, McConnell, and Odom

Preparation of this chapter was supported by U.S. Office of Special Education Programs (Grant # G008730527.)

The authors thank Peggy Davis, Norma Morrison, and Patty Cronin for their assistance with drafts of this chapter.

(1991) noted that children with disabilities performed significantly below similar-age children without disabilities on a multi-measure assessment of social competence. In a national survey, preschool special education teachers noted that 75% of the children with disabilities in their classes would benefit from learning more age-appropriate social skills (Odom, McConnell, & Chandler, 1991). In fact, leaders in the field have proposed that early intervention programs should include the development of young children's social competence as a central mission (Guralnick, 1990; Strain, 1990).

Programs designed to teach social interaction skills for young children with disabilities must include typically developing peers as participants (i.e., as models or active interveners). In such programs, typically developing children may provide a responsive and socially active context in which children may observe, practice, and acquire more advanced social interaction skills. The inclusion of such a peer group affects both the acquisition (Odom & Strain, 1986) and the cross-setting generalization of skills (Strain, 1983a).

Given the ready access to typically developing peers that they make available, mainstreamed preschools could serve as effective settings for acquiring social interaction skills and developing positive social relationships (Haring, 1992). Unfortunately, one of the most frequently replicated findings in the research literature on integration is that social interaction between children with and without disabilities will not occur automatically (see Odom & McEvoy, 1988, for a review). Typically developing children tend to select other typically developing children as social partners in integrated settings, often to the exclusion of the children with dis-

abilities (Guralnick & Groom, 1987, 1988). Thus, a context that seems essential for promoting social interaction skills for young children with disabilities many be limited by the nature of social interaction patterns in such settings, unless specific intervention programs are designed to address directly the skill deficits of the children with disabilities.

The purpose of this chapter is to examine research on social interaction skills training for young children with disabilities, and to draw from this examination potential implications for promoting effective early intervention programs in mainstreamed settings. In this chapter, the authors present a conceptual framework that underlies most social interaction interventions, distinguish between the concepts of social integration and social interaction interventions, review a range of specific intervention approaches, and propose implications of employing these interventions in mainstreamed, community-based settings.

CONCEPTUAL ISSUES IN SOCIAL INTERACTION INTERVENTION

A variety of conceptual issues serve as a foundation for social interactions intervention approaches for young children with disabilities. Understanding the terminology associated with these interventions, their conceptual foundation, and the nature of the social problem is essential for professionals interested in employing such interventions in mainstreamed settings.

Terminology

In this chapter, the authors refer to *social interaction* as the direct exchange of words, gestures, toys, or other materials between two or more children (unless indicated otherwise, all definitions are taken from Vanderbilt-Minnesota Social Interaction Project, in press). Social interaction can be thought of as a chain of social behaviors in which social partners contribute different behaviors or links in the chain. The first behavior in a social interaction chain is often called a *social initiation,* and subsequent behaviors in the chain are called *social responses.* These behaviors are *bidirectional* or *reciprocal* in nature, in that different partners in social interactions direct social behaviors to the other partner, who in turn directs social behaviors back to the original child (Strain & Shores, 1977). Researchers have identified a number of social behaviors that occur during young children's peer interactions; in a recent review, Odom and Ogawa (1991) found that more than 400 behavioral categories have been used in peer social interaction research conducted primarily in the 1980s. The term *social competence* is used to refer to children's effective and appropriate use of social behavior in their social interactions with peers. A child's level of competence is often judged by significant social agents in the child's life, such as teachers, parents, or peers (Odom & McConnell, 1985).

The distinction between social integration and social interaction interventions is important to the discussions in this chapter. *Social integration* refers to the degree to which children with disabilities are active social participants within a social group containing typically developing peers (e.g., a classroom, childcare center). The most common measure of such social integration is the magnitude and nature of social interaction that occurs between children with and without disabilities.

If children with disabilities interact with nondisabled peers with the same frequency and quality as nondisabled peers do with one another, one can argue that social integration has been accomplished.

Social interaction interventions refer to specific procedures that teach social behavior that is necessary for active participation in social groups, and that also support the use of those behaviors in such groups. As noted above, such interventions are most effectively employed in settings with nondisabled peers, although such interventions have also taken place in classes containing only children with disabilities (Odom & Strain, 1986).

Conceptual Framework for Social Interaction Interventions

Most social interaction interventions designed for preschool-age children with disabilities operate from the theoretical base of applied behavior analysis. Children engage in social interaction with peers because these interactions result in positive effects (i.e., are reinforcing). For example, Mary may ask Scott to share his glue, and as a result, Scott gives Mary the glue, which she can then use to complete her collage. The positive effect in this interaction is Mary's receiving the glue. Judy may suggest to Charlie that they pretend to be trout fishing, and as a result, Charlie starts to play with her, which Judy thinks is fun. In this example, the positive and playful response is itself the positive effect. Baer and Wolf (1970) originally noted that such peer responses to social behaviors serve as the natural community of reinforcement in preschool group settings. It should also be noted that through a history of positive interactions with specific peers, positive social relationships may form. In such situations, these specific peers (i.e., friends) may serve as more generalized positive reinforcers, in that play with the friend-peer may be intrinsically rewarding regardless of the outcome of individual interactions.

The absence of social interaction with peers may occur for several reasons. Children may not have the entry-level skills for engaging in such interactions. Being isolated from such interactions, in turn, allows little opportunity for children to experience positive effects from their social behavior. Some children may attempt to interact with peers, but the peers may not respond positively—either because the child's behavior is unskilled, or because of other characteristics that the child exhibits (e.g., stereotypic behavior, appearance, reputation). Still other children may engage in negative or aggressive behavior that alienates peers and reduces the opportunity for the child to receive positive social behaviors from peers. In each of these cases, the children with disabilities do not experience the positive effects that are associated with engaging in social exchanges.

Most behavioral social interaction interventions attempt to increase children's positive social interactions with peers. The assumption is that positive interaction will become reinforcing, which in turn will lead to participation in interactions in other settings and across time (i.e., cross-setting generalization and maintenance). McConnell (1987) has noted that the notion of *entrapment,* in which the reinforcing status of the peers' interaction increases the likelihood of future interaction, is a concept that underlies such interventions. As children learn social skills that allow them to participate in peer social interactions, the positive or reinforcing qualities of the peers' social behavior increase the likelihood that the child will use the social behavior in the future.

TYPES OF SOCIAL INTERACTION INTERVENTIONS

Researchers have investigated a variety of procedures for fostering the social interaction skills of young children with disabilities. These interventions have involved arranging the environment to support peer interaction, directly teaching social skills to children with disabilities, promoting and/or reinforcing social interactions of young children with disabilities, teaching children with disabilities to monitor their own behavior, and teaching peers to begin social interactions with children with disabilities.

Environmental Arrangement

One strategy for facilitating children's social interactions is the systematic arrangement of environments (cf. Sainato & Carta, 1992; Twardosz, 1984). Although modification of specific adult and child social contingencies is technically a re-arrangement of one's environment, those procedures are reviewed in subsequent sections. For the purposes of this chapter, environmental arrangement includes alteration of the physical and social context of a setting (e.g., classroom, playground).

Arrangement of the Physical Environment Quilitch and Risley (1973) demonstrated that specific types of toys were influential in increasing young children's social interactions. In a well-controlled study, these investigators found that the availability of some toys, such as checkers and pick up sticks (i.e., social toys), resulted in more social interactions among school-age children than did other toys, such as puzzles and crayons (i.e., isolate toys). Their comparison of toy types demonstrated the effect that careful selection of toys can have on the likelihood of children's social interactions. In a more recent study with preschool children, Beckman and Kohl (1984) investigated the effects of social and isolate toys on the social interactions of children in both integrated and segregated play groups. Their findings replicated those of Quilitch and Risley (1973), with children's social interactions occurring at higher rates in both integrated and segregated play groups when social toys, as opposed to isolate toys, were made available.

The manipulation of the amount of space made available for children within a setting is another type of environmental arrangement. McGrew (1970) proposed that the amount of space made available to persons be conceptualized along two dimensions. *Social density* can be altered by increasing or decreasing the number of persons within the same-size setting. *Spatial density* can be manipulated by changing the amount of space made available to the same number of persons within a setting. In an early study, Hutt and Vaizey (1966) increased the number of children in a freeplay setting (i.e., social density) and found decreased positive social responding and increased aggressive behavior. Loo (1972) investigated changes in spatial density and, similar to Hutt and Vaizey (1966), found that children's positive social interactions decreased as less space was made available. When McGrew (1970) manipulated both spatial and social density, he did not find effects on the frequency of children's social interactions. These investigations of spatial and social density have yielded inconsistent findings (Hartup, 1983).

In a more recent study that controlled for the type of toys made available, teacher interactions with children, and familiarity of the children, Brown, Fox, and Brady (1987) found that limiting the amount of space made available to preschool children during play (i.e., 19 vs. 58 square feet per child) resulted in systematic increases in their social interactions. Moreover, in contrast to the findings of Hutt and Vaizey (1966), no increase in aggressive responses occurred in the restricted spatial condition.

In another study of spatial arrangements in a classroom, Spiegel-McGill, Bambara, Shores, and Fox (1984) demonstrated that the proximity of children influenced their social responsiveness; when children were placed close to one another they became more interactive with classmates. Because the participants of this study had disabilities that necessitated prosthetic seating and positioning, the environmental arrangement of their chairs appears to have been of even greater importance to their social behavior than it would be for children without significant motor disabilities.

Arrangement of Social Environment
The studies discussed above used manipulations of the physical environment to improve children's social responding; researchers have also studied the effects of alterations of the social environment. For example, Shores, Hester, and Strain (1976) examined the effects of teacher-imposed structure (e.g., introducing the activity, suggesting sociodramatic roles) during an activity on the social interactions of preschool children with behavior disorders. When children were exposed to three levels of teacher participation (i.e., direct teacher involvement, no teacher involvement, and teacher-structured play), the children had the highest rates of social interactions when the teacher initially structured the play activity. In contrast, when teachers were directly involved throughout the activity, children were less likely to interact with peers. DeKlyen and Odom (1989) also found that rates of peer interaction among young children

with and without disabilities were related to the level of activity structure employed by teachers. Highly structured play activities, which were defined by the extent to which teachers pre-arranged the activity (e.g., discussion of the activity, teacher assignment of roles or expectations), resulted in a higher percentage of social interactions.

In another manipulation of social environmental arrangements, Strain (1983a) reported that the inclusion of children without disabilities in play activities with children with autism (i.e., heterogeneous play groups) produced generalization of newly acquired social interaction skills from training sessions to nontraining play periods. He argued that in freeplay settings composed only of children with disabilities (i.e., segregated environments) peers were not as responsive to and supportive of social behavior of the children with autism who had participated in social-skills training. This positive generalization finding with heterogeneous play groups strongly suggests the importance of providing integrated circumstances for children who need, or who have received, social skills training.

Several investigators have shown that environmental arrangements can be effective in improving young children's social behavior. Rogers-Warren (1984) noted, however, that environmental arrangements often produce only modest effects. Indeed, McEvoy, McConnell, Odom, and Skellenger (1991) failed to obtain positive effects for preschool children with disabilities when implementing an environmental arrangement intervention package composed of limited space assignment, structured play activities, and integrated groupings in four classrooms. Also, Hecimovic, Fox, Shores, and Strain (1985) did not achieve generalization of social responding with heterogeneous play groups.

Despite mixed results, environmental arrangement interventions may have potential benefits for children with disabilities. First, many environmental arrangements are easily achieved, and deleterious findings have not been reported (Brown et al., 1987). Second, in a recent survey, teachers rated highly the feasibility and current use of environmental arrangements as an intervention strategy in their classrooms (Odom et al., 1991). Finally, environmental alterations may interact with more intensive social skills interventions—which have specific social contingencies, such as teacher- or peer-mediated social skills training, as components—to produce improved social responding (Odom & Strain, 1984).

Naturalistic Approaches to Social Skills Intervention

Another approach to improving young children's social interactions has been to intervene within naturally occurring contexts and situations during the preschool day. The circumstances for intervention are different from the procedures described later in that they occur in routine activities or situations in the classroom. Moreover, the approach is less structured than traditional social skill training, which involves teachers modifying classroom activities so that they become more supportive of children's social interactions (Brown, McEvoy, & Bishop, 1991).

Group Affection Activities   One naturalistic approach for improving young children's social interactions has been to intervene within typically occurring contexts. For example, Twardosz, Nordquist, Simon, and Botkin (1983) developed and evaluated procedures that encourage children's social interactions during typical preschool activities. Their intervention package, which Twardosz and her colleagues called "group affection activities," provided teachers and children with opportunities to discuss and practice affectionate social initiations, such as hugs, tickles, and compliments, that have a high probability of eliciting and supporting social interactions. The intervention procedures consisted of a teacher leading a discussion on the importance of friends and the designation of special friends (i.e., socially withdrawn children) before the activities; teacher prompts to socially interact during the group activities; and subsequent teacher praise and acknowledgment of any interactions that occurred during the games, stories, and songs.

Group affection activities are noteworthy in that they are easily implemented by teachers during routine large-group activities. Moreover, the intervention often results in generalized changes in children's social responses in unstructured free play periods occurring many hours after the intervention. Since the initial investigation by Twardosz and her colleagues (1983) with children who were socially withdrawn, McEvoy et al. (1988), as well as Brown, Ragland, and Fox (1988), have used similar intervention procedures successfully to increase the social interactions of young children with developmental disabilities in both training and nontraining contexts.

Incidental Teaching of Social Behavior Another naturalistic approach to social skills intervention, one that has received only limited empirical attention up to this time, is incidental teaching of social interactions. For a number of years, incidental teaching has been used effectively to promote young children's language development (for review see Hart, 1985). Incidental teaching is child-initiated and is conducted most effectively in naturally occurring circumstances. Incidental teaching of social behavior is conducted during unstructured activities, for brief periods of time, and usually when children are interested in materials, activities, or other children. Because teaching episodes are short in duration and occur while children are already interested in something, initial problems with children's attention and motivation may be less of a concern.

During incidental teaching of social behavior episodes, teachers can prompt children to initiate to one another, or they can provide models to facilitate children's social interactions. This approach allows teachers to provide additional opportunities throughout the school day to encourage interactions with peers (see, e.g., Brown et al., 1991). Moreover, the procedures might be useful as a tactic to transfer children's newly acquired social skills from more structured training sessions to less structured nontraining classroom activities and settings. In an investigation of this approach, Nordquist, Twardosz, and McEvoy (1985) found that incidental teaching was effective in changing the social behavior of children with autism in integrated preschools. Additional empirical support is needed, however, and the use of incidental teaching of social behavior alone may not prove effective in providing children with significant social skills deficits with sufficient opportunities to learn and practice important social skills.

Teacher-Mediated Interventions

In teacher-mediated interventions, the teachers may play various roles. They may lead social skills training instructional groups, provide prompts for engaging in social interaction, provide reinforcement for social responding, or use a combination of these techniques.

Social Skills Training Groups Teaching skills directly in didactic or instructional groups is a teacher-mediated strategy for promoting social interaction. This approach has been called social skills training. In these groups teachers introduce, describe, and demonstrate social interaction skills, and children may practice or roleplay the skills (Ladd & Mize, 1983; Mize, Ladd, & Price, 1985). Sessions are often conducted in a lesson format. The lessons may occur over an extended period of time or until the students reach a specified performance criterion. The expectation is that children will learn the social skills in the instructional setting and use them in play activities outside of the setting.

Several investigators have examined the use of social skills training lessons. In one social skills training study, McConnell, Sisson, Cort, and Strain (1991) taught 10 positive social skills across 56 sessions to preschoolers with behavior disorders, and observed modest increases in children's social skills effects. In a second study, McConnell, Peterson, and Fox (1992) investigated the effects of a social skills training package in which children with developmental delays were taught 5 initiating and 5 responding skills over a 25-day period. For both of these studies, direct teacher involvement (i.e., prompting and reinforcement) was required to establish robust effects. With preschoolers with hearing impairments, Antia and Kreimeyer (1987) conducted social skills training groups to teach six specific social skills (i.e., greeting, sharing, assisting, complimenting, cooperative play, and inviting). Although these authors found increases in social interaction in freeplay settings, the teachers also provided prompts and models of appropriate playing in those settings.

A related approach has been to teach children with disabilities play behaviors that would be likely to engage children in social interaction. In a series of studies, Goldstein and his colleagues, as well as others (Doctoroff, 1991; Goldstein & Cisar, 1992; Goldstein, Wickstrom, Hoyson, Jamieson, & Odom, 1988), have analyzed sociodramatic play activities and created scripts that they teach to children with and without disabilities. These researchers have found that children can learn the scripts and use them independently in the training settings. However, the children in these studies did not actively use the social scripts in play settings unless teacher prompts were provided. With autistic children, Haring and Lovinger (1989) taught toy play skills and initiations designed to involve the peers in toy play to children with autism, and found increases in social interaction in freeplay settings. It should be noted that in freeplay settings, peers were coached to respond to the children with autism.

Although social skills training groups appear to have been effective with other children and adults with disabilities (Bornstein, Bellack, & Hersen, 1980; Mesibov, 1986; Walker, McConnell, & Clarke, 1985), McConnell's and Goldstein's work suggests that social skills taught in instructional groups may need to be paired with teacher support (e.g., prompts or reinforcement) in play settings, with Haring and Lovinger being the notable exception to this conclusion. Two factors may account for these results. First, social skills lessons tend to be quite verbal, and some young children with social competence deficits may not have the verbal skills to take advantage of the lessons. Second, for preschoolers with disabilities, their behavior may not yet have come under sufficient verbal control (i.e., they may be able to describe the skills presented in the lessons, but not use the skills in interactions with their peers in nontraining settings).

Teacher Prompts Teacher prompting represents a second strategy that promotes social interaction with peers. A prompt generally refers to a verbal or physical cue (i.e., suggestion or gesture) for the child with disabilities to engage in social interactions. Such prompts may signal a child to initiate an interaction or respond to the initiation of others. Teacher prompting, as an intervention strategy, has most often been used directly in play settings with children, rather than in instructional settings outside of the social context. The ultimate purpose of prompting is usually to increase children's engagement in social interactions, with the social responses of the peers to eventually serve as the positive consequence or reinforcer for the interactions. In one study, Odom and Strain (1986) used a prompting procedure to increase social initiations of children with autism, but did not withdraw the prompts before the intervention ended. In an extension of their research with preschoolers with hearing impairments, noted above, Antia and Kreimeyer (1988) used a graduated fading procedure for reducing teacher prompts and models, and found that increases in social interactions maintained after intervention procedures were withdrawn. Although prompting has been used in many more studies, it is combined with teacher reinforcement in most intervention procedures.

Teacher Reinforcement Teachers have also used reinforcement as an intervention tactic when children engage in social interaction with peers. Reinforce-

ment is defined as positive consequences that increase the probability that a social behavior will occur again; it may include verbal praise, tangible reward, opportunities to engage in activities, and so forth. The rationale for this technique is that reinforcement delivered after the interaction will increase the likelihood that children with disabilities will engage in the interaction again. The assumption is that increased participation in positive interactions with peers will then lead to the interactions themselves becoming reinforcing as the external reinforcement is being withdrawn.

In one of the first studies to examine the use of teacher reinforcement on social behavior, Allen, Hart, Buell, Harris, and Wolf (1964) examined the effect of adult praise of social interaction of a preschool child who was socially isolated, and noted increases in her social behavior. In two other early studies, Strain and his colleagues (Strain, Shores, & Kerr, 1976; Strain & Timm, 1974) provided reinforcement for social interaction to young children with disabilities (i.e., behavior disorders) and observed increases in the frequency of interaction. In a recent study, described above, McConnell et al. (1991) provided prompts and reinforcement to children with behavior disorders after they had participated in social skills training, and found increases in the percentage of time spent in social interaction. For a comprehensive review of this literature, see McEvoy, Odom, and McConnell (1992).

The advantage of teacher reinforcement is that it can be provided directly in settings where children may actually use their social interaction skills after the intervention has ended. However, the teacher must be judicious when applying reinforcement. A clear recommendation has been to administer reinforcement only after a social interaction has completely stopped (Peterson, McConnell, Cronin, Spicuzza, & Odom, 1991). Strain and Fox (1981) noted that when teachers provide reinforcement during ongoing social interaction, children will terminate their interactions and orient to the teacher.

Another consideration in using teacher reinforcement and prompts is that they must be faded or withdrawn if the interactions themselves are to assume a reinforcing function. Timm, Strain, and Eller (1979) used a systematic fading procedure for reducing teacher prompts to young children with disabilities in order to promote maintenance of social interactions after the teacher prompting and reinforcement intervention had ended. As noted above, Antia and Kreimeyer (1988) gradually withdrew teacher supports to children with disabilities, which resulted in maintenance of social interactions of preschoolers with hearing impairments. Similary, Fox, Shores, Lindeman, and Strain (1986) systematically withdrew teacher prompts and reinforcement for peer social interaction, with children maintaining their interactions after the intervention ended. From these studies, it appears that teachers must use the children's social behavior as a gauge in deciding how quickly to withdraw their prompts or reinforcement, and that this process should occur gradually.

Peer-Mediated Interventions

Another set of intervention strategies has been called peer-mediated, in that peers are taught to support the social interactions of children with disabilities by making social initiations that are likely to produce a positive response. The rationale for using peers as the primary interveners is

that they are natural participants in the interactions, and thus could more directly serve as the cue for the future interactions. Also, by increasing the opportunity for interactions, children with disabilities may learn appropriate ways of responding to peers and may begin to understand the reinforcing nature of the interactions. Another advantage for peer-mediated interventions is that the teacher does not directly prompt or reinforce the children with disabilities, so there is no need for systematic fading, although teachers may find it necessary to provide support for nondisabled peers.

In one of the first studies to use this approach, Strain, Shores, and Timm (1977) taught a nondisabled child to make several specific types of social initiations to a child with behavior disorders, and found increases in the social interactions of the child with disabilities, as well as in those of other children in the play group. Since this early study, peer-mediated intervention has been used to promote the social interaction skills of preschool children with disabilities in a number of studies (Fantuzzo et al., 1988; Hendrickson, Strain, Tremblay, & Shores, 1982; Lancioni, 1982; Strain, 1983a). In a unique application of this method, Goldstein and his colleagues (Goldstein & Ferrell, 1987; Goldstein & Wickstrom, 1986) have taught peers to make initiations that support the communicative interactions of children with language impairments and other disabilities.

Peer-mediated interventions usually consist of several components. First, children who are socially competent are selected to serve as peer interveners. The social skills of the peers have a substantial effect on the success of the intervention (Odom & Strain, 1986). Second, the peers are taught social initiations or other behaviors that elicit or support the interactions of the children with disabilities. These skills are taught in training sessions similar to the social skills training groups for children with disabilities described above. The number of sessions varies across studies, but there are usually fewer sessions than are required in social skills training for children with disabilities. Teacher prompts and, at times, reinforcement, are provided to the peers for making social initiations in play groups outside of the training session to the children with disabilities (Ostrosky, Chandler, Odom, McConnell, & Peterson, 1991b).

As with teacher-mediated interventions, in peer-mediated intervention, procedures have been included for reducing or eliminating teacher supports for peer interactions. The rationale has been that for these interventions to be truly mediated by the peers, they should be independent from teacher involvement, although teachers would still monitor the effects of the interventions. Odom and Watts (1991) used a visual feedback system (i.e., happy faces drawn on a card after an interaction) and correspondence training (i.e., peers' verbal report to the teacher whether they got their friends to play) (Osnes, Guevremont, & Stokes, 1986) to support peer initiations to children with autism after teacher prompts were withdrawn. Peers did continue to initiate interaction with target children when the teacher withdrew verbal prompts, although neither correspondence training nor visual feedback were faded by the end of the study. In a peer-initiation intervention with three children with disabilities, Sainato, Goldstein, and Strain (1992) designed a procedure in which peers self-monitored four types of initiations to children with autism. In this procedure, peers received reinforcement when their reports matched

an adult observer's report and they made a pre-arranged number of initiations. This self-monitoring procedure allowed the teachers to reduce their verbal prompts to a low level, but again the procedure was not completely faded by the end of the study. To eliminate the use of teacher prompts and visual feedback, Odom, Chandler, Ostrosky, McConnell, and Reaney (1992) systematically faded teacher prompts, and then visual feedback, in peer-mediated interventions with children with disabilities. All support (i.e., teacher prompt, visual feedback) was withdrawn by the end of the intervention. As in teacher-mediated interventions, these studies suggest that teacher involvement must be withdrawn in a systematic fashion if it is to be successful.

Combined Intervention Approaches

In teacher-mediated approaches, direct intervention procedures are provided to children with disabilities, but peers are not involved in the training. Peer-mediated approaches usually include direct training for peers, but do not include target children. However, several recent studies have involved both target children and peers in the same training sessions, which essentially results in a combination of teacher- and peer-mediated approaches to social skills training. With socially withdrawn preschoolers, Hodgens and McCoy (1990) adapted a coaching approach originally developed for older children by Ladd (1981) and Ogden and Asher (1977). This procedure included direct instruction and modeling of three skills in a small group setting containing peers and target children, as well as a visual feedback system used in the play settings. These authors found that the socially withdrawn children acquired all three skills and used them in generalization settings and with untrained peers. In a similar study that included children with disabilities, Odom, Ostrosky, Cronin, and Keetz (1992) taught five skills to peers and target children in a social skills training group, provided teacher prompts to both target children and peers in play activities, and used a visual feedback system to eliminate teacher prompts and induce generalization in a second daily activity. Increases in social interactions were found for five of the six children in the study. To investigate the effect of the timing of visual feedback in combined interventions, Spicuzza, McEvoy, and McConnell (1992) implemented the combined intervention and provided visual feedback either immediately after a social interaction occurred, or at the end of a 30-second interval. They found positive effects for the intervention itself, but little difference between the effects of the two types of visual feedback. Although only a few studies have examined the combination of peer- and teacher-mediated interventions, the results to date appear promising. The possible advantage of such intervention is that both types of children learn the social skills at the same time, and the emphasis on supporting the skills is directed to both children. Thus, neither the target children nor their peers are highlighted as tutors or recipients, and the potential may be greater for creating a more co-equal status among participants and for achieving generalization.

Group Contingencies

Establishing group reinforcement contingencies is another approach to increasing the social interaction of children with disabilities. With this procedure, positive consequences are provided to an entire group of children contingent upon the level of social interaction of either a single member of the group (i.e., in independent contingencies) or the group as a whole (i.e., interdependent contingencies). Lefebvre and Strain (1989) employed group contingencies in a peer-initiation intervention. Peers voted on reinforcers to be received if the target child engaged in a certain level of social interaction in play group triads. Increases in interactions and reductions in teacher prompts resulted from the use of this procedure. In a similar study, Kohler, Strain, Maretsky, and DeCasare (1990) taught social skills to all children in an integrated classroom, and introduced teacher prompts and both individual and group contingencies for engaging in social interactions. When no differences were found between the individual and group contingencies, the authors also introduced a social support condition, in which peers reminded other peers in the group to make social initiations. This type of social support produced moderate increases in social interaction when paired with the group contingency. Although they did not incorporate group contingencies per se, McConnell et al. (1991) examined the effects of providing group-oriented prompts to children in the social skills training study described above and found increases in peer initiations and subject responses, as contrasted with a condition in which prompts were provided only to target children. In summary, group contingencies appear to be promising techniques for supporting social interactions, but as yet there is little information on how to fade the reinforcement and prompting elements of the interventions.

Treatment Comparisons

The direct intervention approaches mentioned above appear to have generally produced positive changes in peer social interaction for children with disabilities. However, it is possible that such interventions might have differential treatment effects for children. To examine the differential effects on immediate behavior, Odom and Strain (1986) compared a peer-initiation and teacher-mediated intervention for promoting the social behavior of three autistic children. They found that peer-initiation intervention resulted in increases in peers' initiation and target children's responses, while the teacher-mediated intervention produced increases in target children's initiations and peers' responses (peers were also taught appropriate responses). Also the teacher-mediated intervention resulted in a longer mean length of interactions than did the peer-initiation intervention. In a similar study, Smith, McConnell, Maretsky, Kudray, and Strain (in press) alternated the prompts given to participants in social interaction and found similar effects. However, when a combined intervention condition was implemented (i.e., teacher prompts were directed to all participants in the interaction), a more equitable and reciprocal rate of social interaction occurred (i.e., similar rates of initiations and responses for each participant). Also, Smith et al. (in press) taught peer responses that extended social interactions, which resulted in a longer mean length of interactions.

In a large group study involving preschool-age children who were neglected and maltreated, Fantuzzo et al. (1988) examined the effects of peer-initiation and adult-mediated interventions. They found significantly greater changes in social interaction for children in the peer-initiation treatment group, as contrasted with the adult-intervention and control groups. These differences occurred in both the treatment and generalization settings. To examine differential treatment effects for preschool-age children with disabilities, Odom and McConnell (1991) randomly assigned children in 20 special education classrooms to four treatment conditions—environmental arrangements, child-specific (i.e., social skills training and adult prompting), peer-mediated (i.e., peer-initiation), and a comprehensive condition (i.e., combination of all the treatments). During pre- and post-intervention sessions, these researchers collected data on a direct observational measure of social interaction, an observer impressions scale, a teacher rating scale, and a peer rating scale. Pre-intervention scores served as covariates for post-intervention scores. On three of the measures the children in the peer-mediated intervention performed significantly higher than children in the control or comprehensive intervention, while children in the child-specific intervention scored higher than the control and comprehensive intervention on two measures. The peer-mediated intervention was significantly higher than the child-specific intervention on only one measure (i.e., teacher ratings). The environmental arrangements interventions differed significantly from (i.e., were higher than) the other treatments in peer ratings. The results of these studies suggest that the type of intervention chosen will affect specific types of social behavior, and that the more directed interventions (i.e., peer-mediated and child-specific) appear to have more powerful effects. A question remaining from the Odom and McConnell (1991) study is why the combined intervention was not more powerful, given the results of subsequent studies that have employed the combined intervention strategies (Odom, Ostrosky, et al., 1992; Spicuzza et al., 1992).

GENERALIZATION AND MAINTENANCE STRATEGIES

Baer, Wolf, and Risley (1968) originally argued that generalization and maintenance of behavior change was a necessary aspect of any effective intervention technology. A decade later, Stokes and Baer (1977) delineated the tactics of an "implicit technology" for promoting the generalization of behavior change across people, responses, settings, and time. More recently, Baer, Wolf, and Risley (1987) reiterated that generalization and maintenance of treatment effects continue to be necessary "for maximal effectiveness" of any intervention technology.

A review of the social interaction training literature indicates that the effects of social interaction training interventions do not readily generalize across settings unless systematic programming for generalization is used. Such programming should include systematic strategies for programming natural reinforcers for interaction (e.g., through prompt fading, providing a socially responsive peer group), training diversely (e.g., providing many examples and opportunities for use of social skills in different settings), and incorporating functional mediators (e.g., employing stimuli in training that are similar to naturalistic settings, correspondence training) (Stokes & Osnes, 1986). Unfortunately, space constraints prevent a comprehensive review of the generalization literature, although the implications of this literature are covered in the next section. For comprehensive reviews of the literature, the reader is referred to the papers and chapters by Brown and Odom (1992); Chandler, Lubeck, and Fowler (1992); McEvoy and Fox (1990); and Stokes and Osnes (1986).

IMPLICATIONS FOR PRACTICE

The literature reviewed above has many implications for supporting the development or acquisition of social interaction skills in integrated, community-based settings. These implications relate to the basic questions of *who* should participate in the intervention, *what* should be taught, *how* the skills should be taught, and *why* teach social interaction skills to some young children with disabilities.

Identification of Children in Need of Intervention (Whom To Teach?)

The social interaction interventions described above are designed for children with peer social interaction skills deficits. Not all children with disabilities will benefit from, or even need to participate in, such interventions. Some children with disabilities may have acquired a level of social competence that meets their needs. Other children may not possess the prerequisite skills necessary to benefit from these interventions. It is important to be able to determine for which children specific intervention activities should be planned.

The characteristics of children who would benefit from the more directed interventions described above (i.e., child-specific, peer-mediated, combined) are listed in Table 1. The primary characteristic is that children do not engage in effective or appropriate social interactions with peers. They may never initiate interactions with others, may ignore initiations from other children, may respond in a manner that discourages further interactions, or may engage in negative behavior (e.g., physical aggression, taking others' toys, verbal abuse) as their primary mode of interaction. By the time children are 3 years old, they should be starting to enjoy interacting with peers during play activities. For that reason, placing a heavy emphasis on social interaction interventions for children with disabilities younger than 3 is not recommended, although teachers can certainly

Table 1. Characteristics of children who would be included in social interaction interventions

Children with disabilities

Infrequent or no social interactions with peers (e.g., child rarely starts an interaction, usually does not respond when others start interactions, or responds negatively)

Chronological age of at least 3 years old

Purposeful play with toys (e.g., uses toys for play rather than banging, chewing, throwing)

One- or two-word utterances used reliably in a communicative fashion (or other form of communication that peers can be taught to understand)

Can understand and follow very short, one-step directions when accompanied by a gesture

Children serving as peers

Age-appropriate or good play skills

Age-appropriate social skills (e.g., makes appropriate and effective initiation to other children, generally responds positively)

No history of negative peer interaction, especially with the children with disabilities

Verbal communication skills that will allow children to make clear and understandable social initiations

Follows teacher directions

Can attend to a task for 10 minutes

Is willing to participate

Attends school on a regular basis

Adapted from Ostrosky, Chandler, Odom, McConnell, and Peterson (1991b).

set up their classroom to encourage social interaction (i.e., employ environmental arrangement interventions) or use incidental teaching of social behavior when opportunities occur. A good rule of thumb is that if children do not interact with their peers on the average of once every 2 minutes when they are observed across several play sessions and are participating in activities that are compatible with social play, then the teacher might note concerns for that child. The next step would be to collect more systematic assessment information to document such concerns. Odom and McConnell (1988) provided a detailed review of approaches for assessing the social interactions of young children with disabilities.

An important prerequisite skill for social skills intervention is that children can use toys in a purposeful manner. Children's play skills do not have to be sophisticated, but they should be beyond banging, chewing on, or throwing as the primary mode of toy manipulation. Children typically begin to acquire such functional play skills after the first year of life (Fewell & Kaminski, 1988). Such play skills serve as the foundation of playful social interactions with peers during the preschool years. An exception to the rule is sometimes made for children with autism. For these children symbolic play is often delayed or nonexistent, but they, too, appear to benefit from peer-mediated intervention (Odom et al., 1985; Sainato et al., 1992; Strain, 1983a).

As noted above, the social competence of typically developing peers directly influences the effectiveness of more structured interventions. Thus, the teacher should carefully select children who will serve as peers. Suggested criteria for selecting peers are provided in Table 1. Age-appropriate social and play skills and willingness to be involved in the intervention seem to be good predictors of which children will serve effectively as peers in these interventions. Although not a specific criteria, typically developing children who are 4 or 5 years old have been better able to serve as peers than children who are 3 years old.

Selection of Target Behaviors (What To Teach?)

As with any individualized program for young children, the choice of skills to be included in an instructional or intervention program should be based on the needs of the child. The choice of skills influences how well the behaviors generalize to other settings and peers and maintain after intervention. For example, if a child never makes a social initiation, but responds well to the initiations of others, then social initiations might be targeted. If a child is completely socially isolated and never engages in social interaction, then beginning with simple responding skills, which are often less difficult to master than initiating skills, would be appropriate. Essentially, teachers should determine what specific skills will help children become most effective and appropriate in their interactions with others.

There are some guidelines for skills selection. Strain, Odom, and McConnell (1984) noted that skills that have a high probability of receiving a positive response from a peer should be chosen. In a descriptive study, Tremblay, Strain, Hendrickson, and Shores (1981) identified a set of social initiations that elicited a positive response from peers (e.g., organizing play, sharing, affection, assistance). A subsequent validation study revealed that these skills, as well as more general positive responding, influenced the social acceptance of children with disabilities by typically developing classmates (Strain, 1983b). Such skills have served as the target behaviors in many directed intervention studies (e.g., Hendrickson et al., 1982; McConnell et al., 1991; Odom, Hoyson, Jamieson, & Strain, 1985). However, a range of other skills have also been identified as being important for young children. Below is a list of skills contained in the intervention studies reviewed by Odom and Ogawa (1991). This list may serve as an initial guide for teachers and consultants when choosing behaviors that should be targeted for intervention:

Affection
Conversation
Dispensing
Initiation (offer toy)

Nonverbal responses
Other initiation strategy
Positive initiations
Positive interaction initiated by peer
Positive interactive responses
Receiving
Speech
Verbal responses

Selecting and Implementing Social Interaction Interventions (How To Teach?)

The intervention strategies described above vary in intensity and in the resources needed for their implementation. To guide professionals in their selection of strategies, it is recommended that decisions about specific strategies proceed in a stepwise manner, a manner similar to the decision process that Evans and Meyer (1985) and Gaylord-Ross (1980) proposed for selecting interventions to decrease aberrant behavior. Such a decision-making process is hierarchical in nature in that teachers would begin with the least intrusive and most normalized intervention (i.e., interventions requiring the least amount of change in the class routine and the least amount of additional resources); evaluate whether a particular level of intervention achieves the goals of the instructional program for the child in question; and then determine if a more intense level of intervention is necessary. This decision hierarchy is presented in Figure 1. Although developed independently, the decision hierarchy is similar to and compatible with early childhood educators' recommendations to use less directive procedures to facilitate social interaction whenever possible (cf. Nourot & Van Hoorn, 1991).

Level I At this level the child with disabilities is physically integrated into a mainstreamed, community-based setting.

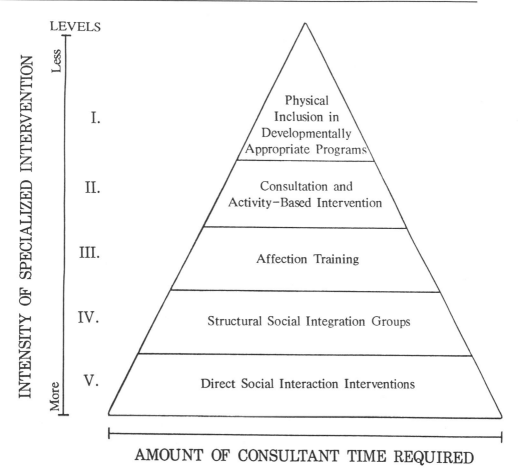

Figure 1. Amount of consultant time required for different levels of intervention.

We would expect that for such integration to be successful, efforts would be made to ensure that the preschool followed high-quality early childhood education practices and provided a developmentally appropriate program for typically developing young children (Bredekamp, 1987; NAEYC and NAECE/SDE, 1991; Richarz, chap. 5, this volume).

Level II In Level II, a program consultant would collaborate with the early childhood education staff to design an individualized program for each of the children with disabilities. Hanson and Widerstrom (chap. 8, this volume) describe different strategies for fostering collaboration between special education and early childhood education professionals. More specifically, in their research, Peck, Killen, and Baumgart (1989) demonstrated the positive effects of a collaborative consultation approach. Following this consultation model at the proposed second level of intervention, a special education consultant and early childhood education personnel would collaboratively design a plan for supporting social integration across the day. Such a plan could employ

alized Curriculum Sequenc-
1, as Doctoroff, McEvoy, and
) have proposed, or the Activity Based Intervention approach designed
by Bricker and her colleagues (Bricker &
Cripe, 1992). When opportunities for social integration are provided during the
day, the teacher should then make a decision about whether this level of intensity
results in the child's social interaction
with peers. If the child remains socially
isolated, or rebuffs interactions, the third
level of intervention should be considered.

Level III At the third level of intensity, the teacher could consider implementing affection activity intervention
(McEvoy et al., 1988), described above.
This intervention could be implemented
at the beginning of the day, and the effects
could be monitored during integrated
freeplay period.

Level IV If the child remains socially
isolated after affection activities are implemented, the teacher could next implement one of the environmental arrangement interventions described above. This
intervention could take the form of structured social integration play activities
(DeKlyen & Odom, 1989) that would occur
for brief periods of time during the day.
Procedures for conducting these integrated play groups have been described
in detail elsewhere (Odom et al., 1988;
Skellenger, McEvoy, McConnell, & Odom,
1991). The purpose of these groups would
be to provide intensive but brief opportunities for children with disabilities to
interact with their typically developing
peers.

Level V If the child remains socially
isolated during the structured play groups,
the teacher should consider implementing
one of the more intensive interventions
noted above (e.g., child-specific, peer-
mediated). Although intensive in nature,

these interventions also appear to be the
most effective for children with substantial disabilities (e.g., mental retardation,
autism). Most of the interventions are designed to be implemented in the structured play groups described in Level IV.
In addition, the teacher and consultant
should collaboratively design an activity-
based or ICS model plan for promoting the
generalization of the skills learned in the
intervention settings to other settings
during the day.

***Role of the Special Education Con-
sultant*** To deliver an individualized intervention program to young children
with disabilities in mainstreamed settings, early intervention programs must
provide consultation and support to early
childhood education personnel (see Hanson & Widerstrom, chap. 8, this volume).
Ideally, the needs of the child would dictate the nature and magnitude of this consultation. In the decision model described
above, the amount of direct participation
by the consultant increases with the level
of intervention. The authors propose that
Level II be the minimal level of intervention for any child with disabilities integrated into mainstreamed settings. At
Level III, the classroom teacher or other
staff would conduct the affection training
activities, but the consultant would probably need to provide training and materials
to the teacher, and might participate in
monitoring the child's progress. At Level
IV, again, the special education consultant would provide training and materials. The person who leads the structured
play group would depend on the amount of
time the consultant had to devote to in-
class activities. One possibility might be
for the consultant and the classroom staff
to alternate days. At Level V, the special
education consultant would probably need
to deliver the interventions. Most of the

intensive interventions described in this chapter require training in delivering prompts and reinforcement on specific schedules and would require more time than early childhood teachers may have. However, in balancing their caseloads, the special education consultants would have to recognize the time investment required. It should be noted that most in ter vention procedures are designed to include two or three children with disabilities in each training session (Odom, Kohler, & Strain, 1987; Ostrosky et al., 1991b; Peterson et al., 1991).

Resources Curriculum guides for implementing social interaction intervention represent a translation of research-based interventions into practical procedures (Odom & McConnell, 1989). Described below are a number of curriculum and intervention manuals that could serve as resources for teachers. Importantly, each of the manuals has gone through a systematic research, development, and validation process.

The *Social Competence Intervention Package for Preschool Youngsters* (SCIPPY) (Day, Powell, & Stowitschek, 1980) was one of the first guides for implementing peer-mediated interventions in classroom settings. This package included a manual for training peer helpers to initiate three skills (i.e., sharing, organizing play, and assisting) and activities that serve as the context for social interaction. The manual entitled *Teaching Strategies for Promoting Social Skills* (Odom et al., 1987) represents an extension of the work begun with SCIPPY. In this manual, scripted lessons are provided for teaching social initiation to peers. The target behaviors taught in this program are: share, share request, play organizer, assistance, assistance request, affection, and complimentary statements. In addition, the authors pro-

vide information about assessing children's social interaction and identifying children who would benefit from participating in the intervention.

The Vanderbilt-Minnesota Social Interaction Project has extended this curriculum development effort and recently generated a series of intervention manuals that describe environmental arrangements (Skellenger et al., 1991), child-specific (i.e., teacher-mediated) (Peterson et al., 1991), peer-mediated (Ostrosky et al., 1991b), and comprehensive (Ostrosky et al., 1991a) interventions. Each of these manuals contain instructions for arranging the classroom to accommodate the intervention, procedures for selecting children to participate, a schedule for implementing the interventions over a 100-day period, scripted lessons for conducting social skills training lessons, detailed instructions for withdrawing teacher prompts, and a set of 20 activities that would serve as the context for intervention activities and peer social interaction.

A Socialization Curriculum for Preschool Programs that Integrate Children with Handicaps (Brown, Ragland, & Bishop, 1989) includes directions for conducting affection training/socialization activities in regular early childhood education classrooms. These activities are designed to occur in large groups (i.e., up to 10 children) and 17 scripts, which include preschool games and songs, are provided. This manual also includes instructions for using incidental teaching to promote peer interactions involving young children with disabilities in integrated settings.

The Social Integration Project (1989) at Utah State University has developed a curriculum, called *Let's Be Social,* for promoting social interaction skills in mainstreamed settings. This curriculum guide contains 10 units, which include skills such as greeting, helping others, making requests, listening, and so forth. Instructions for implementing this program for individual children or for the entire class are provided in the guide.

The *Integrated Preschool Curriculum* (Odom et al., 1988) was developed to promote the social integration of young children with disabilities in integrated classrooms. The curriculum represents an environmental arrangement intervention approach. The guide contains instructions for establishing social integration groups, as well as 48 structured play activities, most of which are written at two levels (i.e., Level 1 to promote play skills and Level 2 to promote social integration). Procedures for assessing social interaction and screening for children with social skill deficits are also included. A set of intervention strategies for directly intervening to promote social interaction is also provided, as are recommendations for using this curriculum in the mainstreamed classroom and with children with different disabling conditions.

Philosophical Considerations (Why To Teach?)

The intervention strategies at Level IV and V differ both practically and philosophically from activities that typically occur in mainstream early childhood education classes (Richarz, chap. 5, this volume). Such interventions are behavioral in nature, but they also represent an effective practice from a special education perspective (Wolery, Bailey, & Strain, in press). They are designed to support the acquisition of skills for children with disabilities; most of these children with disabilities would probably not acquire these skills through active participation in developmentally appropriate environments alone. As such, these interventions could

be seen as prosthetic (Lindsley, 1964), just as wheelchairs may be prostheses for children with cerebral palsy, or glasses are prostheses for children with visual impairments. However, they differ from these more permanent forms of prostheses in that they are designed to be eventually withdrawn. A teacher and consultant may decide to provide an intensive level of intervention (Level V), but the assumption is that as the child acquires social interaction skills, the intensity of intervention will be reduced, potentially back to Level II.

SUMMARY

In this chapter, the authors have presented a rationale for conducting social interaction interventions for some children with disabilities; examined the conceptual/theoretical bases for these intervention strategies; described the research on these interventions, which spans nearly 25 years; and proposed a strategy for selecting interventions for use in community-based programs. From the research literature, it appears that the necessary instructional/curriculum technology has already been developed, although it will continue to be refined, particularly with respect to the generalization and maintenance of social behavior. The ultimate test of the usefulness of these interventions will be their use by teachers. There is some evidence that teachers see social skills as an area of special need for their students, but it appears that few curricula or programs are actually employed in classrooms (McConnell, McEvoy, & Odom, 1992). The next step in this area of inquiry will be to move the intervention procedure from the drawing board (i.e., research investigation) to actual use in mainstreamed, community-based settings containing children with and without disabilities.

REFERENCES

Allen, K.E., Hart, B., Buell, J.S., Harris, F.R., & Wolf, M.M. (1964). Effects of social reinforcement on isolate behavior of a nursery school child. *Child Development, 35,* 511–518.

Antia, S.D., & Kreimeyer, K.H. (1987). The effects of social skills training on the peer interaction of preschool hearing-impaired children. *Journal of the Division for Early Childhood, 11,* 206–216.

Antia, S.D., & Kreimeyer, K.H. (1988). Maintenance of positive peer interaction in preschool hearing-impaired children. *The Volta Review, 90,* 325–337.

Baer, D.M., & Wolf, M.M. (1970). The entry into natural communities of reinforcement. In R. Ulrich, H.H. Sachnik, & J. Mabry (Eds.), *Control of human behavior* (pp. 319–324). Glenview, IL: Scott, Foresman.

Baer, D.M., Wolf, M.M., & Risley, T.R. (1968). Some current dimensions of applied behavior analysis. *Journal of Applied Behavior Analysis, 1,* 91–97.

Baer, D.M., Wolf, M.M., & Risley, T.R. (1987). Some still-current dimensions of applied behavior analysis. *Journal of Applied Behavior Analysis, 20,* 313–327.

Beckman, P., & Kohl, F.L. (1984). The effects of social and isolate toys on the interactions and play of integrated and nonintegrated groups of preschoolers. *Education and Training of the Mentally Retarded, 19,* 169–174.

Bornstein, M., Bellack, A.S., & Hersen, M. (1980). Social skills training for highly aggressive children: Treatment in an inpatient psychiatric setting. *Behavior Modification, 4,* 173–186.

Bredekamp, S. (1987). *Developmentally appropriate practice.* Washington, DC: National Association for the Education of Young Children.

Bricker, D., & Woods Cripe, J.J. (1992). *An activity-based approach to early intervention.* Baltimore: Paul H. Brookes Publishing Co.

Brown, W.H., Bryson-Brockmann, W., & Fox, J.J. (1986). The usefulness of J.R. Kantor's setting event concept for research on children's social behavior. *Child & Family Behavior Therapy, 8,* 15–25.

Brown, W.H., Fox, J.J., & Brady, M. (1987). Effects of spatial density on 3- and 4-year-old children's socially directed behavior during freeplay: An investigation of a setting factor. *Education and Treatment of Children, 10,* 247–258.

Brown, W.H., McEvoy, M.A., & Bishop, N. (1991). Incidental teaching of social behavior: A naturalistic approach for promoting young children's peer interactions. *Teaching Exceptional Children, 24,* 35–38.

Brown, W.H., & Odom, S.L. (1992). *Strategies for promoting generalization of social interaction training programs for young children with disabilities.* Manuscript submitted for publication.

Brown, W.H., Ragland, E.U., & Bishop, N. (1989). *A socialization curriculum for preschool programs that integrate children with handicaps.* Unpublished manuscript, Vanderbilt University, John F. Kennedy Center, Nashville.

Brown, W.H., Ragland, E.U., & Fox, J.J. (1988). Effects of group socialization procedures on the social interactions of preschool children. *Research in Developmental Disabilities, 9,* 359–376.

Chandler, L.K., Lubeck, R.C., & Fowler, S.A. (1992). The generalization and maintenance of young children's social skills: A retrospective review and analysis. *Journal of Applied Behavior Analysis, 25,* 415–428.

Day, R.M., Powell, T.H., & Stowitschek, J.J. (1980). *SCIPPY: Social competence intervention package for preschool youngsters.* Nashville, TN: Vanderbilt University.

DeKlyen, M., & Odom, S.L. (1989). Activity structure and social interaction with peers in developmentally integrated play groups. *Journal of Early Intervention, 13,* 342–351.

Doctoroff, S. (1991). *Effects of sociodramatic script training and peer role prompting on the sociodramatic role play and social interaction of socially isolated preschool children.* Unpublished doctoral dissertation, Vanderbilt University, Nashville, TN.

Doctoroff, S.A., McEvoy, M.A., & Alpert, C.L. (1991). Increasing peer interaction using the Individualized Curriculum Sequencing model. *Education and Treatment of Children, 14,* 142–150.

Evans, I.M., & Meyer, L.H. (1985). *An educative approach to behavior problems: A practical decision model for interventions with severely handicapped learners.* Baltimore: Paul H. Brookes Publishing Co.

Fantuzzo, J.W., Jurecic, L., Stovall, A., Hightower, A.D., Goins, C., & Schachtel, D. (1988). Effects of adult and peer social initiations on the social behavior of withdrawn, maltreated preschool children. *Journal of Consulting and Clinical Psychology, 56,* 34–39.

Fewell, R.R., & Kaminski, R. (1988). Play skills development and instruction for young children with handicaps. In S. Odom & M. Karnes (Eds.), *Early intervention for infants and children with disabilities: An empirical base* (pp. 145–158). Baltimore: Paul H. Brookes Publishing Co.

Fox, J., Shores, R., Lindeman, D., & Strain, P. (1986). Maintaining social initiations of withdrawn handicapped and nonhandicapped preschoolers through a response-dependent fading tactic. *Journal of Abnormal Child Psychology, 14,* 387–396.

Gaylord-Ross, R. (1980). A decision model for the treatment of aberrant behavior in applied settings. In W. Sailor, B. Wilcox, & L. Brown (Eds.), *Methods of instruction for severely handicapped students* (pp. 135–158). Baltimore: Paul H. Brookes Publishing Co.

Goldstein, H., & Cisar, C.L. (1992). Promoting interaction during sociodramatic play: Teaching scripts to typical preschoolers and classmates with disabilities. *Journal of Applied Behavior Analysis, 25,* 265–280.

Goldstein, H., & Ferrell, D.R. (1987). Augmenting communicative interaction between handicapped and nonhandicapped preschool children. *Journal of Speech and Hearing Disorders, 19,* 200–211.

Goldstein, H., & Wickstrom, S. (1986). Peer intervention effects on communicative interactions among handicapped and nonhandicapped preschoolers. *Journal of Applied Behavior Analysis, 19,* 209–214.

Goldstein, H., Wickstrom, S., Hoyson, M., Jamieson, B., & Odom, S. (1988). Effects of sociodramatic script training on social and communicative interaction. *Education and Treatment of Children, 11,* 97–111.

Guralnick, M.J. (1990). Social competence and early intervention. *Journal of Early Intervention, 14,* 3–14.

Guralnick, M.J., & Groom, J.M. (1987). The peer relations of mildly delayed and nonhandicapped preschool children in mainstreamed playgroups. *Child Development, 58,* 1556–1572.

Guralnick, M.J., & Groom, J.M. (1988). Friendships of preschool children in mainstreamed playgroups. *Developmental Psychology, 24,* 595–604.

Guralnick, M.J., & Weinhouse, E.M. (1984). Peer-related social interactions of developmentally delayed young children: Development and characteristics. *Developmental Psychology, 20,* 815–827.

Haring, T.G. (1992). The context of social competence: Relations, relationships, and generalization. In S. Odom, S. McConnell, & M. McEvoy (Eds.), *Social competence of young children with disabilities: Issues and strategies for intervention* (pp. 307–320). Baltimore: Paul H. Brookes Publishing Co.

Haring, T.G., & Lovinger, L. (1989). Promoting social interaction through teaching generalized play initiation responses to preschool children with autism. *Journal of The Association for Persons with Severe Handicaps, 14,* 255–262.

Hart, B.M. (1985). Naturalistic language training techniques. In S.F. Warren & A.K. Rogers-Warren (Eds.), *Teaching functional language* (pp. 63–88). Austin, TX: PRO-ED.

Hartup, W.W. (1983). Peer relations. In M. Heatherington (Ed.), *Handbook of child psychology* (Vol. IV, pp. 103–196). New York: John Wiley & Sons.

Hecimovic, A., Fox, J.J., Shores, R.E., & Strain, P.S. (1985). An analysis of developmentally integrated and segregated free play setting and the generalization of newly-acquired social behaviors of socially withdrawn preschoolers. *Behavioral Assessment, 7,* 367–388.

Hendrickson, J.M., Strain, P.S., Tremblay, A., & Shores, R.E. (1982). Functional effects of peer social initiations on the interactions of behaviorally handicapped children. *Behavior Modification, 6,* 323–353.

Hodgens, J.B., & McCoy, J.F. (1990). Effects of coaching and peer utilization procedures on the withdrawn behavior of preschoolers. *Child & Family Behavior Therapy, 12*(2), 25–47.

Howes, C. (1988). *Peer interaction of young children.* (Monographs of the Society of Research in Child Development, No. 217) Chicago: University of Chicago.

Hutt, C., & Vaizey, M.J. (1966). Differential effects of group density on social behavior. *Nature, 209,* 1371–1372.

Kohler, F.W., Strain, P.S., Maretsky, S., & DeCasare, L. (1990). Promoting positive and supportive interactions between preschoolers: An analysis of group-oriented contingencies. *Journal of Early Intervention, 14,* 327–341.

Ladd, G.W. (1981). Effectiveness of a social learning method for enhancing children's social interaction and peer acceptance. *Child Development, 52,* 171–178.

Ladd, G.W., & Mize, J. (1983). A cognitive-social learning model of social-skill training. *Psychological Review, 90,* 127–137.

Lancioni, G.E. (1982). Normal children as tutors to teach social responses to withdrawn mentally retarded schoolmates: Training, maintenance, and generalization. *Journal of Applied Behavior Analysis, 15,* 17–40.

Lefebvre, D., & Strain, P.S. (1989). Effects of a group contingency on the frequency of social initiations among autistic and nonhandicapped preschool children: Making LRE efficacious. *Journal of Early Intervention, 13,* 329–341.

Lindsley, O.R. (1964). Direct measurement and prosthesis of retarded behavior. *Journal of Education, 147,* 62–81.

Loo, C.M. (1972). The effects of spatial density on the social behavior of children. *Journal of Applied Social Psychology, 2,* 372–381.

McConnell, S.R. (1987). Entrapment effects and the generalization and maintenance of social skills training for elementary school students with behavior disorders. *Behavioral Disorders, 12,* 252–263.

McConnell, S.R., McEvoy, M.A., & Odom, S.L. (1992). Implementation of social competence interventions in early childhood special education classes: Current practices and future directions. In S. Odom, S. McConnell, & M. McEvoy (Eds.), *Social competence of young children with disabilities: Issues and strategies for intervention* (pp. 277–306). Baltimore: Paul H. Brookes Publishing Co.

McConnell, S.R., & Odom, S.L. (1986). Sociometric: Peer-referenced measures and the assessment of social competence. In P. Strain, M. Guralnick, & H. Walker (Eds.), *Children's social behavior: Development, assessment, and modification* (pp. 215–286). New York: Academic Press.

McConnell, S.R., Peterson, C., & Fox, J.J. (1992). *Effects of child specific interventions on social interaction rates of young children with disabilities: Selection of treatment compo-*nents. Manuscript submitted for publication.

McConnell, S.R., Sisson, L.A., Cort, C.A., & Strain, P.S. (1991). Effects of social skills training and contingency management on reciprocal interaction of preschool children with behavioral handicaps. *Journal of Special Education, 24,* 473–495.

McEvoy, M.A., & Fox, J.J. (1990, May). *Generalization, maintenance and social interaction: Ten years after Stokes and Baer.* Paper presented at the annual conference of the Association for Behavior Analysis, Nashville, TN.

McEvoy, M.A., McConnell, S.R., Odom, S.L., & Skellinger, A. (1991). *Analysis of an environmental arrangements intervention for young children with disabilities.* Unpublished manuscript.

McEvoy, M.A., Nordquist, V.M., Twardosz, S., Heckaman, K., Wehby, J.H., & Denny, R.K. (1988). Promoting autistic children's peer interaction in an integrated early childhood setting using affection activities. *Journal of Applied Behavior Analysis, 21,* 193–200.

McEvoy, M.A., Odom, S.L., & McConnell, S.R. (1992). Peer social competence intervention for young children with disabilities. In S. Odom, S. McConnell, & M. McEvoy (Eds.), *Social competence of young children with disabilities: Issues and strategies for intervention* (pp. 113–133). Baltimore: Paul H. Brookes Publishing Co.

McGrew, P.L. (1970). Social and spatial density effects on spacing behavior in preschool children. *Journal of Child Psychology and Psychiatry, 11,* 197–205.

Mesibov, G.B. (1986). A cognitive program for teaching social behaviors to verbal autistic adolescents and adults. In E. Schopler & G. Mesibov (Eds.), *Social behavior in autism* (pp. 265–284). New York: Plenum Press.

Mize, J., Ladd, G.W., & Price, J.M. (1985). Promoting positive peer relations with young children: Rationales and strategies. *Child Care Quarterly, 14,* 221–237.

National Association of Early Childhood Specialists in State Departments of Education. (1991). Guidelines for appropriate curriculum content and assessment in programs serving children ages 3 through 8. *Young Children, 46*(3), 21–38.

Nordquist, V.M., Twardosz, S., & McEvoy, M.A. (1985, April). *Promoting social interaction of autistic children through peer-mediated af-*

fection activities and incidental teaching. Paper presented at the annual conference of The Council for Exceptional Children, Anaheim, CA.

Nourot, P.M., & Van Hoorn, J.L. (1991). Symbolic play in preschool and primary settings. *Young Children, 46,* 40–50.

Oden, S., & Asher, S.R. (1977). Coaching children in social skills for friendship making. *Child Development, 48,* 495–506.

Odom, S.L., Bender, M., Stein, M., Doran, L., Houden, P., McInnes, M., Gilbert, M., DeKlyen, M., Speltz, M., & Jenkins, J. (1988). *Integrated preschool curriculum.* Seattle: University of Washington Press.

Odom, S.L., Chandler, L., Ostrosky, M., McConnell, S.R., & Reaney, S. (1992). Fading teacher prompts from peer-initiation interventions for young children with disabilities. *Journal of Applied Behavior Analysis, 25,* 307–318.

Odom, S.L., Hoyson, M., Jamieson, B., & Strain, P.S. (1985). Increasing handicapped preschooler's peer social interactions: Cross-setting and component analysis. *Journal of Applied Behavior Analysis, 18,* 3–16.

Odom, S.L., Kohler, F.W., & Strain, P.S. (1987). *Teaching strategies for promoting social skills.* Unpublished intervention manual, Early Childhood Research Institute, University of Pittsburgh.

Odom, S.L., & McConnell, S.R. (1985). A performanced-based conceptualization of social competence of handicapped preschool children: Implications for assessment. *Topics in Early Childhood Special Education, 4*(4), 1–19.

Odom, S.L., & McConnell, S.R. (1988). Assessing social interaction skills. In D. Bailey & M. Wolery (Eds.), *Assessing infants and preschoolers with handicaps* (pp. 390–427). Columbus, OH: Charles E. Merrill.

Odom, S.L., & McConnell, S.R. (1989, May). *Translative research and development of social interaction interventions: Closing the gap between research and practice.* Paper presented at the Annual Convention of the Association for Behavior Analysis, Milwaukee, WI.

Odom, S.L., & McConnell, S.R. (1991). *Social interaction intervention programs for young children with disabilities: A comparison of treatments.* Paper presented at the Biennial Meeting of the Society for Research in Child Development, San Francisco, CA.

Odom, S.L., McConnell, S.R., & Chandler, L.K. (1991). *Acceptability, feasibility, and current use of social interaction interventions for preschool children with disabilities.* Manuscript submitted for publication.

Odom, S.L., & McEvoy, M.A. (1988). Integration of young children with handicaps and normally developing children. In S. Odom & M.B. Karnes (Eds.), *Early intervention for infants and children with handicaps: An empirical base* (pp. 241–267). Baltimore: Paul H. Brookes Publishing Co.

Odom, S.L., & Ogawa, I. (1991). *A methodological review of observational measurement systems of young children's social interactions with peers.* Unpublished manuscript.

Odom, S.L., Ostrosky, M., Cronin, P., & Keetz, A. (1992). *Experimental analysis of a comprehensive intervention to promote social interactions of young children with and without disabilities: Treatment and induced generalization effects.* Manuscript submitted for publication.

Odom, S.L., & Strain, P.S. (1984). Classroom-based social skills instruction for severely handicapped preschool children. *Topics in Early Childhood Special Education, 4,* 97–116.

Odom, S.L., & Strain, P.S. (1986). A comparison of peer-initiation and teacher-antecedent interventions for promoting reciprocal social interaction of autistic preschoolers. *Journal of Applied Behavior Analysis, 19,* 59–71.

Odom, S.L., & Watts, E. (1991). Reducing teacher prompts in peer-initiation interventions through visual feedback and correspondence training. *Journal of Special Education, 25,* 26–43.

Osnes, P.G., Guevremont, D.C., & Stokes, T.F. (1986). "If I say I'll talk more, then I will": Correspondence training to increase peer directed talk by socially withdrawn children. *Behavior Modification, 10,* 287–299.

Ostrosky, M., Chandler, L., Odom, S., McConnell, S., & Peterson, C. (1991a). *Comprehensive intervention manual.* Unpublished curriculum manual, Vanderbilt-Minnesota Social Interaction Project, Vanderbilt University, John F. Kennedy Center, Nashville, TN.

Ostrosky, M., Chandler, L., Odom, S., McConnell, S., & Peterson, C. (1991b). *Peer-mediated intervention manual.* Unpublished curriculum manual, Vanderbilt-Minnesota Social Interaction Project, Vanderbilt University, John F. Kennedy Center, Nashville, TN.

Parker, J.G., & Asher, S.R. (1987). Peer relations and later personal adjustment. *Psychological Bulletin, 102,* 357–389.

Peck, C.A., Killen, C.C., & Baumgart, D. (1989). Increasing implementation of special education instruction in mainstreamed preschools: Direct and generalized effects of nondirective consultation. *Journal of Applied Behavior Analysis, 22,* 197–210.

Peterson, C., McConnell, S., Cronin, P., Spicuzza, R., & Odom, S. (1991). *Child-specific intervention manuals.* Unpublished curriculum manual, Vanderbilt-Minnesota Social Interaction Project, Vanderbilt University, John F. Kennedy Center, Nashville, TN.

Quilitch, H.R., & Risley, T.R. (1973). The effects of play materials on social play. *Journal of Applied Behavior Analysis, 6,* 573–578.

Rogers-Warren, A.K. (1984). Ecobehavioral analysis. *Education and Treatment of Children, 7,* 283–303.

Sainato, D.M., & Carta, J.J. (1992). Classroom influences on the development of social competence in young children with disabilities. In S. Odom, S. McConnell, & M. McEvoy (Eds.), *Social competence of young children with disabilities: Issues and strategies for intervention* (pp. 93–109). Baltimore: Paul H. Brookes Publishing Co.

Sainato, D.M., Goldstein, H., & Strain, P.S. (1992). Effects of self-monitoring on preschool children's use of social interaction strategies with their autistic peers. *Journal of Applied Behavior Analysis, 25,* 127–141.

Shores, R.E., Hester, P., & Strain, P.S. (1976). The effects of the amount and type of teacher-child interaction on child-child interaction during free-play. *Psychology in the Schools, 13,* 171–175.

Skellenger, A., McEvoy, M., McConnell, S., & Odom, S. (1991). *Environmental arrangments intervention manual.* Unpublished curriculum manual, Vanderbilt-Minnesota Social Interaction Project, Vanderbilt University, John F. Kennedy Center, Nashville, TN.

Smith, J., McConnel, S.R., Maretsky, S.R.,

Kudray, R.M., & Strain, P.S. (in press). Promoting reciprocal social interactions among autistic and normally developing children in an integrated preschool. *Journal of the Multihandicapped Person.*

Social Integration Project. (1989). *Let's be social.* Tucson, AZ: Communication Skill Builders.

Spiegel-McGill, P., Bambara, L.M., Shores, R.M., & Fox, J.J. (1984). The effects of proximity on socially directed behaviors of severely multiply handicapped children. *Education and Treatment of Children, 7,* 365–378.

Spicuzza, R.J., McConnell, S.R., & Odom, S.L. (1991, May). *Normative analysis of social interaction behaviors for children with and without handicaps: Implications for evaluation and design of interventions.* Paper presented at the annual conference of the Association for Behavior Analysis, Atlanta, GA.

Spicuzza, R., McEvoy, M.A., & McConnell, S.R. (1992, May). *Effects of immediate versus intermittent feedback on social interactions of children with behavior disorders.* Paper presented at the annual conference of the Association for Behavior Analysis, San Francisco, CA.

Stokes, T.F., & Baer, D.M. (1977). An implicit technology of generalization. *Journal of Applied Behavior Analysis, 10,* 349–367.

Stokes, T.F., & Osnes, P.G. (1986). Programming generalization of children's social behavior. In P.S. Strain, M.J. Guralnick, & H.M. Walker (Eds.), *Children's social behavior: Development, assessment, and modification* (pp. 407–443). Orlando, FL: Academic Press, Inc.

Strain, P.S. (1983a). Generalization of autistic children's social behavior change: Effects of developmentally integrated and segregated settings. *Analysis and Intervention in Developmental Disabilities, 3,* 23–34.

Strain, P.S. (1983b). Identification of social skill curriculum targets for severely handicapped children in mainstreamed preschools. *Applied Research in Mental Retardation, 4,* 369–382.

Strain, P.S. (1990). LRE for preschool children with handicaps: What we know, what we should be doing. *Journal of Early Intervention, 14,* 291–296.

Strain, P.S., & Fox, J.J. (1981). Peers as behavior change agents for withdrawn classmates. In A. Kazdin & B. Lahey (Eds.), *Advances in child clinical psychology* (167–198). New York: Plenum Press.

Strain, P.S., Odom, S.L., & McConnell, S.R. (1984). Promoting social reciprocity of exceptional children: Identification, target behavior selection, and intervention. *Remedial and Special Education, 5,* 21–28.

Strain, P.S., & Shores, R.E. (1977). Social reciprocity: A clinical teaching perspective. *Exceptional Children, 43,* 526–530.

Strain, P.S., Shores, R.E., & Kerr, M.M. (1976). An experimental analysis of "spillover" effects on social interaction among behaviorally handicapped preschool children. *Journal of Applied Behavior Analysis, 9,* 31–40.

Strain, P.S., Shores, R.E., & Timm, M. (1977). Effects of peer social initiations on the behavior of withdrawn preschool children. *Journal of Applied Behavior Analysis, 10,* 289–298.

Strain, P.S., & Timm, M.A. (1974). An experimental analysis of social interaction between a behaviorally disordered preschool child and her classroom peers. *Journal of Applied Behavior Analysis, 7,* 583–590.

Timm, M.A., Strain, P.S., & Eller, P.H. (1979). Effects of systematic, response dependent fading and thinning procedures on the maintenance of child-child interaction. *Journal of Applied Behavior Analysis, 12,* 308.

Tremblay, A., Strain, P.S. Hendrickson, J.M., & Shores, R.E. (1981). Social interactions of normally developing preschool children: Using normative data for subject selection and target behavior selection. *Behavior Modification, 5,* 237–253.

Twardosz, S. (1984). Environmental organization: The physical, social, and programmatic context of behavior. In M. Hersen, R.M. Eisler, & P.M. Miller (Eds.), *Progress in behavior modification* (Vol. 18, pp. 123–161). Orlando, FL: Academic Press.

Twardosz, S., Nordquist, V.M., Simon, R., & Botkin, D. (1983). The effects of group affection activities on the interaction of socially isolate children. *Analysis and Intervention in Developmental Disabilities, 3,* 311–338.

Vanderbilt-Minnesota Social Interaction Project. (in press). *Social interaction skills training.* Tucson, AZ: Communication Skills Builders.

Walker, H.M., McConnell, S.R., & Clarke, J.Y. (1985). Social skills training in school settings: A model for the social integration of handicapped children in less restrictive settings. In R. McMahon & R. Peters (Eds.), *Childhood disorders: Behavioral-developmental approaches* (pp. 142–168). New York: Bruner/Mazel.

Wolery, M.R., Bailey, D.B., & Strain, P.S. (in press). Applying the framework of Developmentally Appropriate Practice to children with special needs. In S. Bredekamp (Ed.), *Guidelines for appropriate curriculum content and asessment in programs serving children ages 3 through 8.* Washington, DC: NAEYC.

Chapter 4

PROVIDING FAMILY SUPPORT IN INTEGRATED SETTINGS
Research and Recommendations

Pamela J. Winton

Providing services to children in the least restrictive environment (currently known as most inclusive environment) and involving parents in those services are two themes that have shaped the research and practice landscape of early intervention services for the last 10 years. Interestingly, the terminology and assumptions surrounding those two themes have shifted and changed as a broader understanding of both issues has developed.

Historically, the concept of least restrictive environment (LRE) has been defined as an educational issue related to placement. Recently the definition of LRE has been broadened to include a child's full integration into his or her family, home, and community (National Early Childhood Technical Assistance System [NEC*TAS], 1990). This provides an expanded context within which to consider providing family support in integrated settings.

The concept of parent involvement has also undergone change. The basic assumption concerning parent involvement was that the primary reason for involving parents in their child's intervention program was to enhance the child's education (Turnbull & Winton, 1984); therefore, much effort was spent improving parents' skills in teaching and managing their children. This concept has now been replaced by the broader assumptions underlying the family support movement. These assumptions include the following: 1) family support should be a primary goal of early intervention, and 2) families' values, interests, and priorities should guide intervention.

Not only is there philosophical support for redefining how families are involved in services, the passage of PL 99-457 (Part H) in 1986 established a strong legislative mandate to do so. This law requires that an individualized family service plan

Preparation of this article was supported in part by Grant #G0087C3064, Special Education Program, Office of Special Education and Rehabilitative Services, U.S. Department of Education.

The author would like to thank Robin McWilliam, Don Bailey, and Pat Wesley for feedback on an outline of this chapter.

(IFSP) be developed by a multidisciplinary team, which is to include the family, for each child and family enrolled in an early intervention program. In addition to the child-related components required by the individualized education program (IEP), the IFSP must include a statement of family strengths and needs, and a description of a plan to meet those needs. The regulations emphasize the interrelationships among children, families, and community services, and establish family support as a key goal for intervention services.

The changing definitions and conceptualizations of LRE and family support have created challenges for professionals designing and implementing community-based early childhood programs. One of these challenges is that of translating the assumptions underlying family-centered intervention into specific practices. Recent publications addressing this issue make it clear that providing family support entails more than learning a certain set of procedures or offering families a specific set of services (Winton & Bailey, in press a, in press b); it requires a willingness to develop a collaborative relationship with each family and to provide services based on each family's values and priorities.

A second challenge is that of defining the relationship between family-centered early intervention and the LRE. It has been suggested in an earlier publication (Winton, 1990a) that allowing families' values and priorities to guide intervention ensures that services will be provided within the LRE as it is defined by each family. Defining LRE as "a total process and concept that involves decisionmaking about the type, nature, and location of services" (NEC*TAS, 1990, p. 1), with families being at the center of that process, integrates the two concepts.

The primary purpose of this chapter is to identify ways that programs and communities can structure services that support family choices. This chapter begins with a brief overview of research on family perspectives on integration at the early childhood level, and then provides a series of recommendations from a systems-oriented perspective for developing and implementing community-based programs that are supportive of families and the choices they make.

SUMMARY OF RESEARCH ON FAMILIES AND EARLY CHILDHOOD INTEGRATED PROGRAMS

The research conducted in the late 1970s on the issue of families and early childhood integrated settings reflected the dominant thinking of the time, which held that LRE was strictly an educational and placement issue. Researchers examined family perspectives on LRE in order to understand how placement in a mainstreamed setting affected child outcome. In one of the early studies, parents who had chosen either integrated or specialized early childhood placements for their child were interviewed about their perspectives on those settings (Turnbull & Winton, 1983; Winton, 1981). The data from this study did not indicate that one type of setting was superior to another, but they did suggest the following: 1) parents who had selected integrated placements were satisfied with those choices, and 2) a common reason why parents selected integrated settings for their children was the exposure to "the real world" that these programs provided.

Further research efforts included gathering information on the perspectives of parents of children without disabilities who had experience with integrated programs (Bailey & Winton, 1987; Green & Stoneman, 1989; Reichart et al., 1989; Turnbull, Winton, Blacher, & Salkind, 1983). This research indicated that these parents, in general, also viewed integration in a positive light.

Data that suggested that mainstreaming worked better for children than it did for families (Bailey & Winton, 1987; Turnbull & Winton, 1983; Winton, 1981) led to several studies that addressed the issue of social support in integrated settings. A sociometric study by Blacher and Turnbull (1983) indicated that in an integrated preschool setting, interactions between families whose children have disabilities and those whose children do not have disabilities may be limited. A subsequent study of patterns of friendship and acquaintance between families in integrated daycare substantiated the earlier findings (Bailey & Winton, 1989). Generally, families of children with disabilities were more likely to meet and become friends with other families of children with disabilities, and were less satisfied with their acquaintance with other families in the daycare center than were families of typically developing children.

One of the overall conclusions that must be drawn from the research summarized above is that there are substantial individual differences among parents' expectations and experiences in integrated programs (Bailey & Winton, 1987, 1989; Turnbull & Winton, 1983; Winton, 1981). Because of the methodological approach used in one of the original studies, in which in-depth interviews were conducted (Turnbull & Winton, 1983; Winton, 1981), it was quite clear from the beginning of this line of research that the choice between integrated and specialized placement was a complex issue influenced by

variables such as family values and beliefs, presence or absence of siblings, neighborhood and community options for integration, parent employment, and the need for daycare and respite. All families seek to be integrated into the community, but each family has a unique definition of what integration means and how it should be accomplished. The selection of a preschool may be only one of many factors that families consider in their attempts to meet the special needs of their child.

RECOMMENDATIONS FOR PROVIDING FAMILY SUPPORT IN INTEGRATED SETTINGS

If one goal of integrated programs is to encourage family support, then the following broad considerations are especially important:

1. Each family has unique service needs. Understanding the interests, priorities, and resources of each family, and taking an individualized approach to family support based on this information are critical.
2. The means of providing family support should be formulated within a broad social context that takes into account existing support networks and the family's definition and perception of support.
3. Services should be made available in ways that promote the integration, as defined by the family, of the child and family into the community.

These broad recommendations are consistent with current definitions (Dunst, Trivette, & Deal, 1988; Johnson, McGonigel, & Kaufmann, 1991) and legal mandates (PL 99-457, Part H) for best practices in working with families in early intervention programs. These new ideas about working with families pave the way for changes in the structures of community services and programs. Because the law is not specific about how to implement the federal mandates, many important programmatic decisions are left in the hands of states and local communities. Such flexibility is expected to facilitate the development of implementation strategies that truly work within the context of each unique community and program. However, a research study by Bailey, Buysee, Edmondson, and Smith (1992) indicates that the translation of family-centered ideas into actual practice is difficult. The barriers identified by the early interventionists surveyed in this study were more likely to be systems problems, rather than problems related to individual knowledge or skill. This suggests that the provision of family support cannot be ensured by simply addressing the skills, knowledge, and attitudes of individual interventionists (Bailey et al., 1992; Winton, 1990b). Providing family support in integrated settings requires that professionals be aware of multiple sources of influence.

Parents identify two areas of concern unique to integrated settings (Peck, Hayden, Wandschneider, Peterson, & Richarz, 1989; Winton, 1986, 1990a): 1) finding and deciding upon appropriate services and; 2) having confidence in the adequacy of staff and services in integrated settings. These two topics are the central focus of the remainder of this chapter. Within each content area the assumptions underlying the family support movement and the relevant policy initiatives in PL 99-457 (Part H) are briefly outlined. Specific recommendations for developing community-based programs that are supportive of families are also presented. This chapter will not provide detailed information on specific programmatic or individual prac-

tices related to family support, since those are the subjects of other publications (Winton & Bailey, in press a, in press b).

Finding and Deciding upon Appropriate Services

Integrating a baby into the fabric of the family is an immediate challenge for the family of any newborn. When the baby has special needs, the process of integration is usually more complicated for a number of reasons, one being the presence of the professionals providing assistance to the baby and the family. In some cases families may not feel that they have a choice about accepting services. In a 1978 article Doernberg cautioned professionals to consider the possibility that the benefits of therapy provided to the young child might be outweighed by the stress placed on the family by their being involved in the intervention program. Doernberg's clinical judgment on this issue is supported by recent research. A study conducted by Affleck, Tennen, Rowe, Roscher, and Walker (1989) indicates that the benefits of intervention provided to families after the transition of their premature babies from hospital to home are mediated by the extent to which mothers feel the need for intervention support. Mothers who have lower levels of need for support actually experience greater stress as a result of receiving intervention. When applied to family-centered intervention LRE should mean using the least intrusive, yet still effective, approach (NEC*TAS, 1990).

When parents and other family members understand that several choices are available, deciding which services are appropriate can be a complex, stressful, and time-consuming task (Bernheimer, Young, & Winton, 1983; Winton, 1986). Families have been told or may feel that their young children have special needs requiring extra assistance, yet too often they get scant or conflicting information about which services to look for and about how to find them. Parents who have been through this process have reported a fragmented, uncoordinated system of services with no single person or place where information on community programs is readily available (Suelzle & Keenan, 1981).

Certain policy initiatives emanating from the family support movement and culminating with PL 99-457 directly address the parental concerns about finding and selecting services. These policy initiatives include: 1) supporting families in their decisionmaking role, 2) promoting inter-agency collaboration and community-based services, 3) providing case management or service coordination services to families to assist them in accessing community services, and 4) providing a transition plan as part of the individualized family service plan. The recommendations that follow focus on how communities and programs might put these initiatives into practice in ways that will provide support to families as they decide upon and locate services.

Adopting a Family-Centered Philosophy To Guide Broad-Based Community Planning

The assumptions underlying the family support movement and PL 99-457 are substantially different from those underlying parent involvement, especially as previously interpreted in PL 94-142. The emphasis on strengthening the decisionmaking role of families challenges a basic assumption about who is in charge of intervention services. The interests and priorities of families are often substantially different from those that professionals traditionally identify in that they are usually related to the ways that families live their normal lives. For example, a priority for a family might be attending their typically developing child's little league games, attending church, or taking a family camping trip. A family's major concerns might relate to basic needs, such as getting job training or finding safe housing. What families might want from intervention is help in deciding how to accomplish those things.

Many professionals question whether it is realistic to assume that families want to or are able to participate in a family-centered intervention process as it is described in current literature (Bailey et al., 1992). There is considerable debate, especially among public school personnel, over the extent to which the recommendations for IFSP development should serve as a basis for developing IEPs (Fowler, Hains, & Rosenkoetter, 1990). In other words, the adoption of family choice principles has raised troubling questions for many professionals. For example, if families identify needs outside of the traditional definition of family services, who is going to be responsible for meeting those needs? And what if families choose services that are not available in their community? Or, if the family and the professional do not agree about priorities for child and family needs and intervention goals, then whose ideas should prevail?

The literature on the change process (Havelock & Havelock, 1973) suggests that without a common philosophical framework and values base it is very difficult for an organization to make the decisions necessary to implement innovative ideas, such as those suggested by current policy initiatives. Questions like those mentioned above must be addressed by community leaders in order to effectively plan community-based programs that truly support families. If community leaders are in agreement that families should have choices about the level and type of intervention that they receive, then it follows that a comprehensive and coordinated system of services that is responsive to a broad array of family interests would be a community priority. This leads to the next recommendation.

Creating a Continuum of Service Options within the Community

A dilemma that always emerges in discussions of the least restrictive environment for preschool children with disabilities is the difficulty of addressing this issue when most states do not provide regular preschool education for typically developing children. Approaching the issue from a solely educational perspective provides only a limited view of possible options. As a result, achieving the goal of providing services to children with special needs in normalized settings has met with only limited success (Peck, Richarz, et al., 1989).

The policy initiatives of PL 99-457 present an opportunity to states and local communities to expand options for providing services. Ensuring that services are expanded in ways that promote normalization is a concern often voiced. Polly Arango (1990) addresses this issue from a parent's perspective:

> If P.L. 99-457 follows the lead of P.L. 94-142, we will end up with all these thousands of babies who are developmentally disabled or even potentially disabled, and their families, placed in categories that set them on a different track for life. Will they go to preschools and pediatricians and day-care centers that are separate from our other children and our neighbors' children? Look at what has happened—outright segregation, sometimes in special education programs that are based on P.L. 94-142. Certainly P.L. 99-457 itself tried to ensure mainstreaming and family centeredness, but I think we need to be wary. (p. 58)

Creating collaborative arrangements with existing daycare and regular preschools presents a seemingly attractive and perhaps cost-effective way of broadening integrated options for preschoolers. In fact, federal regulations related to Part B of PL 99-457 published in the *Federal Register* (April, 1989) provide three options for meeting the LRE needs of preschoolers:

1. Providing opportunities for the participation (even part-time) of preschool children with disabilities in other preschool programs operated by public agencies (e.g., Head Start)
2. Placing children with disabilities in private school programs for nondisabled preschool children or private school preschool programs that integrate children with disabilities and nondisabled children
3. Locating classes for preschool children with disabilities in regular elementary schools

A case study report by Peck and his associates (Peck, Hayden, et al., 1989; Peck, Richarz, et al., 1989) makes it clear that for collaborative programs of the sort described in the first and second options to succeed, social and political support within the community is critical. According to the model proposed by Peck and his colleagues, the movement toward integrated programs might be seen as a threat to the comfort and stability of the status quo. This makes generating community support a complex process that must include all those with vested interests in the status quo. In order for this process to work, many administrative issues must first be clarified. For example, who will pay for services, such as daycare, that are not specified in the IEP or IFSP? How will coordination and communication between programs occur when a child is being served by more than one program? Who will be in charge of transportation between programs? To address these issues adequately, informal and formal agreements about philosophy, curriculum, and instruction must be renegotiated.

The same resistances and fears that Peck and his colleagues (Peck, Hayden, et al., 1989) identified as being associated with a community's attempt to integrate programs (i.e., relinquishing control of decisionmaking, changes in role definitions, and negotiating agreements with other community agencies) are likely to be operating when the changes mandated in the family-centered components of Part H are taking place. Peck, Richarz, et al. (1989) described a process model for generating community support and planning for community innovations. It is clear that this sort of effort requires leadership from a group willing to foster community participation in the planning process. Local Interagency Coordinating Councils (ICCs) may be the logical group to undertake such activities.

Facilitating a Smooth Transition from Early Intervention to Preschool Services for Children and Their Families

There is a wealth of literature on the importance of helping families during program transitions (see entire issue of Neisworth [1990] and Hanline, chap. 7, this volume). PL 99-457 reflects the importance of this issue. One of the requirements of Part H is that each individualized family service plan must include a description of the steps to be taken to support the transition of the service responsibility from the early intervention system to a preschool program. This emphasis should help alleviate the difficulties parents report in choosing and locating services. However, because precise information about how such planning should be

accomplished is not being provided by the federal government, states will need to develop policies, guidelines, and interagency agreements to facilitate transitions between programs.

One of the acknowledged barriers to smooth transitions is the two-part structure of PL 99-457. Through amendments to Part B of PL 94-142, PL 99-457 extends the right to a free, appropriate education to all eligible 3- to 5-year-olds. This has generally been interpreted to mean that the policies and practices in place for school-age children should now be applied to preschoolers. Part H of PL 99-457 encourages states to create an innovative, comprehensive, and coordinated system of early intervention services. The effect of having two separate sets of policies—the one for infants and toddlers (through Part H) being family-centered, and the one for 3- to 5-year-olds being an extension of Part B policies—has created havoc for most states (Division for Early Childhood, February-March, 1991). Families and professionals are left wondering if suddenly, when the child reaches age 3, the means by which services are provided should revert to what some professionals recognize as inappropriate practice (Division for Early Childhood, February-March, 1991). The natural resistance of public school personnel to making changes is only reinforced by the two sets of requirements. It is much easier to extend the IEP process downward to the 3–5 age group than it is to deal with the new assumptions and practices related to the family-centered approaches being recommended in Part H.

Recommendations being made for the reauthorization of PL 99-457 have emphasized the need for a single set of requirements for children up to 5 years old. These requirements should reflect what is currently mandated in Part H, since this represents state-of-the-art knowledge (Division for Early Childhood, February-March, 1991; Gallagher et al., 1991). Until states and local comunities have clear directives from the federal level on the issue of coordination between Part H and Part B, many communities will continue to struggle with the problem.

At the programmatic level, curricula have been developed and articles written providing guidelines and recommendations for involving families in transition planning (see Hanline, chap. 7, this volume). Another resource available to families during transitions is the guarantee, through Part H, of a service coordinator (previously known as a case manager) to assist in locating appropriate services. One of the recommendations being made for the reauthorization of PL 99-457 is that this service be extended to the 3–5 age group as well.

Creating a Clearinghouse for Information about Community Services

The service delivery landscape is everchanging. Professionals are notorious for not knowing what services are available in their own community. The most natural information resource for families—neighbors, friends, and extended family (Powell, 1980)—are not usually aware of programs for children with special needs. A central clearinghouse for information about existing resources, programs, and services would provide families with the information they need to act as informed decisionmakers. Printed materials quickly become outdated; looseleaf notebooks that would allow for a constant updating of information would be more useful. In addition, identifying parents who know about the different service options and would be willing to share that information with other families would greatly add to the

value of the written information. Parents would also be more likely to know about normalizing types of community activities—such as swim lessons, tumbling classes, or music or art experiences—that have worked well with children with special needs. The local interagency coordinating council is a logical group to support this kind of effort.

Availability of Adequately Trained Staff and Related Services

The quality of a mainstreamed program for young children depends on the expertise of the teachers and staff (Klein & Sheehan, 1987). Unfortunately, research has documented that parents of children with and without disabilities (Bailey & Winton, 1987; Green & Stoneman, 1989; Turnbull & Winton, 1983) have concerns about the training and qualifications of teachers in integrated programs. These concerns are supported by reports in professional journals indicating that many early childhood educators (Odom & McEvoy, 1990) and daycare providers (Klein & Sheehan, 1987) lack specialized training in teaching and caring for young children with special needs. Parents of children with disabilities sometimes take on the extra burden of trying to train teachers themselves or coordinate additional special services outside of the preschool program to make up for the teachers' lack of training or the absence of related services (Winton, 1986). For some families, integrated placements for their children might become more restrictive for family members if they feel they must constantly supplement services or provide inservice for staff. Research has suggested that an important factor for many parents in their selection of a preschool setting is the opportunity that the setting provides for relaxing from the daily responsibility of teaching their children (Winton & Turnbull, 1981). It is difficult to relax if teacher competence is a concern.

Unfortunately, the qualifications of staff members is an important issue in all early intervention programs, not just those that are integrated. Moderate-to-high staff turnover in such programs has already been documented (Palsha, Bailey, Vandiviere, & Munn, 1990). In addition, there are major shortages of occupational, physical, and speech therapists (Yoder, Coleman, & Gallagher, 1990).

Because of the importance of well-trained staff to the successful implementation of PL 99-457, the law addresses the issue of personnel preparation. Each state must develop a comprehensive system of personnel development (CSPD) to ensure a systematic state-wide effort at meeting the needs for qualified staff in early childhood programs. The legislation mandates that the CSPD must do the following: 1) include both preservice and inservice training, 2) be conducted on an interdisciplinary basis when appropriate, and 3) address the needs of a variety of personnel, including public and private providers, primary referral sources, parents, paraprofessionals, and persons who will serve as case managers.

While these policy initiatives are promising, documentation of progress indicates that states are struggling in their attempts to carry out the federal mandates for personnel preparation (Gallagher et al., 1991). The recommendations that follow are meant to increase the competence of staff members in integrated settings with children with special needs and their families.

Integrating Training in Early Childhood Education and Early Childhood Special Education Odom and McEvoy (1990) declare that "creating a main-

streamed professional" educator is one of the tasks that must be accomplished if mainstreaming at the preschool level is to become a viable service delivery option. One way to accomplish this is through state certification requirements. An effort is underway in North Carolina to create a single certificate for teachers who work with young children (birth through kindergarten) that combines competencies for working with typically and atypically developing children and their families. The rationale for this effort is twofold: 1) increasing numbers of young children with special needs will be served in mainstreamed settings, and 2) staff who work with young children need to have a thorough knowledge of the development of the whole child and of all of the variations in that development.

Creating a single certification program for all educators of young children would support a second strategy: the integration of training of early childhood educators (ECE) and early childhood special educators (ECSE) at the preservice level. Odom and McEvoy (1990) listed the benefits that might be gained for both groups if coursework was integrated. The student of ECE would be exposed to information about individual differences in learning, and about instructional strategies for addressing those differences. The student of ECSE would be exposed to information on typical child development, and on strategies for providing consultation.

This recommendation for a broader early childhood training program might be countered by those who feel that training programs should provide for even greater specialization, such as is offered by programs with an infancy focus. Perhaps each type of training program has its place. What may be of greater importance is the extent to which the coursework provided is up-to-date and reflects the current emphasis on interdisciplinary and family collaboration. A report by Bailey, Palsha, and Huntington (1990) reflects this concern. Their survey of faculty in early childhood special education found the primary content priority to be materials for family assessment and developing the IFSP.

A graduate-level interdisciplinary families curriculum focusing on early intervention has been developed and field tested through the Carolina Institute for Research on Infant Personnel Preparation (Winton, 1991). A curriculum of this sort might provide ECE/ECSE students with information useful in working with families of all young children. Mandating certification requirements, and providing integrated early childhood training programs and up-to-date training materials, are strategies for helping to address parents' concerns about the availability of trained teachers in integrated settings.

Embedding Infancy and Family Content into Existing Preservice Training Programs for Related Services Personnel and Paraprofessionals The three strategies outlined above do not address those professionals and paraprofessionals working in integrated settings who are not certified through the schools. Paraprofessionals frequently work as teachers' aides in integrated educational settings, or as daycare providers. A recent nation-wide survey of high-quality early childhood programs (U.S. General Accounting Office, 1990) indicated that 48% of the teacher's aides working in such programs had associate's degrees, or at least some college training. Many states require only a high school diploma and minimal additional training for daycare providers (Klein & Sheehan, 1987). Community colleges are likely to be the settings where paraprofes-

sionals receive such training. Providing the faculty of community colleges with state-of-the-art training materials and curricula related to young children with special needs and their families might be an appropriate way of reaching the entry-level paraprofessional.

One parental concern identified in the literature (Turnbull & Winton, 1983) is the lack of availability of related services in integrated programs. The fact that PL 99-457 mandates related services for infants and toddlers should help address this concern; however, the current model for providing those services, as well as the information on the preservice training of related service personnel, suggests that problems may lie ahead.

Surveys of preservice training programs in the related services (PT, OT, & speech-language pathology) indicate that students completing entry-level programs are minimally prepared to work effectively with infants who are at risk, or with their families (Bailey, Simeonsson, Yoder, & Huntington, 1990). Moreover, data from these surveys suggest that this situation is not likely to change in any dramatic manner. Coordinators of most programs stated that they were only willing to add from 1 to 6 hours of coursework because existing curricula are already filled with requirements. Curricula for learning to work with families are currently being developed through the Carolina Institute for Research on Infant Personnel Preparation for graduate training programs in the related services of PT (Sparling, 1991), OT (Hanft, Humphry, Burke, Cahill, & Miller, in preparation), and speech-language pathology (Crais, 1991). These curricula meet the criteria identified through the surveys; that is, the family content has been developed in such a way that it is embedded within existing coursework that is part of the requirements for each of the target disciplines. Since change within preservice programs for related personnel is apt to be minimal, recommendations for changes at the service delivery level may be more effective.

Promoting an Integrated Delivery of Related Services In order to address parents' concerns about the availability of trained staff and related services in integrated settings, it is necessary to look at models of service delivery. Most early childhood integrated settings are located in the community, rather than near specialized facilities where therapy is likely to be provided (e.g., hospitals, clinics). Providing therapy services obviously poses a number of problems. Difficulties in coordinating time, people, equipment, and facilities create frustration for everyone involved. This has given rise to the need to consider alternative options for the delivery of related services. Odom and McEvoy (1990) suggest using the therapist as an assessor, program designer, and consultant for the child's program, rather than as a direct service provider. Templeton, Fredericks, and Udell (1989), stating that the traditional "pull out" therapy seems especially out of place in regular preschool and daycare settings, have described an integrated daycare program in which related services were successfully provided through a consultation model.

It should be pointed out that there is much debate over the relative worth of various models for providing related services. Those that support a consultative or integrated approach maintain that therapy provided within the ongoing classroom or childcare routine will be more effective than therapy provided in a treatment room for a short period of time every week (Giangreco, York, & Rainforth, 1989). Those who support the pull-out approach

would argue that the direct contact time between child and therapist is too important to give up (Geiger, Bradley, Rock, & Croce, 1986). In a qualitative study of resistance to integration at the preschool level, Peck and his associates (Peck, Hayden, et al., 1989) found that many professionals have a vested interest in maintaining the status quo due to their fears over loss of control. Having someone suggest that his or her role was being changed from direct service provider to consultant certainly might be perceived as threatening to someone who did not wish to change roles or did not feel that he or she had the skills and knowledge to work as a consultant. Research on models of related services delivery is needed so that these important decisions can be made on the basis of data rather than emotions. In the meantime, the documented shortage of therapists working in early intervention (Yoder et al., 1990), coupled with the increased demand (resulting from the new law) for related services for infants and preschoolers, mean that alternative approaches to the delivery of services must be considered.

Providing Inservice Training that Is Geared Toward Systems Change The challenges related to providing family support in integrated settings are enormous. This topic entails addressing two areas of early intervention in which simultaneous changes are taking place. Creating structures and mechanisms for facilitating those changes is critical as communities struggle with providing family support and integrating programs at multiple levels.

Planning and training are two mechanisms that Peck, Hayden, and colleagues (1989) view as being helpful when communities deal with innovation. Peck's model of community participation (Peck, Richarz, et al., 1989) illustrates a planning approach that might be replicated in other communities. As mentioned earlier, local Interagency Coordinating Councils, set up through PL 99-457, might support a planning effort. The question of who would fund such an effort would have to be addressed, since most local ICCs operate on a volunteer basis. For example, many local ICCs do not have funds for even a secretary unless they request resources from United Way or some other charity.

A more usual approach in helping professionals deal with new information and ideas is the provision of inservice training, funded primarily through state agencies or federally supported outreach or demonstration projects. Because of the magnitude of the changes associated with family support in integrated programs, the typical 1- or 2-day workshop is not likely to be effective. In an earlier publication (Winton, 1990b), it was argued that inservice training related to an innovation such as the family-centered components of PL 99-457 should have the following characteristics: 1) involve "organizational families," or all of those individuals who are affected by the changes being recommended; 2) focus on specific practices in order to identify the gaps between current practices and what is being recommended; 3) provide ongoing support, reflective of the fact that the process of change takes time; and 4) involve participants in creating their own plan of change for further staff development.

An approach to training that fits some of the characteristics listed above is the onsite consultation model. There have been descriptions in the literature of the success of this model in providing support to regular preschool teachers (Hanline, 1990) and daycare providers (Klein & Sheehan, 1987) who are willing to serve children with special needs. This model tends to be limited, however, to changes at the individual or program level.

If the innovative ideas associated with family support and integration are to be realized, inservice efforts must focus on systems-level change as well. A team-based, decisionmaking model of inservice training related to the family-centered approaches of PL 99-457 has been developed and field tested through the Carolina Institute for Research on Infant Personnel Preparation (Bailey, McWilliam, Winton, & Simeonsson, 1991). The curriculum was developed to target existing early intervention teams consisting of direct service providers, families, and administrators. The goal of the training is for each team to develop an action plan for becoming more family-centered in their work. The format for training is a 4-day workshop.

The following results of field testing suggest that this may be a promising approach for dealing with systems changes related to family support in integrated settings: 1) although families are the focus of the curriculum, issues concerning community-based integration options quickly emerge, often within the context of discussions related to providing families with choices; and 2) as a result of participating in a workshop based on this approach, some teams decide that they want to engineer change in other parts of the community or the service delivery system. Follow-up evaluation will tell the extent and level to which community and programmatic changes do occur as results of staff development based on this curriculum.

SUMMARY

It is clear that providing family support in integrated settings is a complex issue. The numerous articles currently being written on the subject of family support and

PL 99-457 will raise knowledge and awareness levels; however, systems changes will be required in order to address the recommendations made in this chapter. Community structures will need to be created to support programs and individual practitioners who implement the family-centered practices recommended in the current literature. Without such a foundation, individual professionals will find themselves trying to provide broad-based family support without a broad base of community support to back them up. This is bound to lead to frustration and failure; one individual or one agency cannot do it all. In addition, the community network must extend beyond the traditional formal services and include parks and recreation, transportation, churches, community centers, community colleges—all of the contexts in which families live.

A significant factor that may influence community change is the increasing number of families who have been served under the family-centered policies in Part H. Families who have been given choices about where and how services are provided, and whose choices have been respected, are going to have a hard time accepting the more traditional approach to parent involvement and the limited options for services available for their children. Historically, parents have wielded considerable public policy influence when acting in concert as advocates for their children (Turnbull & Winton, 1984). The direction that communities take in supporting families and providing integrated programs may well depend on families' abilities to continue to advocate for themselves and for broader community options. Perhaps it will be families who bring an even broader definition of the least restrictive environment into being, one that is based on a collaborative, ongoing, decisionmaking process that takes into account the nature, type, and extent of intervention appropriate for each child and family. This definition suggests a coordinated, comprehensive, flexible network of community services, programs, and resources that is responsive to the evolving interests and needs of families and children.

REFERENCES

Affleck, G., Tennen, H., Rowe, J., Roscher, B., & Walker, L. (1989). Effects of formal support on mothers' adaptation to the hospital-to-home transition of high-risk infants: The benefits and costs of helping. *Child Development, 60,* 488–501.

Arango, P. (1990). A parent's perspective on "Family-centered care": Making it a reality. *Children's Health Care, 19*(1), 57–62.

Bailey, D., Buysee, V., Edmondson, R., & Smith, T. (1992). Creating a family focus in early intervention: Professional perceptions of typical practices, ideal practices and barriers to change. *Exceptional Children, 58*(4), 298–309.

Bailey, D., McWilliam, P., Winton, P., & Simeonsson, R. (in press). *Implementing family-centered services in early intervention: A team-based model for change.* Cambridge, MA: Brookline Books.

Bailey, D., Palsha, S., & Huntington, G. (1990). Preservice preparation of special educators to serve infants with handicaps and their families: Current status and training needs. *Journal of Early Intervention, 14*(1), 43–54.

Bailey, D., Simeonsson, R., Yoder, D., & Huntington, G. (1990). Preparing professionals to serve infants and toddlers with handicaps and their families: An integrative analysis across eight disciplines. *Exceptional Children, 57*(6), 26–35.

Bailey, D., & Winton, P. (1987). Stability and change in parents' expectations for mainstreaming. *Topics in Early Childhood Spe-*

cial Education, 7(1), 73–88.

Bailey, D., & Winton, P. (1989). Friendship and acquaintance among families in a mainstreamed day care center. *Education and Training of the Mentally Retarded, 24,* 107–113.

Bernheimer, L., Young, M., & Winton, P. (1983). Stress over time: Parents with young handicapped children. *Journal of Developmental and Behavioral Pediatrics, 4*(3), 177–181.

Blacher, J., & Turnbull, A.P. (1983). Are parents mainstreamed? A survey of parent interactions in the mainstreamed preschool. *Education and Training of the Mentally Retarded, 18,* 10–16.

Crais, E. (1991). *A practical guide to embedding family-focused content into existing speech-language pathology coursework.* Chapel Hill: Carolina Institute for Research on Infant Personnel Preparation, Frank Porter Graham Child Development Center, University of North Carolina, Chapel Hill.

Division for Early Childhood. (1991, February-March). Statement and recommendations with respect to reauthorization of Part H and amendments to Part B of the Individuals with Disabilities Education Act. *DEC Communicator, 17*(3), p. 6.

Doernberg, N. (1978). Some negative effects on family integration of health and educational services for young handicapped children. *Rehabilitation Literature, 39*(4), 107–110.

Dunst, C., Trivette, C., & Deal, A. (1988). *Enabling and empowering families: Principles and guidelines for practice.* Cambridge, MA: Brookline Books.

Education for All Handicapped Children Act of 1975, PL 94-142. (August 23, 1977). Title 20, U.S.C. 1401 et seq: *U.S. Statutes at Large, 89,* 773–796.

Education of the Handicapped Act Amendments of 1986, PL 99-457. (October 8, 1986). Title 20, U.S.C. 1400 et seq: *U.S. Statutes at Large, 100,* 1145–1177.

Federal Register. (1989, April/Sections 300 & 552.).

Fowler, S., Hains, A., & Rosenkoetter, S. (1990). The transition between early intervention services and preschool services: Administrative and policy issues. *Topics in Early Childhood Special Education, 9*(4), 55–65.

Gallagher, J., Harbin, G., Clifford, R., Eckland, J., Place, P., Fullagar, P., & Huntington, K. (1991). *Recommendations for reauthorization Part H of P.L. 99-457.* Chapel Hill: Carolina Policy Studies Program, Frank Porter Graham Child Development Center, University of North Carolina, Chapel Hill.

Geiger, W., Bradley, R., Rock, S., & Croce, R. (1986). Commentary. *Physical Occupational Therapy Pediatrics, 6*(2), 16–21.

Giangreco, M., York, J., & Rainforth, B. (1989). Providing related services to learners with severe handicaps in educational settings: Pursuing the least restrictive option. *Pediatric Physical Therapy, 1,* 55–63.

Green, A., & Stoneman, Z. (1989). Attitudes of mothers and fathers of nonhandicapped children. *Journal of Early Intervention, 13*(4), 292–304.

Hanft, B., Humphry, R., Burke, J., Cahill, P., & Miller, K. (1992). *Working with families: a curriculum guide for pediatric therapists.* Chapel Hill: Carolina Institute for Research on Infant Personnel Preparation, Frank Porter Graham Child Development Center, University of North Carolina, Chapel Hill.

Hanline, M.F. (1990). Project Profile: A consulting model for providing integration opportunities for preschool children with disabilities. *Journal of Early Intervention, 14*(4), 360–366.

Havelock, T., & Havelock, M. (1973). *Training for change agents.* Ann Arbor: University of Michigan.

Johnson, B., McGonigel, M., & Kaufmann, R. (Eds.). (1991). *Guidelines and recommended practices for the Individualized Family Service Plan* (2nd. ed.). Washington, DC: Association for the Care of Children's Health.

Klein, N., & Sheehan, R. (1987). Staff development: A key issue in meeting the needs of young handicapped children in daycare settings. *Topics in Early Childhood Special Education, 7,* 13–27.

National Early Childhood Technical Assistance System (NEC*TAS). (1990). *NEC*TAS Resource Packet: Least Restrictive Environment for Infants, Toddlers and Preschoolers.* Chapel Hill: Frank Porter Graham Child Development Center, University of North Carolina, Chapel Hill.

Neisworth, J. (Ed.). (1990). Transition [Special issue]. *Topics in Early Childhood Special Education, 9*(4).

Odom, S., & McEvoy, M. (1990). Mainstreaming at the preschool level: Potential barriers and tasks for the field. *Topics in Early Childhood Special Education, 10*(2), 48–61.

Palsha, S., Bailey, D., Vandiviere, P., & Munn, D. (1990). A study of employee stability and turnover in home-based early intervention. *Journal of Early Intervention, 14*(4), 342–351.

Peck, C., Hayden, L., Wandschneider, M., Peterson, K., & Richarz, S. (1989). Development of integrated preschools: A qualitative inquiry into sources of resistance among parents, administrators, and teachers. *Journal of Early Intervention, 13*(4), 353–363.

Peck, C.A., Richarz, S.A., Peterson, K., Hayden, L., Mineur, L., & Wandschneider, M. (1989). An ecological process model for implementing the least restrictive environment mandate in early childhood programs. In R. Gaylord-Ross (Ed.), *Integration strategies for students with handicaps* (pp. 281–298). Baltimore: Paul H. Brookes Publishing Co.

Powell, D. (1980). *Finding child care: A study of parents' search processes*. Detroit: The Merrill-Palmer Institute.

Reichart, D., Lynch, E., Anderson, B., Svobodny, L., DiCola, J., & Mercury, M. (1989). Parental perspectives on integrated preschool opportunities for children with handicaps and children without handicaps. *Journal of Early Intervention, 13*(1), 6–13.

Sparling, J. (1992). *Embedding family material into an entry level physical therapy curriculum*. Chapel Hill: Carolina Institute for Research on Infant Personnel Preparation, Frank Porter Graham Child Development Center, University of North Carolina, Chapel Hill.

Suelzle, M., & Keenan, V. (1981). Changes in family support networks over the life cycle of mentally retarded persons. *American Journal of Mental Deficiency, 86*(3), 267–274.

Templeton, T., Fredericks, H., & Udell, T. (1989). Integration of children with moderate and severe handicaps into a day care center. *Journal of Early Intervention, 13*(4), 325–328.

Turnbull, A.P., & Winton, P. (1983). A comparison of specialized and mainstreamed preschools from the perspectives of parents of handicapped children. *Journal of Pediatric Psychology, 8*, 57–71.

Turnbull, A., & Winton, P. (1984). Parent involvement policy and practice: Current research and implications for families of young, severely handicapped children. In J. Blacher (Ed.), *Severely handicapped children and their families: Research in review* (pp. 374–395). New York: Academic Press.

Turnbull, A.P., Winton, P., Blacher, J., & Salkind, N. (1983). Mainstreaming in the kindergarten classroom: Perspectives of parents of handicapped and nonhandicapped children. *Journal of the Division for Early Childhood, 6*, 14–20.

US General Accounting Office. (1990). *Early childhood education: What are the costs of high-quality programs?* (Report No. GAO/HRD -90-43BR). Gaithersburg, MD: Author.

Winton, P. (1981). Descriptive study of parents' perspectives on preschool services: Mainstreamed and specialized (Doctoral dissertation, University of North Carolina, Chapel Hill, 1981). *Dissertation Abstracts International, 42*, 356A. (University Microfilms No. 42-08)

Winton, P.J. (1986). The consequences of mainstreaming for families of young handicapped children. In C.J. Meisel (Ed.), *Mainstreaming handicapped children: Outcomes, controversies, and new directions* (pp. 129–148). Hillsdale, NJ: Lawrence Erlbaum Associates.

Winton, P. (1990a). Promoting a normalizing approach to families: Integrating theory with practice. *Topics in Early Childhood Special Education, 10*(2), 90–103.

Winton, P. (1990b). A systemic approach for planning inservice training related to Public Law 99-457. *Infants and Young Children, 3*(1), 51–60.

Winton, P. (1991). *Working with families in early intervention: An interdisciplinary curriculum*. Chapel Hill: Carolina Institute for Research on Infant Personnel Preparation, Frank Porter Graham Child Development Center, University of North Carolina, Chapel Hill.

Winton, P., & Bailey, D. (in press a). Communicating with families: Examining practices and facilitating change. In J. Paul & R. Simemsson (Eds.), *Understanding and working with parents of children with special needs* (2nd ed.). New York: Holt, Rinehart & Winston.

Winton, P., & Bailey, D. (in press b). Family-centered practices in early intervention for children with hearing loss. In J. Roush & N. Matkin (Eds.), *Infants and toddlers with hearing loss: Identification and family-centered intervention.* Parkton, MD: York Press.

Winton, P., & Turnbull, A. (1981). Parent involvement as viewed by parents of handicapped children. *Topics in Early Childhood Special Education, 1*(2), 11–20.

Yoder, D., Coleman, P., & Gallagher, J. (1990). *Personnel needs: Allied health personnel meeting the demands of Part H, P.L. 99-457.* Chapel Hill: Carolina Policy Studies Program, Frank Porter Graham Child Development Center, University of North Carolina, Chapel Hill.

SECTION II

PLANNING FOR DEVELOPMENT
ISSUES IN CURRICULUM AND TRANSITIONS

The kinds of interactions and experiences described in Section I, and others that are of benefit to children in integrated programs, are not likely to occur without the careful planning of activities and interventions by early childhood professionals and parents. The quality of this planning, and the collaborative relationships among professionals and parents on which it is based, are integral to the success of integrated programs. Section II addresses issues surrounding the planning and coordinating of experiences for young children that reflect current knowledge from the fields of early childhood education and early intervention. In Chapter 5, Richarz describes the overall design of high-quality early childhood programs, based on the principles of developmentally appropriate practice. In Chapter 6, Wolery and Fleming review strategies for addressing individual needs within integrated programs, drawing from the knowledge base of early intervention.

Thoughtful planning and coordination of children's experiences may also extend across programs. As Brofenbrenner (1979) noted, active facilitation of transitions of children and families into new social settings can make a positive contribution to their adaptation to the new activities, demands, and opportunities of those settings. Research and program development work describing practices that support children and families during transitions into or out of integrated early childhood programs are reviewed by Hanline in Chapter 7.

Chapter 5

Innovations in Early Childhood Education
Models that Support the Integration of Children of Varied Developmental Levels

Sherrill Richarz

One of the key components of an effective integrated classroom is the program model or curriculum. A carefully planned and well managed early childhood experience can facilitate the successful integration of normally developing children and children with disabilities from a variety of cultural, economic, and ethnic backgrounds. Bronfenbrenner (1979) described direct interactions among children, teachers, and families and the concept of the program or curricular model as microenvironment in his ecological framework of child development. This chapter addresses issues related to the microenvironment of mainstream programs and the relationships between the microenvironment and other ecological levels.

The planned integration of children with and without disabilities into the same educational setting is a rather recent phenomenon. Curricular models and programs designed for the normally developing child and the child with disabling conditions have evolved from different educational perspectives; traditionally, early childhood educators and special educators have espoused somewhat different positions on what the curriculum should include. Each reflects the historical perspectives of the particular field, the values of society at the time, and the public attitude toward education for typical children and for children with special needs. Traditional early childhood educators advocate models that are based on the naturally emerging competencies and interests of the child and the concerns of society for a specific population of children and that have an academic skills—oriented content with specific cognitive target outcomes for the children (Elkind, 1987; Osborn, 1991; Spodek, 1991; Widerstrom, 1986). Special education, with its history of medical and therapeutic intervention, has focused more on the remediation of skill deficits in children who were not developing normally (Barbour, 1987; Hildebrand, 1991;

Safford, 1978; Widerstrom, 1986). Both groups of educators were concerned with the welfare of children, but the broader cultural and social perspective of development has frequently been overlooked in implementation of the program practices and curriculum.

Many definitions for the term *curriculum* have been proposed over the years, and each one adds perspective to the concept. Most include both the content of a program and the procedures for its implementation. It appears at first that curricula for regular early childhood programs and for special education have been thought of as being quite different because of the varied perspectives of scholars in the two fields. However, on closer examination it is evident that there is actually no clear dichotomy between the two groups, for both agree on the foundations for the development of quality program models and curricula. In this chapter, the points of convergence and divergence between early childhood special education and regular early childhood education are explored.

DEFINITIONS OF CURRICULUM

Hendrick (1990) defines curriculum from a traditional regular early childhood education perspective as "the design of experience and activities to help children increase their competence" (p. 2). She sees it as total learning for the whole child, and bases her program model on this view. The position statement *Guidelines for Appropriate Curriculum Content and Assessment in Programs Serving Children Ages 3 through 8* (National Association for the Education of Young Children and the National Association of Early Childhood Specialists in State Departments of Education [NAEYC & NAECS/SDE], 1991)

proposes a broad definition of curriculum as "an organized framework that delineates the content children are to learn, the processes through which children achieve the identified curricular goals, what teachers do to help children achieve these goals, and the context in which teaching and learning occur" (p. 21). The model is a design for the environment that provides for skill development and intellectual challenges for the children.

From a special education perspective, Cook, Tessier, and Armbruster (1987) define curriculum as "all of the specific features of a master teaching plan that have been chosen by a particular teacher for his or her classroom" (p. 388). They describe the challenge of early education as that of helping children to realize their full potential. Saracho (1984), in writing about mainstreaming, describes a curriculum as "a set of organized experiences to promote learning that has been judged appropriate" (p. 18).

In reviewing these definitions, curriculum, from both regular early childhood education and special education perspectives, emerges as a vital part of the educational program for both children with disabilities and normally developing children. Many educators plan curriculum without seeing it as the total educational experience of the children, and thus fail to include the other microlevel participants in the planning process—the children themselves, the parents, and the community.

MODELS OF EARLY CHILDHOOD PROGRAMS: IMPORTANT INFLUENCES ON CURRICULUM

Historical Perspectives

The historical antecedents in the care and education of young children in the United

States have contributed to the diversity in program models, as well as to the variety of philosophical bases, fiscal and legal sponsorship, and approaches to teaching (Katz, 1987; McKee & Paciorek, 1988; Powell, 1987; Seefeldt & Barbour, 1990). The curricula of the major models of early education reflect the purposes for which they were initiated, the separate institutional histories of the concepts of care and education, the population being served, and the views of society on childrearing and education for all children. Lazerson (1971) describes early childhood education as having different focuses at different times—as social reform, as a facilitator of children's development, or as preparation for further education. Each of these purposes had a major impact on the development of curriculum content.

Early childhood programs in the United States evolved primarily from the traditional nursery school and kindergarten movements that began with Locke, Rosseau, Pestalozzi, Froebel, Peabody, and Hill (Bloch, 1991; Hildebrand, 1991; Osborn, 1991). Concern for the natural emergence of interests and abilities as a part of the maturation process of childhood has historically dominated the education of very young children. However, intervention for specific deficits, as defined by the values of society of the day, required different program models. For example, such programs were instituted for the children of immigrants arriving in the United States in the 19th century. Social welfare settlement house programs were begun with the goals of physical care, safety, and health for immigrant children, and to foster their integration into the dominant culture of American society (Leeper, Witherspoon, & Day 1984). Early in the 1900s in Italy, poor children and children with deficits were the focus of Montes-

sori's program model in which specifically designed environments promoted the development of the whole child. Although she was a physician, Montessori believed that "mental deficiency" was an educational problem rather than a physical one (Orem & Coburn, 1978; Osborn, 1991) and that specific curricula and specially designed materials could ameliorate the problem. Ironically, application of the Montessori model to the education of children with special needs or to the integration of children with and without disabilities has not occurred in Montessori programs to any great extent, despite the fact that one of her original goals was to develop an educational approach appropriate for all children (Orem & Coburn, 1978; Osborn, 1991).

In the United States, the child study movement of the 1920s and the parent-cooperative nursery schools that soon followed were major influences on subsequent curriculum development. Programs arising from these movements provided a number of benefits, including social experiences for children from homes where cognitive growth was being addressed by well-educated parents, research settings for students in child development, sites for teacher education programs, and settings in which mothers could learn about childrearing practices and share their experiences with other mothers. The public nursery school programs, begun in the economic depression of the 1930s, were designed primarily to provide employment for the many out-of-work school teachers. Leaders of this movement paid little attention to program development, and the curricula often resembled those of kindergarten and first grade. During World War II, social welfare childcare was operated to provide 24-hour care for children whose mothers were employed in war production plants. The goal was good custodial care for the children of thousands of "Rosie the Riveters," and in some of these programs excellent models for curriculum and program implementation were developed. In many, however, curriculum was not a high priority (Allen & Hart, 1984; Leeper et al., 1984; Osborn, 1991).

The Impact of Head Start

The compensatory education movement of the 1960s spawned Head Start to serve economically disenfranchised children and their families. The original goal of Head Start was to provide early educational intervention for children who were "disadvantaged"—an ambiguous term viewed by some as referring to income deficit and to others as also indicating a cultural deficit (Weiss, 1981; Widerstrom, 1986). From the beginning, leaders conceptualized Head Start as an ecological model of program design in which parent and community involvement, health care, education, and social service all served as critical components (Greenberg, 1990; Zigler & Valentine, 1979). In Head Start, both children with disabilities and normally developing children have been served in the same classrooms, but there is no standard Head Start curriculum. Head Start is now over 25 years old, and even though much has been learned about its limits and about the effectiveness of various curricular models in early childhood education, the program continues to include a broad range of curricula that reflect the diversity of cultural, social, and ethnic contexts in which it operates (Hymes, 1991; Peters, Neisworth, & Yawkey, 1985; Powell, 1987; Zigler & Lang, 1983).

Contemporary Perspectives on Early Childhood Programs

In the 1980s, a growing number of preschool programs reflected middle- and upper-class parents' concerns about their children's later success in school, and as a result, programs for these children emphasized academic skills and intellectual development (Gallagher & Coche, 1987). Neither the cognitive/social development preschools for children of low socioeconomic status (SES) nor the academically focused early childhood programs were originally planned with the integration of children with special needs in mind. Some accommodated children with physical limitations, but other types of disabilities were generally not addressed in program philosophy, policy, or curriculum design (Allen & Hart, 1984; Elkind, 1987; Leeper et al., 1984; Osborn, 1991; Zigler, 1987).

The most striking development in recent years is the increase in mothers of children under 6 in the labor force and the subsequent demand for childcare. The early childhood programs that care for children of employed parents often do not provide care for children with disabilities, and parents, regardless of income level, have a difficult time arranging for full-time care for these children. For all groups, the quality of childcare ranges from exemplary to abysmal (Trawick-Smith, 1991; Willer et al., 1991).

In recent years in the United States, the general public, educators, public policy experts, parents, and others have been calling for changes in the educational system (Committee for Economic Development, 1987; National Association of State Boards of Education [NASBE], 1988; National Governors' Association, 1986; Rothman, 1989). Restructuring is being demanded in areas of public education that have long been held constant, including teacher education, accountability, program structure, and curriculum design. The parameters of concern over education have also broadened to include early childhood programs (NASBE, 1988). Curriculum content and implementation have become targets of change as well, and in response to general concerns about appropriate experiences for young children, the National Association for the Education of Young Children (NAEYC) issued a position statement entitled *Developmentally Appropriate Practices for Children from Birth through Age Eight* (Bredekamp, 1987). In this statement, NAEYC identified practices and curricular content that they felt were developmentally appropriate for young children.

DAP and the Curriculum—What Does it Mean?

Developmentally appropriate practice, commonly referred to as DAP, influenced not only those in the early childhood profession, but also other types of educators, political and business leaders, and parents. The need to incorporate current knowledge about human learning into practices in the field is another important consideration during program model and curriculum planning. But developmentally appropriate practices became a catchall phrase that has frequently been misused by educators, other professionals, and businesses to achieve a measure of acceptance, to imply knowledge of child growth and development, or to market curriculum materials, workshops, and other profit-making offerings. What was introduced to identify a position on the education of young children and begin a dialogue on quality components in early childhood education often became a label used to justify a variety of both good and bad program practices.

The more recent document, *Guidelines for Appropriate Curriculum Content and Assessment in Programs Serving Children Ages 3 through 8* (NAEYC & NAECS/SDE, 1991), further delineates the components of quality program models for typical chil-

dren and children with disabilities and describes the importance of combining program model design with ongoing assessment of children and evaluation of programs. The debate over the theoretical groundings of DAP, its application to constituent groups, and the inclusion or exclusion of specific components continues (Bloch, 1991; Bredekamp, 1991; Katz, 1991; Kessler, 1991; Lubek, 1991; Spodek, 1991). For example, Bloch (1991) argues that early childhood education needs to be reconceptualized to include alternative perspectives and research paradigms, and Kessler (1991) proposes re-examining the basic tenets of schooling for democracy as the desired approach to a child-centered curriculum, while Bredekamp (1991) encourages building early childhood education on the common ground shared by developmental theorists and curriculum theorists. This dialogue provides opportunities for reflection and discourse from a variety of perspectives, and such discourse will ultimately benefit early childhood curriculum. The NAEYC documents on DAP provide an overview of best practices for early childhood programs. However, program developers must be cautious about applying the guidelines in an inflexible or dogmatic manner; these guidelines are not meant to be a one-size-fits-all model of educational practice.

CURRICULA FOR CHILDREN WITH SPECIAL NEEDS

Curricula for young children with disabilities have evolved from multiple perspectives (Shonkoff & Meisels, 1990); they have been strongly influenced by the traditions and practices of the public school system, the health care field, institutional social services, and others. Legislation such as PL 94-142 and PL 99-457 mandated more extensive early childhood special education and encouraged providing services in the least restrictive environment, and the educational system found itself providing education for very young children with disabilities, often in an integrated setting. The beliefs in the importance of the early years and in the early socialization of children outside the family have been combined with numerous resources, materials, and known strategies to develop curricula for early intervention programs for children with special needs (Shonkoff & Meisels, 1990).

The idea that deficits could be remedied through repeated drills and exercises, such as those used in old model institutions for "the retarded and infirm," frequently persisted into the school setting, and resulted in highly teacher-directed methods (Allen & Hart, 1984; Peterson, 1987). Legal restraints, as well as traditional attitudes about atypical development, discouraged change in curriculum strategies at the level of institutional practices or social policy. Special educators recognized the importance of the development of the whole child, but past close association with remedial education and speech, physical, and occupational therapy resulted in a strong clinical tradition in the design of curricula (Allen & Hart, 1984; Peterson, 1987; Safford, 1978; Widerstrom, 1986). In addition, behavioral psychology exerted a strong influence on special education with its approach to teaching as individualistic (learning in a one-on-one mode) but not necessarily individualized (designed to meet the specific differences and needs of each child), skill-focused, and adult-directed (Widerstrom, 1986).

Early childhood intervention continues to evolve and change as sociopolitical and academic influences respond to the needs of children, their families, and society. The curricula in intervention programs reflect the various levels of the ecological system, and no single system provides all the answers for curriculum design.

THEORETICAL MODELS OF EARLY CHILDHOOD PROGRAMS

Models of early childhood education differ in curriculum content and method of presentation. The way that the developmental process and the role of the environment are viewed are reflected in such differences (Powell, 1987). The many viewpoints on program design mirror a variety of theories of human development, the United States's broad social and economic goals, society's commitment to individual differences, the degree of discrimination and prejudice operating in society, the resources and abilities of the families and institutions involved, and the legal definitions imposed through the political system. The curriculum often epitomizes beliefs about the influences within the ecological system operating on individual children in any given program. The theoretical grounding of curriculum in early childhood education has been dominated by psychology and child development perspectives, while learning theory is more influential in the field of special education (Carta, Schwartz, Atwater, & McConnell, 1991; Spodek, 1991; Swadener & Kessler, 1991).

Examining Specifics of the Theories

No single theory can entirely explain human development, but several important influences on curriculum development in early childhood education can be ascribed to a limited number of theoretical models. Any framework that organizes these models in a broad way generally parallels the maturationist/socialization perspective (Elliott, 1972; Jipson, 1990; Kohlberg & Mayer, 1972; Verma & Peters, 1975), the learning/behavioristic view (Bissell, 1973a; Kohlberg & Mayer, 1972; Peters et al., 1985; Powell, 1987; Verma & Peters, 1975), and the cognitive-developmental theoretical perspectives (Powell, 1987; Verma & Peters, 1975; Weikert, 1987). Maturationist/socialization theory proposes that children are emotionally involved, adaptive, need limited structuring of the environment, and respond in a predetermined, genetically programmed sequence to a supporting environment. It also specifies that learning is both externally and internally driven. Some of the better known maturationist programs are the Bank Street College model and the traditional nursery school model espoused by Hymes and others of the 1950s and 1960s (Bissell, 1973a; Peters et al., 1985; Powell, 1987; Seefeldt & Barbour, 1990). Learning/behavioral theory describes children as being under the control of environmental contingencies, responsive to structuring of curriculum by the teacher, and product-oriented. Curriculum from this perspective focuses on the cultural transmission of knowledge and behavior. The didactic DARCEE model, Bereiter-Engleman's direct instruction model, and the University of Kansas model follow behaviorist theory (Bissell, 1973a; Peters et al., 1985; Powell, 1987). The cognitive-developmental perspective, which has been the dominant focus of early childhood curriculum in recent years, is described as being child-focused, with a limited amount of teacher structure, and one in which the child is viewed as being intrinsically motivated and an active learner. Children are seen as constructing knowledge through interactions with people and materials in their en-

vironment. The best known cognitive-developmental model is the High/Scope curriculum (Powell, 1987; Weikert, 1987). The assumptions implicit in these theories influence curriculum in both design and practice. Curriculum is shaped by the theoretical roles of the teacher and the child. Powell (1987) describes these roles as forming a continuum from child-initiated and child-directed involvement to teacher-originated and -directed activities.

Miller and Seller (1985) proposed three overarching organizational categories of curriculum that correspond to the broad theoretical bases of education: transmission (e.g., direct instruction, skills-based, traditional elementary school curriculum), transaction (e.g., the child's learning opportunities and the child's interactions with teachers combine to construct knowledge), and transformation (e.g., social contexts rooted in issues of equity and justice). These models also differ in the amount of group versus individual instruction that they involve, and in the amount of information the teacher gives the child versus the amount the teacher elicits or expects from the child.

Integration of children with special needs and normally developing children in the same setting brings a variety of professionals in close contact with each other. Often, the theoretical orientation of these professionals is very different, and program design and implementation present numerous challenges (Allen & Hart, 1984).

The variation in the application of theory to curriculum strategy and design becomes apparent when observing practices and procedures in different classrooms or early childhood centers. The crucial concern today is to include what is known about program effectiveness and to apply the underlying theoretical framework of these programs to curriculum design and implementation. Relevant theories must influence decisions about models. When integrating young children with and without disabilities into a single program, the importance of a solid theoretical base becomes even more evident.

RESEARCH ON EFFECTIVE CURRICULA

The variety of program models and curricula designed for young children requires that educators examine the effectiveness of early education models, and such scrutiny needs to be based on the results of empirical research. Much of the rhetoric from both regular early childhood education and special education is based more on personal experience or emotional response than on a solid foundation of carefully constructed research.

Research on curriculum models can serve several purposes. It can have a positive influence on changes that should occur in integrated programs; it can suggest conceptual changes that need to be made in curriculum design; and it can legitimize and sustain predetermined positions (Musick & Barbera-Stein, 1988). There is a need for more empirical research on program approaches and curriculum comparisons in integrated programs; thus, there are only limited results on which to base inferences about best practices. There have been studies on both model early childhood programs and on programs for children with special needs, but more precise studies are needed prior to making inferences about the most effective curriculum for integrated programs. Both early childhood special education and early childhood regular education attempt to fill this void by drawing conclusions about

curriculum needs without the benefit of research. A data base has been difficult to assemble in both special education and early childhood education, because distinguishing between the effects of natural maturation and those of treatment is difficult, as early childhood is a period of such rapid growth and development for all children. In addition, parenting styles, child characteristics, and teacher variables cannot be isolated from program variables (Clarke-Stewart & Fein, 1983; Katz, 1977; Powell, 1987). Katz (1987) stated that "It is a general principle that any field characterized by a weak data base has a vacuum which is filled by ideologies" (p. 151).

With the heightened involvement of public schools in early childhood programs (i.e., as a result of public laws concerning young children with special needs and at-risk children) and the growing interest of parents in the value of early education, questions have arisen about curriculum practices and program models that make a real difference in children's lives (Shonkoff & Meisels, 1990; Sigel, 1987). When providing early education and intervention for preschoolers, what approach should be used? Should the curricular approach be different for the various children being served? If so, how should this affect integrated preschool programs?

Early Studies on Learning

The research of Bloom (1964), Bruner (1966), and Hunt (1961) stimulated educators' interests in the first 5 years of life. Each supported the idea that children's environments greatly influence the acquisition of skills and basic coping strategies, and that such early environmental experience is important in later development. From these ideas, from the compensatory programs that emerged as part of the war on poverty, and from existing early childhood programs, Bissell (1973a) identified four curriculum models that could be linked to major theories or philosophies of child development. The *Permissive model* emphasized the whole child, had primarily a child-initiated curriculum with teacher response, contained low-to-moderate program structure, and was based mainly on Erikson, Gesell, and other maturationists. The *Structured Cognitive model* emphasized aptitudes and attitudes related to learning processes, balanced teacher- and child-initiated experiences, and included moderate structure (i.e., cognitive-developmental theory). The *Structured Information model* emphasized the acquisition of information and skills and included a high degree of teacher direction and program structure (i.e., behaviorist/learning theory). The *Structured Environment model* included a process-oriented approach with the teacher as a mediator or facilitator, provision of self-instructing materials, and moderate structure (i.e., based on the philosophy of Montessori). In a study of program practices with these models, Bissell (1973b) found that structured cognitive and structured information models were more effective than the permissive or structured environment models in producing cognitive gains. The effectiveness varied with the population being served, the objectives of the program, the competencies of the teachers, and the child:adult ratio. Bissell also noted a specificity of effects: in programs with concrete objectives and well-defined, well-formulated strategies for achieving these objectives "there was somewhat more growth in areas related to the stated objectives than was found in these areas in other programs" (p. 105). Other early research on curriculum comparison led to the conclusion that any well-planned and administered early childhood program could benefit the child (Smith, 1975; Weikert, 1972). The strategy for implementation, not the curriculum itself, was identified as the most important component for effectiveness.

Recent Contributions to Research

Subsequent curriculum comparison studies and long-term follow-up of earlier studies now suggest that different preschool curricula produce different outcomes for children (see Powell, 1987, for an in-depth review of this topic). A number of studies on the different curricular approaches in early childhood education support the hypothesis that preschoolers do best in programs that provide interaction with other children and adults; active, rather than passive, experiences; and opportunities for child-initiated activities (Fry & Addington, 1984; Gertsen, 1986; Miller, Bugbee, & Hybertson, 1985; Powell, 1987). Others have reported gender differences in response to curricular approaches, with boys being more sensitive to teaching method than girls, but both demonstrating gains of different types with group participation or teacher involvement (Fagot, 1973; Miller et al., 1985; Stallings & Stipek, 1986). Results of the Perry Preschool Project (Schweinhart, Weikart, & Larner, 1986; Weikart, 1987) have frequently been cited as evidence of the effectiveness of child-initiated learning activities for low-income preschoolers, although some have seriously challenged the methodology of these studies (Bereiter, 1986; Gertsen, 1986). The High/Scope researchers have emphasized the need for restraint in the interpretation and generalization of the findings and have urged that additional research with different populations be conducted before final conclusions are drawn.

Research on quality early childhood model programs and Head Start has indicated that both have immediate positive impact on tests of intellectual performance and social competence, but that early gains are not necessarily retained (Haskins, 1989; Lee, Brooks-Gunn, Schnur, & Liaw, 1990). Children from model programs show improvement in later school performance, and there are fewer placements in special education (Jordan, Grallo, Deutsch, & Deutsch, 1985; Lazar & Darlington, 1982), but little evidence for such effects has been found for children who have been enrolled in the broader array of programs in Head Start.

Head Start is one of the oldest and largest programs that integrates children with disabilities and normally developing children. However, few studies have examined the effects of the different curriculum models used in these Head Start programs on the intellectual, physical, or social competence of either group of children in these integrated settings. Rather, the major focus of most Head Start studies has been on the impact a preschool experience has on the behavior and achievement in elementary school of children from low-income families (Jordan et al., 1985; Powell, 1987; Zigler & Lang, 1983).

The lack of substantive research on curriculum effect in Head Start is not surprising, considering the numerous program sites throughout the United States and the vast differences in curriculum design and practices at these sites. Without specifically identified comparison variables, few general conclusions can be made about curriculum in Head Start, either for children with special needs or for children whose development is progressing normally. Raver and Zigler (1991), in a recent commentary on program evaluation in Head Start, feel that Head Start

curricula reflect the evaluative measures used; if Head Start truly aims for the development of the whole child, then this goal should be reflected in program evaluations of curricula.

DAP—Does it Make a Difference?

Several studies have examined the effects of DAP-oriented curricula for young children. Oakes and Caruso (1990) examined the use of developmentally appropriate activities in kindergartens and found that teachers who felt that they were willing to share authority used more DAP activities than did teachers who were more authority-controlling. However, they found that fewer than 50% of the classroom activities in any classroom could be considered developmentally appropriate. Hamilton and Gordon (1978) found that authoritarian teachers tend to discourage children from developing persistence and independence in task behavior, two areas frequently mentioned as being especially important in working with children with disabilities (Allen & Hart, 1984; Cook et al., 1987). Gelfer (1990) used developmentally appropriate practices, based on the High/Scope model, with language or learning impaired children, and reported the equivalent of 1.4 years of growth in the children in the first 6 months.

Children with Disabilities and the Curriculum

Early childhood special educators contend that children with disabilities need intervention early in their lives, and that it should be comprehensive in nature and delivered efficiently (Bricker, 1989; Carta et al., 1991). Preferred curriculum models for children with special needs have tended to include a structured environment with moderate-to-high adult intervention. Researchers have also found that children with special needs may not engage in spontaneous interaction with objects, activities, and people in the environment (Allen & Hart, 1984; Beckman, Robinson, Jackson, & Rosenberg, 1988; Bricker, 1989; Carta et al., 1991). A study by Kysela, Hillyard, McDonald, and Ahlston-Taylor (1981) on intervention for preschoolers with Down syndrome in programs that included both direct and incidental teaching in school and home settings showed that the children in this program exhibited greater improvement in cognitive and linguistic development than comparable children who did not receive such intervention. Fredericks et al. (1978), in a study of integration in a community childcare, found that social interaction between children with and without disabilities increased with staff intervention and a modicum of structure. Bricker (1989) stated that structured intervention can be effective with young children with disabilities. Odom and McEvoy (1988) examined the research on integrated program models and concluded that children with disabilities gain as much in mainstreamed settings as in those serving only children with special needs. The process of integration itself did not appear to be the key factor in producing beneficial outcomes; specific curricula and the quality of instruction were identified as the crucial elements in a successful integrated program.

Increasingly, early childhood programs, especially at the kindergarten level, are academically or skill-oriented. Hatch and Freeman (1988), in an enthnographic study of kindergarten-associated staff, found that kindergarten curriculum is frequently academically focused, but that teachers and administrators may not believe that this best serves the needs of the children. There is thus a philosophy–reality conflict for many practitioners.

The Importance of Curriculum in Integrated Programs

In reviewing the research on curriculum design and program practices, Powell (1987) pointed out two major themes: "preschool curriculum does matter and preschool effects appear to be a function of interaction between child characteristics and preschool practices" (p. 205). Research on integrated programs is limited, and conclusions about segregated early childhood program practices are often based on outcomes that cannot be generalized to integrated programs. Additional limitations of research are the lack of attention to the effects of parental attitude, gender, culture, child temperament, teacher role and attitude, and family characteristics other than socioeconomic level (Powell, 1987).

At first glance, educational practices in early childhood regular and special education appear to differ substantially. Yet, how great are the differences in what research indicates about program practices and curriculum? The major difference appears to be the position on the continuum of child–teacher initiation and involvement in curriculum. This polarization parallels the historical foundations of special education (didactic) and regular early childhood programs (less didactic). In general, these issues need to be put into perspective. Curricula for integrated programs should provide what children need to learn to become as competent as their biological limits allow, and the program practices should provide opportunities for sequenced growth within a framework of development. Early childhood programs for all types of children should reflect the knowledge base of child development theory, take individual child characteristics into account, include sequenced learning activities, support the development of the whole child, respond to current parental needs, and be partly based on the cultural milieu of the children and the society in which they live.

SYNTHESIS OF RESEARCH OUTCOMES: IMPLICATIONS FOR CURRICULUM DEVELOPMENT

A mainstreamed early childhood program must be of high quality if it is to benefit children, and it should reflect a philosophy compatible with the ecological framework in which it exists. The unique educational and social needs of young children should be the most important guidelines in program development, and not whether the child is disabled or developing normally (see Wolery & Fleming, chap. 6, this volume). Allen and Hart (1984) describe the importance of developing a curriculum that interrelates opportunities for intellectual stimulation, the development of physical skills, and encouragement of social and emotional well-being. This principle of interrelatedness can serve to guide parents, teachers, the community, and others in planning curriculum.

Selecting Curricula

Guidelines for the development of an appropriate curriculum for integrated early childhood programs include a series of assumptions (Richarz & Peterson, 1990; Seefeldt & Barbour, 1990). First, all young children in an integrated setting can share a common curriculum. It is not necessary for teachers to juggle content and strategies found in the variety of curricula that might be used. Second, adaptations and modifications must be made to the curriculum to meet the different competency levels, learning styles, and cultural needs of specific subgroups or individuals within

the larger group (see Wolery & Fleming, chap. 6, this volume). If the similarities and differences of the children in the integrated classroom have been carefully identified through screening and assessment, then adaptations flow from the needs, and logical target outcomes guide the modifications. Third, instructional techniques should include both teacher- and child-directed experiences. Different children respond to different kinds of learning experiences. Some appropriate activities evolve from children's initiations, while best practices for others are teacher-directed experiences. Teacher-directed activities for promoting specific-skill acquisition may include directions, task analysis, and modeling by the teacher. Child-directed activities may involve peer teaching, observation of other children, or sharing special interests. Another example of child-directed learning comes through group discovery when children share their newly acquired knowledge. Fourth, the curriculum needs to protect, maintain, and enhance the integrity of each child. The gain or outcome for the child must outweigh the cost of any learning experience (i.e., the emotional, physical, and intellectual involvement of the child must be considered in developing any curriculum). Last, an ecological framework can be applied to decisionmaking about curricula. Teachers, parents, and others involved in the educational process need to be aware of the responsibilities and functions that each has in planning for the children's needs, and must coordinate the curriculum in response.

Child Characteristics and the Curriculum

Since research indicates that curriculum is an important determinant of benefits for children, and that children's characteristics are also important determinants, it follows that children's learning will reflect, to some extent, how well curriculum and child characteristics are matched. A child's knowledge about his or her world is gained in different ways; some of it is child-constructed and some is societally determined (Elkind, 1987; Piaget, 1950; Vygotsky, 1978). Thus, an early childhood curriculum must achieve a balance between child-initiated and teacher-directed activities. Vygotsky (1981) views the teacher as the one who understands the distance between what children can accomplish alone and what they can do when helped by an adult or a more competent peer; he referred to this distance as the "zone of proximal development" (p. 117).

Katz (1988) described the content of curriculum as focusing on intellectual activities, not academic ones. She writes that young children should be involved in activities that have more *horizontal* relevance than *vertical* relevance. Horizontal relevance means that children are dealing with experiences relevant to what they do outside school, while vertical relevance means that what they are learning is preparing them for the next level of schooling. Katz argues that experiences in the curriculum need to relate more to familiar experiences to be meaningful to the young child. This has special significance for integrated programs, in that horizontally relevant curricula may be more likely to support and stimulate the development of children with disabilities.

The curriculum must not be so difficult that individual children lose their sense of mastery; such mastery results from struggling with something difficult and subsequently learning how to deal with it. Children with disabilities have experienced repeated failures and frustration not so much because of the difficulty of a challenge, but because they do not have the strategies or skills to attack the problem. The curriculum must include bridges that take the child from the known to the unknown. Many of these bridges are teacher-planned experiences and activities that increase the child's skills or put previous knowledge into a new context. Stimulating and maintaining the child's involvement and interest, especially with the diversity found in an integrated program, frequently depends on the teacher's interpreting cues from the child and arranging activities that result in child-initiated participation. Katz (1987) cautions that the use of a single teaching approach or curriculum with groups of children with diverse backgrounds and levels of ability produces heterogeneous outcomes, and may cause a significant proportion of the children most in need of successful intervention to struggle and fail. The need for both adult-planned and child-motivated elements in the curriculum can be identified through the various forms of individual and group assessment available to the educator, and through contacts with parents or other service providers (Bagnato, Neisworth, & Capone, 1986; Bailey & Wolery, 1984; NAEYC & NAECS/SDE, 1991).

Curriculum should be constructed to achieve specific goals and objectives derived from an assessment of the children and the ecological milieu. An organized framework and strategies for reaching the set goals are essential. As valuable as play is in a learning medium, a curriculum should not be limited to a haphazard collection of play experiences that may or may not benefit the child. The "cookbook" approach to curriculum (e.g., the use of activity books for planning) may offer a variety of worthwhile ideas, but as the sole source of curriculum this method fails to provide the opportunity for rich conceptual development or for building increasingly complex skill levels. Another inappropriate curriculum plan is to use whatever materials and activities are available (i.e., the cupboard approach), some being age- or individually appropriate, but most failing to meet individual needs of children or program goals (NAEYC & NAECS/SDE, 1991).

THE ROLE OF ASSESSMENT AND EVALUATION IN CURRICULUM DEVELOPMENT

Differing Views—Similar Goals

One area related to curriculum that elicits controversy between early childhood educators and special educators is the assessment of children, including the evaluation of how well individual and group goals have been met (Carta et al., 1991; NAEYC & NAECS/SDE, 1991; Parker & Zuckerman, 1990; Schultz, 1989). Educational decisions that affect children must be based on the analysis of documentation of the children's strengths and weaknesses. For children without disabilities, formal measures of successful mastery of learning experiences have not traditionally begun until first grade. Preschoolers have generally been evaluated subjectively, and reports to parents have been informal. This began to change rapidly with the passage of federal legislation that provided early education to preschoolers with disabilities through the public school system and mandated procedures for screening and diagnosis, accountability for child progress, and program evaluation. Systems for the developmental evaluation of young children evolved rapidly, and many of these systems were based on the standardized testing instruments and procedures used

with older children. Developmental considerations in testing young children presented new challenges. Inappropriate placements and inadequate monitoring of children and programs led to an outcry from parents and many educators. Children were sometimes judged as being intellectually disabled merely because they did not speak English or were unable to respond to the testing situation (Bailey & Wolery, 1984; Kamii, 1990; NAEYC & NAECS/SDE, 1991; National Commission on Testing and Public Policy [NCTPP], 1990; Shepard & Smith, 1988). The informal system for monitoring the progress of preschoolers was also inappropriate, but little was done to improve the systems being used. Recently, advocates have begun a movement calling for revisions of testing procedures in order to eliminate the inappropriate use and interpretation of instruments that appears to be occurring (Meisels, 1985; NAEYC, 1988; NAEYC & NAECS/SDE, 1991; NCTPP, 1990; Schultz, 1989).

Accountability for child progress and program effectiveness are issues that must be considered when planning or implementing a curriculum for young children. Providing an appropriate curriculum requires that teachers learn about children's individual needs, as well as the needs of the group. This information should be used to adapt the curriculum effectively, to help parents understand the role of curriculum for their children, and to evaluate the effects of the curriculum. The regulations in PL 99-457 and PL 102-119 are explicit, and they provide a framework for the assessment of children with specific disabilities in integrated programs. But the effective use of this framework requires that the teacher use appropriate instruments for such assessment and properly interpret the results.

Assessments should be made both formally and informally, and should incorporate multiple methods. Such assessment should include the use of periodic observations conducted in children's day-to-day environments, incorporate a variety of processes and tools for assessment, and actively solicit parental contributions. The procedures should assess all areas of the child's development in order to allow the educator to select and implement the most efficient and effective curriculum. Records of assessment and evaluation must be consistently maintained to be of value (Illinois Association for Supervision and Curriculum Development [ILASCD], 1989; Meisels, 1985; NAEYC & NAECS/SDE, 1991; Shonkoff & Meisels, 1990).

Resolving Dilemmas in Assessment

Educators and other professionals who work in integrated programs may have different perspectives on the assessment of children's progress (e.g., how it should be done, what instruments should be used, and how the results should be interpreted). A major concern for many is the danger of labeling the child with a specific disability or learning behavior that may or may not accurately reflect the quantitative measures or the qualitative aspects of the child's overall development (Bricker & Veltman, 1990; McCune, Kalmanson, Fleck, Glazewski, & Sillari, 1990; Odom & Shuster, 1986). Teachers from a regular early childhood education background have tended to undervalue the role of objective, formalized evaluation and assessment, and instead, emphasize informal observation in judging children's progress. Early childhood special educators are required by law to rely on diagnostic and comprehensive evaluation of the child's educational progress, yet sometimes fail to recognize the value of the

qualitative aspects of development (Bagnato et al., 1986; Bricker & Veltman, 1990; Shepard & Smith, 1988). Bricker and Veltman (1990) observed that diagnostic assessments often do not provide the specific information about the child's level of functioning that educators need when planning the curriculum for intervention.

In response to developmentally appropriate practices, Carta et al. (1991) critiqued the attitude of regular early childhood educators toward assessment as "rejecting active promotion of developmental progress toward a program goal" (p. 5), yet in the DAP document, Bredekamp (1987) states that "assessment of children's development and learning is essential for planning and implementation of developmentally appropriate practices" (p. 12). It appears that the role of assessment in DAP is interpreted differently by various groups. Perhaps early childhood regular and special educators underestimate the complexity of meeting the needs of all children in integrated settings, and fail to fully understand the different perspectives on assessment. For example, early childhood special educators may not understand that children within the normal range of development are as diverse in their responses to teaching strategies and ability to accept a different cultural experience as are children with identified disabilities. Similarly, early childhood educators may not be aware that children with disabilities also desire social interaction or unstructured play and that these needs may have to be met before the child will move on to a higher level of physical skill or concept development (Allen & Hart, 1984; Feeney, Christensen, & Moravcik, 1991). To accurately monitor the progress of the children and the curriculum practices, a systematic and continuous system of assessment needs to be developed and maintained for all early childhood programs (NCTTP, 1990; Schultz, 1989).

CULTURAL, ECONOMIC, AND ETHNIC INFLUENCES ON THE PROGRAM MODEL

As the United States population rapidly becomes more diverse in ethnicity, cultural background, and economic composition, it is important to recognize that "American culture is, in fact, many cultures, its history, many histories" (Lee, 1991, p. 2). Yet the ecological system tends to reflect EuroAmerican values and beliefs about childhood and education. Early childhood programs need to be implemented with a fresh outlook and new considerations that foster an atmosphere of mutual respect, tolerance, and an understanding of differences among children and families. Children are bringing a broader range of family and cultural diversity to programs, and familial values may differ from the teachers' values and from institutional EuroAmerican practices.

Many professionals involved in reconceptionalizing early childhood education argue that rational approaches to curriculum are never scientifically and politically neutral or objective. Rather, curriculum embodies fundamental beliefs about what is "good and important," and these beliefs are based on dominant middle-class cultural values and traditions (Swadener & Kessler, 1991; Vincent, Salisbury, Strain, McCormick, & Tessier, 1990). Peterson and Ellis (1986) describe two forms of cultural myopia that should be considered when planning curriculum: ethnocentrism and mainstream thinking. Both help explain barriers that interfere with a broad-based curriculum. Ethnocentrism refers to an exaggerated preference for one's own group and a concomitant dislike of other groups (LeVine & Campbell, 1972) while mainstream thinking reflects a focus, whether intentional or not, on the traditions, customs, and values of the dominant culture, which is usually EuroAmerican. Williams (1991) stated that adults need to understand more about their own cultural structures, and recognize possible discontinuities in their own attitudes and behaviors as sources of negative or mixed cultural messages. Richarz (1984) emphasized the importance of considering the cultural and ethnic backgrounds of all children and families in a program, as well as recognizing the special circumstances of some families (e.g., refugee families, immigrants, and newer family forms such as single parents or gay or lesbian couples).

Diversity and Program Practices

Program practices often reflect the inequities of society, and intervention for children with disabilities may not be a high priority in some cultures (Campbell, Goldstein, Schaefer, & Ramey, 1991; Miller & Seller, 1985). This raises challenging and difficult issues concerning values about intervention, the role of the family and institutions, and the rights of the child.

Those involved in curriculum planning should take into account the "relationship between each child's personal and cultural history and the social environment of the classroom" (Jipson, 1991, p. 133). The curriculum must be culturally salient, locally relevant, and meaningful within the context of a specific community (NAEYC & NAECS/SDE, 1991). Respect and esteem for different peoples is not reflected in a curriculum that is developed without considering varied cultural values about atypical development, attitudes toward formal education, or special traditions or customs (Derman-Sparks & The A.B.C. Task Force, 1989; Ramsey, Vold, & Williams, 1989; Williams, 1989). Educational, familial, and human services settings should act as equal partners in the delivery of a meaningful curriculum.

Communication styles between families and teachers or other direct service providers may be quite different, yet they are crucial to the understanding and subsequent acceptance of specific curriculum. Interpreting the nature and purpose of the curriculum for parents appears to be an important element in encouraging their involvement (Harrison, Wilson, Pine, Chan, & Buriel, 1990). The Task Force on Parent Involvement and Choice (National Governors' Association, 1990) asserts that interaction between these participants helps to establish programs that draw parents into decisionmaking, and thus enhances parent commitment to education.

Appropriate cultural interaction styles are always important when communicating about overall program issues or children's day-to-day activities (Bowman, 1989; West, 1986). Examining the diversity of family types, abilities, cultural practices, and economic levels currently found in the families served by early childhood programs makes it apparent that helping families to understand their children's program is a challenging task for teachers. Yet family support for curriculum practices, intervention strategies, and subsequent family involvement is widely recognized as a key element in the effectiveness of an educational experience for young children (Bowman, 1989; Comer, 1989; West, 1986).

Accounting for individual differences is a cornerstone of effective program planning and implementation in an integrated program. Aside from the identified physical, intellectual, and social characteristics of the child that are considered atypical,

unique family and child characteristics are also crucial determinants of curriculum design. The linkages between the program model and the levels of the ecological system in which the families and children operate dictate culturally appropriate responses that expand or limit program accomplishments (Comer, 1989).

Family Involvement in Program Planning

Families' responses to a child's program are often influenced by their own experience and culture. "Culture forms a prism through which members of a group see the world and create shared meanings" (Bowman, 1989, p. 118). Many parents find the curriculum does not meet their expectations in the area of academics or in the correction of deficits. Some cultural traditions dictate that the extended family should be involved in important conferences or in monitoring the outcomes of the child. "Family" may refer to something different from the traditional unit, and may be specified by the culture. Families who share a common background with teachers and other service providers at the mesolevel may move more easily to the next ecological level; they may be able to face institutional pressure or confusing regulations that control the operation and maintenance of the program and effectively articulate their concerns about curriculum or program practices (National Governors' Association, 1990). Cultural, economic, and ethnic differences have an influence on which prism families use to view and interpret their experience, and this, in turn, influences their responses.

The transmission of information between the institutional level and the family is one area of communication that appears to need strengthening. In most cultures, the educational institution commands a higher status than that of many families. In having the rationale for the curriculum explained to them, low-income parents, refugee families, or families from an ethnic group different from that of the teacher may feel disadvantaged. They may be reluctant to express a view about their children's needs that differs from that of the authority figure from the institution. Previous interaction experiences between a family and a teacher (i.e., the direct interaction level) or a principal or director (i.e., the institutional practices level) will naturally influence the family's acceptance or rejection of the recommended curriculum or other institutional recommendations. Negative contacts with educational agencies have dominated many minority families' communication with such programs. They bring this experience to future interactions and see the reflection of the inequities of the greater society (Jipson, 1991; Miller & Seller, 1985). Those professionals at the direct interaction level have a responsibility to ascertain the most acceptable approaches for different cultural or ethnic groups and for individual families within those groups and to implement appropriate communication strategies (Bowman, 1989; Derman-Sparks & The A.B.C. Task Force, 1989; Froschel & Sprung, 1988; Richarz, Peck, & Peterson, 1986; West, 1986). Respect for a variety of views, interest in new ideas, and discussion of values and attitudes can help clarify communication between those at the same ecological level or even those from different levels.

A RECOMMENDED APPROACH TO CURRICULUM DECISIONS

No single model or design for curriculum can be applied to all integrated programs, but the basic conditions described in this chapter support the concept of developmental appropriateness. Developmentally appropriate practices include a curriculum that is individually, and culturally, age-appropriate. The document that describes the specific curriculum components is *Guidelines for Appropriate Curriculum and Assessment in Programs Serving Children Ages 3 through 8* (NAEYC & NAECS/SDE, 1991). This paper is more specific to curriculum content than was the earlier DAP document (Bredekamp, 1987), emphasizes the importance of planned assessments, contains fewer ambiguous statements, and better integrates curriculum and assessment. It is broad enough to allow adaptations to individual beliefs, yet contains a set of principles of best practice that protects the intellectual, social, and cultural integrity of children and their families.

Interpretation of intent, examination of content, and judgments about DAP will continue, and can be used in discourse to strengthen the position of early intervention and to diminish the polarization of special education and early childhood education. Agreement will not evolve quickly, and changes will require compromise and cooperation. Walsh (1991) observed that the current discussions on DAP are based on agreements that may not actually exist, (e.g., that the ages and stages approach to development is valid) and present only a limited perspective on learning. Challenges to a position taken by such professionals help refine and revise its component strengths and lead to careful study.

Many educators respond to a second-hand interpretation of DAP; they have not actually read the material, but merely accept or reject another's view. Others expect DAP to provide an outline for day-to-day procedures. Jipson (1991), in an ethnographic examination of early childhood teachers' perceptions of DAP, concluded that educators approached DAP as a teacher's manual or curriculum guide, rather than as a general guide to what children need and to what constitutes best practices in early childhood programs. DAP does provide strategies that assist in making decisions about curriculum content and assessment, but it is not a manual for day-to-day operation. Its principles are applicable to a broad range of diverse groups of children. It also addresses both content and process, a dichotomy that is at the center of a long-running debate in curriculum studies. DAP is not a curriculum model in itself but offers a framework that can be applied to making decisions about specific program practices.

Early childhood programs that are to be effective must involve the whole child, whether he or she is a normally developing youngster or one with disabilities. The NAEYC and NAECS/SDE (1991) document proposes that the curriculum should address children's needs in the following areas: 1) social interactions and social skill development; 2) cognitive development, concept formation, and increasingly complex understandings in relation to prior experience and cultural expectations; 3) attention to emotional responses; and 4) integration of physical competence or physical limitations and other areas of curriculum.

A Screening Process

With the increase in early childhood programs for both children with special needs and normally developing children, commercial publishers of curriculum activity books and distributors of packaged curricula have multiplied rapidly. Educators are inundated with curriculum material from which choices may be made. When making decisions about the appropriateness and applicability of curricular materials, it is helpful to initially screen materials to see if an in-depth examination is warranted. Richarz and Peterson (1990) developed helpful criteria for evaluating curricula; a curriculum should:

1. Represent a theoretical base and have a conceptual framework.
2. Address all areas of development—physical, social, emotional, and cognitive.
3. Contain clear statements of goals and objectives that can be expected of the children.
4. Allow for instruction and learning in different configurations of child-child-adult interaction that include solitary, small group, and large group experiences both with and without adult interaction.
5. Allow for a wide range of developmental levels and flexibility in implementation.
6. Allow for both skill development and understanding of ideas and concepts and be based on prior knowledge and experience of the children.
7. Contain activities that are suitable for use with different ethnic and cultural groups, children from multiple family income levels and family configurations, and children who have special needs and normally developing children.
8. Provide a nonsexist approach and activities.
9. Promote the personal independence of children through the development of adaptive skills, skills in problem solving in social interactions, and the development of responsibility.
10. Contain material of intellectual integrity, knowledge that is worth having.

11. Use constructive correction in response to children's errors.

By focusing attention on the selection and implementation of curricula for integrated early education, the needs of the children can be more fully met, and more positive outcomes for children can be anticipated.

SUMMARY

Recognizing the complexity of the issues involved in the development of curriculum and the variety of individuals who influence the selection is essential to the process of curriculum development. The basic consideration should be what is right for each child or group of children involved. The educational services provided through the curriculum should show respect for the individual child's developmental level and emerging capabilities, as well as offer appropriate stimulation and challenge for each child. The curriculum should also reflect the values of the family, the cultural background of the children's communities, and the overall involvement of the service institutions.

Curriculum should not be static, but should be continually revised to meet the changing needs of the group and the individual children. It should be a process of constant building, evaluating, and adapting based on the impact of the curriculum on the students.

With careful examination and thoughtful application, developmentally appropriate practices as described in *Guidelines for Appropriate Curriculum Content and Assessment in Programs Serving Children Ages 3 through 8* (NAEYC & NAECS/SDE, 1991) can provide a practical and theoretically sound framework for curriculum development in integrated early childhood programs.

REFERENCES

Allen, K.E., & Hart, B. (1984). *The early years: Arrangements for learning.* Englewood Cliffs, NJ: Prentice Hall.

Bagnato, S.J., Neisworth, J.T., & Capone, A. (1986). Curriculum-based assessment for the young exceptional child: Rationale and review. *Topics in Early Childhood Special Education, 6,* 97–110.

Bailey, D.L., & Wolery, M. (1984). *Teaching infants and preschoolers with handicaps.* Columbus, OH: Charles E. Merrill.

Barbour, N. (1987). Curriculum concepts and priorities. *Childhood Education, 63,* 331–336.

Beckman, P.J., Robinson, C.C., Jackson, B., & Rosenberg, S.A. (1988). Translating developmental findings into teaching strategies for young handicapped children. *Journal of the Division for Early Childhood, 12,* 45–52.

Bereiter, C. (1986). Does direct instruction cause delinquency? *Early Childhood Research Quarterly, 1,* 289–292.

Berrueter-Clement, J., Schweinhart, L., Barnett, W.S., Epstein, A.S., & Weikart, D.P. (1984). Changed lives: The effects of the Perry Preschool Program on youths through age 19. Ypsilanti, MI: *Monographs of the High/Scope Educational Research Foundation,* No. 8.

Bissell, J. (1973a). The cognitive effects of preschool programs for disadvantged children. In J. Frost (Ed.), *Revisiting early childhood education* (pp. 223–240). New York: Holt, Rinehart & Winston.

Bissell, J. (1973b). Planned variation in Head Start and Follow Through. In J.C. Stanley (Ed.), *Compensatory education for children ages two to eight: Recent studies of educational intervention* (pp. 63–107). Baltimore: Johns Hopkins Press.

Bloch, M.N. (1991). Critical science and the history of child development's influence on early education research. *Early Education and Development, 2,* 95–108.

Bloom, B.S. (1964). *Stability and change in human characteristics.* New York: John Wiley & Sons.

Bowman, B. (1989). Educating language minority children: Challenges and opportunities. *Phi Delta Kappan, 71,* 118–120.

Bredekamp, S. (Ed.). (1987). *Developmentally appropriate practices in early childhood programs serving children from birth through age 8* (expanded ed.). Washington, DC: National Association for the Education of Young Children.

Bredekamp, S. (1991). Redeveloping early childhood education: A response to Kessler. *Early Childhood Research Quarterly, 6,* 199–209.

Bricker, D.D. (1989). *Early intervention for at risk and handicapped infants, toddlers, and preschool children.* Palo Alto, CA: VORT.

Bricker, D.D., & Veltman, M. (1990). Early intervention programs: Child-focused approaches. In S.J. Meisels & J.P. Shonkoff (Eds.), *Handbook of early childhood intervention* (pp. 373–399). New York: Cambridge University Press.

Bronfenbrenner, U. (1979). *The ecology of human development: Experience by nature and design.* Cambridge, MA: Harvard University Press.

Bruner, J. (1966). *The process of education.* Cambridge, MA: Harvard University Press.

Campbell, F.A., Goldstein, S., Schaefer, E.S., & Ramey, C.A. (1991). Parental beliefs and values related to family risk, educational intervention, and children's academic competence. *Early Childhood Research Quarterly, 6,* 167–182.

Carta, J.J., Schwartz, I.S., Atwater, J.B., & McConnell, S.R. (1991). Developmentally appropriate practice: Appraising its usefulness for young children with disabilities. *Topics in Early Childhood Special Education, 11,* 1–20.

Clarke-Stewart, K., & Fein, G. (1983). Early childhood programs. In P. Mussen (Ed.), *Manual of child psychology* (pp. 917–999). New York: John Wiley & Sons.

Comer, J.P. (1989). Racism and the education of young children. *Teachers' College Record, 90,* 352–361.

Committee for Economic Development. (1987). *Children in need.* New York: Author.

Cook, R.E., Tessier, A.T., & Armbruster, V.B. (1987). *Adapting early childhood curricula for children with special needs* (2nd ed.). Columbus, OH: Charles E. Merrill.

Derman-Sparks, L., & The A.B.C. Task Force. (1989). *Anti-bias curriculum: Tools for empowering young children.* Washington, DC: National Association for the Education of Young Children.

Education for All Handicapped Children Act of 1975, PL 94-142. (August 23, 1977). Title 20, U.S.C. 1401 et seq: *U.S. Statutes at Large, 89,* 773–796.

Education of the Handicapped Act Amendments of 1986, PL 99-457. (October 8, 1986). Title 20, U.S.C. 1400 et seq: *U.S. Statutes at Large, 100,* 1145–1177.

Elkind, D. (1987). *Miseducation: Preschoolers at risk.* New York: Alfred A. Knopf.

Elliott, D.L. (1972). *Early childhood education: How to select and evaluate materials.* New York: Education Products Information Exchange Institute.

Fagot, B. (1973). Influence of teacher behavior in the preschool. *Developmental Psychology, 9,* 198–206.

Feeney, S., Christensen, D., & Moravcik, E. (1991). *Who am I in the lives of children?* (4th ed.). New York: Charles E. Merrill.

Fredericks, H.D, Baldwin, V., Grove, D., Moore, W., Riggs, C., & Lyons, B. (1978). Integrating moderately and severely handicapped preschool children into a normal day care center. In M.J. Guralnick (Ed.), *Early intervention and the integration of handicapped and nonhandicapped children* (pp. 191–206). Baltimore: University Park Press.

Froschel, M., & Sprung, B. (1988). *Resources for educational equity: A guide for grades pre-k-12.* New York: Garland.

Fry, P.S., & Addington, J. (1984). Comparison of social problem solving of children from open and traditional classrooms: A two-year longitudinal study. *Journal of Educational Psychology, 76,* 318–329.

Gallagher, J., & Coche, J. (1987). Hothousing: The clinical and educational concerns over pressuring young children. *Early Childhood Research Quarterly, 2,* 203–210.

Gelfer, J.I. (1990). An early education pilot program using a developmentally appropriate practice for children with language and learning problems: The guidelines for the early learning (GEL) program. *Early Education and Development, 1,* 458–464.

Gertsen, R. (1986). Response to "Consequences of three preschool curriculum models through age 15." *Early Childhood Research Quarterly, 1,* 293–302.

Greenberg, P. (1990). Head Start . . . Before the beginning: A participant's view. *Young Children, 45,* 40–52.

Hamilton, V.J., & Gordon, D.A. (1978). Teacher–child interactions and task persistence. *American Educational Research Journal, 15,* 459–466.

Harrison, A.O., Wilson, M.N., Pine, C.J., Chan, S.Q., & Buriel, R. (1990). Family ecologies of ethnic minority children. *Child Development, 61,* 347–362.

Haskins, R. (1989). Beyond metaphor: The efficacy of early childhood education. *American Psychologist, 44,* 274–282.

Hatch, J.A., & Freeman, E.B. (1988). Kindergarten philosophies and practices: Perspectives of teachers, principals, and supervisors. *Early Childhood Research Quarterly, 3,* 151–166.

Hendrick, J. (1990). *Total learning for the whole child* (3rd ed.). Columbus, OH: Macmillan/Charles E. Merrill.

Hildebrand, V. (1991). *Introduction to early childhood education* (5th ed.). New York: Macmillan.

Hunt, J.M. (1961). *Intelligence and experience.* New York: Ronald Press.

Hymes, J.L., Jr. (1975). *Early childhood education: An introduction.* Washington, DC: National Association for the Education of Young Children.

Hymes, J.L., Jr. (1991). *Early childhood education: Twenty years in review.* Washington, DC: NAEYC.

Illinois Association for Supervision and Curriculum Development. (1989). *Early childhood screening.* Normal, IL: Author.

Individuals with Disabilities Education Act Amendments of 1991, PL 102-119. (October 7, 1991). Title 20, U.S.C. 1400 et seq: *U.S. Statutes at Large, 105,* 587–608.

Jipson, J. (1990, April). *Developmentally appropriate practices: Limiting possibilities.* Paper presented at the annual conference of the American Educational Research Association, Washington, DC.

Jipson, J. (1991). Developmentally appropriate practices: Culture, curriculum, connections. *Early Education and Development, 2,* 120–136.

Jordan, T., Grallo, R., Deutsch, M., & Deutsch, C. (1985). Long-term effects of early enrichment: A 20 year perspective on persistence and change. *American Journal of Community Psychology, 13*(4), 393–415.

Kamii, C. (Ed.). (1990). *Achievement testing in early childhood education: The games grown-ups play.* Washington, DC: National Association for the Education of Young Children.

Katz, L.G. (1977). Early childhood programs and ideological disputes. In L.G. Katz (Ed.), *Talks with teachers* (pp. 148–171). Washington, DC: National Association for the Education of Young Children.

Katz, L.G. (1987). Early education: What should young children be doing? In S.L. Kagan & E.F. Zigler (Eds.), *Early schooling: The national debate* (pp. 151–167). New Haven, CT: Yale University Press.

Katz, L.G. (1988). *Early childhood education: What research tells us.* Bloomington, IN: Phi Delta Kappa.

Kessler, S.A. (1991). Alternative perspectives on early childhood education. *Early Childhood Research Quarterly, 6,* 183–197.

Kohlberg, L., & Mayer, R. (1972). Development as an aim of education. *Harvard Educational Review, 42,* 449–496.

Kysela, G., Hillyard, A., McDonald, L., & Ahlston-Taylor, J. (1981). Early intervention: Design and evaluation. In R.L. Schiefelbusch & D.D. Bricker (Eds.), *Early language: Acquisition and intervention* (pp. 341–388). Baltimore: University Park Press.

Lazar, I., & Darlington, R.B. (1982). Lasting effects of early education: Report from the Consortium for Longitudinal Studies. *Monographs of the Society for Research in Child Development,* No. 47 (2-3, Serial No 195).

Lazerson, M. (1971). Social reform and early childhood education: Some historical perspectives. In R.H. Anderson & H.G. Shane (Eds.), *As the twig is bent: Readings in early childhood education* (pp. 22–33). Boston: Houghton Mifflin.

Lee, L.C. (1991). The opening of the American mind: Educating leaders for a multicultural society. *Human Ecology Forum, 19,* 2–5.

Lee, V.E., Brooks-Gunn, J., Schnur, E., & Liaw, F-R. (1990). Are Head Start effects sustained? A longitudinal follow-up comparison of disadvantaged children attending Head Start, no preschool, and other preschool programs. *Child Development, 61,* 495–507.

Leeper, S.H., Witherspoon, R.L., & Day, B. (1984). *Good schools for young children* (5th ed.). New York: Macmillan.

LeVine, R., & Campbell, D. (1972). *Ethnocen-*

trism: *Theories of conflict, ethnic attitudes and group behavior.* New York: John Wiley & Sons.

Lubek, S. (1991). Reconceptualizing early childhood education: A response. *Early Education and Development, 2,* 168–173.

McCune, L., Kalmanson, B., Fleck, M.B., Glazewski, B., & Sillari, J. (1990). An interdisciplinary model of infant assessment. In S.J. Meisels & J.P. Shonkoff (Eds.), *Handbook of early childhood intervention* (pp. 219–245). New York: Cambridge University Press.

McKee, J.A., & Paciorek, K.M. (1988). *Curricular applications in early childhood education 88/89.* Guilford, CT: Dushkin.

Meisels, S.J. (1985). *Developmental screening in early childhood: A guide* (rev. ed.). Washington, DC: National Association for the Education of Young Children.

Miller, J.L., & Seller, J. (1985). *Curriculum perspectives and practice.* New York: Longman.

Miller, L.B., Bugbee, M.R., & Hybertson, D.W. (1985). Dimensions of preschool: The effects of individual experience. In I.E. Sigel (Ed.), *Advances in applied developmental psychology* (Vol. 1, pp. 25–90). Norwood, NJ: Ablex.

Musick, J., & Barbera-Stein, L. (1988). The role of research in an innovative preventive initiative. In D. Powell (Ed.), *Parent education as early childhood intervention: Emerging directions in theory, research, and practice* (pp. 209–227). Norwood, NJ: Ablex.

National Association for the Education of Young Children. (1988). Position statement on standardized testing of young children 3 through 8 years of age. *Young Children, 43,* 42–47.

National Association for the Education of Young Children, & National Association for Early Childhood Specialists in State Departments of Education. (1991). *Guidelines for appropriate curriculum content and assessment in programs serving children ages 3 through 8.* Washington, DC: National Association for the Education of Young Children.

National Association of State Boards of Education. (1988). *Right from the start. The report of the NASBE Task Force on Early Childhood Education.* Alexandria, VA: Author.

National Commission on Testing and Public Policy. (1990). *From gatekeeper to gateway: Transforming testing in America.* Chestnut Hill, MA: Author.

National Governors' Association. (1990). *Time for results: The Governors' 1991 Report on Education* (No. 3049). Washington, DC: Author.

Oakes, P.B., & Caruso, D.A. (1990). Kindergarten teachers' use of developmentally appropriate practices and attitudes about authority. *Early Education and Development, 1,* 445–457.

Odom, S.L., & McEvoy, M.A. (1988). Integration of young children with handicaps and normally developing children. In S.L. Odom & M. Karnes (Eds.), *Early intervention for infants and children with handicaps: An empirical base* (pp. 241–267). Baltimore: Paul H. Brookes Publishing Co.

Odom, S.L., & Shuster, S. (1986). Naturalistic inquiry and the assessment of young handicapped children and their families. *Topics in Early Childhood Special Education, 6,* 68–82.

Orem, R.C., & Coburn, M. (1978). *Montessori prescription for children with learning disabilities.* New York: G.P. Putnam's Sons.

Osborn, D.K. (1991). *Early childhood education in historical perspective* (3rd ed.). Athens, GA: Education Associates.

Parker, S.J., & Zuckerman, B.S. (1990). Therapeutic aspects of the assessment process. In S.J. Meisels & J.P. Shonkoff. (Eds.), *Handbook of early childhood intervention* (pp. 350–369). New York: Cambridge University Press.

Peters, D.L., Neisworth, J.T., & Yawkey, T.D. (1985). *Early childhood education: From theory to practice.* Monterey, CA: Brooks/Cole.

Peterson, G., & Ellis, G. (1986). Countering ethnic and cultural myopia in the study of families. *Family Perspectives, 20,* 227–239.

Peterson, N. (1987). *Early intervention for handicapped and at-risk children: An introduction to early childhood–special education.* Denver: Love.

Piaget, J. (1950). *The psychology of intelligence.* London: Routledge & Kegan Paul.

Powell, D. (1987). Comparing preschool curricula and practices: The state of research. In S.L. Kagan & E.F. Zigler (Eds.), *Early schooling: The national debate* (pp. 190–211). New Haven: Yale University Press.

Ramsey, P.G., Vold, E.B., & Williams, L.R. (1989). *Multicultural education: A source book.* New York: Garland.

Raver, C.C., & Zigler, E.F. (1991). Three steps

forward, Two steps back: Head Start and the measurement of social competence. *Young Children, 46,* 3–9.

Richarz, S. (1984). *Exploring children's roots: Ethnic and cultural heritage.* Moscow, ID: News Review Publishing Co.

Richarz, S., Peck, C.A., & Peterson, K. (1986). *Developing integrated preschools in rural communities.* Proposal funded by the U.S. Department of Education, Handicapped Children's Early Education Program. Pullman: Washington State University.

Richarz, S., & Peterson, K. (1990). *DAP Checklist: A process for selecting developmentally appropriate curriculum.* Pullman: Washington State University.

Rothman, R. (1989). What to teach: Reform turns finally to the essential question. *Education Week, 1,* 10–11.

Safford, P.L. (1978). *Teaching young children with special needs.* St. Louis: Mosby.

Saracho, O. (1984). Mainstreaming: The role of the teacher. *Day Care and Early Education, 12,* 17–23.

Schultz, T. (1989). Testing and retention of young children: Moving from controversy to reform. *Phi Delta Kappan, 71,* 125–129.

Schweinhart, L.J., Weikert, D.P., & Larner, M.B. (1986). Consequences of three preschool curriculum models through age 15. *Early Childhood Research Quarterly, 1,* 15–45.

Seefeldt, C., & Barbour, N. (1990). *Early childhood education: An introduction* (2nd ed.). Columbus, OH: Charles E. Merrill.

Shepard, L.A., & Smith, M.L. (1988). Escalating academic demand in kindergarten: Some nonsolutions. *Elementary School Journal, 89,* 135–146.

Shonkoff, J.P., & Meisels, S.J. (1990). Early childhood intervention: The evolution of a concept. In S.J. Meisels & J.P. Shonkoff (Eds.), *Handbook of early childhood intervention* (pp. 3–31). New York: Cambridge University Press.

Sigel, I.E. (1987). Does hothousing rob children of their childhood? *Early Childhood Research Quarterly, 2,* 211–225.

Smith, M.S. (1975). Evaluation findings in Head Start Planned Variation. In A.M. Rivlin & P.M. Timpane (Eds.), *Planned variation in education: Should we give up or try harder?* (pp. 101–111). Washington, DC: Brookings Institution.

Spodek, B. (1991). Reconceptualizing early childhood education: A commentary. *Early Education and Development, 2,* 161–167.

Stallings, J., & Stipek, D. (1986). Research in early childhood and elementary school teaching programs. In M.C. Wittrock (Ed.), *Handbook of research on teaching* (3rd ed.) (pp. 727–753). New York: Macmillan.

Swadener, B.B., & Kessler, S. (1991). Introduction to special issue. *Early Education and Development, 2,* 85–94.

Trawick-Smith, J. (1991). Executive summary. In J. Trawick-Smith (Ed.), *Child-care programs: Raising the standards.* Bloomington, IN: Phi Delta Kappa.

Verma, S., & Peters, D.L. (1975). Day care teacher practices and beliefs. *The Alberta Journal of Educational Research, 21,* 46–55.

Vincent, L., Salisbury, C.L., Strain, P., McCormick, C., & Tessier, A. (1990). A Behavioral–Ecological Approach to Early Intervention: Focus on Cultural Diversity. In S.J. Meisels & J.P. Shonkoff (Eds.), *Handbook of early childhood intervention* (pp. 173–195). New York: Cambridge University Press.

Vygotsky, L.S. (1978). *Mind in society: The development of psychological processes.* Cambridge, MA: Harvard University Press.

Vygotsky, L.S. (1981). The development of higher forms of attention in childhood. In J.V. Wertsch (Ed.), *The concept of activity in Soviet Psychology* (pp. 189–240). Armonk, NY: M.E. Sharpe.

Walsh, D.J. (1991). Extending the discourse on developmental appropriateness: A developmental perspective. *Early Education and Development, 2,* 109–119.

Weikert, D.P. (1972). Relationship of curriculum, teaching, and learning in preschool education. In J.C. Stanley (Ed.), *Preschool programs for the disadvantaged* (pp. 22–66). Baltimore: Johns Hopkins University Press.

Weikert, D.P. (1987). Curriculum quality in early education. In S.L. Kagan & E.F. Zigler (Eds.), *Early schooling: The national debate* (pp. 168–189). New Haven, CT: Yale University Press.

Weiss, R. (1981). INREAL intervention for language handicapped & bilingual children. *Journal of the Division for Early Childhood, 4,* 24–27.

West, B. (1986). Culture before ethnicity. *Childhood Education, 62,* 175–181.

Willer, B., Hofferth, S.L., Kisker, E.E., Divine-Hawkins, P., Farquhar, E., & Slantz, F.B.

(1991). *The demand and supply of child care in 1990.* Washington, DC: National Association for the Education of Young Children.

Widerstrom, A.H. (1986). How important is play for handicapped children? *Childhood Education, 60,* 39–50.

Williams, A.H. (1989). Diverse gifts: Multicultural education in the kindergartern. *Childhood Education, 66,* 2–3.

Williams, L. (1991). Curriculum making in two voices: Dilemmas of inclusion in early childhood education. *Early Childhood Research Quarterly, 6,* 303–311.

Zigler, E. (1987). Formal schooling for four-year-olds? No. In S.L. Kagan & E.F. Zigler (Eds.), *Early schooling: The national debate* (pp. 27–44). New Haven, CT: Yale University Press.

Zigler, E., & Lang, M. (1983). Head Start: Looking toward the future. *Young Children, 38,* 3–6.

Zigler, E., & Valentine, J. (Eds.). (1979). *Project Head Start: A legacy of the War on Poverty.* New York: Free Press.

Chapter 6

IMPLEMENTING INDIVIDUALIZED CURRICULA IN INTEGRATED SETTINGS

Mark Wolery
and Lucy A. Fleming

Young children with developmental delays and disabilities have two broad categories of needs. First, they have needs that are similar to all other children; for example, they need to be safe, nourished, accepted, nurtured, and challenged. But they also have a unique set of needs that is *not* shared by children who are free of developmental delays and disabilities. The first set of needs implies that they should be included in early education programs for typically developing children, and, indeed, they are enrolled in such programs with increasing regularity. The second set implies that to meet their unique needs, their early education experiences must be individualized. This chapter focuses on how the unique needs of young children with developmental delays and disabilities can be addressed within the context of an early education environment designed for typically developing children.

This chapter has three purposes: 1) to define terms and identify issues related to individualizing instruction for young children with disabilities in integrated settings, 2) to summarize relevant instructional research, and 3) to draw implications for practice and research.

DEFINITION OF TERMS AND IDENTIFICATION OF ISSUES

Definition of Terms

Three terms—curriculum, instruction, and individualization—are particularly important to any discussion about integrated programming for children with disabilities. *Curriculum* has four elements (Bailey, Jens, & Johnson, 1983; Dunst,

Preparation of this chapter was made possible by cooperative agreement H024K90005, Early Childhood Research Institute—Integrated Programs, between the Office of Special Education Programs, U.S. Department of Education and the Allegheny-Singer Research Institute. However, the opinions expressed herein do not necessarily reflect the position or policy of the U.S. Department of Education, and no official endorsement should be inferred.

1981; Wolery, 1983). First, it refers to the *content* or target outcomes of teaching (i.e., the skills, strategies, and processes being taught). The content is usually organized in sequence, and moves from what is easy to learn to more difficult lessons, or from prerequisites to skills that build upon those prerequisites. In many cases, the content includes the domains of social, motor, adaptive, communication, and cognitive development (Bailey & Wolery, 1989, 1992; Bricker, 1989; Hanson & Lynch, 1989; Odom & Karnes, 1988; Peterson, 1987; Thurman & Widerstrom, 1990), and is arranged in an order that corresponds to the order in which typical children appear to acquire knowledge and skills. In other cases, the content may not be "developmental," but rather, is formulated to teach skills that are needed in specific environments (Noonan & Kilgo, 1987; Salisbury & Vincent, 1990). Sometimes the content is not dependent upon the context in which instruction is provided. For example, a child who needs to learn to feed herself may be taught this skill at home, in a segregated program, or in a mainstreamed setting. Other skills, however, may require specific types of environments. For example, learning to engage in sustained social interactions with peers, or to have conversations with peers that include six or more exchanges, requires contexts that include peers who have the skills necessary to support the child's learning of the targets.

With the increased emphasis being placed on mainstreaming, particularly in programs that apply the developmentally appropriate practice guidelines described by the National Association for the Education of Young Children (NAEYC) (Bredekamp, 1987; Bredekamp & Rosegrant, in press), the sources of curricular content need to be re-evaluated. A recent (Novem-

ber, 1990) policy statement by NAEYC and the National Association of Early Childhood Specialists in State Departments of Education (NAECS/SDE) provides an expanded list of desired outcomes—many of which are less skill-oriented than those that have traditionally been sought. The list includes such targets as curiosity, creativity, early literacy, critical thinking, understanding others' perspectives, understanding cultural diversity, developing a positive attitude toward learning, appreciation for the fine arts, and many others. Professionals have little information about encouraging these traits in young children with disabilities. Clearly, there are still substantial challenges to face in identifying relevant curriculum content.

Second, the curriculum should include a set of *assessment strategies* to identify the content that is most appropriate for each learner. This element is central to the individualization of instruction, because it identifies what each child should be taught. Third, the curriculum should contain a set of *instructional manipulations* designed to ensure the acquisition and use of the content that was deemed important for each child. Finally, the first three elements should be tied together by *compatible perspectives* on child development (Dunst, 1981). The content, the assessment procedures, and the instructional strategies should be logically and philosophically consistent with one another. A primary weakness in past curricular practices of early childhood special education has been the tendency to approach these three elements from incompatible perspectives. Specifically, the developmental milestones model was used to define the universe of possible curriculum content. Adaptations of norm-referenced measures that were designed to identify children of different developmental capabilities, rather than to identify instructional targets, were used to determine the content needed by each learner. And the instructional manipulations were derived from various cultural transmission perspectives, particularly the behavioral model. This mixing of incompatible perspectives led to the teaching of skills of questionable value (see Brinker, 1985; Dunst, 1981, for more complete discussions).

Instruction refers to the purposeful manipulations of the environment that allow children to acquire and use important skills. Three comments about this definition are important. First, it refers to a broad range of manipulations, including structuring of the physical and social environment (e.g., having typical peers present) and providing specific types of activities (Bailey & Wolery, 1992; Odom & Strain, 1984), using naturalistic teaching procedures (Warren & Kaiser, 1988), using peer-mediated interventions (Strain & Odom, 1986), using response prompting strategies (Wolery, Ault, & Doyle, 1992; Wolery, Bailey, & Sugai, 1988), and using stimulus modifications (Etzel & LeBlanc, 1979). Second, this definition specifies that these manipulations are made purposefully. Depending more on logic and experience than on empirical evidence, the authors argue that a central difference between mainstreamed programs that produce few desirable (i.e., defined individually for each child) outcomes and those that produce substantial and meaningful outcomes is the extent to which the instructional decisionmakers have designed and manipulated the environment to foster skill acquisition and use. The more intentional the manipulations, the greater the benefits to the children involved. Third, the definition specifies that the manipulations are aimed at fostering both acquisition and use of skills. Instruc-

tion is provided to promote acquisition (i.e., learning how to use skills), fluency (i.e., learning to use skills smoothly and rapidly, or at natural rates), maintenance (i.e., learning to use skills after instruction has stopped), and generalization (i.e., learning to use the skills when and where they are needed) (Wolery, Ault, & Doyle, 1992; Wolery, Bailey, et al., 1988).

Individualization refers to the extent to which the: 1) curriculum content is customized for each learner, 2) instructional manipulations are carried out to influence skill acquisition and use, and 3) manipulations are adjusted based on children's needs and performance. The development of customized content requires a thorough assessment of the child's developmental abilities, his or her independence and interactions in relevant environments, the influence of assistance and adaptations, and consideration of family values and perspectives. The instructional manipulations are made based on a number of guidelines (listed later), children's performance is monitored, and instruction is adjusted to ensure that the desired outcomes are obtained efficiently. It should be noted that individualization is not synonymous with one-on-one instruction; rather, it implies purposeful planning and adjustment of the activities, routines, and interactions in which each child participates.

Conceptual Foundation

Establishing a conceptual foundation for the individualization of curriculum is essential to providing an effective program in mainstreamed settings. Specifically, *mainstreaming is a context or setting variable, rather than the primary independent or treatment variable.* Mainstreaming is justifiable on several grounds (cf. Bricker, 1978; Peck & Cooke, 1983), and mainstreamed placement appears to be defensible for most children (Guralnick, 1990). However, mainstreaming alone is not sufficient to produce the most desirable outcomes for children (Fewell & Oelwein, 1990; McLean & Hanline, 1990). Ecological analyses of mainstreamed programs clearly indicate that children in a mainstreamed program can experience very different opportunities for interaction and learning (Carta, Sainato, & Greenwood, 1988). The benefits that accrue to children are directly related to the extent to which important skills are identified, environmental manipulations are individualized, and instruction is adjusted.

To make mainstreaming a legitimate practice, the field is faced with two global tasks. First, interventionists must ensure that young children with disabilities are enrolled in mainstreamed settings; and second, they must ensure that what occurs within those settings is individualized for each child. Recent data suggest that the field has done well with the first task, at least with children who have mild disabilities. In fact, the authors' survey of nearly 900 randomly selected preschool programs for typical children from every geographic region of the nation indicated that 75% of the responding programs reported integrating at least one child with a diagnosed disability during the 1989–1990 school year (Wolery, Fleming, & Venn, 1990). These respondents were from Head Start, private not-for-profit, private for-profit, church/synagogue, corporate, hospital, childcare chains, military, public school pre-kindergarten, and public school kindergarten programs. The return rate of the questionnaire was adequate (i.e., in excess of 55%) and returned questionnaires were reliably coded (i.e., inter-coder agreement in excess of 96%). What occurs within those programs and how adequately children's needs are being met are

less clear. This chapter focuses on the second global task: Ensuring that mainstreamed settings engage in practices that individualize instruction for children.

Individualization Issues Associated with Assessment

Functional assessment is the foundation of the individualization of curricular content and instruction. Adequate assessment requires that information be gathered in three crucial areas: 1) child needs and current functioning, 2) family concerns and priorities, and 3) appropriateness of the instructional environment.

Assessment that provides information about present levels of functioning has a direct effect on each child's individualized education program (IEP) or individualized family service plan (IFSP). Several characteristics of effective, ecologically valid assessments have been specified (Bailey, 1989). The first characteristic is the inclusion of *multiple developmental and behavioral domains*. A comprehensive assessment provides information about cognitive, communication, motor, social, and adaptive skills. A second characteristic is the use of *multiple measures* to ensure a broad perspective. A variety of direct testing procedures is often recommended, including norm-referenced, curriculum-based, clinical judgment scales, (Neisworth & Bagnato, 1988; Simeonsson, Huntington, & Parse, 1980), play scales (Fewell, 1983), and measures of information processing, coping, and attending ability (Bagnato, Neisworth, & Munson, 1989). Information should also be derived from structured naturalistic observations and from formal and informal interviews with significant others. A third characteristic is the gathering of information from *multiple independent sources* such as parents, teachers, and therapists. This practice increases the likelihood of observing skills that are emerging, person- or situation-specific, or inconsistent. A related practice is interdisciplinary assessment in which a variety of personnel, including special educators, speech-language pathologists, occupational therapists, physical therapists, psychologists, social workers, classroom aides, and family members, collaborate in the evaluation process. PL 99-457 requires interdisciplinary/multisource assessment as a method for increasing both parent–professional agreement and the effectiveness of team decisionmaking. A variety of team compositions and strategies has been identified and described (Fordyce, 1981; Wolery & Dyk, 1984). A fourth characteristic of quality assessment is *parental involvement*. Involving parents can increase families' competence, encourage trust in professionals, and provide valuable information about the child's functioning in the broader ecology of home and community routines (Bailey, 1989; Brinkerhoff & Vincent, 1986). A fifth characteristic is that measures are *nondiscriminatory*. This means that information-gathering procedures should not be biased against children of a particular race, gender, cultural background, or religious affiliation. Evidence of nondiscriminatory practice can be determined by examining test items and manuals. Using multiple measures and sources in a variety of natural contexts also reduces the possibility of unfair bias.

Another important part of assessment is determining family concerns and priorities. As in child assessment, assessment of families should cover all important domains (Bailey, 1988). Two of these domains are the family's perceptions of their needs and the needs of their child, and family priorities for early intervention services. Professionals should be aware that families of children with dis-

abilities may have concerns and needs in a variety of areas, not all of which are directly related to their child's instructional program. Several instruments for assessing the needs and concerns of families have been developed. The Family Needs Survey (Bailey & Simeonsson, 1988) provides information in six categories: 1) the need for information related to child disability or behavior, 2) the need for support, 3) the need for help in explaining about their child to others, 4) the need for help in obtaining available services, 5) the need for financial help or resources, and 6) the need for help in intrafamily functioning. The Family Needs Survey also includes an open-ended statement, "Please list your five greatest needs as a family."

Another instrument for gathering data on family needs is the Family Information Preference Inventory (Turnbull & Turnbull, 1986). This scale assesses need in five areas: 1) teaching the child at home, 2) advocacy and working with professionals, 3) planning for the future, 4) helping the whole family relax and enjoy life, and 5) finding and using more support. The Family Needs Scale (Dunst, Cooper, Weeldreyer, Snyder, & Chase, 1988) identifies needs in nine areas: 1) basic resources, 2) specialized childcare, 3) personal and family growth, 4) financial and medical resources, 5) child education, 6) meal preparation, 7) future childcare, 8) financial budgeting, and 9) household support. These instruments provide a mechanism to help families identify important concerns. Families' priorities should be the basis for individualizing goals and services. To deny families' ownership of goals can lead to mistrust or overdependence on professionals (Dunst, 1985). Moreover, parents are less likely to pursue goals that they feel do not address pressing needs (Bailey, 1987). Thus, a key aspect of individualizing curriculum content is understanding which skills are valued by families.

Individualization Issues Associated with Teachers' Roles

A number of environmental variables can influence the individualization of curriculum content. One of these variables is teacher behavior. Recently, the roles that teachers in mainstreamed settings assumed during classroom activities were measured and analyzed (Fleming, Wolery, Weinzierl, Venn, & Schroeder, 1991). Results showed that teachers engaged in a variety of roles. Of the eight roles observed, the most frequent roles were *instructor* (i.e., teaching specific content and directing or leading activities) and *monitor* (i.e., checking on progress, suggesting variations, and encouraging persistence). Specific activities did not predict particular roles, and a variety of roles was assumed during each activity. Teachers often switched roles within, as well as between, activities. Those selecting instructional strategies and scheduling daily activities to ensure effective individualization must take this variability into account.

Fleming et al. (1991) proposed a four-step model for this process. The first step is to assess and analyze the teachers' roles. A teacher who begins activities in the instructor role and then moves to an observer role might use a different teaching strategy than one who alternated between monitor and observer several times during an activity. The second step is to select effective teaching strategies. Response-prompting strategies such as constant time delay would be appropriate procedures for a teacher who spends a great deal of time in the instructor role. Naturalistic teaching procedures such as incidental teaching, mand-model, or natu-

ralistic time delay would be more appropriate for teachers who frequently engaged in the monitor, observer, or co-player role. Teachers who remain in the instructor or monitor, rather than materials-manager or behavior-manager, role during transition could effectively use transition-based teaching strategies. The third step is to provide teachers with information and training. Many early childhood teachers may not be familiar with strategies developed and disseminated by special education teachers/researchers. Teachers should be trained to integrate specific teaching procedures into current classroom activities. The fourth step in this model is to monitor and evaluate the adaptations. Monitoring performance as teachers implement changes in their classroom routines is necessary. As teachers become more adept at implementing changes in their roles, their ability to generalize to new activities and different children should be assessed.

SUMMARY OF RESEARCH ON THE INSTRUCTION OF CHILDREN WITH DISABILITIES

In this section, general guidelines for selecting high-priority objectives and for selecting and implementing instructional manipulations are presented. This is followed by a summary of potential manipulations, and the research on selected manipulations. Finally, an overview of developmentally appropriate practice is presented.

General Guidelines for Individualization

Most instructional models involve at least four steps (with many variations and substeps): 1) collecting assessment information, 2) planning instruction and monitoring systems, 3) implementing instruction, and 4) monitoring/evaluating the effects of instruction and making adjustments as needed (Bricker, 1989; Wolery, 1989). These steps are linked together to ensure that several important issues are addressed (Bricker & Veltman, 1990), such as: identifying high-priority target behaviors; organizing the physical dimensions of the classroom; selecting materials; structuring routines, activity areas, and schedules; meshing high-priority objectives with particular activity areas and times for instruction, based on teachers' roles; implementing the class-wide and individualized curriculum; monitoring children's learning and classroom operation; and making adjustments in the physical space, materials, activity areas, activity schedules, routines, and instructional practices, based on children's performance.

In Table 1 several general guidelines are presented for identifying high-priority objectives and for making decisions about selecting instructional strategies and organizing individualized instruction. Three comments about these guidelines are pertinent. First, the outcomes of individualized instruction drive the process. Thus, family values and the usefulness and long-term benefits of skills are critical considerations. Second, the instruction is designed to achieve the desired outcomes; thus, teams must repeatedly evaluate whether acquisition is occurring, generalization is being displayed, and independence and participation are being promoted. Efficient strategies, which assume effectiveness, are given precedence over other strategies. Simpler, more normalized, and less intrusive and restrictive strategies are selected on the basis of their effects on child learning. No justification

Table 1. General guidelines for implementing instruction with children who have disabilities

Determining the priority of skills for instructional goals

1. Family values, goals, and perspectives should be a central consideration in determining whether a given skill is targeted for instruction.
2. The immediate usefulness of a skill is critical to the identification of that skill as an instructional priority.
3. Long-term benefit of a skill is critical to the identification of that skill as an instructional priority.
4. Analysis of the function of the skill in the environment is important in determining whether and how it should be taught.

Planning and implementing individualized instruction

1. Instruction should be organized to promote acquisition, fluency, maintenance, and generalization.
2. Instruction should be organized to promote independent performance, but adapted performance (partial participation) is preferred over dependency and nonparticipation.
3. The effectiveness (whether children learn) and efficiency (how rapidly and broadly children learn) of instructional procedures and arrangements are more important than their naturalness (normalization), their intrusiveness, or their restrictiveness.
4. If child benefit in terms of learning (independence, generalization, engagement, and developmental performance) is equal, then more natural, more normalized, less restrictive, and less intrusive strategies should be employed.
5. If child benefit in terms of learning is equal, then more child-direct strategies and arrangements are preferred.
6. If child benefit in terms of learning is equal, then parsimonious (simpler/simplest) strategies and arrangements are preferred.
7. Instructional strategies and arrangements should encourage integration across developmental domains and environments.
8. Fluent performance and performance maintained by natural contingencies are necessary for enduring skill use and application.
9. Existing behaviors should be used to teach new functions (effects), and existing functions are the proper context for teaching new behaviors.
10. Existing behaviors should be replaced with more normative, adaptive, and developmentally advanced behaviors that produce the same environmental effects (functions).

Adapted from Bailey and Wolery (1992).

exists for employing instructional manipulations, even those that are easy to implement, are used with typical children, or are considered minimally intrusive and restrictive, if they result in *in*efficient learning. Third, when structuring instruction, both forms (i.e., behaviors) and functions (i.e., effects) must be described (Carr, 1988; Neel & Billingsley, 1989; Wolery, 1989). The new behaviors or new functions should be taught using children's existing behaviors and functions. Children should not be taught new behaviors *for* new functions; rather, instruction should focus *either* on a new function *or* a new form. For example, if a child crawls (existing form) to get from one place to another (existing function), then walking (new form) should be taught in the context of getting from place to place. Conversely, if a child does not request objects (new function), the child should be taught using objects that he or she already labels (i.e., existing form), rather than those that he or she does not (new form).

Instructional Decisions

Teaching young children with disabilities involves a range of potential manipulations that can be divided into three broad teacher functions: 1) organization of the physical, social, and temporal dimensions of the classroom; 2) selection and use of materials; and 3) selection and use of intervention strategies. The organization of mainstreamed classrooms should, for the most part, be similar to that found in high-quality programs for typically developing children. It is clear that particular physical arrangements, activity schedules, and social groupings influence children's play, behavior, and learning (Bailey & Mc-William, 1990). Because these issues are discussed in detail in other sources, they are not addressed here (Bailey, Harms, & Clifford, 1983; Bailey & Wolery, 1992; Johnson, Christie, & Yawkey, 1987; Musselwhite, 1986; Odom & Strain, 1984).

Selection of materials and children's preferences for particular materials and activities are issues of considerable importance. Although materials do not "teach," they set the stage for interactions that result in learning. For example, some materials appear to give rise to more social exchanges than others (Odom & Strain, 1984). An issue that has received little attention in the instructional research on preschoolers is the use of *general case programming* for selecting materials (Albin & Horner, 1988). General case programming is a means of organizing instruction to promote generalization. General case programming requires identification of variations in stimuli and responses in the natural environment and selection of instructional examples (i.e., materials) that include those variations. Its success with older students who have severe disabilities suggests that fruitful applications with young children may be possible (Horner & McDonald, 1982; Sprague & Horner, 1984).

Teachers must determine which strategies to use and how those strategies should be implemented. Available strategies can be grouped into five types: 1) peer-mediated interventions, 2) milieu or naturalistic strategies, 3) stimulus modifications, 4) response shaping, and 5) response prompting. *Peer-mediated interventions* have been used primarily for social skills development (Odom & Strain, 1984) but occasionally have been used to teach communication skills (Goldstein & Wickstrom, 1986). The strategies have been discussed in numerous sources (cf. Odom & Brown, chap. 3, this volume; Strain, 1981; Strain & Odom, 1986). *Naturalistic strategies* such as incidental teaching, mand-model procedure, and naturalistic time delay are used primarily for promoting communication skills. As with peer-mediated interventions, they too have been discussed authoritatively in other sources (Cipani, 1991; Kaiser, Alpert, & Warren, 1987; Notari & Cole, chap. 2, this volume; Warren & Kaiser, 1988; Warren & Rogers-Warren, 1985). *Stimulus modification procedures* have been used primarily to teach academic skills, and with older children. Their complexity, the extensive material-preparation time required, and their infrequent use in applied contexts preclude their discussion here (cf. Etzel & LeBlanc, 1979; LeBlanc, Etzel, & Domash, 1978). *Response shaping* is a well known, frequently used, but understudied strategy (Cooper, Heron, & Heward, 1987). It involves differentially reinforcing successive approximations of the target behavior. It is substantially beneficial in settings where child-directed learning is used. It can be used to increase both the complexity of child behavior and the duration of children's engagement, participation, and play. However, few recent studies have demonstrated its effects with young children, primarily because it is such a well established and accepted procedure.

Response prompting refers to a number of strategies that are designed to transfer stimulus control from controlling stimuli (i.e., response prompts) to natural or target stimuli (Wolery, Ault, & Doyle, 1992). In reality, some of the peer-mediated interventions and all of the naturalistic teaching procedures are response-prompting strategies. Response-prompting strategies share at least three common characteristics. First, prompts are used to encourage the learner to perform the target behavior in the presence of the target stimulus. Second, reinforcement is provided contingent on the occurrence of the target behavior when the target stimulus is present. Third, the prompts are system-

atically faded. The procedures differ in the manner in which prompts are provided and faded. Descriptions of some response prompting strategies appear in Table 2.

Several summary statements can be made about these procedures, and are based on research conducted in mainstreamed settings and in other settings, and with both preschool children and older children:

Most of the response-prompting procedures, when they are adjusted as needed, result in effective learning (Wolery, Bailey, & Sugai, 1988).

The system of least prompts is used widely (perhaps more than any other strategy), especially for chained responses (Doyle, Wolery, Ault, & Gast, 1988).

Antecedent response-prompting strategies are more efficient than error correction (i.e., fewer errors are produced) (Ault, Wolery, Doyle, & Gast, 1989).

Stimulus modification procedures tend to be more error-free than response-prompting procedures (Ault et al., 1989).

Most-to-least prompting may be more efficient than the system of least prompts and constant time delay (Ault et al., 1989; McDonnell & Ferguson, 1989), although one study shows constant time delay to be more efficient than most-to-least prompting (Miller & Test, 1989).

Constant time delay and simultaneous prompting appear to produce about equally efficient learning (Schuster, Griffen, & Wolery, 1992).

Progressive time delay and constant time delay are more efficient than the system of least prompts with both discrete and chained responses (Ault et al., 1989; Schoen & Sivil, 1989; Wolery, Ault, Gast, Doyle, & Griffen, 1990).

Table 2.   Procedural parameters of commonly used response-prompting procedures

Error correction
The teacher provides the target stimulus (discriminative stimulus) and presents an opportunity for the child to respond. Correct responses are differentially reinforced, and errors result in a prompt.

Antecedent prompt and test
The teacher presents a prompt simultaneously with the target stimulus before the learner responds, presents an opportunity to respond, and reinforces correct responses. In subsequent trials, the prompt is removed and a "test" is given to determine if the behavior occurs when the learner is presented with the target stimulus alone. During test trials, error responses may or may not receive a prompt.

Antecedent prompt and fade
The teacher presents a prompt simultaneously with the target stimulus, presents an opportunity to respond, and reinforces correct responses. Over trials, the prompt is systematically faded until the learner responds to the target stimulus alone. Fading may occur both in frequency and intensity.

Simultaneous prompting
The teacher provides a prompt simultaneously with the target stimulus, presents an opportunity to respond, and reinforces correct responses. In daily probe trials, the target stimulus is presented alone.

Most-to-least prompting (decreasing assistance)
The teacher uses a hierarchy of prompts ordered from most to least intrusive. Initially the most intrusive prompt is presented simultaneously with the target stimulus, and correct responses are reinforced. This continues until the child attains a specified criterion level of performance. When criterion is reached with the most intrusive prompt, the next less intrusive prompt is provided until performance meets criterion. This process continues until the child responds to the target stimulus alone.

System of least prompts (increasing assistance)
The teacher uses a hierarchy of prompts ordered from least to most intrusive. On each trial, the teacher presents the target stimulus alone, and provides an opportunity for a response. If no response, or an error, results, the least intrusive prompt is presented, as is an opportunity to respond. Again, if no response is forthcoming, or an error occurs, the next most intrusive prompt is presented with an opportunity to respond. This continues until the child responds correctly. Reinforcement is provided, and the trial is terminated when the child responds correctly to any level of the hierarchy.

Constant time delay
Initially, for a specified number of trials, the teacher presents the target stimulus simultaneously with a controlling prompt, followed by an opportunity to respond. Correct responses are reinforced. For subsequent trials, the interval between the delivery of the target stimulus and presentation of the prompt is increased by a fixed number of seconds. Correct responses before and after the prompt are usually reinforced.

Progressive time delay
Initially, for a specified number of trials, the teacher presents the target stimulus simultaneously with a controlling prompt followed by an opportunity to respond. Correct responses are reinforced. For subsequent trials, the interval between the delivery of the target stimulus and presentation of the prompt is *gradually* increased. Correct responses before and after the prompt are usually reinforced.

Adapted from Ault, Wolery, Doyle, and Gast (1989).

Progressive and constant time delay appear to result in nearly equally efficient learning (Ault, Gast, & Wolery, 1988). Constant time delay has been used widely with preschoolers and results in effective learning with minimal procedural modifications (Wolery, Holcombe, et al., 1992).

Although much of the original research with these strategies occurred in one-on-one settings, some of these strategies (e.g., constant time delay, system of least prompts) have been effective with small groups in mainstreamed classrooms (Cybriwsky, Wolery, & Gast, 1990). Guidelines and teacher decisions for structuring group instruction also have been described (Collins, Gast, Ault, & Wolery, 1991). This research has documented that specific skills are acquired during group instruction and that broad developmental changes can result from it in mainstreamed preschool settings (Hoyson, Jamieson, & Strain, 1984). Group instruction can increase the number of opportunities to learn, and thereby increase skill acquisition (Sainato, Strain, & Lyon, 1987) and result in observation learning (Cybriwsky et al., 1990). A variation on direct instruction in groups is to embed the response-prompting procedures in other activities (e.g., circle time). The authors' initial research on this practice, using constant time delay (Fleming, Wolery, & Venn, 1991) and simultaneous prompting, (Wolery, Fleming, Venn, Domjancic, & Thornton, 1991) has produced effective learning.

In addition to instruction provided in group arrangements, some research has evaluated the use of these procedures in distributed-trial formats in mainstreamed preschool programs. Specifically, it appears that error correction implemented during transitions between activities is as efficient as progressive time delay in one-on-one instructional sessions for teaching preacademic content (Wolery, Doyle, Gast, Ault, & Lichtenberg, in press). Similarly, Chiara (1990) demonstrated that constant time delay resulted in efficient learning when instructional trials on preacademic content were distributed throughout the day.

Thus, it appears that systematic instruction using response-prompting procedures can be provided in small, direct instruction groups; embedded within other instructional activities; or implemented at transitions or distributed throughout other times of the day. These statements are particularly true for preacademic and discrete tasks, although evidence suggests that chained skills (e.g., transitions) also can be taught in these ways (Venn, Wolery, & Fleming, 1991).

Context of Individualization: Developmentally Appropriate Practices Framework

In recent years, NAEYC has attempted to disseminate information that encourages early educators to use practices that are based on the way children learn and are sensitive to their developmental levels. Because many mainstreaming efforts will be conducted in programs using the NAEYC guidelines, they are identified below (Bredekamp, 1987). It should be noted, however, that considerable research is needed before the appropriateness of the NAEYC guidelines for young children with disabilities is understood (cf. Carta, Shwartz, Atwater, & McConnell, 1991; Wolery, Strain, & Bailey, in press).

Developmental appropriateness consists of two concepts: age appropriateness and individual appropriateness. *Age appropriateness* is based on the predictable growth and change sequences in cognitive, physical, emotional, and social domains that occur in all children (Bredekamp, 1987). The learning environment and experiences are correlated to the development of children within the age span served by a given program. *Individual appropriateness* is a belief that "each child is a unique person with an individual pattern and timing of growth, as well as individual personality, learning style, and family background" (Bredekamp, 1987, p. 2). Experience with materials, ideas, and people should match the child's individual abilities and interests.

Developmentally appropriate practice programs comprise four components: 1) curriculum, 2) adult–child interaction, 3) relations between home and program, and 4) developmental evaluation of children. Curriculum is planned to be appropriate for the age span, developmental levels, and interests of the children enrolled in the program. There are several guidelines to ensure that curriculum complies with the principles of developmentally appropriate practice; these are described in Table 3.

Adults base their interactions with children on their knowledge of age appropriateness and individual appropriateness. Guidelines for achieving developmentally appropriate interactions are described here (Bredekamp, 1987):

Children's initiations are responded to immediately and directly. Adults adapt their responses to the child's age and individual abilities. Adults respond to infants and toddlers by physical contact, singing, and talking. Adults repeat words and paraphrase to show toddlers they have been understood. As children get older and more interactive, adults use less physical communication and more verbal communication.

Many opportunities for communication are provided. Children develop communication skills by hearing and using language. Individual and small group arrangements are most apt to facilitate interaction with adults and peers.

Adults facilitate completion of tasks by providing attention, proximity, and encouragement. Children learn from trial and error, and their misconceptions reflect their developing thought processes. Materials and activities are presented in an open-ended way, with more than one answer, and unique responses are valued.

Adults are aware of signs of stress and provide stress-reducing activities when needed. Expectations for, and demands on, children should not be excessive. Books, quiet time, water play, body movement, physical comfort, and active listening are used to soothe children who are distressed.

Self-esteem is fostered when adults show respect for, and acceptance of, all children, regardless of behavior. Behaviors such as messiness, aggression, or resistance are not unusual for very young children. Adults help children develop self-control and the ability to become progressively more responsible for their own behavior.

Adults facilitate the development of self-control in children. Clear and consistent limits on classroom behavior are set. Children are redirected to more acceptable activities if needed. Children are encouraged to resolve conflicts on their own.

All children are closely supervised at all times. Children are always protected from unauthorized adults and older children. Some older children may be mature enough to be granted permission to leave the classroom while remaining in the building.

In classrooms using developmentally appropriate practices, teachers and parents are viewed as partners. Communication is open and frequent. Guidelines for relations between the home and program are described here (Bredekamp, 1987):

Parents have the right to participate in their child's educational program. Parents share in making educational decisions and planning for activities such as toilet training, transitions to school programs, and developing peer relationships.

Teachers and family members engage in regular communication and conferences. Teachers seek information from parents about individual children, and engage in mutual problem solving.

Table 3. Developmentally appropriate curriculum guidelines

Guideline	Description
Goals for all developmental domains are addressed in an integrated manner.	Activities should include physical, cognitive, social, and emotional components. Domains are interrelated and activities that stimulate one area will affect learning in other areas.
Curriculum planning is based on regular assessment of individual strengths, interests, and needs.	Teachers observe and record special interests and developmental progress.
Learning is interactive.	Active interaction with materials and people in the environment results in learning. Learning should not be limited by adult concepts of completion, achievement, or failure.
Learning activities and materials should be concrete, real, and related to the children's lives.	Children should touch and manipulate objects and interact with people. Related pictures and stories are used to broaden real experiences. Workbooks, dittos, coloring books, and adult models of art projects are not considered appropriate materials for the preschool classroom.
Programs should meet the needs of children who exhibit skills and interests outside the normal developmental range.	If the range of exhibited developmental skills exceeds 18 months, there is a need for a wide variety of furnishings, equipment, complexity of materials, and teaching strategies.
The difficulty and complexity of activities and materials should increase as children develop skills and comprehension.	Learning and involvement can be facilitated by teachers asking questions, making suggestions, and adding more complex materials.
Children are given the opportunity to choose from a variety of activities and materials. The teacher's role is to facilitate engagement.	Engagement is facilitated by providing a variety of materials, the opportunity for small group and solitary activity, assistance for children who have difficulty making choices, and opportunity for child-directed practice of newly acquired skills.
Materials should be multicultural and nonsexist.	Providing a variety of nonsexist and multicultural experiences that includes aspects of food, music, and family life, increases children's knowledge, acceptance, and appreciation of others, enhances self-esteem, and supports the value of the family.
Quiet or restful activities should be balanced with more active periods.	This is accomplished by alternating activities across the day. However, the schedule should be flexible enough to take advantage of unscheduled serendipitous events.
Daily outdoor experiences should be provided.	Outdoor activities should be as carefully planned as other experiences and should integrate practicing motor skills, experiencing freedom, and learning about outdoor environments.

Adapted from Bredekamp (1987).

Teachers recognize and respect parents' points of view.

Transitions are eased through the sharing of developmental information among teachers, parents, and agencies. Continuity of educational experience is enhanced by communication as children move within programs or to other settings.

In developmentally appropriate settings, programs are planned and implemented based on information about individual children's development. Direct observation and anecdotal descriptions of behavior are viewed as the most valid measures of child development. Guidelines for assessing children are described here (Bredekamp, 1987):

Multiple measures are used, particularly observations by teachers and parents. Curriculum decisions are not made on the basis of performance on standardized tests.

Children with special needs are identified through developmental assessment and observation. This information is used to help develop appropriate programming and to make professional referrals to families.

The validity of comparative data analysis is questionable for many standardized measures. Normative information in standardized tests must be age-, gender-, culture-, and socioeconomically matched to be useful.

As a cautionary note, the validity and utility of these practices for teaching young children with developmental delays and disabilities awaits more research (Carta et al., 1991). However, it is clear that they must be expanded in the areas of transition practices and the involvement of multiple disciplines in the individualization process. Reconceptualization may be needed to increase the emphasis on family-focused services and to increase the emphasis on producing specific outcomes for children (Wolery, Strain, & Bailey, in press). Nonetheless, mainstreaming efforts are probably best implemented in high-quality environments for typically developing children. Thus, understanding that particular context is critical in individualizing curriculum experiences for young children with special needs.

Summary

From the research, several logical conclusions can be made about individualizing curriculum in mainstreamed settings. First, individualization requires careful assessment of the student and identification of high-priority objectives. Second, individualization requires careful design and analysis of the intervention setting and schedule. Third, a broad range of instructional interventions have been shown to positively influence the behavior of young children with disabilities. Fourth, individualization requires careful monitoring and continuous adjustment of the curriculum based on children's performance.

IMPLICATIONS FOR PRACTICE AND RESEARCH

In the first part of this section, standards are listed against which the success of the individualized curriculum can be judged. These are followed by a set of questions that teachers and program leaders can use to evaluate individualized curriculum endeavors in mainstreamed settings. In the second part of this section, broad issues are identified for further research.

Implications for Practice

A legitimate question for practice is: "What are the criteria by which the success of an individualized curriculum is to be judged?" The authors suggest that three standards apply. It should be noted, however, that this question is different from the one that asks, "What are the criteria by which the success of mainstreaming is to be judged?" This second question is broader and more complex. The three standards by which to judge the success of the individualized curriculum are: 1) efficient acquisition and use of important skills, 2) high levels of engagement by children throughout the intervention day, and 3) parents' satisfaction with the manner and outcomes of instruction.

The first measure is different from those usually established for educational endeavors for children with disabilities in at least three ways. First, inclusion in a mainstreamed site is not seen as an indication of success; inclusion is a means by which opportunities for success are possible. Second, the appropriateness of instruction (defined as meeting the requirement of PL 94-142 and 99-457, or as using best practices) is not, in itself, sufficient; the individualization must result in successful skill acquisition and use. Third, the usual provision of effective instruction (i.e., students acquire and use the behaviors taught) is not sufficient; the teaching must result in *efficient* skill acquisition and use. Efficiency can be defined as the relative rapidity with which skills are learned, the extent to which generalization occurs, the extent to which observational and incidental learning occur, and the positive effect of current instruction on future learning (cf. Wolery & Gast, 1990).

The second standard is based on the extent to which children engage in appropriate and meaningful exchanges with the social and physical environment. If the individualized curriculum does not result in high levels of engagement throughout the day, then children's time is being wasted and opportunities for additional instruction are being lost.

The third standard, the parents' satisfaction, has two major parts. First, parents should be satisfied with how instruction is provided, with what happens to their child on a daily basis, with the interactions that occur between their child and the adults and other children in the program, and with the ways in which specialized services are provided. Furthermore, they should be satisfied with the outcomes of instruction; that is, with the extent to which children learn the skills that are valued by families and that make raising the child a more enjoyable and successful endeavor.

Ten questions are provided in Table 4 to guide teachers and program leaders at mainstreamed sites in evaluating their individualized instructional activities. For each question, potential measures for each are listed, as are potential difficulties in mainstreamed settings. Each question should be asked periodically. In the following paragraphs, the authors describe sample procedures for ensuring that the tasks implied by each question are addressed.

The first issue, identification of instructional targets, was addressed earlier, and is not repeated here. The second issue, scheduling times for instruction, does not imply that times are specified for one-on-one instruction in isolated therapy sessions. What is implied is that teachers' roles in instructional activities that occur throughout the day are assessed, and that the activities are identified to determine when each skill could be taught and which instructional strategies are appropriate for those activities and teacher roles. As described by Bricker (1989) and Sailor and Guess (1983), a matrix of activities and high-priority instructional targets is made. For each high-priority objective, a time is found throughout the day when instruction can be provided and when instructional strategies can be embedded in teachers' current roles. The third issue, planning time for instruction on generalization, is addressed in a similar manner.

Table 4.   Ten tests for evaluating individualized curriculum endeavors

Question	Potential measures for answering questions	Potential difficulties in mainstreamed settings
1. Have important skills been identified?	Ratings of importance by parents and professional members of the intervention team Description by team members of how each skill will increase developmental performance and independence, increase access to less restrictive placements, allow child to learn more complex skills, and/or increase the ease with which families can care for child	Staff may perceive the identification of specific skills as being inappropriate and inconsistent with the developmentally appropriate practice (DAP) guidelines. Staff may use inappropriate measures and measurement strategies to identify instructional targets. Staff may not have skills for conducting ecological inventories and for involving family members in assessments.
2. Are times scheduled for instruction to ensure acquisition of important skills?	Staff members can identify times each day when instruction can be provided for each skill. Instruction of each skill can be identified through direct observation in the classroom. Direct observation of child engagement in activities designed to promote acquisition of targeted behaviors	Staff may view scheduling of instruction for specific skills as inconsistent with DAP guidelines. Staff may schedule time but fail to implement activities or the instructional strategies within the activities. Staff may implement strategies, but child may not attend or participate. Staff may not know how to schedule instruction for specific skills.
3. Are times scheduled to ensure use and application (generalization) of important skills?	Staff members can identify times when generalization of skills is appropriate. Opportunities for generalization can be identified through direct observation in classroom. Direct observation of child engagement in activities designed to promote generalization	Staff may not understand the need to program generalization. Staff may view programming for generalization as being incompatible with the DAP guidelines. Staff may not know how to program for generalization. Staff may schedule time and strategies for promoting generalization, but fail to implement them. Staff may implement the strategies, but the child does not participate.
4. Are times scheduled to train intervention agents to implement strategies?	Schedule of staff training that identifies specific strategies Documentation that training occurred Direct measures (attendance, paper/pencil tests, direct observation) of staff members' participation in training	There may be no skilled individual available to provide training. Staff cannot attend/participate in training at scheduled times. Staff does not perceive the need for training or the interventions.
5. Is child engaged in instructional activities throughout the day?	Direct observation of randomly selected times using momentary time sampling Staff members' ratings of child engagement	Child may not have skills to be engaged in the activities. Activities may be too difficult/easy or too long/short. Child waiting for materials or adult direction.

(continued)

Table 4. (*continued*)

Question	Potential measures for answering questions	Potential difficulties in mainstreamed settings
		Staff may believe reinforcement of engagement is inconsistent with DAP guidelines.
		Staff may view engagement as child, rather than adult, responsibility.
6. Are staff using the strategies correctly?	Staff members' ratings of their use of the strategies Direct observation of staff use of strategies	Training was inadequate for staff to learn procedural parameters of strategies. Staff may believe strategies are inconsistent with DAP guidelines. Staff may have tried strategies, experienced failure, and stopped use. Lack of follow-up may lead staff to believe strategies are unimportant. Classroom demands preclude use of the strategies. Strategies may be inconsistent with the roles staff use in the identified activities.
7. Is the child acquiring the important skills?	Staff and parents' ratings of child's acquisition Collection of probe data on child performance Collection of daily data on child performance	Staff may not be implementing strategies or may do so incorrectly. Staff may view strategies as inconsistent with DAP guidelines. Staff may not be aware that acquisition is not occurring, and may not adjust interventions appropriately.
8. Is the child using and applying the important skills?	Staff and parents' ratings of child's skill use Collection of probe data on child performance Collection of daily data on child performance	Staff may not be implementing generalization facilitating strategies, or may be doing so incorrectly. Staff may view generalization promoting strategies as inconsistent with DAP guidelines. Staff may be unaware that generalization is not occurring, and may not adjust interventions appropriately.
9. Are interventions adjusted when they are not working?	Staff reports of intervention adjustment Documentation from review of records that interventions are adjusted	Staff may be unaware of when to adjust programs; need instruction in data decision rules. Staff may recognize need for adjustment, but not know how to adjust program.
10. Are parents satisfied with the manner of instruction and its outcomes?	Parents' ratings of satisfaction with instructional procedures Parents' ratings of satisfaction with outcomes Comparison of outcomes with parents' previous statements of desired outcomes	Staff may lack communication skills to describe methods to families. Staff may not involve families appropriately in selecting strategies or in developing adjustments. Staff may not communicate outcomes appropriately to parents.

Adapted from Bailey and Wolery (1992).

Importantly, opportunities for generalization should be identified clearly; these should be realistic times when children could apply and use the skills taught in other contexts.

The fourth question, concerning scheduling times for staff training, requires consideration of many issues. The inservice training literature is replete with examples of ineffective inservice training (Guskey, 1986). However, effective models for training do exist (cf. Reid, Parsons, & Green, 1989; Venn & Wolery, in press). These are frequently characterized by individualization, active involvement in training as compared to passive listening, demonstration and modeling of strategies, immediate feedback, and an integrated longitudinal staff development program (Klein & Sheehan, 1987).

The fifth question deals with children's engagement in activities. While engagement is not, in itself, sufficient to ensure learning, it is viewed as necessary. Furthermore, the extent of engagement corresponds to the approximate extent to which learning is likely to occur. In addition, engagement is a highly valued skill in classrooms following the developmentally appropriate practice guidelines. McWilliam and Bailey (1992) describe a number of procedures to facilitate engagement by young children with disabilities.

The sixth issue, the correct use of intervention strategies by staff, requires careful monitoring, and is an extension of staff-training activities. Billingsley, White, and Munson (1980) describe a process for measuring intervention fidelity. It requires specification of the procedural parameters of the instructional manipulation, identification of the teacher behaviors needed to implement the strategy (e.g., set-up behaviors, delivery of antecedent events, and delivery of consequent events), and direct observation to determine whether the strategy is used as planned.

The seventh and eighth questions are similar; both deal with whether children are acquiring *and* using the skills that are considered important. This requires staff to monitor the outcomes of instruction for skills acquisition and use. The authors are not advocating collecting daily data on every instructional program; rather, new programs for high-priority objectives, programs that have been in place for some time but for which progress is minimal, and programs where the teacher is unsure about the child's progress, should receive more frequent monitoring. However, all objectives should be monitored on a periodic basis (i.e., every 1 or 2 weeks). To minimize the demands on teachers during instructional activities, short (i.e., 1–3 minutes) probes or assessments can be used to collect data on children's acquisition and use of skills.

The ninth issue, adjustment of ineffective interventions, is based on the data collected on children's performance, and the use of data-decision rules is relevant. Data-decision rules tell staff not only when adjustments are needed, but also what the nature of those adjustments should be (cf. Haring, Liberty, & White, 1980; Liberty, 1988; Wolery, Bailey, & Sugai, 1988). Finally, the tenth issue, parents' satisfaction with both the manner in which instruction is implemented and the outcomes of that instruction, were discussed earlier as a standard by which the success of individualized curricular interventions are judged.

Implications for Research

Numerous areas for additional research could be identified; four are mentioned here. First, research is needed to discover the extent to which the instructional strategies shown to be efficient can be embedded in the instructional activities of mainstreamed preschool teachers. It is important to monitor the fidelity with which they are implemented and the effects they have in such contexts. Second, research is needed in which attempts are made to teach children with disabilities the skills identified by NAEYC and NAECS/SDE as being important. This will require the generation of sequences of behavior for poorly operationalized constructs. Such research should identify the procedures required to teach those skills and the effects of children's learning of them. Third, considerable research is needed to evaluate the extent to which developmentally appropriate practices produce positive outcomes for children, to define changes that need to be made, and to determine the effects of those practices on children's social interactions and relationships. Fourth, research is needed to determine how best to train staff to implement individualized interventions in mainstreamed settings. Staff skill is seen as a major barrier to effective and widespread mainstreaming in preschool settings (Odom & McEvoy, 1990). Such research must consider the caregiving demands of those settings, child-to-staff ratios, and the roles that teachers currently assume.

Retention of trained staff is also a research priority.

SUMMARY

Individualization of curriculum requires careful specification of the skills to be taught, precise and systematic implementation of instructional strategies, and persistent monitoring and adjustment of the interventions based on children's progress. To specify the skills to be taught, assessments should be conducted, and should address multiple domains, use multiple strategies, secure information from multiple sources, involve family members, and be nondiscriminatory. The instructional strategies should be implemented within the context of teachers' current roles and instructional skills. A wide variety of instructional strategies have already been developed, but it is not yet known how best to apply them in developmentally appropriate practice programs. This chapter describes one model for implementing individualized instructional programs in mainstreamed contexts. Individualization efforts should be judged against three standards: 1) efficient acquisition and use of important skills by the child, 2) high levels of engagement throughout the intervention day, and 3) parental satisfaction with the manner and outcomes of instruction.

REFERENCES

Albin, R.W., & Horner, R.H. (1988). Generalization with precision. In R.H. Horner, G. Dunlap, & R.L. Koegel (Eds.), *Generalization and maintenance: Life-style changes in applied settings* (pp. 99–120). Baltimore: Paul H. Brookes Publishing Co.

Ault, M.J., Gast, D.L., & Wolery, M. (1988). Comparison of progressive and constant time delay procedures in teaching community-sign word reading. *American Journal of Mental Retardation, 93*, 44–56.

Ault, M.J., Wolery, M., Doyle, P.M., & Gast, D.L. (1989). Review of comparative studies in instruction of students with moderate and severe handicaps. *Exceptional Children, 55*, 346–356.

Bagnato, J.T., Neisworth, J. T., & Munson, S.M. (Eds.). (1989). *Linking developmental assessment and early intervention: Curriculum-based prescriptions*. Rockville, MD: Aspen Systems.

Bailey, D.B. (1987). Collaborative goal setting with families: Resolving differences in values and priorities for services. *Topics in Early Childhood Special Education, 7*(2), 59–71.

Bailey, D.B. (1988). Assessing family stress and needs. In D.B. Bailey & R.J. Simeonsson (Eds.), *Family assessment in early intervention* (pp. 95–118). Columbus, OH: Charles E. Merrill.

Bailey, D.B. (1989). Assessment and its importance in early intervention. In D.B. Bailey & M. Wolery (Eds.), *Assessment of infants and preschoolers with handicaps* (pp. 1–21). Columbus, OH: Charles E. Merrill.

Bailey, D.B., Harms, T., & Clifford, R.M. (1983). Matching changes in preschool environments to desired changes in child behavior. *Journal of the Division for Early Childhood, 7*, 61–68.

Bailey, D.B., Jens, K.G., & Johnson, N. (1983). Curricula for handicapped infants. In S.G. Garwood & R.R. Fewell (Eds.), *Educating handicapped infants: Issues in development and intervention* (pp. 387–415). Rockville, MD: Aspen Systems.

Bailey, D.B., & McWilliam, R.A. (1990). Normalizing early intervention. *Topics in Early Childhood Special Education, 10*(2), 33–47.

Bailey, D.B., & Simeonsson, R.J. (Eds.). (1988). *Family assessment in early intervention*. Columbus, OH: Charles E. Merrill.

Bailey, D.B., & Wolery, M. (Eds.). (1989). *Assessing infants and preschoolers with handicaps*. Columbus, OH: Charles E. Merrill.

Bailey, D.B., & Wolery, M. (1992). *Teaching infants and preschoolers with handicaps* (2nd ed.). New York: Macmillan

Billingsley, F.F., White, O.R., & Munson, R. (1980). Procedural reliability: A rationale and an example. *Behavioral Assessment, 2*, 229–241.

Bredekamp, S. (Ed.). (1987). *Developmentally appropriate practice in early childhood programs serving children from birth through age 8*. Washington, DC: National Association for the Education of Young Children.

Bredekamp, S., & Rosegrant, T. (in press). *Reaching potentials: appropriate curriculum and assessment for young children*. Washington, DC: National Association for the Education of Young Children.

Bricker, D. (1978). A rationale for the integration of handicapped and nonhandicapped preschool children. In M.J. Guralnick (Ed.), *Early intervention and the integration of handicapped and nonhandicapped children* (pp. 3–26). Baltimore: University Park Press.

Bricker, D. (1989). *Early intervention for at-risk and handicapped infants, toddlers, and preschool children*. Palo Alto, CA: VORT.

Bricker, D., & Veltman, M. (1990). Early intervention programs: Child-focused approaches. In S.J. Meisels & J.P. Shonkoff (Eds.), *Handbook of early childhood intervention* (pp. 373–399). Cambridge: Cambridge University Press.

Brinker, R.P. (1985). Curricula without recipes: A challenge to teachers and a promise to severely mentally retarded students. In D. Bricker & J. Filler (Eds.), *Severe mental retardation: From theory to practice* (pp. 208–229). Reston, VA: Division on Mental Retardation of the Council for Exceptional Children.

Brinkerhoff, J.L., & Vincent L.J. (1986). Increasing parental decision making at the individualized educational program meeting. *Journal of the Division of Early Childhood, 11*, 46–58.

Carr, E.G. (1988). Functional equivalence as a mechanism of response generalization. In R.H. Horner, G. Dunlap, & R.L. Koegel, (Eds.), *Generalization and maintenance: Life-style changes in applied settings* (pp. 221–241). Baltimore: Paul H. Brookes Publishing Co.

Carta, J.J., Sainato, D.M., & Greenwood, C.R. (1988). Advances in the ecological assessment of classroom instruction for young children with handicaps. In S.L. Odom & M.B. Karnes (Eds.), *Early intervention for infants and children with handicaps* (pp. 217–239). Baltimore: Paul H. Brookes Publishing Co.

Carta, J.J., Schwartz, I.S., Atwater, J.B., & McConnell, S.R. (1991). Developmentally appropriate practice: Appraising its usefulness for young children with disabilities. *Topics in Early Childhood Special Education, 11*(1), 1–20.

Chiara, L. (1990). *Comparison of a massed group instructional trial format and a dis-*

tributed 1:1 instructional trial format using a constant time delay to teach picture naming to handicapped and nonhandicapped preschool-aged children. Unpublished master's thesis, University of Kentucky, Lexington.

Cipani, E. (1991). A guide for developing language competence in preschool children with severe and moderate handicaps. Springfield, IL: Charles C Thomas.

Collins, B.C., Gast, D.L., Ault, M.J., & Wolery, M. (1991). Small group instruction: Guidelines for teachers of students with moderate to severe handicaps. Education and Training in Mental Retardation, 26, 18–32.

Cooper, J.O., Heron, T.E., & Heward, W.L. (1987). Applied behavior analysis. Columbus, OH: Charles E. Merrill.

Cybriwsky, C.A., Wolery, M., & Gast, D.L. (1990). Use of a constant time delay procedure in teaching preschoolers in a group format. Journal of Early Intervention, 14, 99–116.

Doyle, P.M., Wolery, M., Ault, M.J., & Gast, D.L. (1988). System of least prompts: A review of procedural parameters. Journal of The Association for Persons with Severe Handicaps, 13, 28–40.

Dunst, C.J. (1981). Infant learning: A cognitive-linguistic intervention strategy. Hingham, MA: Teaching Resources.

Dunst, C.J. (1985). Rethinking early intervention. Analysis and Intervention in Developmental Disabilities, 4, 287–323.

Dunst, C.J., Cooper, C.S., Weeldreyer, J.C., Snyder, K.D., & Chase, J.H. (1988). Family Needs Scale. In C.J. Dunst, C.M. Trivette, & A.G. Deal (Eds.), Enabling and empowering families: Principles and guidelines for practice (pp. 149–151). Cambridge, MA: Brookline Books.

Education for All Handicapped Children Act of 1975, PL 94-142. (August 23, 1977). Title 20, U.S.C. 1401 et seq: U.S. Statutes at Large, 89, 773–796.

Education of the Handicapped Act Amendments of 1986, PL 99-457. (October 8, 1986). Title 20, U.S.C. 1400 et seq: U.S. Statutes at Large, 100, 1145–1177.

Etzel, B.C., & LeBlanc, J.M. (1979). The simplest treatment alternative: Appropriate instructional control and errorless learning procedures for the difficult-to-teach child. Journal of Autism and Developmental Disorders, 9, 361–382.

Fewell, R.R. (1983). New directions in the assessment of young handicapped children. In C.R. Reynolds & J.H. Clark (Eds.), Assessment and programming for young children with low incidence handicaps (pp. 1–41). New York: Plenum.

Fewell, R.R., & Oelwein, P.L. (1990). The relationship between time in integrated environments and developmental gain in young children with special needs. Topics in Early Childhood Special Education, 10, 104–116.

Fleming, L.A., Wolery, M., & Venn, M. (1991). Use of constant time delay in circle time with preschoolers who have developmental delays. Unpublished manuscript, Allegheny–Singer Research Institute, Pittsburgh, PA.

Fleming, L.A., Wolery, M., Weinzierl, C., Venn, M.L., & Schroeder, C. (1991). Model for assessing and adapting teachers' roles in mainstreamed preschool settings. Topics in Early Childhood Special Education, 11(1), 85–98.

Fordyce, W. (1981). On interdisciplinary peers. Archives of Physical Medicine, 62(2), 51–53.

Goldstein, H., & Wickstrom, S. (1986). Peer intervention effects on communicative interaction among handicapped and nonhandicapped preschoolers. Journal of Applied Behavior Analysis, 19, 209–214.

Guralnick, M.J. (1990). Major accomplishments and future directions in early childhood mainstreaming. Topics in Early Childhood Special Education, 10, 1–17.

Guskey, T.R. (1986). Staff development and the process of teacher change. Educational Research, 15, 5–12.

Hanson, M.J., & Lynch, E.W. (1989). Early intervention: Implementing child and family services for infants and toddlers who are at risk or disabled. Austin, TX: PRO-ED.

Haring, N.G., Liberty, K.A., & White, O.R. (1980). Rules for data-based strategy decisions in instructional programs. In W. Sailor, B. Wilcox, & L. Brown (Eds.), Methods of instruction for severely handicapped students (pp. 159–192). Baltimore: Paul H. Brookes Publishing Co.

Horner, R.H., & McDonald, R.S. (1982). A comparison of single instance and general case instruction in teaching a generalized vocational skill. Journal of The Association for the Severely Handicapped. 7, 7–20.

Hoyson, M., Jamieson, B., & Strain, P.S. (1984). Individualized group instruction of normally developing and autistic-like children: The

LEAP curriculum model. *Journal of the Division for Early Childhood, 8*, 157–172.

Johnson, J.E., Christie, J.F., & Yawkey, T.D. (1987). *Play and early childhood development*. Glenview, IL: Scott, Foresman.

Kaiser, A.P., Alpert, C.L., & Warren, S.F. (1987). Teaching functional language: Strategies for language intervention. In M.E. Snell (Ed.), *Systematic instruction of persons with severe handicaps* (pp. 247–272). Columbus, OH: Charles E. Merrill.

Klein, N., & Sheehan, R. (1987). Staff development: A key issue in meeting the needs of young handicapped children in day care settings. *Topics in Early Childhood Special Education, 7*(1), 13–27.

LeBlanc, J.M., Etzel, B.C., & Domash, M.A. (1978). A functional curriculum for early intervention. In K.E. Allen, V.A. Holm, & R.L. Schiefelbusch (Eds.), *Early intervention—A team approach* (pp. 331–381). Baltimore: University Park Press.

Liberty, K. (1988). Decision rules and procedures for generalization. In N.G. Haring (Ed.), *Generalization for students with severe handicaps: Strategies and solutions* (pp. 177–204). Seattle: University of Washington Press.

McDonnell, J., & Ferguson, B. (1989). A comparison of time delay and decreasing prompt hierarchy strategies in teaching banking skills to students with moderate handicaps. *Journal of Applied Behavior Analysis, 22*, 85–91.

McLean, M., & Hanline, M.F. (1990). Providing early intervention services in integrated environments: Challenges and opportunities for the future. *Topics in Early Childhood Special Education, 10*, 62–77.

McWilliam, R., & Bailey, D.B. (1992). Promoting engagement and mastery. In D.B. Bailey & M. Wolery (Eds.), *Teaching infants and preschoolers with handicaps* (2nd ed., pp. 229–255). Columbus, OH: MacMillan.

Musselwhite, C.R. (1986). *Adaptive play for special needs children: Strategies to enhance communication and learning*. San Diego: College-Hill.

Neel, R.S., & Billingsley, F.F. (1989). *IMPACT: A functional curriculum handbook for students with moderate to severe disabilities*. Baltimore: Paul H. Brookes Publishing Co.

Neisworth, J.T., & Bagnato, S.J. (1988). Assessment in early childhood special education: A typology of dependent measures. In S.L. Odom & M.B. Karnes (Eds.), *Early intervention for infants and children with handicaps: An empirical base* (pp. 23–50). Baltimore: Paul H. Brookes Publishing Co.

Miller, U.C., & Test, D.W. (1989). A comparison of constant time delay and most-to-least prompting in teaching laundry skills to students with moderate retardation. *Education and Training in Mental Retardation, 24*, 363–370.

Noonan, M.J., & Kilgo, J.L. (1987). Transition services for early age individuals with severe mental retardation. In R.N. Ianacone & R.A. Stodden (Eds.), *Transition issues and direction* (pp. 25–37). Reston, VA: Council for Exceptional Children.

Odom, S.L., & Karnes, M.B. (Eds.). (1988). *Early intervention for infants and children with handicaps: An empirical base*. Baltimore: Paul H. Brookes Publishing Co.

Odom, S.L., & McEvoy, M.A. (1990). Mainstreaming at the preschool level: Potential barriers and tasks for the field. *Topics in Early Childhood Special Education, 10*(2), 48–61.

Odom, S.L., & Strain, P.S. (1984). Classroom-based social skills instruction for severely handicapped preschool children. *Topics in Early Childhood Special Education, 4*(3), 97–116.

Peck, C.P., & Cooke, T.P. (1983). Benefits of mainstreaming at the early childhood level: How much can we expect? *Analysis and Intervention in Developmental Disabilities, 3*, 1–22.

Peterson, N.L. (1987). *Early intervention for handicapped and at-risk children: An introduction to early childhood–special education*. Denver: Love.

Reid, D.H., Parsons, M.B., & Green, C.W. (1989). *Staff management in human services*. Springfield, IL: Charles C Thomas.

Sailor, W., & Guess, D. (1983). *Severely handicapped students: An instructional design*. Boston: Houghton Mifflin.

Sainato, D.M., Strain, P.S., & Lyon, S.R. (1987). Increasing academic responding of handicapped preschool children during group instruction. *Journal of the Division for Early Childhood, 12*, 23–30.

Salisbury, C.L., & Vincent, L.J. (1990). Criterion of the next environment and best practices: Mainstreaming and integration 10 years later. *Topics in Early Childhood Special Education, 10,* 78–89.

Schoen, S.F., & Sivil, E.O. (1989). A comparison of procedures in teaching self-help skills: Increasing assistance, time delay, and observational learning. *Journal of Autism and Developmental Disorders, 19,* 57–72.

Schuster, J.W., Griffen, A.K., & Wolery, M. (1992). A comparison of constant time delay procedure and simultaneous prompting in teaching food words to elementary-aged students with moderate mental retardation. *Journal of Behavioral Education, 2,* 305–325.

Simeonsson, R.J., Huntington, G.S., & Parse, S.A. (1980). Expanding development assessment of young handicapped children. In J. Gallagher (Ed.), *New directions for exceptional children* (pp. 51–74). San Francisco: Jossey-Bass.

Sprague, J.R., & Horner, R.H. (1984). The effects of single instance, multiple instance, and general case training on generalized vending machine use by moderately and severely handicapped students. *Journal of Applied Behavior Analysis, 17,* 273–278.

Strain, P.S. (1981). *The utilization of classroom peers as behavior change agents.* New York: Plenum.

Strain, P.S., & Odom, S.L. (1986). Peer social initiations: Effective intervention for social skills development of exceptional children. *Exceptional Children, 52,* 543–551.

Thurman, S.K., & Widerstrom, A.H. (1990). *Infants and young children with special needs: A developmental and ecological approach* (2nd ed.). Baltimore: Paul H. Brookes Publishing Co.

Turnbull, A.P., & Turnbull, H.R. (1986). *Families, professionals, and exceptionality: A special partnership.* Columbus, OH: Charles E. Merrill.

Venn, M.L., & Wolery, M. (in press). Increasing day care staff members' interactions during caregiving routines. *Journal of Early Intervention.*

Venn, M.L., Wolery, M., & Fleming, L.A. (1991). *Using progressive time delay to teach children with autism to take transitions.* Unpublished manuscript, Allegheny-Singer Research Institute, Pittsburgh, PA.

Warren, S.F., & Kaiser, A.P. (1988). Research in early language intervention. In S.L. Odom & M.B. Karnes (Eds.), *Early intervention for infants and children with handicaps: An em-*pirical base (pp. 89–108). Baltimore: Paul H. Brookes Publishing Co.

Warren, S.F, & Rogers-Warren, A. (Eds.), (1985). *Teaching functional language: Language intervention series.* Austin, TX: PRO-ED.

Wolery, M. (1983). Evaluating curricula: Purposes and strategies. *Topics in Early Childhood Special Education, 2*(4), 15–24.

Wolery, M. (1989). Using assessment information to plan instructional programs. In D.B. Bailey & M. Wolery (Eds.), *Assessing infants and preschoolers with handicaps* (pp. 478–495). Columbus, OH: Charles E. Merrill.

Wolery, M., Ault, M.J., & Doyle, P.M. (1992). *Teaching students with moderate and severe disabilities: Use of response prompting procedures.* White Plains, NY: Longman.

Wolery, M., Ault, M.J., Gast, D.L., Doyle, P.M., & Griffen, A.K. (1990). Comparison of constant time delay and the system of least prompts in teaching chained tasks. *Education and Training in Mental Retardation, 25,* 243–257.

Wolery, M., Bailey, D.B., & Sugai, G.M. (1988). *Effective teaching: Principles and procedures of applied behavior analysis with exceptional students.* Boston: Allyn and Bacon.

Wolery, M., Doyle, P.M., Gast, D.L., Ault, M.J., & Lichtenberg, S. (in press). Comparison of progressive time delay and transition based teaching. *Journal of Early Intervention.*

Wolery, M., & Dyk, L. (1984). Arena assessment: Description and preliminary social validity data. *Journal of The Association for the Severely Handicapped, 3,* 231–235.

Wolery, M., Fleming, L., & Venn, M. (1990). *Year 01 report: Curriculum Modification Component of the Research Institute on Preschool Mainstreaming* (Grant No. H024K90002). Pittsburgh, PA: Allegheny Singer Research Institute.

Wolery, M., Fleming, L., Venn, M., Domjancic, C., & Thornton, C. (1991). *Effects of simultaneous prompting during circle time.* Manuscript submitted for publication.

Wolery, M., & Gast, D.L. (1990). *Efficiency of instruction: Conceptual framework and research directions.* Manuscript submitted for publication.

Wolery, M., Holcombe, A., Cybriwsky, C., Doyle, P.M., Schuster, J.W., Ault, M.J., & Gast, D.L. (1992). Constant time delay with discrete responses: A review of effectiveness and demographic, procedural, and methodological parameters. *Research in Developmental Disabilities, 13,* 239–266.

Wolery, M., Strain, P.S., & Bailey, D.B. (in press). Applying the framework to children with special needs. In S. Bredekamp & T. Rosegrant (Eds.), *Reaching Potentials: Appropriate curriculum and assessment for young children.* Washington, DC: National Association for the Education of Young Children.

Chapter 7

FACILITATING INTEGRATED PRESCHOOL SERVICE DELIVERY TRANSITIONS FOR CHILDREN, FAMILIES, AND PROFESSIONALS

Mary Frances Hanline

As children grow and develop throughout their early childhood years, they experience a number of transitions in the area of service delivery. These transitions may include going home from the hospital, entering the early intervention service delivery system, changing programs or agencies within the system, and exiting the system. Family members and professionals must negotiate these transitions along with the children. Two critical service delivery transitions in the preschool years are the entry into, and the exit out of, a preschool program. These critical transitions take various forms and may include entry into a preschool program upon exiting a toddler program; entry into a preschool program with no infant/toddler intervention; exit from early intervention services to regular education services at the kindergarten level, or at any other time during the preschool years; and exit from early intervention services to kindergarten special education services.

These transitions often include entry into integrated settings. A transition may involve placement for the first time into a program that provides opportunities for interactions between children with and without disabilities, or there may be a system-wide reorganization from segregated to integrated programming. When transitions to integrated settings are made, unique issues, beyond those of other types of transitions, must be considered.

While these changes present challenges for everyone involved, the implementation of procedures that meet individual and community needs can ease transitions for children, families, and professionals. Such transition support is considered best practice (Bredekamp, 1991; McDonnell & Hardman, 1988), and its importance is highlighted by the fact that PL 99-457 mandates that steps for assisting the family and child to make the transition from infant/toddler intervention to preschool services be incorporated into the individualized family service plan (IFSP). Those providing transition support must consider the resources and needs of children, families, and professionals, and must recognize that transitions do not occur in isolation from the social supports on which families and professionals normally rely, or from community attitudes toward children with disabilities (Rice & O'Brien, 1990).

TRANSITION CHALLENGES

During times of transition, individuals are confronted with many new challenges as change requires that they make decisions, assume new roles, cope with a sense of loss for the past, and deal with uncertainties about the future. People must restructure their way of looking at the world, as well as their plans for living in it (Golan, 1980; Parkes, 1971). Children, families, and professionals involved in service delivery transitions also face changes in relationships, physical and social environments, roles and status, and assumptions about the future.

Challenges Facing Children

When young children with disabilities make the transition from one intervention setting to another, they are faced with many challenges. Some children will respond eagerly and confidently to these challenges; others may be more hesitant. During this time, the children must adjust to a new physical, social, and learning environment, and expectations for them will probably also be different. They may have a new degree of freedom of movement or opportunity to make choices. The amount and type of structure, individualization, and teacher attention may differ, as may the curriculum emphasis (Fowler, 1982; Rosenkoetter & Fowler, 1986; Vincent et al., 1980). Learning new classroom rules, making new friends, responding to a new teacher, and navigating a new physical environment can be frightening to a young child, particularly if the change reduces contact with his or her parents or other familiar caregivers.

Most children adapt positively to a new educational setting. Nevertheless, the transition requires a period of adjustment that may highlight behavior and learning problems. Children with disabilities may not readily transfer skills from one setting to another, or from one teacher to another (Brown et al., 1981). "Difficult" or "noncompliant" behaviors in new environments may indicate a failure of generalization of skills from previous settings or a lack of understanding of expectations and rules (e.g., Drabman & Lahey, 1974). Furthermore, the stress of moving to a new s1school may cause a temporary loss of skills, and inappropriate behavior may be the child's way of telling adults that he or she is anxious and insecure. In addition, the recent trend of increasing standards in kindergartens to a level approaching those that were formerly applied to the first grade puts additional pressure on young children to conform to standards that may be unrealistic and inappropriate (May & Welch, 1986; NAEYC, 1990).

When young children with disabilities make a transition to an integrated setting, their nondisabled peers may also be required to make adjustments. Nondisabled preschool children often recognize that the behavior and appearance of children with disabilities are different from their own (e.g., Esposito, 1989), and may have questions and fears about the causes and outcomes of disabilities. Because many nondisabled children will not have had previous contact with children with disabilities, they will be dependent on adults to help them form accepting attitudes, develop friendships, and learn to communicate with their classmates who are disabled.

Challenges Facing Families

The families of children with disabilities have different strengths and resources available, and varying priorities and concerns, when making preschool transitions (Fowler, Chandler, Johnson, & Stella, 1988). Some families have been actively involved in infant/toddler programs, others have been attending daycare or preschool programs for typically developing children, and yet others have never been involved with any education or daycare program. Some parents know how to be effective advocates for their children; others may require assistance in choosing the role that they will assume. Although each situation is unique, transitions into preschool programs are often difficult for families, particularly in the beginning (Bray, Coleman, & Bracken, 1981; Wikler, 1981).

Many of the uncertainties that parents of children with disabilities face during the transition to preschool are shared by parents of nondisabled children as their own children first enter school or daycare. While families are usually excited about the increased learning opportunities available, parents often wonder: Will my child still need me? Can others take care of my child as well as I can? Will the teacher or daycare provider enjoy and appreciate my child? Will my child make friends? How will my child's time be spent? What changes in my family's routine will be necessary?

In addition to the apprehensions that all parents must face, parents of children with disabilities also have unique concerns. Families must make important decisions regarding their child's education that often require a modification of goals and expectations. Parents must also confront issues surrounding their child's special needs, as transitions may serve to re-affirm their child's differences. Parents may need to learn about their legal rights and responsibilities, and about the services available in the new setting. With each transition, parents may also have concerns about the development and implementation of their child's individualized education program (IEP); about establishing a relationship with a new group of professionals; about "letting go" of the supports that were developed in the program that the child is leaving; about variations in labeling policies and eligibility criteria; and about potential changes in parent–professional collaboration, the service delivery model, and the types of services provided (Hains, Rosenkoetter, & Fowler, 1991; Hanline, 1988).

Transitions to integrated preschool settings may also present an additional set of concerns. Although they are usually pleased with their child's experiences in integrated settings, parents of children with disabilities often have ongoing concerns about such matters as the acceptance of their children by nondisabled peers and adults, the safety of their child, the delivery of services, and the effect that integration has on their child's behavior (Hanline & Halvorsen, 1989; Reichart, Lynch, Anderson, Svobodny, & Mercury, 1989; Winton & Turnbull, 1981). In addition, parents of young children with disabilities may not feel that they share common interests with parents of nondisabled children, may be anxious about answering questions concerning their child's disabilities, and may feel isolated from other families (Chen, Hanline, & Friedman, 1989; Turnbull & Blacher-Dixon, 1980). Parents of nondisabled preschool children, while generally supportive of integration, express concern that regular educators may not be adequately prepared to deal with integration, and that their children may imitate the child who is disabled. Parents of nondisabled young children also express their desire that their child's experiences with children with disabilities be positive ones, in order to foster sensitivity and tolerance in their child (Green & Stoneman, 1989; Peck, Hayden, Wandschneider, Peterson, & Richarz, 1989).

Siblings may also face challenges during a transition to an integrated setting. These might include informing friends and family about the transition, dealing with possible stigma and embarrassment, and feeling responsible for the child with a disability if he or she is integrated into the sibling's own school (Turnbull & Turnbull, 1990).

Challenges Facing Professionals

Service delivery transitions also present challenges to professionals. Just as family members must "let go" of the support and friendships provided by the program that the child is leaving, professionals must also "let go" of children and families who are making the transition. Professionals have often collaborated with family members, and may have worked with the child throughout the entire infant, toddler, or preschool period, forming strong attachments to both the child and his or her family over the years. Furthermore, professionals in the program that the child is leaving must trust that the new program will offer services adequate to meet the needs of the child and his or her family. At the same time, professionals in the new program must begin to establish a collaborative relationship with the family and begin to understand the strengths and needs of the new child (Hains, Fowler, & Chandler, 1988).

Often, professionals from receiving and sending programs may be unable to communicate with each other about children and families who are making the transition. Professionals from the program that the child is leaving may be unaware of available services, the eligibility criteria for these services, or the philosophy and curriculum of the next placement. Professionals from the new program may lack adequate information about the incoming child and his or her family (Hains et al., 1988; Hanline, 1989). This lack of communication is often worst during the toddler-to-preschool transition, as this transition often involves a transition between agencies, while the preschool-to-kindergarten transition usually occurs within the same agency, the public school system.

However, when the service-delivery change involves a transition to an integrated setting, the lack of communication between regular and special educators may be even worse than when both professionals are special educators. Furthermore, educators or daycare providers who will be providing services to the child in the integrated setting may have concerns about the adequacy of their preparation to teach children with disabilities or the availability of sufficient resources, or they may be unsure of what their specific responsibilities will be (Blacher & Turnbull, 1982; Peck et al., 1989). In addition, special educators and educators who work with typically developing children often have different perspectives on which skills are necessary for a successful transition to a mainstream setting, with special educators typically establishing higher standards than do regular educators (e.g., Beckoff & Bender, 1989). Basic differences in the philosophies of regular and special early educators (Odom & McEvoy, 1990) may also create difficulties during times of transition to integrated settings.

FACILITATING TRANSITIONS

The challenges facing children, families, and professionals during preschool service delivery transitions provide both a reason and a framework for the development of transition procedures. Transition is more complex than the mere physical relocation of a child (Polloway, 1987). According to Noonan and Kilgo (1987):

> transition is (a) a longitudinal plan, (b) a goal of smooth/efficient movement from one program to the next, (c) a process including preparation, implementation, and follow-up, and (d) a philosophy that movement to the next program implies movement to a program that is less restrictive than the previous program. (p. 26)

Thus, transition procedures must include preplanned, well-orchestrated activities imbedded in an ongoing process that facilitates the transition for children, families, and professionals, and that takes into account the social and cultural influences that affect the process.

Facilitating the Transition for Children

Although preparing children for preschool transitions is often seen as a task that should begin only months before the change in placement, preparation for transition is best approached as an integral part of a total early intervention program. Embedding systematic instructional methods that promote the generalization of skills throughout the entire program curriculum may help facilitate a child's eventual transition to new settings. Some of the most effective of these strategies are: teaching with sufficient exemplars, program-

ming common stimuli, teaching skills that are likely to be used in natural settings and reinforced through natural consequences, teaching skills that will be used in environments where models of behavior are available, and teaching in multiple settings with multiple teachers (Fox, 1989; Wolery & Gast, 1984).

In addition, using an ecologically referenced curriculum (with consideration for skills that may be needed in future settings) throughout the early childhood years may also help prepare a child for transition. The ecological inventory strategy may be used to identify and teach an individual child specific skills required in his or her next environment (Falvey et al., 1979). This approach is very individualized and requires that a child's next placement be identified well in advance of the transition. A second approach (Fowler, 1982) involves collaboration by the personnel of the sending and receiving programs in three tasks: 1) the identification of differences between the programs, 2) the addition of certain elements to each program in order to minimize these differences, and 3) continual evaluation of the effectiveness of these steps.

A third ecologically referenced curriculum approach involves the identification of requirements, beliefs, and expectations (often called "survival skills") appropriate to a particular type of educational environment (McCormick & Kawate, 1982; Walter & Vincent, 1982; Vincent et al., 1980). This approach has been used predominantly in the preschool-to-kindergarten transition. Survival skills for kindergarten classrooms center on independent task work, following class routine, joining and participating in groups, classroom behavior, adaptive behavior, following directions, social and play skills, and functional communication. The underlying assumption about the importance of survival skills is that children who are capable of exhibiting these skills will be more likely to be placed in regular educational settings.

The use of one of the three types of ecologically referenced curriculum strategies has been suggested in preschool-to-kindergarten transition models (e.g., Conn-Powers, Ross-Allen, & Holburn, 1990; Rule, Fiechtl, & Innocenti, 1990) and in infant/toddler-to-preschool transition models (e.g., Gallagher, Maddox, & Edgar, 1984; Kilgo, Richard, & Noonan, 1989). To date, however, only one study has attempted to evaluate the effectiveness of such an approach. Rule and colleagues (1990) demonstrated that: 1) survival skills (e.g., saying the pledge of allegiance and mastering an entry routine) could be taught to 4- and 5-year-olds with disabilities, 2) the performance of these skills generalized to daycare settings while the children were still preschoolers, and 3) the children continued to apply the survival skills in educational settings beyond preschool. In addition, the need for the inclusion of survival skills training in a preschool curriculum is supported by research that documents the importance of independent work abilities and appropriate classroom behavior in maintaining placement in mainstreamed environments (e.g., Carden-Smith & Fowler, 1983; Walker, Hops, & Johnson, 1975). Furthermore, skills in the areas of communication and independence were judged by daycare providers to be critical for success in integrated daycare programs (Murphy & Vincent, 1989).

There has been only limited research on specific strategies for embedding instructional methods throughout an early intervention curriculum, or using an ecologically referenced curriculum, to foster the generalization of skills, and no research findings support the conclusion that the mastery of survival skills will ensure transition to a mainstreamed kindergarten. However, Conn-Powers and colleagues (1990) demonstrated that in five school districts in Vermont that implemented comprehensive transition procedures with the assistance of Project TEEM (Transitioning into the Elementary Education Mainstream), all children made a transition to full-inclusion settings in their local home schools. However, no comparison data on children in districts where transition procedures were not implemented were reported. Additional research in this area is clearly needed.

Supporting Families

The stress often associated with transitions may be reduced through individualized family support. A wide range of services and participation options must be made available, giving individual families the opportunity to participate in the transition in ways that they themselves welcome. This is especially important because positive experiences with early transitions may help families when transitions occur at various points later in their child's lifecycle (Lazzari & Kilgo, 1989; Ziegler, 1985). The supports should: 1) provide for the advance preparation of families, the inclusion of families in the process itself, and support after the transition has been made (Hains et al., 1991; Hanline & Knowlton, 1988); and 2) promote the family's independence (Dunst, Trivette, & Deal, 1988), partly by assisting families in identifying and developing skills that will facilitate the current transition, as well as those that occur in the future (Turnbull, 1988). Although it is recommended that preparations begin several months prior to the transition, the timing of the transition support should be flexible, as factors such as the child's age and the severity of the disability may influence the family's ability to prepare for transition(Kilgo et al., 1989; McDonald, Kysela, Siebert, McDonald, & Chambers, 1989).

Providing families with information on the transition process, rights and responsibilities, eligibility criteria, and placement and service options prior to the transition is vital, as parents who are better informed report more satisfaction (Hamblin-Wilson & Thurman, 1990; Johnson, Chandler, Kerns, & Fowler, 1986). Parents may also want assistance in updating and organizing information to be shared at IEP meetings, formulating their ideas for IEP goals, and learning strategies to ensure their inclusion in the decisionmaking process. Although families may be provided with information through multiple methods and sources (e.g., books and other written materials, parent meetings, audiovisual materials, locally developed manuals or resource packets, parent-to-parent contacts), families have reported that the opportunity to talk individually with professionals was more useful than group discussions, presentations, written handouts, or worksheets (Spiegel-McGill, Reed, Konig, & McGowan, 1990). Parents have also preferred to have one person available within the receiving agency/ program to whom they could turn for assistance (Hanline, 1988). In addition, the opportunity to visit potential next placements may serve to reduce anxiety by reassuring parents that appropriate programs are available (McDonald et al., 1989).

During the actual meetings in which IFSP/IEPs are developed and placement is determined, including parents as equals in the decisionmaking process and using the information that they provide serve as tools to empower parents for future transitions. Avoiding professional jargon, using terminology common to both the sending and receiving programs, and encouraging parents to bring friends and advocates (including someone from the sending program) may help facilitate parental participation (Turnbull & Turnbull, 1990). Informing parents as quickly as possible about their child's new placement allows them to begin to establish a relationship with the professionals in the new program and to plan for possible changes in their family routine.

After the transition is made, follow-up parent contact by professionals from the sending program is crucial (Johnson et al., 1986; Spiegel-McGill et al., 1990). This follow-up contact allows parents to begin to form a partnership with a new group of professionals without feeling abandoned by the professionals with whom they are already familiar. Professionals in the receiving programs can also help facilitate the transition by respecting parental concerns, forming a partnership with parents, creating a normalized classroom environment, and allowing sufficient time for adjustment (Hanline, Suchman, & Demmerle, 1989).

Models to support families during preschool transitions share common components (identified above) that are considered to be best practice when providing comprehensive support for families. Available research indicates that parents typically report satisfaction with such services, identify specific components as being more helpful (i.e., easy access to professionals, information about services, and follow-up support), and feel more prepared for the transition (e.g., Hanline & Knowlton, 1988; Spiegel-McGill et al., 1990).

However, more direct evaluation of the effects of specific transition procedures is needed.

Promoting Professional Participation

Direct service professionals usually play key roles in the transition process, as they are the professionals who have the most contact with children and their families. The role of the professional (usually the teacher) from the sending program is to: 1) prepare the child for a successful transition through the implementation of an appropriate individualized program and classroom curriculum, 2) collaborate with family members by acknowledging the role they have chosen and supporting them in that role, and 3) act as a liaison with professionals in the receiving program. The receiving teacher must: 1) learn about the strengths, needs, and background of the child who is making the transition; 2) adjust the demands of the classroom to facilitate the child's transition; 3) begin to establish a relationship and communication pattern with parents; and 4) act as liaison with professionals in the sending program. In order to effectively fulfill these responsibilities, professionals in the sending program must have adequate and accurate information about receiving programs and professionals of the receiving program must have adequate and accurate information about the child (and family) who is making the transition, so communication is of the utmost importance. Administrative support is also necessary if sending and receiving professionals are to have adequate time to learn about each others' programs, provide support to families, and adequately prepare the child. Making transition procedures part of the official administrative policies of agencies/programs involved in

transitions may help ensure that these procedures are recognized as an integral part of an early interventionist's professional role. Administrative support is also needed to foster cooperation between agencies and to develop standard interagency agreements (Gallagher et al., 1984).

Interagency Collaboration

Interagency collaboration is particularly critical when the infant/toddler program that a child is attending is administered by an agency different from that administering the preschool program into which the child is to be placed. In addition, if states adopt an "at risk" label for infants and toddlers, many of these children may not qualify for services under the criteria for preschool programs. Thus, it becomes essential for community agencies to develop a mechanism for sharing information about all available services and the eligibility criteria of those services. In this way, service delivery transitions will be made without interruptions in service, and the full range of potential services will be accessible to children and their families (Fowler, Hains, & Rosenkoetter, 1990).

Interagency collaboration helps to ensure that information will be exchanged between sending and receiving programs in a timely manner, to identify the resources within each program/agency that cover transition activities, and to provide consistent information to families (Peterson, 1991). In addition, because most school districts do not provide services to nondisabled preschool children, interagency collaboration may serve to provide opportunities for preschool children with disabilities to be served in integrated settings with same-age peers in private daycare or preschool settings, Head Start programs, and so on (McLean & Hanline, 1990). See Hanson and Widerstrom (chap.

8, this volume) for a more extended discussion of interagency issues.

Research documenting the effects of interagency agreements on the preschool transition process is not yet available. Furthermore, although professionals reported that implementing best practices contributed to successful preschool-to-kindergarten transitions (Conn-Powers et al., 1990), studies are needed to document effective strategies for ensuring the timely exchange of information between sending and receiving programs and providing support to professionals during transitions.

PRESCHOOL TRANSITIONS: FUTURE DIRECTIONS

In recent years, the issue of preschool transitions has received considerable attention in the professional literature. The literature suggests that the overall goals of transition procedures are to promote collaboration among all individuals and programs/agencies involved in the transition, support and empower the family as equal partners in preschool and future transitions, increase the likelihood of an integrated placement, and enhance the child's adjustment to the new educational setting. Data documenting parental concerns during preschool transitions and data evaluating parent and professional satisfaction with transition models are available in limited amounts and indicate that the components of transition support identified in the literature have been evaluated as being helpful and as contributing to successful transitions. However, research is needed to more substantially validate identified curriculum, family support, and interagency collaboration strategies, as well as to help resolve issues related to transition in these three areas.

Curriculum Issues

Curriculum strategies for facilitating children's preschool transitions have thus far focused on preparing the preschool child for the demands of a kindergarten setting. This has caused many early childhood special educators to emphasize the development of survival skills in preparation for the preschool-to-kindergarten transition. These skills sometimes serve as the primary curriculum content for preschool programs, raising concerns that these programs are not developmentally appropriate. But the development of survival skills was never meant to be the sole purpose of a preschool curriculum (Salisbury & Vincent, 1990). In addition, establishing developmentally inappropriate expectations for preschool children in preparation for the child's transition to a new setting that is equally developmentally inappropriate is a "misguided attempt to ease the child's transition" (Bredekamp, 1987, p. 60).

The field of early intervention faces two challenges related to curriculum and transition. One is to work with early childhood educators to develop infant/toddler, preschool, and kindergarten programs that are developmentally appropriate, and yet still include instruction that will facilitate the development and inclusion of all children (Burton, Hains, Hanline, McLean, & McCormick, 1992; Odom & McEvoy, 1990; Salisbury & Vincent, 1990). If early intervention programs begin to more closely resemble developmentally appropriate early childhood education programs, more opportunities to learn through child-initiated play and exploration, choicemaking, and interactions between peers may become available. Furthermore, although differences in programs for children of different ages are both expected and desirable, sending and receiving programs should strive to be developmentally appropriate, as "the more developmentally appropriate different programs are, the smoother and more successful children's transitions will be between different programs or groups" (Bredekamp, 1987, p. 60).

The second challenge is to begin to emphasize preparing the receiving program for the child, rather than solely preparing the child for the site (Conn-Powers et al., 1990). In this way, early intervention's goal of preparing all children for integration will be more easily realized, and the failure to master survival skills will not be used as a basis for exclusion from regular education settings. Models emphasizing the preparation of future settings and empirical validation of their effectiveness are also needed. Preparation of the new setting, however, must not be limited to the provision of the resources needed to make integration successful and the inclusion of regular educators or daycare providers in the transition process. Preparation must also include methods of encouraging nondisabled children to befriend children with disabilities. As the effects that "disability awareness" and other pre-enrollment activities have on the behavior of preschool children are variable, these activities must be implemented only with caution (Odom & McEvoy, 1988). Additional research is needed to identify the optimal timing of such activities and the types of disabilities for which they are appropriate, and to explore other issues surrounding the preparation of typically developing young children for the transition of peers with disabilities into their classrooms.

Family Issues

Parental concerns about preschool transitions are well-documented in the professional literature. However, many questions concerning family transition issues remain unresearched and unanswered. For example, what skills and coping mechanisms are needed during transitions? How can the transition from family-focused services in infancy to child-focused services in the preschool years be facilitated? Will the empowerment of families during their child's infancy change the type of transition support that is needed in the future? What is the appropriate time to begin transition planning? And how is the timing influenced by family and child variables? What factors influence a family's choice as to whether placements should be integrated or segregated?

In addition to answering these questions, research is also needed to discover whether supports provided during times of transition actually reduce parent anxiety, empower parents, and accelerate the adjustment to a new setting. Furthermore, although all family members are likely to be affected by preschool service delivery transitions, the ways that siblings and extended family members are affected and the services from which they could possibly benefit are not known.

Professional and Interagency Collaboration Issues

Interagency collaboration is the cornerstone of efficient and effective transition procedures. However, the conditions necessary to ensure interagency collaboration during preschool transitions are not known. While it is logical to assume that the conditions that facilitate interagency collaboration for other purposes (e.g., formal written agreements, common goals and joint decisionmaking, administrative commitment, positive working relationships [Peterson, 1991; Rogers & Farrow, 1983]) will encourage and maintain collaboration during preschool transitions, data supporting the effectiveness of these aspects of collaboration are still needed. Furthermore, although the issue of transition has not been emphasized in early intervention disciplines other than education, it is relevant to all disciplines, and should become more interdisciplinary in focus.

In addition, the role of professionals who provide services to infants, toddlers, preschoolers, and their families must be expanded to include the implementation of comprehensive transition procedures. In most communities, early intervention professionals are still viewed primarily as classroom teachers, and their job responsibilities and work hours are assigned accordingly. Thus, many transition support services provided to families and many efforts to exchange information with other local programs occur during professionals' own time. Furthermore, many funding patterns prevent local agencies from receiving financial support for services other than those that involve direct contact with children. As many transition procedures require professionals to engage in activities other than the instruction of children (e.g., attending interagency council meetings, home visits to parents) funding patterns must be altered to allow agencies/programs to receive funding for transition-related services other than those that involve direct contact with children.

SUMMARY

Appropriate and effective comprehensive transition procedures must include pre-planned and coordinated procedures that provide support for children, families, and professionals. Treating preschool service delivery transitions as an integral part of ongoing learning activities for children, support provisions for families, and professional responsibilities helps ensure that the challenges faced by everyone involved in the transition will be met successfully. With comprehensive transition procedures that meet local community and individual child, family, and professional needs, preschool service delivery transitions can open doors to new learning opportunities for children, to the development of family coping skills that will assist in negotiating transitions throughout the family lifecycle, and to avenues for continued learning for professionals through collaboration.

Future research on transition should focus on the empirical validation of the effectiveness of curriculum strategies, family support, and interagency collaboration in facilitating preschool transitions. Expanding transition planning to include regular educators and professionals from other relevant disciplines, developing effective methods of teaching young children with disabilities in developmentally appropriate environments endorsed by regular educators, exploring methods for preparing the receiving environment to meet the needs of children with disabilities, and more fully understanding parental perspectives on mainstreaming will help ensure successful transitions to integrated settings.

REFERENCES

Beckoff, A.G., & Bender, W.N. (1989). Programming for mainstream kindergarten success in preschool: Teachers' perceptions of necessary prerequisite skills. *Journal of Early Intervention, 13*(3), 269–280.

Blacher, J., & Turnbull, A.P. (1982). Teacher and parent perspectives on selected social aspects of preschool mainstreaming. *The Exceptional Child, 29,* 191–199.

Bray, N., Coleman, J., & Bracken, M. (1981).

Critical events in parenting handicapped children. *Journal of the Division for Early Childhood, 3,* 26–33.

Bredekamp, S. (1991). *Developmentally appropriate practice in early childhood programs serving children from birth through age 8.* Washington, DC: National Association for the Education of Young Children.

Brown, L., Pumpian, I., Baumgart, D., VanDeventer, P., Ford, A., Nisbet, J., Schroeder, J., & Gruenewald, L. (1981). Longitudinal transition plans in programs for severely handicapped students. *Exceptional Children, 47,* 624–630.

Burton, C.G., Hains, A.H., Hanline, M.F., McLean, M., & McCormick, K. (1992). Early childhood intervention and education: The urgency of professional unification. *Topics in Early Childhood Special Education, 11*(4), 53–69.

Carden-Smith, L.K., & Fowler, S.A. (1983). An assessment of student and teacher behavior in treatment and mainstreamed classes for preschool and kindergarten. *Analysis and Intervention in Developmental Disabilities, 3,* 35–37.

Chen, D., Hanline, M.F., & Friedman, C.T. (1989). From playgroup to preschool: Facilitating early integration experiences. *Child: Care, Health, and Development, 15,* 283–295.

Conn-Powers, M.C., Ross-Allen, J., & Holburn, S. (1990). Transition of young children into the elementary education mainstream. *Topics in Early Childhood Special Education, 9*(4), 91–105.

Drabman, R.S., & Lahey, B. (1974). Feedback in classroom behavior modification: Effects on the target and her classroom. *Journal of Applied Behavior Analysis, 7,* 591–598.

Dunst, C., Trivette, C., & Deal, A. (1988). *Enabling and empowering families.* Cambridge, MA: Brookline Books.

Education of the Handicapped Act Amendments of 1986, PL 99-547. (October 8, 1986). Title 20, U.S.C. 1400 et seq: *U.S. Statutes at Large, 100,* 1145–1177.

Esposito, B. (1989). *Disability awareness and attitudes of young children in an integrated environment: A naturalistic case study.* Unpublished doctoral dissertation, Florida State University, Tallahassee.

Falvey, M., Ferrara-Parrish, P., Johnson, F., Pumpian, I., Schroeder, J., & Brown, L. (1979). Curricular strategies for generating comprehensive, longitudinal and chronological age-appropriate functional individual vocational plans for severely handicapped adolescents and young adults. In L. Brown, M. Falvey, D. Baumgart, I. Pumpian, J. Schroeder, & L. Gruenewald (Eds.), *Strategies for teaching chronological age-appropriate functional skills to adolescent and young adult severely handicapped students* (Vol. 9, Part 1) (pp. 102–161). Madison, WI: Madison Metropolitan School District.

Fowler, S.A. (1982). Transition from preschool to kindergarten for children with special needs. In K.E. Allen & E.M. Goetz (Eds.), *Early childhood education: Special problems, special solutions* (pp. 309–334). Rockville, MD: Aspen Systems.

Fowler, S.A., Chandler, L.K., Johnson, T.E., & Stella, M.E. (1988). Individualizing family involvement in school transitions: Gathering information and choosing the next program. *Journal of the Division for Early Childhood, 12,* 208–216.

Fowler, S.A., Hains, A.H., & Rosenkoetter, S.E. (1990). The transition between early intervention services and preschool services: Administration and policy issues. *Topics in Early Childhood Special Education, 9*(4), 55–65.

Fox, L. (1989). Stimulus generalization of skills and persons with profound mental handicaps. *Education and Training in Mental Retardation, 24*(3), 219–229.

Gallagher, J., Maddox, M., & Edgar, E. (1984). *Early Childhood Interagency Transition Model.* Bellevue, WA: Edmark.

Golan, N. (1980, May). Intervention at times of transition: Sources and forms of help. *Social Casework,* pp. 259–266.

Green, A.L., & Stoneman, Z. (1989). Attitudes of mothers and fathers of nonhandicapped children toward preschool mainstreaming. *Journal of Early Intervention, 13*(4), 292–304.

Hains, A.H., Fowler, S.A., & Chandler, L.K. (1988). Planning school transitions: Family and professional collaboration. *Journal of the Division for Early Childhood, 12*(2), 108–115.

Hains, A.H., Rosenkoetter, S.E., & Fowler, S.A. (1991). Transition planning with families in early intervention programs. *Infants and Young Children, 3*(4), 38–47.

Hamblin-Wilson, C., & Thurman, S.L. (1990).

The transition from early intervention to kindergarten:Parental satisfaction and involvement. *Journal of Early Intervention, 14*(1), 55–61.

Hanline, M.F. (1988). Making the transition to preschool: Identification of parent needs. *Journal of the Division for Early Childhood, 12*(2), 98–104.

Hanline, M.F. (1989). *Facilitating pre-kindergarten special education service delivery transitions* [Guidebook]. Tallahassee: Florida Department of Education, Bureau of Education for Exceptional Students. (Project No. 371-26790-89640)

Hanline, M.F., & Halvorsen, A. (1989). Parent perceptions of the integration transition process: Overcoming artificial barriers. *Exceptional Children, 55*(6), 487–492.

Hanline, M.F., & Knowlton, A. (1988). A collaborative model for providing support to parents during their child's transition from infant intervention to preschool special education public school programs. *Journal of the Division for Early Childhood, 12*(2), 98–107.

Hanline, M.F., Suchman, S., & Demmerle, C. (1989). Beginning public preschool. *Teaching Exceptional Children, 21*(2), 61–62.

Johnson, T.E., Chandler, L.K., Kerns, G.M., & Fowler, S.A. (1986). What are parents saying about family involvement in transitions? A retrospective transition interview. *Journal of the Division for Early Childhood, 11*(1), 10–17.

Kilgo, J.L., Richard, N., & Noonan, M.J. (1989). Teaming for the future: Integrating transition planning with early intervention services for young children with special needs and their families. *Infants and Young Children, 2*(2), 37–48.

Lazzari, A.M., & Kilgo, J.L. (1989). Practical methods for supporting parents in early transitions. *Teaching Exceptional Children, 22*, 40–43.

May, D.C., & Welch, E. (1986). Screening for school readiness: The influence of birthdate and sex. *Psychology in the Schools, 23*, 100–105.

McCormick, L., & Kawate, J. (1982). Kindergarten survival skills: New directions for preschool special education. *Education and Training of the Mentally Retarded, 17*(2), 247–252.

McDonald, L., Kysela, G.M., Siebert, P.,

McDonald, S., & Chambers, J. (1989, Fall). Parent perspectives: Transition to preschool. *Teaching Exceptional Children*, 4–8.

McDonnell, A., & Hardman, M. (1988). A synthesis of "best practice" guidelines for early childhood services. *Journal of the Division for Early Childhood, 12*(4), 328–341.

McLean, M., & Hanline, M.F. (1990). Providing early intervention services in integrated environments: Challenges and opportunities for the future. *Topics in Early Childhood Special Education, 10*(2), 62–77.

Murphy, M., & Vincent, L.J. (1989). Identification of critical skills for success in day care. *Journal of Early Intervention, 13*(3), 221–229.

National Association for the Education of Young Children. (1990). NAEYC position statement on school readiness. *Young Children, 46*(1), 21–23.

Noonan, M.J., & Kilgo, J.L. (1987). Transition services for early age individuals with severe mental retardation. In R.N. Ianacone & R.A. Stodden (Eds.), *Transition issues and directions* (pp. 25–37). Reston, VA: Council for Exceptional Children.

Odom, S.L., & McEvoy, M.A. (1988). Integration of young children with handicaps and normally developing children. In S.L. Odom & M.B. Karnes (Eds.), *Early intervention for infants and children with handicaps: An empirical base* (pp. 241–268). Baltimore: Paul H. Brookes Publishing Co.

Odom, S.L., & McEvoy, M.A. (1990). Mainstreaming at the preschool level: Potential barriers and tasks for the field. *Topics in Early Childhood Special Education, 10*(2), 48–61.

Parkes, C.M. (1971). Psycho-social transitions: A field for study. *Social Science and Medicine, 5*, 101–115.

Peck, C.A., Hayden, L., Wandschneider, M., Peterson, K., & Richarz, S. (1989). Development of integrated preschools: A qualitative inquiry into sources of resistance among parents, administrators, and teachers. *Journal of Early Intervention, 13*(4), 353–364.

Peterson, N. (1991). Interagency collaboration under Part H: The key to comprehensive, multidisciplinary, coordinated infant/toddler intervention services. *Journal of Early Intervention, 15*(1), 89–105.

Polloway, E.A. (1987). Transition services for early age individuals with mild mental retardation. In R.N. Ianacone & R.A. Stodden (Eds.), *Transition issues and directions* (pp. 11–24). Reston, VA: Council for Exceptional Children.

Reichart, D.C., Lynch, E.C., Anderson, B.C., Svobodny, L.A., & Mercury, M.G. (1989). Parental perspectives on integrated preschool opportunities for children with handicaps and without handicaps. *Journal of Early Intervention, 13*(1), 6–13.

Rice, M.L., & O'Brien, M. (1990). Transitions: Times of change and accommodation. *Topics in Early Childhood Special Education, 9*(4), 1–14.

Rogers, C., & Farrow, F. (1983). *Effective state strategies to promote interagency collaboration.* A report of the handicapped public policy analysis project (Vol. 1-4; Contract No. 300-82-0829). Center for the Study of Social Policy, 236 Massachusetts Avenue, N.E., Washington D.C. 20002 (ERIC Documents Reproduction Services No. ED 245 467; EC 162 746).

Rosenkoetter, S.E., & Fowler, S.A. (1986). Teaching mainstreamed children to manage daily transitions. *Teaching Exceptional Children, 19,* 20–23.

Rule, S., Fiechtl, B.J., & Innocenti, M.S. (1990). Preparation for transition to mainstreamed post-preschool environments: Development of a survival skills curriculum. *Topics in Early Childhood Special Education, 9*(4), 78–90.

Salisbury, C.L., & Vincent, L.J. (1990). Criterion of the next environment and best practices: Mainstreaming and integration 10 years later. *Topics in Early Childhood Special Education, 10*(2), 78–89.

Spiegel-McGill, P., Reed, D.J., Konig, C.S., & McGowan, P.A. (1990). Parent education: Easing the transition to preschool. *Topics in Early Childhood Special Education, 9*(4), 66–77.

Turnbull, A.P. (1988). The challenge of providing comprehensive support for families. *Education and Training in Mental Retardation, 23*(4), 261–272.

Turnbull, A.P., & Blacher-Dixon, J. (1980). Preschool mainstreaming: Impact on parents. In J. Gallagher (Ed.), *New directions for exceptional children: Ecology of exceptional children, 1* (pp. 25–46). San Francisco: Jossey-Bass.

Turnbull, A.P., & Turnbull, H.R. (1990). *Families, professionals, and exceptionality: A special partnership.* Columbus, OH: Charles E. Merrill.

Vincent, L.J., Salisbury, C., Walter, G., Brown, P., Gruenewald, L.J., & Powers, M. (1980). Program evaluation and curriculum development in early childhood/special education. In W. Sailor, B. Wilcox, & L. Brown, (Eds.), *Methods of instruction for severely handicapped students* (pp. 303–328). Baltimore: Paul H. Brookes Publishing Co.

Walker, H.M., Hops, H., & Johnson, S.M. (1975). Generalization and maintenance of classroom treatment effects. *Behavior Therapy, 6,* 188–200.

Walter, G., & Vincent, G. (1982). The handicapped child in the regular kindergarten classroom. *Journal of the Division for Early Childhood, 6,* 84–95.

Wikler, L. (1981). Chronic stresses of families of mentally retarded children. *Family Relations, 30,* 281–288.

Winton, P.J., & Turnbull, A.P. (1981). Parent involvement as viewed by parents of preschool handicapped children. *Topics in Early Childhood Special Education, 1,* 11–19.

Wolery, M., & Gast, D.L. (1984). Effective and efficient procedures for the transfer of stimulus control. *Topics in Early Childhood Special education, 4*(3), 52–77.

Ziegler, P. (1985). Saying good-bye to preschool. *Young Children, 41,* 11–15.

ORGANIZATIONAL SUPPORTS FOR INTEGRATION

Patterns of interaction that take place on a daily basis, such as those described in Section I, as well as the broader programmatic features of integrated programs described in Section II, are largely shaped by the characteristics of the schools and other community agencies that deliver the programs. Some of the many aspects of these organizations that clearly affect the design and implementation of integrated programs are the self-perceived mission and priorities of the organization, the structure of the organization, the nature of organizational leadership, and the available staffing resources, including training. In this section, research and development work on organizational factors influencing the implementation of integrated programs is reviewed. Hanson and Widerstrom (Chapter 8) summarize work on the development of collaborative specialized services through indirect means such as consultation. Kontos and File (Chapter 9) analyze some of the needs and issues in conducting staff development for integrated programs and review a number of model staff development projects. In Chapter 10, Peck, Furman, and Helmstetter review a broad body of research on the implementation of change in educational organizations and recommend strategies for moving forward with the kinds of organizational systems change necessary to support the development of integrated programs.

Chapter 8

CONSULTATION AND COLLABORATION
Essentials of Integration Efforts for Young Children

Marci J. Hanson
and Anne H. Widerstrom

Clapping with the right hand only will not
produce a noise
—Malay Proverb

Few educational efforts can be conducted without collaboration. In fact, by its very nature, the educational process involves many people and a variety of resources. Educational exemplars are often characterized by the creative incorporation of resources from outside the educational community and by the degree to which resources can be maximized. In order to reach, and be maintained at, their fullest potential, such efforts require, above all, consultation and collaboration.

Collaboration is the *sine qua non* of successful integration efforts for young children with disabilities. The importance of placing young children with disabilities in integrated educational settings with their nondisabled peers has been attested to both by legislative actions (PL 94-142 and

PL 99-457) and in the research literature (see literature review by Odom and McEvoy, 1988). Though accepted as an element of "best practice" in early education, the goal of providing educational services to very young children with disabilities in the most inclusive environment presents special challenges. Many young children with special needs are denied access to these integrated settings because of special caregiving and development needs, and the lack of appropriate settings. To ensure that children receive better access to these integrated settings, creative solutions can be achieved through collaborative community efforts.

Designing integrated settings for very young children poses unique problems. Most infants and toddlers spend their time in their homes or in childcare settings in family homes or childcare centers. At age 3 a growing number of children begin to attend preschool or nursery school programs, often for several sessions a week, with the remainder of their days also spent at their homes or in childcare settings. Thus, prior to the age of 5, highly structured, day-long formal school experiences outside the home are not typically available, nor are they considered desirable by most early childhood education professionals and parents.

For young children with special needs, more carefully planned and specialized instructional sessions may be needed. These services may be delivered during visits by infant/toddler or preschool specialists to the children's homes, or at centers specializing in the provision of these services. Regardless, few typically developing children are present in the settings in which children with special needs receive services, and, likewise, relatively few children with special needs attend childcare or preschool centers serving typically developing young children. Although parents of children with special needs require the resources of childcare homes and centers and preschools as much as do parents of typically developing children, fewer opportunities are available to them due to such circumstances as special caregiving requirements (e.g., feeding requirements), lack of staff training in handling children with special needs (e.g., appropriate positioning and handling), delays in children's development (e.g., walking, talking, toilet training), and negative attitudes or fears about serving children with disabilities. While the nature of most current service systems does not enhance the opportunities for very young children with disabilities to receive care and/or educational services in settings designed for typically developing children, exemplary models of these integrated programs do exist. These models were developed through extensive collaboration among service providers, and they depend on continued collaboration and consultation to address the needs of individual children and families and to maintain their levels of service.

The purpose of this chapter is to review the relevant literature on consultative and collaborative efforts for integrating young children with disabilities with their typically developing peers. Furthermore, those models that demonstrate cooperative endeavors between service providers for children with disabilities and those for typically developing children are described. Finally, guidelines and recommendations for enhancing cooperative service delivery systems gleaned from these models are discussed.

DEFINITIONS OF CONSULTATION AND COLLABORATION

The terms *consultation* and *collaboration* are frequently referred to during discussions of service delivery systems for young children with disabilities and their families. Various definitions of these terms have been offered. For purposes of this discussion, those presented by Pryzwansky in West (1990) will be adopted:

> Consultation is a term defined as the process of giving advice or information . . . the assumption on which it is based is that a professional (the consultee) seeks assistance from a professional resource who is considered an "expert" . . . Collaboration . . . is another type of helping relationship . . . in which one professional is an active partner with the professional seeking assistance . . . collaborative consultation suggests to me that the "expert" is much more involved with the consultee. (p. 1)

Although these terms have often been used in reference to early childhood programs and services, in recent years greater attention has also been given to more collaborative efforts across agencies and among different types of service providers in discussions of school restructuring. For instance, the process of collaborative consultation has been proposed by Thousand, Villa, Paolucci-Whitcomb, and Nevin (1990) as a means of redefining the operation of schools and the relationships among school personnel, community members, and students. Collaborative consultation is defined as "an interactive process which enables people with diverse expertise to generate creative solutions to mutually defined problems" (Idol, Paolucci-Whitcomb, & Nevin, 1986, p. ix).

Because of the dearth of research and demonstration literature on collaborative or consultative efforts in early education, levels or types of collaboration and consultation are not differentiated or evaluated in this chapter. In most cases in the literature, descriptions of models are not sufficiently detailed, nor are types of models experimentally compared in order to conduct an evaluation of the effectiveness of different types of consultative or collaborative efforts. Thus, in this discussion the terms consultation and collaboration will be used in the most generic sense to indicate joint planning, direct service, and evaluation and refinement efforts conducted by several professionals working together. All forms of consultation and collaboration are considered valid for the purposes of this review.

APPROPRIATE SERVICE DELIVERY SETTINGS AND PREFERRED PRACTICES

The principles of least restrictive environment and normalization were developed primarily to address issues concerning school-age children and older individuals.

Little attention has been given to what they mean for the very young child, particularly for the child under 3 years old. The authors adopt the position articulated by the National Early Childhood Technical Assistance Team (NEC*TAS) Expert Team (1989) that for infants and toddlers (children under age 3) the least restrictive and most normative environment is among their families. It is within the family that the very young child develops socially and emotionally, and there that the child becomes attached to parents and siblings and learns the rituals and practices of the family and the culture. Thus, integrative efforts are defined as those that support the family and the community services and systems with which the family interacts. A home-based early intervention model aimed at supporting families and providing consultative assistance to families as needed and desired may fall under this description, as may models that provide assistance, training, and support to existing community-based childcare facilities. Other community-based services that are available in a given locale for infants, toddlers, and their families, such as parent–child groups, play groups, special interest groups (e.g., swimming), and church groups, should be considered as potential opportunities for children with disabilities to join in programs with their typically developing peers.

For preschool-age children (ages 3–5 years) there are more community-based opportunities for children with disabilities to participate in programs with typically developing peers. It is at this age that children typically demonstrate the ability to separate from their parents for part of the day and play with other children. These opportunities for social exploration and interaction may be particularly fruitful. In many communities a wide range of "preschool" experiences are available, including publicly funded preschool programs (e.g., Head Start); private preschools found in schools, churches, and community centers; and childcare programs found in private homes and community settings. Since most states do not provide publicly funded educational experiences for all preschool-age children, developing least restrictive placement, integrative opportunities for this age group most often requires establishing both formal and informal collaborative ties with other existing services. Research on the effects of these integrated program efforts indicates that positive outcomes are possible when the programs are carefully planned and monitored (Odom & McEvoy, 1988; Strain, 1988).

RESEARCH ON CONSULTATION AND COLLABORATION

There is a relatively small body of literature on the topic of consultation and collaboration in early education settings. It appears that little effort has been put into systematically exploring and empirically testing collaborative and/or consultative efforts. The following discussion presents a review of the literature that is available. This discussion is divided into three segments: interagency collaboration in early childhood programs and settings, implications of collaboration efforts for school-age children, and methods and models of collaboration in early childhood education.

Interagency Collaboration in Early Childhood Programs and Settings

While a number of articles have established the importance of interagency collaboration and cooperation, as well as the

methods for achieving this coordination (e.g., Elder & Magrab, 1980; Johnson, McLaughlin, & Christensen, 1982), few have identified the components needed for collaborative efforts in early childhood education (Hanson, 1985; Mulvenon, 1980).

A recent study by Stegelin and Jones (1991) sought to document interagency collaboration efforts among early childhood service providers in Ohio, a heavily populated state. This study used survey and interview techniques to identify existing collaborative efforts, interagency collaboration training needs, and facilitators of and barriers to collaboration. Survey questions were developed through structured interviews with 50 members of an Early Childhood Task Force from a consortium of four Special Education Regional Resource Centers (SERRCs). A statewide survey of 1,044 agencies and service providers of early childhood regular and special education programs in Ohio was also conducted. Those surveyed included Head Start programs, Mental Retardation/Developmental Disabilities agencies, Preschool Incentive Grant programs, Early Childhood Collaborative Councils, Chartered Preschool Foundation programs, and licensed daycare centers. Three hundred representatives, or 29% of the sample, responded to the survey. Results indicated that a large percentage of early childhood providers, nearly 62%, did engage in collaborative efforts. Furthermore, over 49% reported that these efforts were successful. When those surveyed were asked to name the one factor responsible for successful collaboration, the following elements were reported most often: networking with others (12.7%), commitment to collaboration (9.7%), a common focus (7.7%), support from technical assistance groups (6%), and identifying and sharing resources (4.3%). The following factors received the highest rankings from respondents when asked to indicate the importance of specific elements in successful collaboration: knowledge of service and resource providers, identification of children's needs, involvement of key community representatives, establishment of a collaborative network, and development of common goals. The top five barriers listed were: lack of understanding of the policies of other agencies, lack of communication, lack of time for collaboration, unclear goals, and gaps in screening and diagnostic services. The respondents also identified a need for training in interagency collaboration skills.

In another recent study Harrison, Lynch, Rosander, and Borton (1990) evaluated an early childhood education program designed to increase interagency collaboration. Project IINTACT (Infant Interagency Network Through Accessing Computer Technology) was federally funded through the Handicapped Children's Early Education Program network. The project was designed to increase collaboration among agencies serving at-risk infants and their families, to develop a comprehensive computer-based directory of services, and to provide intervention and parent training to several identified groups of hard-to-reach infants and their families. A critical-incident technique was used to evaluate the effectiveness of the project in attaining these goals. Thirty key informants—professionals, parents, and project staff—were identified and asked to report critical incidents throughout a 3-year period. Each was asked to explain incidents that either inhibited or enhanced the attainment of the project's chief goals. Study results suggested that five factors were important to successful interagency coordination and collaboration: "(1) developing new ways to meet community needs, (2) communicating, (3) networking and increasing awareness, (4) being responsive, and (5) neutralizing territory issues" (Harrison et al., 1990, p. 73).

In a study of the interagency coordination process at sites of High Risk Infant Follow-up (HRIF) projects in California, Jeremy and Korenbrot (1987) found that agency representatives who were given an explicit charge to increase their interagency collaboration efforts, and were provided with additional funds for this purpose, rated their relationships with other agencies more positively than agency representatives who had served as controls. To carry out this study the authors developed instruments to rate relationships between agencies and to rate the functioning of their interagency councils. Using these instruments, structured interviews were conducted with representatives from both the "experimental" group, consisting of the three HRIF projects and three other agencies serving high-risk infants (each of which received special funding from the Maternal and Child Health Branch of the California Department of Health Services), and the "comparison" group, consisting of four agencies that did not receive additional funding for coordination. All agencies were either departments of health, hospitals, special education infant programs, regional centers for persons with developmental disabilities, or social service agencies. The ratings showed better communication and conflict management among the agency representatives at the experimental (interagency collaboration) sites. Only the sharing of fiscal and personnel resources did not seem to improve among the experimental groups. The study also found that increased value was placed on interagency collaboration by those agencies that had participated in the experimental groups.

Implications of Collaboration Efforts for School-Age Children

Given the small body of literature on collaborative and/or consultative efforts in early childhood education, the authors have also chosen to review studies of collaborative efforts in settings for school-age children. It is likely that most of these findings are applicable to many settings serving younger children as well.

Collaboration and consultation efforts for school-age children have been addressed in a fairly extensive body of literature (e.g., Heron & Harris, 1987; Idol, 1990; Idol et al., 1986; Thousand et al., 1990; West & Idol, 1990). The *Journal of Educational and Psychological Consultation*, which published its first issue in 1990, is one example of the high level of interest that this topic has generated.

In the field of early childhood education the term "consultation" usually implies interagency cooperation. In the public school special education arena, however, consultation is more often used to describe a process that takes place within a single classroom, usually between regular and special educators. Public school models of collaborative consultation that have been used successfully include the consulting-teacher model, the teacher-assistance team, the pre-referral intervention team, the school-based resource team, the child-study team, and the triadic model (Heron & Harris, 1987, Thousand et al., 1990; West & Idol, 1990). These models are self-explanatory, except perhaps the triadic model, which denotes a linear relationship among consultant (e.g., special education teacher), mediator (e.g., regular education classroom teacher), and student (Heron & Harris, 1987).

Since the passage of PL 94-142, the use of these models of consultation has mush-roomed in response to the need to effectively mainstream a large number of children with disabilities into the regular education system (Johnson, Pugach, & Hammitte, 1988; Salend, 1984). Although many of these models have been used successfully to facilitate mainstreaming efforts, a number of barriers to effective consultation have also been revealed. Johnson et al. (1988) identified both pragmatic and conceptual barriers to the consultation process, and in their view the former were more easily overcome than the latter. For example, insufficient time for teachers and other professionals to carry out consultation due to large class sizes and overwhelming caseloads were two of the largest potential barriers that teachers and other professionals would have to face. Yet, as the researchers explained, this barrier may be more easily overcome than a conceptual barrier such as negative attitudes, on the part of either regular or special education teachers, toward mainstreaming. The first may be resolved fairly quickly by adequate funding, but the second may take several years to change. Other conceptual barriers identified by Johnson et al. (1988) included the lack of credibility of special educators among regular classroom teachers (e.g., special educators may not understand what it is like to have a large classroom of children all day) and the belief held by many special educators that regular classroom teachers lack knowledge about children with special needs. A related barrier was the different knowledge bases that regular and special educators have. Not only may these primary knowledge bases differ, but few educators, either regular or special, receive training in the consultation process (i.e., strategies for consultation, instructional methods and techniques, clinical knowledge).

In another study Whitted, Cohen, and Katz (1983) sought to identify barriers to and facilitators of state- and local-interagency cooperation in delivering special education and related services to children of school age in three midwestern states: Indiana, Wisconsin, and Louisiana. These investigators reviewed documents in each state that described the structure of the state education agency (SEA), and the structures that had been developed to promote interagency cooperation on both state and local levels. The monitoring systems in place in each state were also studied. Data on placement decisions for special education students, including residential placement decisions made by agencies other than the SEA, were also reviewed. In addition, interviews were conducted with SEA representatives and representatives of collaborating agencies in each state. Several barriers to collaboration were noted, including: 1) a lack of pressure on local agencies from the state level, 2) a lack of guidance from the state level, and 3) a lack of funds necessary to carry out the interagency activities. In addition, when setting priorities, a lack of coordination between those at the state and local levels, and among agencies at the local level, was seen as a serious barrier to interagency efforts, as was distrust among agencies. An important facilitating factor for collaboration, as identified by Whitted et al. (1983), is one agency's taking a leadership role in establishing the initial interagency linkage. Other elements found necessary for developing effective interagency cooperation included clear-cut delineation of responsibility, continuing evaluation of benefits for all participating agencies, and mechanisms for resolving disputes by minimizing confrontations and maximizing negotiations.

The literature on collaboration among those serving school-age children has yielded further suggestions for achieving successful joint efforts. Conducting a staff-needs assessment and then providing meaningful ongoing staff development were identified as critical factors by West and Idol (1990). Scheduling adequate time for professionals to consult with each other (Idol et al., 1986) and using case management as a vehicle for bringing various agencies together to serve the needs of an individual family (Morrill & Gerry, 1990) were also found to be useful. Additionally, the work of Thousand et al. (1990) suggested that the collaborative process must be multidirectional, with the participants acknowledging that all members of the collaborative team have unique and necessary expertise to contribute, and with members being held accountable for any commitments that they make.

As stated above, collaborative efforts are receiving widespread attention in current efforts to restructure and reform school systems (Harris, 1990; Patterson, Purkey, & Parker, 1986; Skrtic, 1987, 1988; Thousand & Villa, 1990; Thousand et al., 1990). Highly collaborative and interactive partnerships across agencies, as well as among professionals traditionally employed by public schools, are likely to be the wave of the future (Cohen, 1989; Kirst & McLaughlin, 1989; Schorr, 1989). The inclusion of members previously excluded from the collaboration process, particularly in school-age programs, such as the parents and the students themselves, is also being advocated. Thousand et al. (1990) propose using models of collaborative consultation to achieve a paradigm shift in defining the schools of the future. Three reasons are given: 1) to prepare students for life in the 21st century in a highly complex society; 2) to enable school personnel to meet the needs of the diverse student body, regardless of the students' race, gender, intellectual development or cultural or socioeconomic background; and 3) to shift the educational focus to a more "adhocratic" school, where the staff uses collective team efforts to meet the needs of individual students. These discussions of school restructuring and reform for the future all highlight the critical importance of collaborative efforts.

Methods and Models of Early Childhood Collaboration

Several investigations have examined aspects of collaborative efforts that were designed to facilitate integration efforts in early childhood education settings. These aspects include: 1) services developed to enhance the smooth transition of children and families from early intervention programs to preschool programs and from preschool to kindergarten, and 2) implementation strategies for training and supporting teachers in incorporating goals for children with special needs into existing early education curricula.

Given that services for children ages birth to 3 are often found in settings different from those for preschoolers ages 3–5, the transition of children and families from one type of setting or agency to the other typically results in both a need and an opportunity for collaboration. Hanline and Knowlton (1988) described a series of steps to prepare families for the transition and to support them through the process. At the infant program site, a staff member functioning as a transition coordinator provides families with information on preschool referral both through a written parent manual and through discussion at infant–parent support group meetings. Prior to the transition, the transition coordinator assists families in developing suggestions for their children's individualized

education programs (IEPs) and in learning about existing community preschool resources. The transition coordinator remains available to parents throughout the intake and the development of the IEP, as well as for follow-up contacts after the preschool placement. Follow-up evaluation data obtained from parents' responses to questions on a Likert scale indicate that parents' were satisfied with both the amount and quality of transition services they received.

Hains, Fowler, and Chandler (1988) identified key elements in the transition process from preschool to kindergarten. Of chief concern were the roles of the sending and receiving teachers. The sending teacher is responsible for preparing the child for the next environment by adjusting curricula to foster the necessary skills. He or she also serves as a liaison between the receiving teacher and the child's parents. The receiving teacher also establishes communication strategies with the child's parents and evaluates and adjusts classroom routines to accommodate entering students. Hains et al. (1988) acknowledge the importance of collaborative planning and the need for establishing lines of communication between agencies. The reader is referred to Chapter 7 of this volume for a more complete discussion of transition models.

Several investigations have also examined the effects of consultative techniques aimed at enhancing integration opportunities for preschool-age children. Hanline (1990) described Project STIP, Supported Transition to Integrated Preschool, in which a consulting teacher, referred to as an integration specialist, assisted regular education preschool teachers in integrating children with disabilities into their public education preschool programs. The regular education teachers were asked what information and services they needed for support in integrating children with special needs. They requested that the consulting teacher provide information on managing and teaching children with disabilities and on the needs of parents. The consulting teacher met with the teachers regularly and modeled the necessary techniques. An evaluation of this model found that a high degree of satisfaction was reported for both teachers and parents. A more thorough discussion of this model is presented in Chapter 7.

Peck, Killen, and Baumgart (1989) used a single-subject, multiple-baseline across subjects research design to systematically examine the effects of a nondirective consultative model. Two studies were conducted in which preschool and daycare center teachers were supported by trained staff members to include IEP goals in their curricula. In the first, the consultation intervention involved teachers viewing a video recording of their own interaction with children. The facilitator informed the teacher of the targeted objective and asked her or him to suggest ways in which the objectives could be incorporated in the regular routine. The strategies were self-generated by the teacher and supported by the facilitator. In the second study, the facilitator, a trained special education teacher, gave the teacher a verbal review of the instructional activity. In both studies the nondirective consultative techniques were found to increase the amount of IEP-related instruction. Improvements in child behavior targeted in the IEP goals were also observed. This research suggests that a nondirective approach may be effective for training teachers to incorporate specific special education goals into their curricula, and that a consulting special education teacher can effectively implement this type of training and support.

Summary

Although there has been relatively little research on or evaluation of collaborative models in early childhood education, studies of consultative and collaborative efforts involving school-age populations strongly support the use of these processes. The few investigations of early education programs or settings that have been conducted suggest that collaborative models were well-received by participants, and that collaborative efforts enhanced professionals' ability to meet community needs. Furthermore, consultation and linkages were facilitative as children made transitions across programs or as children with special needs were integrated into the most inclusive setting. Some specific models for consultation and collaboration are discussed below.

COLLABORATIVE AND CONSULTATIVE MODELS

Around the country numerous innovative collaborative efforts are underway that focus on integrating young children with special needs with their typically developing peers. The authors have chosen two general models for discussion. One model involves training and support for childcare providers attempting to include children with special needs in their childcare programs. Three examples of this model are presented. Second, an extensive discussion of Head Start and its provision for the inclusion of children with special needs is provided. The Head Start Model was chosen because it represents one of the oldest and best-established models for preschool-age integration. The issues, procedures, and experiences identified through these examples are most likely generalizable to a number of other community-based programs serving children under 5 years of age.

Collaboration and Consultation in Childcare Settings

The only settings other than their homes in which children, particularly children from birth through 2 years, are likely to receive care and spend large amounts of time with other children is in childcare homes or centers. Because of the great number of parents in the United States today who work outside of the home, the need for childcare is enormous. Thus, service providers for children with special needs increasingly consider childcare providers to be colleagues and providers of care and treatment. While the advantages of collaborative efforts are obvious to both families and professionals, until recently relatively few models have attempted or examined these cooperative efforts. The following discussion describes three such childcare models.

Day Care Training Project, University of Connecticut Health Center (Bruder, 1989; Bruder, Deiner, & Sachs, 1990) A survey of the families of children with special needs in Connecticut conducted by the University of Connecticut Health Center, Department of Pediatrics, Division of Child and Family Studies, revealed that 40% of the families surveyed were in need of childcare or respite services. In response, this model was developed to provide inservice training for daycare center providers in an effort to coordinate and enhance early intervention and special education services for young children with disabilities who are receiving daycare services. The model consists of three components. First, *on-site workshops* are conducted at daycare centers on topics specific to the center's defined needs. These workshops are designed to foster awareness of, and information exchange on, issues related to providing services to children with disabilities. Second, several *long-term institutes* are offered. The first are 12-week institutes that are provided throughout the year and focus on consultation and collaboration skills and the coordination of special education services. On-site follow-up support is provided to institute participants. Furthermore, participants who complete these institutes are eligible to participate in the second long-term institute, where they will learn to train others. The third component is *individualized technical assistance* provided on-site or via telephone for daycare providers. A toll-free telephone number is available for use by the providers. Bruder (personal communication, February 20, 1991) reports that primary considerations in launching these collaborative efforts are attaining the support of individuals at the policymaking or systems level, getting players together, and giving the early educators and staff members the confidence to include children with disabilities in their services.

Projects: Delaware FIRST and Del Care Project (Bruder, Deiner, & Sachs, 1990; Deiner, 1988) Delaware FIRST was funded as a Handicapped Children's Early Education Project (U.S. Department of Education) from 1986–1989, and Del Care is funded by the Delaware Department of Public Instruction under Part H of PL 99-457. Both projects were funded in order to provide training and support to family daycare providers so that they could provide services to children with disabilities. Training to providers consists of a 20-hour general training course on four major topics: 1) infant and toddler development of typical children and children with disabilities, 2) teaching the infant or toddler with disabilities, 3) communicating with families and helping parents and caregivers handle stress, and 4) utilizing community resources and maintaining professionalism. This general training is followed by approximately 6 hours of specific on-site training, that is focused on particular child and family needs at the daycare center. In addition to the training activities, the support services include: newsletters, a toy-lending system, a professional lending library, a toll-free number for problem-solving and consultation, and regular visits to home daycare providers. Experiences from these projects highlighted the importance of on-site inservice training as an effective training technique. Furthermore, the following technical assistance items were identified as being necessary: reading materials on specific disabilities, activity ideas, regularly scheduled daycare visits, additional training, and telephone support.

Colorado Department of Education/ Douglas County School District (Colorado Department of Education, 1991). An example of a successful collaborative model between childcare and public schools is the one developed in Douglas County, Colorado, by the Colorado Department of Education, working jointly with the Douglas County School District and several private childcare centers. In this reverse-mainstreaming model, typically developing children of ages 3–5 years from local childcare centers are enrolled in school district special education preschool classrooms. Currently, three elementary school buildings house these classrooms, and children are assigned to the site closest to their own neighborhood. Each special education class enrolls five or six typically developing children and seven or eight children with disabilities. Children are assigned to classes according to age—with

groupings of 3- and 4-year-olds and 4- and 5-year-olds—regardless of severity of disability. The special education classrooms use the High Scope curriculum, for which all public school staff members have been fully trained.

The special education preschools are in session four mornings per week. In the afternoons all the children attend the childcare centers nearest their homes. The programs are implemented at each public school site by transdisciplinary teams consisting of a certified early childhood special education teacher, a speech-language pathologist, and an occupational therapist. These specialists are assigned as consultants to the childcare centers in the afternoons, training the child care workers to implement IEP goals and to meet other special needs of the children with disabilities. Weekly team planning sessions are held, and once a month the special education team and the childcare center staff get together for joint planning. Weekly home visits are made by special education staff to those families with disabled children who request it.

The school district provides several incentives to ensure the success of this collaborative effort. First, childcare tuition for nondisabled children is subsidized by the school district, ensuring savings for parents who participate. This has resulted in the need for a waiting list for nondisabled slots since the program began. In addition, the school district subsidizes the salaries of the childcare workers. Second, the district provides a half-time occupational therapist to each of the participating childcare centers, thus facilitating carryover of intervention from the special education preschool to the childcare program. Third, the district is strongly committed to including childcare workers in all IEP meetings, which encourages the sharing of information by all adults involved with the children with special needs.

While the model is seen by parents and other members of the community as being very effective, some problems have been identified. The greatest is the high turnover rate among childcare workers at all three sites. There are several reasons for the turnover rate, including the relatively low rate of pay (despite salary subsidies), workers returning to school, and workers leaving the area to follow spouses in career moves. Whatever the reasons, the fact remains that in order for the program to be truly collaborative, respect and trust must develop between special education and childcare staff members, and this becomes increasingly difficult as turnover rates rise. Strengths of the model, as perceived by the participants, include the heterogeneous mix of the groups, with children with severe needs dispersed throughout all the classrooms; the provision of occupational therapy services in both preschool and childcare classrooms rather than through a pullout model; and the transdisciplinary mode of service delivery. The model recognizes childcare as part of the professional service delivery system and acknowledges the collaborative role childcare programs can play in integrating young children with disabilities and their nondisabled peers.

Summary The experience base from these projects and others like them shows that children with special needs can receive services in childcare settings, both in private homes and at centers. The key elements that appear to be necessary for success are the training of, and continued support and technical assistance to, childcare providers, and the development of a team spirit between early childhood special education and childcare professionals that is based on trust and mutual respect.

Collaboration Between Head Start and Public Schools

Although childcare settings typically serve children of all ages, Head Start programs are generally more limited in scope, primarily serving children 3 through 5 years old. One exception to this rule is the network of parent-child centers located throughout the country that serve children from birth to 3 years old and their families. Due to its comprehensive service model, Head Start has a long history of successful collaboration with various other public agencies. Only recently, however, have these collaborative efforts included public schools.

Head Start is a major resource for mainstreaming for several reasons. First, since 1972 Head Start national policy has required that 10% of available enrollment slots be allocated to children with identified disabilities. This means that the majority of Head Start teachers and assistants have had many years of experience in mainstreaming children with disabilities. Second, a comprehensive model of service delivery characterizes Head Start at the national, regional, and local levels. All children and families served in Head Start programs are provided with nutrition, health, and dental services, and sometimes extended daycare, in addition to the early childhood educational program. In order to implement this comprehensive model, each local Head Start program is required to have specialists on staff who coordinate education, health, parental involvement and special needs services. Therefore, Head Start teachers and administrators have extensive experience in collaboration at the local level, where they must work with representatives from the public health, regular education, special education, and childcare sectors. A third reason for collaboration between Head Start and public school programs when mainstreaming is that formal interagency agreements have already been developed and approved in each state between the regional office of the Administration for Children, Youth and Families (ACYF), which funds Head Start programs in each state, and the state education agency (SEA). The purpose of these agreements is to encourage individual Head Start programs to collaborate with local educational agencies (LEAs) in the provision of services to children of ages 3 through 5 with disabilities. The following excerpt from the interagency agreement currently in force between the California Department of Education and ACYF Region IX illustrates this collaborative process:

It is the intent of this agreement to:
1. Define which service will be provided by each agency.
2. Ensure that all handicapped children have a free and appropriate public education as required by federal and state laws, regardless of which public agency administers the program.
3. Ensure that each agency cooperates to maintain communciation and share leadership responsibilities at the state and local level to ensure that available resources are utilized in the most effective manner.
4. Ensure that cooperative agreements, including formal contracts when appropriate, between local educational agencies and Head Start agencies are developed, implemented, and maintained to ensure that those children needing special education and/or services are provided those services in the least restrictive environment. (California State Department of Education, 1989, p. 1)

As of 1992, all 50 states have written interagency agreements between the ACYF and their state departments of education. In addition to the state agreements, there are also many agreements between local Head Start programs and local public school districts. Both state and local agreements are updated on a regular, often an annual, basis. Although they vary in content and comprehensiveness, the agreements generally address the following topics: child find, assessment, individualized education programs, procedural safeguards, training and technical assistance, and administration, funding, and monitoring.

Child Find   The educational code in each state reflects the requirement in PL 94-142 (now known as IDEA) and PL 99-457 (102-119) of a Child Find system to identify children in need of special education. The interagency agreement may stipulate that Head Start representatives be involved in the procedures established by school districts for Child Find, including annual screenings and referrals for in-depth assessments. The local school district might provide specialists in screening and assessment, including early childhood special educators, speech-language pathologists, psychologists, and physical therapists. Head Start might take responsibility for health screening (medical, dental, nutritional), since Head Start, through special federal funding, can provide joint training and technical assistance to both local school districts and local Head Start programs in order to promote Child Find activities. Thus, each agency contributes something unique to the collaborative process, as reflected in the written interagency agreements.

Assessment   As in the case of Child Find, the collaboration can also benefit both Head Start and the school district in the area of assessments. Head Start programs generally lack funding for individual in-depth assessments of children suspected to have disabilities. However, they have strong parental involvement components and their staff members are usually more in touch with the families they serve than are representatives of the public schools. Interagency agreements may stipulate that the school district conduct the assessment of children referred by Head Start; Head Start, in turn, will gain parental consent for the assessment, support the family during the assessment process, and inform the family of assessment results. Head Start may also provide anecdotal information concerning the child and family that is helpful in the development of the individualized education program (IEP). The California Interagency Agreement stipulates that Head Start personnel, including teachers or coordinators, be included in the development and annual review of all IEPs for children of ages three through five who will be mainstreamed into Head Start classrooms. The IEP must specify which services will be provided by Head Start and which by the school district. Each agency is then responsible for monitoring the services that it provides. Other states have similar language in their interagency agreements.

Procedural Safeguards Procedural Safeguards are important in the formal interagency process. They cover confidentiality of records, protection of individual rights, and due process procedures. The interagency agreement must specify which agency will inform parents of their rights and monitor the establishment of safeguards.

Training and Technical Assistance The agreement may also provide for joint training of Head Start and public school staff in the appropriate provision of special educational services to eligible preschool children and their families. Each of the 10 regions of the United States designated as administrative units by the United States Department of Health and Human Services has a Resource Access Project (RAP) to conduct such training

and provide technical assistance. RAPs have been part of the Head Start network since 1972; together with the United States Department of Public Health in each region, they assist programs to better serve children and families with disabilities. RAPs conduct training at the local, state, and regional levels. They sponsor conferences and provide individual consultations. Their services can be made available at any of the three levels to public schools through the interagency agreements.

Administration, Funding, and Monitoring The interagency agreement may stipulate, as the California agreement does, that local districts and Head Start programs "explore creative methods of financing the costs of the special education and related services, including dual enrollment and itinerant teacher arrangements" (California State Department of Education, 1989, p. 13). It is required that the agreement specify such details as which agency is responsible for providing which services, who pays the bill, who monitors compliance, and who takes responsibility for ensuring a smooth transition from Head Start to a public school program. Nevertheless, it is not difficult to imagine that much creative sharing of resources could occur as a result of the agreement to the benefit of children with disabilities.

Collaboration and Consultation in Head Start Settings

The following section reviews two examples of successful collaborative efforts involving Head Start. The first is similar to many other public school/Head Start projects in progress throughout the country. The second describes a collaborative effort to train parent volunteers for Head Start classrooms.

Merced County Community Action Program (Head Start)/Merced County Office of Education (California) Collaborative Program One example of successful cooperation between public school and Head Start programs is the Merced County, California, experience (S. Brinkley, personal communication, April, 1991). Like many city and county school districts in California, Merced County has turned to established Head Start programs to mainstream 3- to 5-year old children with disabilities. Several of the special education preschool classes are located at sites close to or within a Head Start center; the children with special needs attend the Head Start programs for part of the day, and their special education preschools for the remainder of the day. Early childhood special educators, speech pathologists, and occupational therapists work as consultants in the Head Start classrooms, providing training and technical assistance to Head Start teachers and assistants who are responsible for meeting the special needs of the children with disabilities. Head Start teachers, along with the special needs coordinator, attend all staffings for children who will be enrolled in the Head Start classrooms. Staff development activities are jointly conducted in Merced County, sometimes sponsored by the school district and sometimes by Head Start employee recruitment resources available through RAP. The program appears to be successful because: 1) Head Start and special education staff members have developed mutual respect based on recognition of the unique contribution each makes to the educational process, 2) both groups recognize that without their collaboration the children with special needs would be deprived of an appropraite education, and 3) each group benefits financially from the association.

Project PAVE (Morganton, North Carolina) (Cooper, Helms, Wheeldreyer, & Dunst, 1985) This collaborative effort between Blue Ridge Community action Head Start and the Family, Infant and Preschool Program at Western Carolina Center was designed to accomplish the goals of improving: 1) services to young children with disabilities and their families, 2) the quality of parent involvement in Head Start programs, and 3) mainstreaming opportunities for children with disabilities. To implement the collaborative project, the Head Start center agreed to accept children with moderate to severe needs into their program. Project PAVE (Parents Are Volunteers Who Excel) agreed to train parent volunteers to work in Head Start classrooms and to assist Head Start staff in developing individualized programs for the children with moderate to severe disabilities. As a result of the project, 36 parents were trained and worked in Head Start classrooms as volunteers, which helped to create a richer teacher–child ratio. The training consisted of a series of 6 workshops, lasting 6 hours each. Several of the parents had children of their own enrolled in Head Start. This project illustrates the collaborative working relationship that must develop between two agencies before successful consultation can take place.

Summary Head Start programs provide opportunities for young children with disabilities to participate in classrooms with typically developing peers in a variety of ways. School administrators have only recently begun to include Head Start in the list of placement options available to parents of preschool children with disabilities. Since integrated settings are generally less apparent and available for preschool children than for school-age children, the opportunities afforded by Head Start for creative collaborative efforts that meet the needs of the children and families within given local communities should not be overlooked. The two models reviewed represent only a small sample of the actual range of collaborative efforts that are possible.

RECOMMENDATIONS FOR EFFECTIVE CONSULTATIVE AND COLLABORATIVE EFFORTS

Certain conditions appear to be important for successful collaboration. These include: 1) the desire on the part of one group to accomplish a goal for which necessary resources are unavailable, 2) the ability of a second group to provide the necessary resources to the first group, and 3) willingness on the part of both groups to work together as equals. Given that these conditions exist, the following recommendations are offered for collaborative, consultative efforts to place children under the age of 5 in the most inclusive environment.

Commitment from Decisionmakers

Although initial collaborative efforts may be made at the grass-roots program level, it is necessary to obtain commitment to and ongoing support for those efforts at the highest levels of administration and decisionmaking. Without this system-wide commitment, the collaboration cannot reach maximum effectiveness. This commitment should also be reflected in the recognition of the collaboration as a regular administrative function that should affect the funding of all participating agencies. The work required to imple-

ment the collaboration is time-consuming, and the agencies involved should be suitably reimbursed (Whitted et al., 1983).

There are several steps that state policy makers can take to promote interagency collaboration on mainstreaming (Bruner, 1991). These include: 1) designing requests for proposals that reward collaborative strategies when local demonstration projects are authorized, 2) including both internal accountability measures and family outcome measures in evaluation designs, 3) providing technical assistance and staff support for developing grant programs that foster collaboration, and 4) ensuring that salaries of professionals who are responsible for collaboration are on the same level as those of other employees with comparable training and experience. Such steps at the state level would send a message to local agencies that collaboration is expected and valued and that it will be rewarded.

Commitment, Shared Ownership, and Decisionmaking Among Participants

In order for the collaboration to receive widespread support from all participants, a sense of trust and mutual respect must develop between members of the collaborative groups. It is important, too, that the sense of trust and respect extend to all parents associated with the interagency collaboration. Open communication among all participants and cooperative decisionmaking should be the norm. Communication must be a two-way process, with all participants regarded as equals. Ownership must be shared—ownership of problems and concerns, as well as ownership of the outcomes of collaborative efforts. A consensus model allows for the expression of differing viewpoints, and for differing levels of participation by members. Furthermore it contributes to the development of positive, supportive feelings among all participants. The importance of networking relationships, communicating, and neutralizing territory issues was identified in the research studies previously reviewed (Harrison et al., 1990; Stegelin & Jones, 1991).

Adequate Resources to Support Planning and Coordination of Collaboration

An important consideration for effective collaboration noted in the literature for both school-age and preschool populations is the cost, particularly in terms of professional time. Data suggest that one of the factors that clearly differentiates successful and unsuccessful collaborative efforts is adequate support during planning and coordination (i.e., the actual work of collaboration) (Peck, Furman, & Helmstetter, chap. 10, this volume). This factor seems especially important given the current extent of budget cuts and the resulting increases in the work loads of many professionals. It is unrealistic to expect collaboration, a time-consuming process by any standard, to be undertaken by staff members who already perceive themselves as being overloaded (Johnson et al., 1988).

Ongoing Training and Technical Assistance

The need for ongoing training and technical assistance for staff members involved in integration efforts is critical. Joint training in such areas as promoting play, implementing developmentally appropriate practices, and setting up environments that facilitate learning can stretch the skills of both regular and special educators. Such strategies emphasize the similarities, rather than the differences,

among children. Experienced service providers as well as novices can benefit from training in these and other similar topics.

At some sites the early childhood special education and related services staff members can take a consultative role and provide specialized training in such topics as feeding, positioning and handling, adaptive equipment, sign language, assessment, and so on. This specialized training is often best accomplished using a *trainer of trainers* approach, in which an expert trains a small group of service providers, who then return to their home programs and train other service providers. Ideally, ongoing follow-up technical assistance is also provided. The importance of technical assistance to collaborative efforts is underscored by the sucess of the Connecticut and Delaware projects reviewed above (Bruder et al., 1990).

Another supportive training model is peer-coaching, in which one professional staff member enters into an agreement with another to receive observation and feedback during the course of his or her work (Showers, 1984). Peer coaches may be from the same or different programs, depending on the resources and needs of the agency.

Evaluation

Systematic evaluation of the consultative and collaborative activities should take place on a regular, ongoing basis (e.g., Hanline, 1990). All parties involved should be committed to the evaluative process, and to using the resulting data to make necessary changes in the collaborative process.

Family Input and Involvement

Families should be involved in the interagency efforts at all levels, including the leadership and decisionmaking levels (Schaffner & Buhwell, 1991). Parents may participate in advisory groups and planning and training activities, and may help to lead small group projects. A wide range of activities and several levels of involvement should be made available to family members, so that they have some choice as to the extent and form of their participation.

SUMMARY

The provision of special education services within the most inclusive environment to infants and preschool children poses unique problems, different from those encountered when mainstreaming school-age children. Settings that serve nondisabled populations of similar chronological age are rare in most states for children under 5, whereas all states require universal education for children of ages 6 through 18. Therefore, a 9-year-old with disabilities can quite easily be placed into a regular third or fourth grade classroom, provided administrative support is available, but in many states such public settings are not available for infants and preschool-age children. Those states that do offer public programs to young nondisabled children typically serve only small numbers of children, and may not serve infants. In order to provide services for young children with disabilities in the most inclusive environment, it is necessary for special educators to collaborate with institutions that serve nondisabled children. These include childcare centers, Head Start programs, and private preschools. A wide range of creative models are possible, given existing resources. The key ingredient is commitment to consultative and collaborative efforts to maximize resources and develop successful integrated services that meet the needs of young children and their families.

REFERENCES

Bruder, M.B. (1989). *Day care inservice training model on young children with special needs.* Handicapped Children's Early Education Program Grant Proposal. Farmington: University of Connecticut Health Center, Pediatrics, Division of Child and Family Studies.

Bruder, M.B., Deiner, P., & Sachs, S. (1990). Models of integration through early intervention/child care collaboration. *Zero to Three, 10*(3), 14–17.

Bruner, C. (1991). *Thinking collaboratively: Ten questions and answers to help policy makers improve children's services.* Washington, DC: Institute for Educational Leadership, Educational and Human Services Consortium Series on Collaboration.

California State Department of Education. (1989). *Interagency agreement between the State Department of Education, Special Education Division, and the Administration for Children, Youth and Families, Region IX, Head Start, US Department of Health and Human Services.* Sacramento: Author.

Cohen, D.L. (1989, March 15). Joining Forces: An alliance of sectors envisioned to aid the most troubled young. *Education Week,* p. 7.

Colorado Department of Education, Early Childhood Special Education Unit. (1991). *Douglas County Pilot Integration Project.* Denver: Author.

Cooper, C.S., Helms, G.E., Wheeldreyer, J.C., & Dunst, C.J. (1985, October). *Interagency collaboration and parent empowerment.* Paper presented at the Council for Exceptional Children/Division for Early Childhood, National Early Childhood Conference on Children with Special Needs, Denver.

Deiner, P. (1988, November): *Successful models for mainstreaming disabled children into child care: Delaware FIRST Program and Del Care.* Paper presented at the meeting of the National Association for the Education of Young Children (NAEYC).

Education for All Handicapped Children Act of 1975, PL 94-142. (August 23, 1977). Title 20, U.S.C. 1401 et seq: *U.S. Statutes at Large, 89,* 773–796.

Education of the Handicapped Act Amendments of 1986, PL 99-457. (October 8, 1986). Title 20, U.S.C. 1400 et seq: *U.S. Statutes at Large, 100,* 1145–1177.

Elder, J.O., & Magrab, P.R. (Eds.). (1980). *Coordinating services to handicapped children: A handbook for interagency collaboration.* Baltimore: Paul H. Brookes Publishing Co.

Hains, A.H., Fowler, S.A., & Chandler, L.K. (1988). Planning school transitions: Family and professional collaboration. *Journal of the Division for Early Childhood, 12*(2), 108–115.

Hanline, M.F. (1990). A consulting model for providing integration opportunities for preschool children with disabilities. *Journal of Early Intervention, 14*(4), 360–366.

Hanline, M.F., & Knowlton, A. (1988). A collaborative model for providing support to parents during their child's transition from infant intervention to preschool special education public school programs. *Journal of the Division for Early Childhood, 12*(2), 116–125.

Hanson, M.J. (1985). Administration of private versus public early childhood special education programs. *Topics in Early Childhood Special Education, 5,* 25–38.

Harris, K.C. (1990). Meeting diverse needs through collaborative consultation. In W. Stainback & S. Stainback (Eds.), *Support networks for inclusive schooling: Interdependent integrated education* (pp. 139–150) Baltimore: Paul H. Brookes Publishing Co.

Harrison, P.J., Lynch, E.W., Rosander, K., & Borton, W. (1990). Determining success in interagency collaboration: An evaluation of processes and behaviors. *Infants and Young Children, 3*(1), 69–78.

Heron, T., & Harris, K. (1987). *The educational consultant: Helping professionals, parents and mainstreamed students* (2nd ed.). Austin, TX: Pro-ED.

Idol, L. (1990). The scientific art of classroom consultation. *Journal of Educational and Psychological Consultation, 1*(1), 3–22.

Idol, L., Paolucci-Whitcomb, P., & Nevin, A. (1986). *Collaborative consultation.* Austin, TX: PRO-ED.

Jeremy, R.J., & Korenbrot, C.C. (1987). *Coordination among agencies serving high-risk infants: Evaluation of MCH High-Risk Infant Follow-Up Project: Interagency Coordination, Final Report.* Sacramento: California Department of Health Services, Maternal and Child Health Branch.

Johnson, H.W., McLaughlin, J.A., & Christensen, M. (1982). Interagency collaboration: Driving and restraining forces, *Exceptional Children, 48,* 395–399.

Johnson, L.J., Pugach, M.C., & Hammitte, D.J. (1988). Barriers to effective special education consultation. *Remedial and Special Education, 9*(6), 41–47.

Kirst, M.W., & McLaughlin, M. (1989). *Rethinking children's policy: Implications for educational administration.* Paper prepared for the National Society for the Study of Education Yearbook, 1989.

Morrill, W.A., & Gerry, M.H. (1990, February). Integrating the delivery of services to school-aged children at risk: Toward a description of American experience and experimentation. In *Children and youth at risk.* Conference sponsored by the United States Department of Education, Washington, DC.

Mulvenon, J. (1980). Development of preschool interagency teams. In J.O. Elder & P.R. Magrab (Eds.), *Coordinating services to handicapped children: A handbook for interagency collaboration* (pp. 133–162). Baltimore: Paul H. Brookes Publishing Co.

NEC*TAS Expert Team. (1989). *The concept of least restrictive environment as it applies to infants and toddlers.* Chapel Hill: National Early Childhood Technical Assistance System (NEC*TAS), Frank Porter Graham Child Development Center, University of North Carolina at Chapel Hill.

Odom, S.L., & McEvoy, M.A. (1988). Integration of young children with handicaps and normally developing children. In S.L. Odom & M.B. Karnes (Eds.), *Early intervention for infants and children with handicaps: An empirical base* (pp. 241–267.). Baltimore: Paul H. Brookes Publishing Co.

Patterson, J., Purkey, S., & Parker, J. (1986). *Productive school systems for a nonrational world.* Alexandria, VA: Association for Supervision and Curriculum Development.

Peck, C.A., Killen, C.C., & Baumgart, D. (1989). Increasing implementation of special education instruction in mainstream preschools: Direct and generalized effects of nondirective consultation. *Journal of Applied Behavior Analysis, 22*(2), 197–210.

Salend, S.J. (1984). Factors contributing to the development of successful mainstreaming programs. *Exceptional Children, 50*(5), 409–416.

Schaffner, C.B., & Buswell, B.E. (1991). *Opening doors: Strategies for including all students in regular education.* Colorado Springs, CO: PEAK Parent Center.

Schorr, L.B. (1989). Raising the odds of children's success. In *Expanding the role of the school: Elementary School Center conferences, 1987-89.* New York: Elementary School Center.

Showers, B. (1984). School improvement through staff development: The coaching of teaching. In Far West Laboratory, *Making our schools more effective.* San Francisco: Far West Laboratory for Educational Research and Development.

Skrtic, T. (1987). The national inquiry into the future of education for students with special needs. *Counterpoint, 4*(7), 6.

Skrtic, T. (1988). The crisis in special education knowledge. In E. Meyen & T. Skrtic (Eds.), *Exceptional children and youth: An introduction* (3rd ed.) (pp. 415–448). Denver: Love.

Stegelin, D.A., & Jones, S.D. (1991). Components of early childhood interagency collaboration: Results of a statewide study. *Early Education and Development, 2*(1), 54–67.

Strain, P.S. (1988). *LRE for preschool children with handicaps: What we know, what we should be doing.* Unpublished manuscript, Western Psychiatric Institute and Clinic, Pittsburgh, PA.

Thousand, J.S., & Villa, R.A. (1990). Sharing expertise and responsibilities through teaching teams. In W. Stainback & S. Stainback (Eds.), *Support networks for inclusive schooling: Interdependent integrated education* (pp. 151–166). Baltimore: Paul H. Brookes Publishing Co.

Thousand, J.S., Villa, R.A., Paolucci-Whitcomb, P., & Nevin, A. (1990). Collaborative consultation: A hoax or a grand experiment? *Center for Developmental Disabilities Monograph Series, 11*(1). Burlington: University of Vermont Affiliated Program.

West, J.F., (1990). The nature of consultation vs. collaboration: An interview with Walter O. Pryzwansky. *The Consulting Edge, 2*(1), 1–2.

West, J.F., & Idol, L. (1990). Collaborative consultation in the education of mildly handicapped and at-risk students. *Remedial and Special Education, 11*(1), 22–31.

Whitted, B.R., Cohen, M.D., & Katz, L. (1983, April). *Interagency cooperation: Miracle or mirage? A study of interagency cooperation in the delivery of special education and related services.* Paper presented at the 61st Annual International Convention of the Council for Exceptional Children, Detroit.

Chapter 9

Staff Development in Support of Integration

*Susan Kontos
and Nancy File*

Staff development is a process designed to change teachers' beliefs, knowledge, and practices related to a particular goal (Guskey, 1986). In this chapter, the authors discuss staff development that is aimed at preparing teachers for the integration of young children with special needs into regular community early childhood programs. This discussion focuses on three areas related to staff development: 1) influences on staff development in early childhood programs, and their implications; 2) examples of programs described in the literature that use staff development to enhance integration in early childhood programs; and 3) barriers to effective staff development and recommendations to minimize them. The authors do not discuss the specific content or process of staff development because numerous other resources on these subjects are available (e.g., Hutson, 1981; Wood & Thompson, 1980). In keeping with the

framework of this volume, the authors' intent is to focus on the ecological context of staff development in early childhood programs, and how it affects the successful integration of young children with special needs into classrooms with their nondisabled peers.

INFLUENCES ON STAFF DEVELOPMENT

There are many types of regular early childhood programs, including family daycare homes, childcare centers, and nursery schools. These programs vary in their operating schedules, in the manner in which children are grouped, and in the typical background of the staff. These characteristics, and the ways in which they differ from those of early intervention settings and staff, have implications for the content and process of staff development efforts focused on the integration of young

Appreciation is expressed to Susan Klein Shuster, Georgia Sheriff, and Laura Westberg of the Institute for the Study for Developmental Disabilities, Indiana University, with whom discussions of staff development have benefited our thinking on the issues presented in this chapter.

children with special needs into regular community early childhood programs.

Setting Characteristics

Both family daycare homes and childcare centers provide full-day, year-round care to children. Nursery schools, however, typically operate according to an academic-year calendar and enroll children for half-day programs of 2–4 hours, from 2 to 5 days per week. Although some early intervention programs have adopted a childcare schedule, many operate on a schedule that more closely resembles those of nursery schools.

These operating schedules have certain implications for staff development efforts. Family daycare providers and childcare center staff are responsible for children for longer hours than most nursery school or early intervention staff. Family daycare providers work alone, and staff in childcare centers frequently work staggered schedules because of center hours. This makes scheduling staff development more difficult, unless substitutes can be provided.

Staff Education

Information about early childhood staff qualifications can be gleaned from many small-scale, and several nationwide, studies of childcare centers (Ruopp, Travers, Glantz, & Coelen, 1979; Whitebook, Howes, & Phillips, 1989) and family daycare homes (Divine-Hawkins, 1981). However, there is a dearth of research on nursery school settings. Therefore, in the description of staff below, the authors report only on childcare center staff and family daycare providers.

Family daycare providers are typically educated to the high school level, although some studies report that a small portion of providers have college degrees (Kontos, 1992). The National Child Care Staffing Study (NCCSS; Whitebook et al., 1989) provides the most recent figures on childcare center staff. This study reports that almost 75% of childcare center teachers have some college experience, with 31% of them actually having attained a bachelor's degree.

These figures contrast with those for early childhood special educators. A survey of direct service staff in North Carolina early intervention programs revealed that 57% had bachelor's degrees and 38% held master's degrees (Palsha, Bailey, Vandiviere, & Munn, 1990). Another survey of early intervention programs in Indiana (Kontos & Dunn, 1989) showed that 86% of the teachers had attended at least some college, with 43% of them holding a bachelor's degree and 23% holding a master's degree. However, the majority of aides were educated to the high school level (Kontos & Dunn, 1989). In comparison, then, family daycare providers tend to be less highly educated than early intervention teachers, but about as well-educated as early intervention aides. Childcare teachers appear to be slightly less educated than early intervention teachers, but the differences are not dramatic.

Staff who have invested more years in their formal education may find different staff development activities more suitable to their learning styles than will staff with lower levels of education. Staff members' familiarity and degree of comfort with formal versus informal learning settings should be considered when planning staff development. While it would be tempting to assume for planning purposes that staff with higher levels of education have some background in child development and education, this assumption may well be unfounded, as shown below.

Specialized Training

Family daycare providers have had disparate amounts of specialized training. Based on a review of the literature, Kontos (1992) concludes that the training of family daycare providers is more likely to be informal (e.g., workshops, conferences) rather than formal coursework, and usually totals less than 30 hours. Those with formal training most often received it at the high school level.

Likewise, the NCCSS revealed that the specialized training of childcare center teachers varies widely. The majority of teaching staff, 65% of teachers and 57% of assistant teachers, had some formal coursework in early childhood education or child development at levels ranging from high school to graduate school. For those with formal training in the field, half had received it at the college level. However, only 6.6% of the sample were licensed in early childhood education. The other 18% of the sample who were credentialed were licensed in such fields as elementary education and nursing (Whitebook et al., 1989).

Again, these figures can be compared to those for early childhood special educators. Hanson (1990), from a survey of early intervention workers in California, reported that only half had specialized training in the field of early intervention. Similarly, in the Indiana survey, Kontos and Dunn (1989) found that only 50% of the teachers had majored in early childhood or special education.

In sum, both the early childhood and early intervention fields employ a large percentage of staff who lack specialized professional training in their respective fields. The situation appears to be most extreme among family daycare providers.

There is evidence that many family daycare providers and parents regard childrearing as the best preparation for daycare work (Divine-Hawkins, 1981; Fischer, 1989).

It appears that neither regular early childhood nor early intervention staff are necessarily optimally trained in their respective fields, and that staff development efforts on any number of topics, including intervention, is warranted. Staff development planners must realize that they can expect many staff to lack the knowledge base provided by specialized training in their fields, while still acknowledging that staff members have learned on the job, or through less formal channels. Among the various types of early childhood staff, family daycare providers probably have the most extensive need for staff development.

Licensing and Regulations for Training

States vary with regard to the amount of inservice training they require yearly for childcare providers. Of the five states participating in the NCCSS, one had no requirements for inservice training of center-based staff, while the remaining four states' requirements ranged from 20 hours per year to an unspecified number of hours. The NCCSS reported that, in actuality, only 25% of the teaching staff had participated in 15 or more hours of inservice training during the previous 12 months (Whitebook et al., 1989).

Inservice training regulations for family daycare providers are even more disparate. Twenty-two states have no requirements for either pre- or inservice training for family daycare providers (Children's Foundation, 1990). In states that do require some form of training, the content is frequently CPR and/or first aid, rather than child development or childcare practices.

It is obvious that childcare licensing regulations are likely to provide only minimal incentives for staff to participate in staff development activities. Moreover, as motivators, these regulations represent the "stick" as opposed to the "carrot." A further implication of these data, however, is that states place little value on inservice staff development as an essential part of professional practice. Fortunately, there are other incentives operating within the field to encourage staff development.

Incentives for Staff Development

Many early childhood programs do provide paid time for staff to participate in inservice training. The NCCSS reported that 82% of childcare center staff were allowed paid preparation and training time, although it is not known how time was divided between these two activities (Whitebook et al., 1989). These figures are similar to those reported in an early intervention staff survey; Kontos and File (1992) found that 83% of early intervention staff were paid for inservice training.

Further incentive for early childhood education staff development may be provided by the center accreditation program sponsored by the National Association for the Education of Young Children. This program promotes voluntary compliance with standards of operation that are generally above those of minimal licensing regulations (Phillips, Lande, & Goldberg, 1990). Accreditation costs time and money, but brings prestige to the program. The NCCSS found that accredited centers employed staff with higher educational levels and more specialized training than did centers that were not accredited (Whitebook et al., 1989).

Finally, staff development may be driven

by the motivation of staff to do their jobs well and to meet new challenges. Several studies have reported that the highest levels of job satisfaction for both childcare workers and early intervention staff resulted from their participation in children's development (Kontos & File, 1992; Kontos & Stremmel, 1988; Modigliani, 1986; Whitebook et al., 1989). The desire to serve children and families well may be an incentive for early childhood and early intervention professionals to participate in staff development.

Disincentives for Staff Development

Several factors operate as disincentives for early childhood teachers to participate in staff development activities. Simply finding time for staff development is one of the thorniest problems. Childcare providers who work in full-day programs, whether center- or home-based, have very little time available away from the children. Typically, free time is available only during the children's nap, and it must accommodate multiple adult needs, including breaks, planning and preparation, and staff meetings—not to mention staff development activities.

Also, there is rarely any reward (i.e., salary increase) for participating in staff development activities (and presumably enhancing one's skills). In the words of the NCCSS investigators (Whitebook et al., 1989), "little financial incentive exists for teaching staff to obtain more education, training, or experience." Only 42% of the childcare staff in the NCCSS received merit increases (Whitebook et al., 1989). The same situation appears to exist in early intervention settings, where in a recent survey, only 38% of staff reported receiving merit increases (Kontos & File, 1992).

Finally, the early childhood and early

intervention fields do not provide career ladders that would serve as an incentive for staff to obtain additional training. In the NCCSS, opportunities for advancement ranked in the bottom third of childcare providers' satisfaction with different aspects of their work (Whitebook et al., 1989). Similarly, early intervention staff have expressed a lack of satisfaction with opportunities for promotion (Kontos & File, 1992).

In sum, incentives for participation in staff development are likely to be intrinsic rather than extrinsic. Furthermore, disincentives such as lack of time and formal recognition for staff development need to be addressed (see section on Barriers).

ASSUMPTIONS ABOUT SETTINGS AND BEST PRACTICES

Settings

The function of staff development for regular early childhood staff whose classrooms are integrated will depend not just on their prior training, licensing, and the type of program in which they work. It will also depend on whether regular early childhood education programs are viewed by early intervention professionals as potential integrated early intervention sites as demonstrated below. The opinions of early intervention professionals will also affect the way in which the integrated program fits into children's overall early intervention plans. Regular early childhood programs can serve as the only early intervention site for children with disabilities, or as supplements to segregated programs. They may serve as a comprehensive developmental program for children with disabilities, or purely as a "socialization" experience, with no emphasis on cognitive,

language, or other nonsocial developmental domains. Teachers in a program that serves as the only intervention site for children with disabilities will have different staff development needs than those whose program serves as a supplement.

How do early intervention specialists typically view regular early childhood programs? One key indicator is provided in the Division of Early Childhood (DEC) White Paper on least restrictive environment and social integration (McLean & Odom, 1988). In this paper, McLean and Odom made certain distinctions between mainstreamed educational and noneducational settings. Educational programs included pre-kindergarten, kindergarten, and Head Start. Noneducational programs included nursery school and daycare. From an early intervention perspective, these distinctions are likely to affect community integrated placement decisions. Noneducational early childhood settings will be used, more often than not, as a supplement to the segregated educational site, and will primarily focus on socialization experiences. Educational early childhood settings may be more likely to be used to meet the comprehensive program needs of a child with disabilities. Based on these assumptions regarding typical characteristics of early childhood program types, the vast majority of early childhood settings (i.e., nursery school and childcare programs) may be viewed as being deficient from an educational perspective. As a case in point, Templeman, Fredericks, and Udell (1989) suggested that childcare programs may be considered inappropriate for integration because most lack an educational program. They suggested that, with the involvement of early childhood special educators, a childcare program can be brought up to early intervention standards.

From a regular early childhood educator's point of view, such distinctions are not only pointless, but also inaccurate. To them, how educational a setting is depends less on program type than on program characteristics, such as developmental appropriateness (Bredekamp, 1989). Thus, any type of early childhood program could serve as a comprehensive integrated early intervention site, since the characteristics of good programs cut across the categories of program types. In other words, childcare programs are not, by definition, less educational than any other type of early childhood program.

Practices

One potential reason for disagreement between regular early childhood educators and early intervention specialists about early childhood programs is the fact that they make different assumptions about what is appropriately educational for infants, toddlers, and preschoolers. This is partly due to the fact that the theoretical underpinnings of early intervention are different from those of regular early childhood education. Early intervention curricula have been most heavily influenced by behaviorism (Odom & McEvoy, 1990). Behaviorism, when applied to early intervention, has given rise to a traditional academic, teacher-centered approach with a de-emphasis on play and an emphasis on pre-academic and adaptive skills (Wolery & Brookfield-Norman, 1988).

The regular early childhood approach to infant and preschool programming is at odds with traditional early intervention approaches. Regular early childhood educators are trained to view hands-on learning within the context of play as best practice. Based on maturationist and constructivist theories, play is considered to be the most viable mode of learning for young children (DeVries & Kohlberg, 1987;

Rogers & Sawyers, 1988). Traditional academic approaches to learning (e.g., repetitive teaching of isolated skills out of context, reliance on teacher-directed activities) are considered to be inappropriate (Bredekamp, 1989), stressful (Burts, Hart, Charlesworth, & Kirk, 1990), and unlikely to lead to changes in children's thinking (Kamii, 1982). The preference is for child-centered, rather than teacher-centered, classrooms, where children select their own play/learning materials from the choices made available to them by the teacher, whose role is to facilitate children's learning, rather than to dispense knowledge. The teacher's role of facilitator involves organizing and equipping the classroom to make it a stimulating yet nurturing environment, as well as enhancing children's interactions with peers, adults, and materials (Hendrick, 1990). Programs based on this approach may appear to be noneducational to a person not trained in the methods of early childhood education.

Early interventionists are beginning to extol the value of play and of a focus on age-appropriate skills and instructional strategies for children with disabilities (McDonnell & Hardman, 1988; Odom & McEvoy, 1990; Salisbury & Vincent, 1990). But in practice, play is more likely to be viewed as an assessment device or as an intervention goal (Bailey, 1989; Fewell & Kaminski, 1988) than as a medium for learning. A recent survey of early intervention practices in Connecticut revealed that less than one fourth of the teachers used play as the primary mode of instruction (Mahoney, O'Sullivan, & Fors, 1989). Teachers of infants and toddlers are most likely to use assessment protocols. Thus, while differences in assumptions about settings and practices between regular and special early childhood educators may be slowly diminishing, substantial differences among practitioners remain.

IMPLICATIONS FOR STAFF DEVELOPMENT

It is logical that early interventionists who define best practice as pre-academic instruction would judge most typical early childhood settings with play-based curricula, and childcare in particular, as being noneducational. Using this logic, it is also understandable that early interventionists who integrate children with disabilities into regular early childhood programs would perceive a need to either supplement the noneducational integrated setting with an educational program in another setting, provide staff development to the early childhood educators so that their program can become more educational, or both. There is a pervasive assumption that the primary, if not the only, targets of staff development to promote integration are regular early childhood educators (e.g., Klein & Sheehan, 1987; Peterson, 1983; Templeman et al., 1989). This assumption implies that the attitudes and skills of early intervention specialists that are relevant to integration are not deficient—even if their training and experience has focused on segregated, special education settings. In other words, early childhood special educators are likely to assume the expert role for themselves when implementing integration and assign the novice role to regular early childhood educators. Such a well-meaning but somewhat condescending approach to staff development by early intervention specialists may backfire if regular early childhood educators feel that it is a step in the wrong direction, or that their own expertise is being devalued or disregarded. This could easily happen as a result of the difference in the-

oretical assumptions and in the definitions of best practice espoused by these two groups. Assuming neither field has a lock on the truth, staff development is more likley to be successful if early intervention specialists shed the expert role and take on a collaborative approach that recognizes and values the knowledge and expertise of all participants in the integration process (File & Kontos, in press; Pugach & Johnson, 1989).

The characteristics and assumptions of regular and special early childhood educators suggest that successful integration of children with disabilities into regular early childhood settings will require staff development for both groups. Differences between regular and special early childhood educators in previous training and in their responsibilities to children who are placed in integrated settings dictate differences in the content of the two groups' staff development programs. Previous training is unlikely to have given early childhood educators information on or experience with the development of children with disabilities, with early intervention terminology, or with behavioral strategies. Other areas in which early childhood educators' previous training is likely to be deficient are adapting the environment to meet the needs of children with disabilities, setting specific goals, and tracking students' progress. Early childhood educators have also reported a need to better understand the early intervention service delivery system (Shuster & Kontos, 1991).

Early interventionists, however, are typically trained in general special education programs, without a specialization in early childhood (Kontos & Dunn, 1989). Thus, their needs are generally in the areas of knowledge of, and exposure to, normal development in young children, as well as the rationale for and implementation of developmentally appropriate practices. In a recent survey of early interventionists (Shuster & Kontos, 1991), over half reported a need to learn about the perspective of regular early childhood educators, although most did not express a need to learn about normal child development.

Both groups need to devote attention to the application of developmentally appropriate practices to children with special needs, since, in some instances, changes must be made in teaching strategies (e.g., for children whose physical disabilities make child-initiation of activities in the traditional sense impossible). More work needs to be done in this area, because the guidelines developed by the National Association for the Education of Young Children (Bredekamp, 1989) barely mention children with special needs, and the Division for Early Childhood of the Council for Exceptional Children has not yet formally addressed the issue of developmentally appropriate practices for young children with special needs.

When children with disabilities are placed in integrated community early childhood programs, even for part of their day, early interventionists are no longer the only educators working with the children, and, in many instances, the responsibilities of the early interventionist evolve from those of direct service to those of indirect service to the children. In other words, instead of being a teacher of children with disabilities, an early interventionist becomes a consultant to regular early childhood teachers who are now teachers of children both with and without disabilities. As a result of integration those regular early childhood teachers are not only newly responsible for children with disabilities, they also must now consult with an early interventionist (File & Kontos, in press). Inservice and preservice personnel

training for early childhood special educators rarely includes instruction in integration or collaborative consultation (Bailey, 1989; McCollum, 1987). Staff development that emphasizes the process of collaborative consultation is necessary if the success of integration is to be maximized.

EARLY INTERVENTION PROGRAMS THAT FOCUS ON STAFF DEVELOPMENT

Federal funding has supported the development of several (demonstration and inservice training) early intervention programs with an emphasis on staff development equivalent to that placed on services to children. Interestingly, three of these programs were developed for family daycare settings, the most readily available childcare setting, but the least likely to include trained caregivers. Another focused primarily, but not exclusively, on early interventionists. Below, the authors briefly describe the staff development components of these four programs and report on program evaluations. These descriptions will serve as exemplars of the process and content of staff development for regular and special early childhood educators.

The Family Day Care Project

The Family Day Care Project demonstration program trained family daycare providers in Michigan to care for young children with special needs (Jones & Meisels, 1987). Its goals were three-fold: 1) to teach caregivers about the characteristics of children with special needs; 2) to promote high-quality interactions between caregivers and all children, regardless of developmental status; and 3) to increase caregivers' knowledge of child development, especially knowledge that would be useful when planning appropriate activities and environments for children with and without special needs. To reach these goals, a 1-year training program was developed.

The training year began with a 13-part workshop series focusing on general child development and children with special needs. Following these workshops, one or two children with disabilities were integrated into each caregiver's family daycare home. Most of the children also received early intervention services from their school districts. Following the placement of a child, the caregiver received biweekly visits from a special services coordinator, whose job it was to deal with issues regarding integration of the special needs children into typical home activities, and to promote optimal caregiving in each daycare home. Caregivers also had access to a toy lending library, an information resource center, and medical and educational consultants when necessary.

Jones and Meisels (1987) evaluated the success of the training by comparing the caregivers' attitudes toward children with special needs, their knowledge about integrating children with special needs, and their ability to facilitate children's development through quality childcare prior to, and following, training. Results of the evaluation revealed that the caregivers' attitudes toward young children with special needs did not change following training (they were generally positive to begin with). However, their knowledge about integration was significantly greater, as was the quality of care that they provided. Correlations between the demographic characteristics of the caregivers and the change in scores indicated that these improvements were positively related to experience with children with special needs, amount of formal education, and contact with other caregivers.

These data attest to the efficacy of the training program and suggest that the impact of training may be influenced by caregivers' professionalism and previous experience. However, the design of the study does not allow causal inferences to be made regarding the training, as there was no control group, and the sample size, 13 trainees, was extremely small. Thus, the authors cautioned that results should not be generalized until replicated.

Project Neighborcare

Project Neighborcare was another demonstration project focusing on family daycare (Kontos, 1988). The purpose of this project was to develop a model that would make a full-time family daycare placement viable as an early intervention setting for young children with special needs. The goal was to provide normalized, integrated early intervention services for preschool children with special needs who had working parents in the most prevalent form of childcare, family daycare. Emphasis was placed on maintaining the typical advantages of family daycare (e.g., flexibility, home-like setting), while increasing the rigor of the program to improve its credibility as an early intervention measure. A three-part training program was developed to address these issues.

The first step of training was the initial skills assessment, in which caregivers' strengths and weakness in childcare and early intervention skills were assessed. The initial skills assessment set the stage for the other two components of training and allowed training to be individualized. The second step of training was a series of orientation workshops. Six weekly, 3-hour workshops were conducted in order to increase caregivers' knowledge and awareness regarding each topic and, if necessary, to put caregivers at ease about serving young children with special needs. (Behavior change was not expected to occur as a result of the workshops alone; it was assumed that a more intensive, individualized aproach would be required.) Workshop topics included special needs, quality family daycare, program planning, tracking progress, teaching strategies, behavior management, and working with parents.

The third and most important component of training was the weekly, individual, on-site consultation with each caregiver. This aspect of training was designed to influence the behavior of the caregivers. At the beginning of this step, the consultant and the caregiver developed an individual mastery plan (IMP) based on the initial skills assessment, the needs of the children who were to be served, and the caregiver's personal goals. The purpose of the IMP was to help the consultant individualize the consultation portion of the training, as well as to recognize and reward good work on the part of the caregivers. Consultants could also provide caregivers with support, information, and technical assistance in the form of demonstration, observation and feedback, discussion, or provision of additional resources (e.g., articles to read, adaptive toys).

Project Neighborcare was evaluated in terms of quality of childcare (based on an observation rating scale), early intervention skills (self-ratings of what skills caregivers possessed versus what items on a list of prerequisite skills they felt they still needed to develop), and the social validity of intervention outcomes. Results of the evaluation revealed that 10 months following the initial skills assessment, caregivers' quality of childcare had improved, as had their early intervention skills. Social validity of the intervention was determined by interviews with key adults involved with the program (caregivers,

parents, early intervention professionals in the community). In their interviews, caregivers indicated that they believed the training had prepared them to provide early intervention services, but that they would need the continual support and assistance of the consultant. From their perspective, the training they had received helped them improve the quality of care they provided and benefited all the children, not just the ones with special needs.

The parents of children with special needs were also positive about Project Neighborcare, but did not attribute its successes to the training program itself. Rather, parents simply noticed the benefits of having their child in an integrated setting and tended to attribute their child's recent progress to these benefits. However, they did not perceive of the services that their child received in family daycare as early intervention—to them intervention and segregated programming were synonymous.

In contrast to the caregivers and the parents, early intervention professionals in the community had reservations about Project Neighborcare, perceiving it as an attempt to teach in six workshops what others learn in college degree programs. The professionals did not perceive the ongoing consultation visits as training and questioned the abilities of family daycare providers to understand and deal with children with special needs.

The results of the Project Neighborcare evaluation suggest that training and supervision may make family daycare a viable early intervention setting. As with Jone's and Meisel's work (1987), these inferences were based on a very small sample and a research design that does not allow causal inferences to be made. The results also suggest that, in spite of the intensive training process, special educators may not overcome initial reservations about placing children with special needs in family daycare homes for other than simple supervision or supplemental services. These reservations may also stem from assumptions in the field regarding what kinds of early childhood settings are likely to be educational (McLean & Odom, 1988).

Delaware FIRST

Another demonstration project concerned with family daycare providers, Delaware FIRST (Deiner & Whitehead, 1988) was designed to provide full- or part-time respite care for parents of infants with special needs, an integrated setting for those infants, and training for family daycare providers in providing infant stimulation as outlined in the individualized family service plan (IFSP). This project consisted of recruiting a bank of family daycare providers who were willing to provide services to infants with special needs, and conducting a 16-hour general training course. The general training course included topics such as normal and atypical development, teaching infants and toddlers with special needs, supporting families, utilizing family resources, and getting support. Once a family had been matched with a particular caregiver in the bank, that caregiver was given an additional 6 hours of specific training to prepare her to work with the particular infant. The infant was then placed, and the caregiver received visits from an early childhood special educator twice a month. Caregivers also had access to a toy-lending library and received a monthly newsletter. While no evaluation data were presented, Deiner and Whitehead (1988) reported that they had been successful in meeting the needs of family daycare providers who offered respite services.

Best Practices in Integration

Best practices in integration (BPI) is an inservice training model for persons delivering services to infants, toddlers, and preschool children with special needs within community-based early childhood settings (Shuster & Kontos, 1989). The key components of the model are systems change enacted through community resource networks, a training process to foster knowledge of and skills in collaboration and consultation with early intervention specialists, and a technical assistance process to facilitate both the integration of young children with special needs into regular early childhood programs and successful collaboration between early intervention consultants and early childhood educators (Shuster & Kontos, 1991). This model assumes that successful integration of young children with special needs into regular early childhood programs will require new skills and role changes on the part of early intervention specialists. To assist the direct service provider, early childhood special educators must learn to provide indirect, consultative services to children. The early childhood educator must also learn about consultation, as well as early intervention.

The BPI model was designed, in part, to fill the gap in special and regular early childhood staff knowledge and skills that is created by the role changes necessary for integration. To this end, three modules were developed. Two modules on integration focus on the rationale for and components of successful integration and the role changes required for integration. One module on collaborative consultation focuses on the consultant role, interpersonal and communication skills, and collaborative problemsolving.

Following their introduction to collaborative consultation through the presentation of these modules in workshop format, early childhood special educators becoming consultants are given 2 months of technical assistance as they initiate the integration of young children with special needs into community-based regular early childhood programs. This technical assistance may take many forms, including problemsolving discussions, collaborative review of child or setting data, and, if requested, joint classroom and setting visitations, called *shadowing*. During this time, early childhood special education consultants may also request and receive assistance with planning and implementing training workshops for the regular early childhood staff who provide direct services to the children with special needs. Evaluation of this model is still in progress.

Summary

These four programs have several notable similarities and differences. It may be no coincidence that the three demonstration programs reported here all focused on family daycare. As the most common form of out-of-home care for preschool children, family daycare's schedules are generally more flexible than those of childcare centers, and the service is available in conveniently located neighborhood homes. It is also a mixed-age setting, which means that knowledge of several developmental levels can be expected of the caregiver. Making family daycare available, via staff development, to working parents of children with special needs, is another way to promote the normalization of services. Also, the fact that staff development can succeed with family daycare providers, the least-trained segment of regular early childhood personnel, is encouraging. From a survey of childcare center staff, Powell and Stremmel (1989) reported that mini-

mally trained staff read professional publications and attended conferences less often, and felt that conferences were less helpful, than their more highly trained counterparts. Because they are less entrenched in traditional methods of professional development, minimally trained staff appear to offer the greatest challenge to planning effective staff development activities.

One critical similarity among the four programs is that of extending the notion of training or staff development beyond workshops. Although each program included workshops in some form, they also followed up with some type of individualized assistance on a regular basis. This practice is consistent with that of other model integrated childcare programs (Bagnato, Kontos, & Neisworth, 1987) and with evidence that on-site follow-along with staff is more effective than one-time workshops (Klein & Sheehan, 1987). On-site follow-along for the family daycare providers was conducted by an early intervention specialist, typically an early childhood special educator. This role is similar to the consulting teacher model developed for public school integration efforts (Huefner, 1988).

Each of the three family daycare demonstration projects assumed that the primary staff development needs were those of the regular early childhood staff. The assumption made by the BPI inservice training model was that early intervention specialists also needed new attitudes, knowledge, and skills to successfully facilitate integration, and that the target content should include integration and collaborative consultation. The latter assumption is more in keeping with the position that the authors have taken in this chapter.

A prime difference among the three programs was the rationale for placing a child. The Family Day Care Project supplemented a school-based early intervention program for most of its children. Project Neighborcare was designed to be a full-time childcare/early intervention program for those who needed it. And Delaware FIRST provided respite care for parents, along with infant stimulation for the children. Interestingly, community early intervention specialists had reservations about Project Neighborcare, the full-time program, that they did not have about the other two programs. Perhaps this is an example of training success and marketing failure. In order for staff development to promote successful integration of children with special needs into regular programs, special educators must be willing to entrust the children to these programs. Trust may be easier to come by when an integrated program is supplemental to a more traditional early intervention program and functions purely as social integration. To get beyond this, negative stereotypes of regular early childhood settings may need to be addressed in staff development for early intervention specialists, not just knowledge and skills concerning integration and collaborative consultation.

BARRIERS TO EFFECTIVE STAFF DEVELOPMENT

The authors have taken the position that, as early intervention and early childhood education staff assume new roles associated with the integration of young children with special needs into community-based early childhood programs, a collaborative approach is essential. Moreover, the authors maintain that staff development, rather than reliance on previous experience and training, is necessary for all involved to acquire the knowledge and skills required by their new collaborative roles.

As is often the case, this is easier said than done. Some common barriers to effective staff development must be anticipated and eliminated if they are not to stymie its implementation. This discussion of potential barriers to effective staff development is not meant to be exhaustive, but to highlight some of the most common issues that early intervention and early childhood education professionals implementing staff development should consider.

Resistance to Change

Early childhood and early intervention staff may be resistant to staff development activities because of the changes that they imply. As direct service providers, early childhood education staff may be particularly prone to resistance. They may consider staff development activities intended to facilitate changes in their classroom practices as intrusive (Friend & Bauwens, 1988; Witt, 1986). However, integration leads to many changes in the roles of early intervention staff as well. Staff who do not wholeheartedly embrace their new role as an indirect service provider also tend to resist staff development activities intended to facilitate this role change. Indeed, a recent study based on interviews and participant observation at community planning meetings clearly indicated that concerns about integration and resistance to change were not restricted to any one group, but were expressed by participants from both regular and special education (Peck, Hayden, Wandschneider, Peterson, & Richarz, 1989).

Resistance is likely to be most acute when professionals feel excluded from the change process. Therefore, one task for the field will be to structure the integration process in ways that maximize the involvement of both groups—early interventionists and early childhood educators

—at all phases, including the staff development phase.

To the same extent that the expertise of early childhood educators is not acknowledged, staff development efforts aimed at them are likely to meet with resistance. When efforts are made to acknowledge and make use of the expertise of all those involved in staff development activities, resistance is likely to be reduced. The task for the field will be to design staff development models that build on the existing strengths of staff and are based on the principles of empowerment (Witt & Martens, 1988). This task is obviously more challenging when staff have little or no formal education beyond high school (e.g., family daycare providers and early intervention classroom aides).

Time

As mentioned above, time is a particularly precious commodity for early childhood staff who have full-day responsibilities for children in childcare centers and family daycare homes. It should not be assumed, however, that time for staff development activities is any more plentiful for early intervention staff. Without the assurance that time is available for staff to participate, planning staff development activities is a futile pursuit.

Thus, another task for the field will be to reconfigure job responsibilities to accommodate staff development activities. In view of their normally full slate of responsibilities, staff cannot be expected to subsidize these activities by donating time. Neither can professionals expect children and families to bear the brunt of these activities by closing programs to make time for staff development. Creative solutions to this problem will be required, particularly for family daycare providers who typically have sole responsibility for the

children in their care. Providing substitutes and allowing staff to take "comp time" for time spent in training outside the typical workday hours are two solutions that some programs have used successfully. Finding solutions to the time problem, and the resources to pay for these solutions, may be easier if there is widespread agreement on the importance of staff development to successful integration.

The use of consultation models (Deiner & Whitehead, 1988; Jones & Meisels, 1987; Kontos, 1988) is a partial solution to the time barrier. On-site consultation reduces the amount of time spent in formal workshops away from the children, and results in more individualized facilitation of professional growth. To date, there has been only limited empirical study of the effective use of consultation models in integrated early childhood settings (see Hanson & Widerstrom, chap. 8, this volume; Peck, Killen, & Baumgart, 1989). However, there is a great deal of literature on the use of consultation services in settings with older children (see File & Kontos [in press] for applications of this literature to early intervention settings).

Staff Turnover

Recent surveys of early intervention staff have documented annual turnover rates across personnel categories ranging from 18.5% (Palsha et al., 1990) to 30.5% (Kontos & Dunn, 1989). If these figures are disconcerting, the most recent estimate of 41% annual turnover for childcare center staff (Whitebook et al., 1989) is nothing short of alarming. When personnel changes occur at this rate, the benefits of staff development dissipate almost as fast as they are accrued. Thus, overcoming this barrier is crucial.

Along with increasing salaries and developing career ladders that could promote staff retention (Kontos & File, 1992; Whitebook et al., 1989), the task facing the field is to design staff development models with an ongoing rather than static nature, in order to accommodate staff turnover. Obviously, it would be ineffective to rely solely on periodic formal workshops for staff development. As staff members leave, they take what they have learned with them and, more often than not, are replaced by novices. The use of mentoring and consulting models of staff development will continue to promote the professional growth of staff members in between more formal group experiences.

Incompatible Theories and Practices

As discussed previously, early intervention and early childhood education have traditionally been based on different theories and utilized different practices with young children. When staff development is conducted with the purpose of enhancing integrated environments for young children in community early childhood programs, this difference in approaches becomes an immediate concern. Can staff development models be designed that are sensitive to these differences?

Staff development models that attempt to wholly impose one field's methods on the other are doomed to fail. The challenge, then, is to develop effective programming for young children with special needs that incorporates the strengths of both early intervention and early childhood education. Early intervention professionals cannot assume that all teaching practices from segregated programs will work, or are desirable, in integrated settings. However, early childhood education professionals must adapt to increased needs for accountability in their programs through assessment and tracking of prog-

ress, and must take on new teaching strategies they have previously avoided (e.g., contingency management). Dogmatism on the part of either group is a barrier that will doom staff development efforts before they begin. This particular barrier is a difficult one to resolve and will require candid interdisciplinary discussions between practitioners, those involved in personnel preparation and curriculum development, and leaders of professional organizations (i.e., DEC and NAEYC), as well as flexibility and the willingness on everyone's part to consider new ideas rather than resist change.

SUMMARY

There was no need for the authors to "defend" staff development in this chapter, since there seems to be a consensus in the field that it is a good thing. It is more important to understand the circumstances under which staff development is most likely to be effective. Thus, the primary goal of this chapter is to examine the context in which staff development is likely to take place (i.e., settings, people, assumptions) when its purpose is to promote the successful integration of young children with special needs into community-based regular early childhood programs. Staff development focused on integration may be more complicated than usual, since it typically involves professionals from multiple agencies and disciplines.

There are three reasons why staff development for all professionals involved with the integration of children with special needs is critical: 1) the new skills and purposes required of early childhood and early intervention staff and settings, 2) the differences between early intervention and early childhood specialists in their assumptions about early childhood settings and practices, and 3) the new roles that all staff must assume when early intervention services are delivered in integrated regular early childhood settings. The authors propose that staff development designed to facilitate integration should not only expand the traditional knowledge and skills of staff, but should also focus on integration itself, the role changes it brings about, and the collaborative consultation process that allows all professionals to have a stake in the outcome. Because of the differences in viewpoints between early intervention and early childhood staff brought about by differences in training and theoretical assumptions, in order to achieve a greater unity of perspectives, negotiation may have to be the first step in the staff development process. This implies the use of dialogue, rather than didactic methods, particularly in the early stages of staff development.

The authors' review of the literature suggests that relying on workshops as the sole form of staff development is less efficacious than mentoring or consultation, whether used alone or paired with workshops. Moreover, mentoring or consultation efforts should be collaborative in nature, so that the expertise of all professionals is valued and utilized for successful integrated early childhood programs. The potential barriers to effective staff development are many, and they will require creative problem-solving. But the eventual reward for removing the barriers will be effective collaboration between the separate fields of early childhood and early childhood special education. And the ultimate reward may be the eventual *blending* of the fields, such that not only children's services, but the disciplines as well, are integrated into a single discipline focused on optimal learning and development for *all* young children.

REFERENCES

Bagnato, S., Kontos, S., & Neisworth, J. (1987). Integrated day care as special education: Profiles of programs and children. *Topics in Early Childhood Special Education, 7,* 28–47.

Bailey, D.B., Jr. (1989). Issues and directions in preparing professionals to work with young handicapped children and their families. In J. Gallagher, P. Trohanis, & R. Clifford (Eds.), *Policy implementation and PL 99-457: Planning for young children with special needs* (pp. 97–132). Baltimore: Paul H. Brookes Publishing Co.

Bredekamp, S. (1989). *Developmentally appropriate practice in early childhood programs serving children from birth through age 8* (2nd ed.). Washington, DC: National Association for the Education of Young Children.

Burts, D., Hart, C., Charlesworth, R., & Kirk, L. (1990). A comparison of frequencies of stress behaviors observed in kindergarten children in classrooms with developmentally appropriate versus developmentally inappropriate instructional practices. *Early Childhood Research Quarterly, 5,* 407–423.

Children's Foundation. (1990). *1990 family day care licensing study.* Washington, DC: Author.

Deiner, P., & Whitehead, L. (1988). Levels of respite care as a family support system. *Topics in Early Childhood Special Education, 8,* 51–61.

DeVries, R., & Kohlberg, L. (1987). *Programs of early education: The constructivist view.* White Plains, NY: Longman, Inc.

Divine-Hawkins, P. (1981). *Family day care in the United States: Executive summary.* (Final report of the National Day Care Home Study). (ERIC Document Reproduction Service No. ED 211 224)

Fewell, R.R., & Kaminski, R. (1988). Play skills development and instruction for young children with handicaps. In S.L. Odom & M.B. Karnes (Eds.), *Early intervention for infants and children with handicaps: An empirical base* (pp. 145–158). Baltimore: Paul H. Brookes Publishing Co.

File, N., & Kontos, S. (in press). Indirect service delivery through consultation: Review and implications for early intervention. *Journal of Early Intervention.*

Fischer, J. (1989). *Family day care: Factors in-*

fluencing the quality of caregiving practices. Unpublished doctoral dissertation, University of Illinois, Champaign-Urbana, IL.

Friend, M., & Bauwens, J. (1988). Managing resistance: An essential consulting skill for learning disability teachers. *Journal of Learning Disabilities, 21,* 556–561.

Guskey, T. (1986). Staff development and the process of teacher change. *Educational Researcher, 15,* 5–11.

Hanson, M. (1990). *Final report: California early intervention personnel model, personnel standards, and personnel preparation plan.* Sacramento: California Department of Developmental Services, Community Service Division.

Hendrick, H. (1990). *Total learning: Developmental curriculum for the young child* (3rd ed.). New York: MacMillan Publishing.

Hofferth, S., & Phillips, D. (1987). Child care in the United States, 1970 to 1995. *Journal of Marriage and the Family, 49,* 559–571.

Huefner, D. (1988). The consulting teacher model: Risks and opportunities. *Exceptional Children, 54,* 403–414.

Hutson, H.M. (1981). Inservice best practices: The learning of general education. *Journal of Research and Development in Education, 14,* 1–10.

Jones, S., & Meisels, S. (1987). Training family day care providers to work with special needs children. *Topics in Early Childhood Special Education, 7,* 1–12.

Kamii, C. (1982). *Number in preschool and kindergarten.* Washington, DC: National Association for the Education of Young Children.

Klein, N., & Sheehan, R. (1987). Staff development: A key issue in meeting the needs of young handicapped children in day care settings. *Topics in Early Childhood Special Education, 7,* 13–27.

Kontos, S. (1988). Family day care as an integrated early intervention setting. *Topics in Early Childhood Special Education, 8,* 1–14.

Kontos, S. (1992). *Family day care: Out of the shadows and into the limelight.* Washington, DC: National Association for the Education of Young Children.

Kontos, S., & Dunn, L. (1989). Characteristics of the early intervention workforce: An Indiana perspective. *Early Education and Development, 1,* 141–157.

Kontos, S., & File, N. (1992). Conditions of employment, job satisfaction, and job commitment among early intervention personnel. *Journal of Early Intervention, 16,* 155–165.

Kontos, S., & Stremmel, A. (1988). Caregivers' perceptions of working conditions in a child care environment. *Early Childhood Research Quarterly, 3,* 77–90.

Mahoney, G., O'Sullivan, P., & Fors, S. (1989). Special education practices with young handicapped children. *Journal of Early Intervention, 13,* 261–268.

McCollum, J. (1987). Early interventionists in infant and early childhood programs: A comparison of preservice training needs. *Topics in Early Childhood Special Education, 7,* 24–35.

McDonnell, A., & Hardman, M. (1988). A synthesis of "best practice" guidelines for early childhood services. *Journal of the Division for Early Childhood, 12,* 328–341.

McLean, M., & Odom, S. (1988). *Least restrictive environment and social integration.* Division for Early Childhood White Paper. Reston, VA: Council for Exceptional Children.

Modigliani, K. (1986). But who will take care of the children? Childcare, women and devalued labor. *Journal of Education, 68,* 46–69.

Odom, S., & McEvoy, M. (1990). Mainstreaming at the preschool level: Potential barriers and tasks for the field. *Topics in Early Childhood Special Education, 10,* 48–61.

Palsha, S., Bailey, D., Vandiviere, P., & Munn, D. (1990). A study of employee stability and turnover in home-based intervention. *Journal of Early Intervention, 14,* 342–351.

Peck, C., Hayden, L., Wandschneider, M., Peterson, K., & Richarz, S. (1989). Development of integrated preschools: A qualitative inquiry into sources of resistance among parents, administrators, and teachers. *Journal of Early Intervention, 13,* 353–364.

Peck, C., Killen, C., & Baumgart, D. (1989). Increasing implementation of special education instruction in mainstream preschools: Direct and generalized effects of nondirective consultation. *Journal of Applied Behavior Analysis, 22,* 197–210.

Peterson, N. (1983). Personnel training for mainstreaming young handicapped children. In J. Anderson & T. Black (Eds.), *Mainstreaming in early education* (pp. 23–43). Chapel Hill, NC: Technical Assistance Development System.

Phillips, D., Lande, J., & Goldberg, M. (1990). The state of child care regulation: A comparative analysis. *Early Childhood Research Quarterly, 5,* 151–179.

Powell, D.R., & Stremmel, A.J. (1989). The relation of early childhood training and experience to the professional development of child care workers. *Early Childhood Research Quarterly, 4,* 339–355.

Pugach, M., & Johnson, L. (1989). The challenge of implementing collaboration between general and special education. *Exceptional Children, 56,* 334–342.

Rogers, C., & Sawyers, J. (1988). *Play in the lives of children.* Washington, DC: National Association for the Education of Young Children.

Ruopp, R., Travers, J., Glantz, F., & Coelen, C. (1979). *Child at the center: Final results of the national day care study.* Cambridge, MA: Abt Associates.

Salisbury, C., & Vincent, L. (1990). Criterion of the next environment and best practices: Mainstreaming and integration ten years later. *Topics in Early Childhood Special Education, 10,* 78–89.

Shuster, S., & Kontos, S. (1989). *Best practices in integration.* Proposal for funding submitted to the United States Department of Education Handicapped Children's Early Education Program.

Shuster, S., & Kontos, S. (1991). *Best practices in integration.* Year III continuation proposal submitted to the United States Department of Education Handicapped Children's Early Education Program.

Templeman, T., Fredericks, H.D.B., & Udell, T. (1989). Integration of children with moderate and severe handicaps into a daycare center. *Journal of Early Intervention, 13,* 315–328.

Whitebook, M., Howes, C., & Phillips, D. (1989). *Who cares? Child care teachers and the quality of care in America.* Oakland, CA: Child Care Employee Project.

Witt, J. (1986). Teachers' resistance to the use of school-based interventions. *Journal of School Psychology, 24,* 37–44.

Witt, J., & Martens, B. (1988). Problems with problemsolving consultation: A re-analysis of assumptions, methods, and goals. *School Psychology Review, 17,* 211–226.

Wolery, M.R., & Brookfield-Norman, J. (1988). (Pre)Academic instruction for handicapped preschool children. In S.L. Odom & M.B. Karnes (Eds.), *Early intervention for infants and children with handicaps: An empirical base* (pp. 109–128). Baltimore: Paul H. Brookes Publishing Co.

Wood, F., & Thompson, S. (1980). Guidelines for better staff development. *Educational Leadership, 37,* 374–378.

Chapter 10

INTEGRATED EARLY CHILDHOOD PROGRAMS
Research on the Implementation
of Change in Organizational Contexts

Charles A. Peck,
Gail Chase Furman,
and Edwin Helmstetter

Professionals, parents, and researchers have become increasingly aware of the difficulties of translating the policy initiatives defined in PL 94-142 and PL 99-457 into actual practice (Ballard-Campbell & Semmel, 1981; Winton, 1990). Despite the least restrictive environment (LRE) provisions in these laws, large numbers of children with special educational needs continue to be served in predominantly segregated settings more than 15 years after the passage of the legislation (Danielson & Bellamy, 1989). The limited implementation of early intervention services in integrated settings is particularly ironic because the research on integrated programs at the early childhood level has produced relatively clear evidence that integrated programs can benefit children with disabilities, while doing no harm to typical children (see Guralnick, 1990; Lamorey & Bricker, chap. 13, this volume; Odom & McEvoy, 1988; Peck & Cooke,

1983 for reviews of this research). In addition, research efforts have produced a substantial number of empirically validated intervention practices that help in achieving positive outcomes in integrated programs (e.g., Odom et al., 1988; Peck, Killen, & Baumgart, 1989; Strain & Odom, 1986). It seems that neither awareness of potentially positive outcomes, nor knowledge of relevant processes for achieving these outcomes, has been sufficient to promote widespread and systemic changes in actual practice.

One hypothesis that emerges from this state of affairs is that the aspects of integrated programs that define excellence at the level of children's growth and behavior change, and that have dominated the interest of researchers and program developers, may have relatively little to do with the factors that affect the implementation and maintenance of substantive changes in service delivery programs

(Baer, 1986). Indeed, a consideration of the literature on early childhood mainstreaming and integration, from the seminal Guralnick volume (1978) to the present, suggests that an implicit assumption of most researchers in this area has been that the success of integrated programs depends primarily on the availability of an effective educational technology—knowledge of how to educate children with disabilities in typical early childhood settings. While technical issues of pedagogy (e.g., the development of effective curriculum and instructional models) are obviously fundamental to the quality of integrated programs, they are not necessarily sufficient to guarantee the successful implementation and ongoing maintenance of such programs. On the contrary, the authors of this chapter argue that empirical studies of implementation suggest that sociopolitical rather than pedagogical factors have the greatest effect on the outcomes of implementation efforts. This suggests the importance of a more focused analysis of the integration process, and specifically the underlying sociopolitical issues that shape schools as social organizations, and that mediate the implementation of changes in policy and practice.

This analysis is carried out mainly at the *exosystem* level of Bronfenbrenner's (1979) ecological taxonomy of the factors that affect human development—that is, at the level of social organizations and institutions. The authors describe links between broader social-cultural values and ideology, the structure and process of educational organizations, and some of the practical problems that have been observed in the implementation of integrated programs. The chapter begins with some of the general findings of the research on the implementation of change in educational settings, and then proceeds to focus more directly on research on special education, and on the implementation of integrated programs in early childhood settings. The chapter concludes with some recommendations for those involved in program development efforts.

IMPLEMENTATION OF EDUCATIONAL CHANGE

The research literature on the implementation of changes in educational policy and practice is voluminous and diverse. Although a complete review of this research would be beyond the scope of the present chapter (see Firestone & Corbett, 1987; and Lieberman & Miller, 1986), the authors describe below two major studies of implementation that have important implications for understanding problems in the implementation of integrated programs at the early childhood level.

Perhaps the most widely cited work on the implementation of educational change has been the national evaluation of federal education policy initiatives that was conducted by the Rand Corporation in the 1970s (Berman & McLaughlin, 1976, 1978). The researchers used surveys and interviews to analyze the characteristics and outcomes of 293 educational change projects, and also conducted field-based case studies of 29 of the projects (Berman & McLaughlin, 1976). The results of the Rand study clarified the key role played by organizational dynamics in local education agencies (LEAs), including the motives and ideologies of local participants, in the adoption and institutionalization of changes in policy and practice. Moreover, in cases where the implementation of policy change was successful, the process was recognized as one of mutual adaptation rather than simple implementation of externally developed innovations. That is, the implementing agencies and the new policies or practices themselves were both modified to accommodate one another. The Rand study, as well as others of the same era, shifted the analysis of change efforts away from the rational/technical conceptualization of the implementation process that had dominated policy analysis up until that time. The view that emerged from this and other studies reflected a more sociopolitical perspective, one that recognized the values, beliefs, and culture of educational organizations and communities as powerful contextual conditions that constrain and shape the change process (Firestone & Corbett, 1987; Huberman & Miles, 1984).

A more recent analysis of local perspectives on policy change was carried out as part of a state-level effort to implement innovations in elementary school mathematics curriculum and instruction (Cohen & Ball, 1990; Darling-Hammond, 1990). An important methodological feature of this analysis was its detailed focus on the conceptual and practical responses of individual teachers to the mathematics policy initiative—that is, the study was intended to proceed from "the inside [of the classroom] out" (Cohen & Ball, 1990). The case studies of individual teachers are remarkable in their descriptions of the wide range of mutual adaptations that took place between the teachers' concepts and practices and the state-mandated changes in curriculum and instruction policy. For example, Peterson (1990) described how one teacher's own theories of child development affected her interpretation of the policy guidelines, leading her (with the best of intentions) to adopt practices that were very different from those recommended in the new curriculum framework. Other accommodations between newly mandated policies and existing practices

resulted from conflicts between extant testing and accountability procedures and the curriculum focus of the new approach, leading some teachers to make only a superficial investment in the newer methods, while still placing primary emphasis on traditional practices keyed to accountability policies (Wilson, 1990). Individual reactions to the new policy ranged from token compliance, to co-option of the policy to fit individual preferences and agendas, to serious attempts by some teachers to reconsider the conceptual and practical basis of mathematics education. However, an important finding in all of these case studies was that the implementation of changes in mathematics instruction in response to policy changes was *always* mediated by the teacher's prior beliefs and practices. At this level, as well as at more macro levels of policy implementation (e.g., Berman & McLaughlin, 1978), attempts to make policy changes and innovations are carried out in contexts that are rich with ideological, conceptual, and practical history.

These investigations suggest some basic postulates worthy of consideration during any effort to implement changes in educational policy and practice, including efforts to implement integrated programs in early childhood settings:

1. *Change efforts must entail careful consideration of the role that local sociopolitical conditions play in implementation of new policies.* The results of implementation studies strongly suggest that change is best viewed as transactional—that policy change efforts proceed within contexts that are charged with political agenda, organizational constraints, and social histories that are seldom, if ever, overridden by mandates.

2. *The change process begins where people are—ideologically, conceptually, and practically.* As the studies of individual teachers' responses to new ideas about the teaching of mathematics demonstrate, the practices that they actually implemented were built largely out of their prior knowledge, beliefs, and routines—not simply cut from the cloth of a new policy. This suggests the value of adopting a developmental model for anticipating, interpreting, and evaluating responses to policy change.

3. *The implementation process is deeply affected by the congruence of the values implicit in the policy with those held by local stakeholders in the education system* (Berman & McLaughlin, 1976). This may be particularly important when considering the implementation of change agendas that originate within special education, since the values underlying such agendas may be different from those operating within the larger educational organization, or within society (Sarason & Doris, 1979).

With the foregoing notions about the process of implementing change in mind, the authors now consider several studies of efforts to implement changes in policy and practice within the field of special education.

IMPLEMENTATION OF CHANGE IN SPECIAL EDUCATION

The research literature in the field of special education is notable for the relative lack of attention given to issues that arise during the actual implementation of reform efforts. This is especially interesting in view of the findings of the few studies of

policy implementation that have been carried out, which found major problems in translating the principles embodied in policy enactments such as PL 94-142 and PL 99-457 into actual practice (e.g., Mehan, Hertweck, & Meihls, 1986; Smith, 1982; Weatherley, 1979).

One particularly informative example of research on special education policy implementation was conducted by Weatherley and his associates (Weatherley, 1979; Weatherley & Lipsky, 1977). This study focused on the implementation of changes in special education policy mandated in the Massachusetts Chapter 766 legislation, a prototype for PL 94-142. The Weatherley study utilized an innovative design that described policy implementation activity from two contrasting points of view. One was the top-down viewpoint of state legislators and bureaucrats, who approached the policy implementation process with a traditional rational/technical strategy emphasizing regulation, training, and accountability. The second point of view was that of local implementors, the LEA administrators and teachers who were charged with the actual implementation of the law. Data for the study consisted of surveys, interviews, observations, and document analysis carried out within both the state and local implementation contexts over the course of a year.

The findings of Weatherley's investigation revealed serious problems in implementing the new special education law. For example, while the law called for individualized assessment and instructional planning, districts often resorted to the mass processing of assessments and individualized education program (IEP) decisions. Whereas the law was supposed to stimulate the development of individualized programs, Weatherley observed that children were routinely slotted into existing classroom programs as space was available. And although the law was intended to facilitate the placement of children with disabilities into regular classrooms, the study described the "wholesale shifting of responsibility for troublesome children from the regular class teacher to a specialist" (Weatherley, 1979, p. 116).

Perhaps the most important interpretive finding of the Weatherley study was that these seemingly inappropriate local responses to reform mandates could be seen as "coping" responses to local situations, in which the overwhelming demands of the new law were coupled with a scarcity of new resources to support implementation. Weatherley commented that "school personnel put forth extraordinary effort to comply with the new demands. However, there was simply no way that everything required could be done with the resources available" (Weatherley, 1979, p. 136). In addition, Weatherley observed that many of the goals of the legislation (e.g., its emphasis on assessment of child strengths and on maintaining children in regular classes) were ideologically at odds with the training of many special education and clinical professionals. The training of these professionals emphasized the identification and remediation of child deficits, often using a medical "isolate, fix, and return" model of service delivery. There were thus major questions about the extent to which the policies mandated by the new law were supported by many of the professionals who were responsible for implementing them.

More recent studies of the implementation of special education policies mandated by PL 94-142 attest to the robustness of many of Weatherley's findings. For example, Mehan et al. (1986) studied implementation of special education policy in California using micro-analysis of interactions videorecorded during referral and placement decisions. Decision processes for 140 students were followed over the course of 1 year. The results of this study revealed a sharp and ironic contrast between the highly rationalistic and technical decision processes prescribed in the laws governing special education (e.g., PL 94-142) and the profoundly sociopolitical processes that were found to underly decisions made during the IEP process. The researchers concluded that students were labeled as "handicapped" or not based on complex interactions between traits of the student, characteristics of the school, and personal viewpoints of the decision-makers. They described the career paths of these students as being determined in large part by the institutional practices of the school, which in turn reflected a set of ideological assumptions regarding the nature of disability (which was primarily viewed as residing "in the child") and its appropriate "treatment" (through diagnosis of the child's problem and prescription of educational interventions).

The foregoing studies as well as others (Fulcher, 1989; Reed, 1986; Richardson, Casanova, Placier, & Guilfoyle, 1989; Smith, 1982) suggest a view of special education that departs dramatically from the idealizations of technical precision and rationality outlined in legislation, program descriptions, and introductory textbooks. Studies of implementation suggest that practices within the field are driven as much by their organizational, political, and ideological contexts as they are by the technical considerations that are the focus of most professional discourse. The sociopolitical picture of special education that emerges from this research suggests that concepts such as appropriate education and least restrictive environment are implemented through local political negotiations in which the values, ideology, and needs of organizations and professionals are powerful interests. Such a conclusion does not imply that this state of affairs *necessarily* controverts the interests of children, but simply that it characterizes the sociopolitical ecology in which all implementation efforts take place.

A few studies have focused on the problem of implementing integrated programs from this sociopolitical perspective. The authors describe these studies below, and attempt to identify some of their implications for implementation efforts.

RESEARCH ON IMPLEMENTATION OF INTEGRATED EARLY CHILDHOOD EDUCATION PROGRAMS

The relative lack of systematic study of the actual implementation of integrated early childhood programs may reflect the assumption that programs that produce desirable outcomes for children will be implemented and maintained on their pedagogical merits. The authors' experience with several model demonstration programs that were successful at the level of child behavior change but not successfully maintained (Peck, Richarz, et al., 1989), as well as accounts from other model programs (Barber, Barber, & Clark 1983; Clarke, 1987), suggests that this assumption is problematic. More direct study of the problems of implementation is clearly needed.

One line of policy analysis work that promises to be of great value is currently being conducted by Smith and her colleagues (see Strain, 1991). This research, now in its early stages, will focus on identifying national and state policy incentives and disincentives for the development of integrated programs. Early results of this work indicate that substantial barriers to

integration are perceived by state and local special education administrators (see Strain & Smith, chap. 11, this volume).

Research by the authors and their colleagues (Peck, Furman, Helmstetter, & Reed, in preparation; Peck, Hayden, Wandschneider, Peterson, & Richarz, 1989; Peck, Richarz, et al., 1989) has focused on the problem of implementation at the local level. The work has attempted to clarify some factors affecting the development, implementation, and maintenance of integrated programs within specific school districts and early childhood education programs. Because of the relative lack of formal knowledge in this area, as well as the researchers' hypothesis that factors affecting the implementation of programs operate at multiple levels and in highly interactive ways, this work has relied on a qualitative research strategy. Thus, the authors have attempted holistic descriptions, rather than experimental manipulation of factors hypothesized to affect the success of program development efforts (Peck & Furman, 1992). Two studies of this type are summarized below.

Systemic Sources of Resistance to Integration

The authors' initial work was carried out within the context of efforts to develop integrated programs in eastern Washington State (Peck, Richarz, et al., 1989). A significant feature of the authors' work in these communities was its focus on political as well as pedagogical aspects of implementing integrated programs. The authors utilized interviews and participant observation strategies to investigate the initial concerns and issues arising in three communities involved in the development of integrated preschool programs. It was assumed that an adequate understanding of the sociopolitical ecology of each community would emerge only when the researchers understood the concerns and perspectives of all of the major individuals and interest groups that were required to support the ongoing implementation and maintenance of an integrated program. Thus, specific efforts were made to interview parents, teachers, and administrators from both early childhood and special education programs, as well as other clinical professionals (e.g., speech therapists, occupational therapists) who had a stake in the design of the program.

Analysis of interview data from 30 informants revealed 3 major types of concerns about integration. First, a concern for almost all of the parents, teachers, and administrators who were interviewed was the adequacy of the resources available to support an integrated program. Concerns included the adequacy of staff, materials, and time for coordination of a more complex program. A second category of concerns was the adequacy of preparation for integration (e.g., staff training, logistical planning). The third major type of concern was the potential for conflict among the individuals and groups involved (see Peck, Hayden, et al., 1989, for examples of the specific concerns raised).

While these specific concerns about integration were important in themselves, two additional findings of the study led to insights about the nature of the sociopolitical issues surrounding the integration process. First, interview data demonstrated that many of the individuals who were opposed or resistant to integration were simultaneously supportive of its underlying values and goals, and in many cases indicated that they actually thought that integrated programs would be better for children. One speech therapist articulated the conflicts in her views candidly, stating that while she believed in the social and educational values of integration, and even believed children learned language more readily in such programs, she was concerned that her professional role would be obscured in an integrated program. Several parents expressed concerns about the disruption of childcare arrangements, or loss of therapy time for their child. A second phenomenon, which the authors noticed during longitudinal observation of program planning processes, was that as some initially resistant individuals participated in direct deliberations and negotiations over the design of a new program, they became more willing to accept the ambiguities remaining in the revised program, even in some cases where their initial concerns were not actually resolved.

These dimensions of the study led to a better appreciation of the fact that established local programs represent the dynamic outcomes of a great deal of active but informal negotiation among administrators, teachers, and parents. The local "negotiated order" (Strauss, Schatzman, Ehrlic, Bucher, & Sabshin, 1963) was threatened by the integration process, which represented the destruction of established arrangements and the realignment of political interests within and across local agencies. This perspective clarified the political, rather than pedagogical, nature of many sources of resistance to integration that the authors observed. Specifically, the data suggested that the underlying concern of many of the stakeholders in the integrated program was that they would lose control of aspects of the existing program(s) for which they had informally negotiated favorable arrangements (see Peck, Hayden, et al., 1989, for examples). The authors' interpretation of changes that were observed in concerns about integration over time was that direct participation in the redesign of the program increased knowledge of the politics of the change process, and provided means by which individuals could maintain control of issues which were important to them. The important implications of this interpretation are taken up in the final section of this chapter.

FACTORS AFFECTING THE SURVIVAL OF INTEGRATED PROGRAMS

In a second qualitative study focusing on local implementation, the authors investigated factors affecting the maintenance of integrated preschool programs once they were established (Peck, 1989a; Peck, Furman, et al., in preparation). This retrospective study included interviews with individuals who had been directly involved in seven integrated programs in the states of Washington and California that had "retrenched" to segregation. In order to better understand the characteristics and histories of these programs, the authors also studied three examples of integrated programs that had survived over a period of at least 3 years. Cross-site analyses (Miles & Huberman, 1984) were used to identify factors that differentiated surviving and nonsurviving programs.

The data were interpreted using a context, process, outcome framework. *Context factors* that affected the survival of integrated programs were the background characteristics of the individuals, organizations, and communities involved. *Process factors* consisted of the specific activities implemented to develop and operate the program. *Outcome factors* were changes in the behavior, attitudes, and beliefs of program participants, including children, parents, and professionals. The most salient trends in the data are summarized be-

low. A more comprehensive analysis and interpretation of these data is underway as of 1992 (Peck, Furman, et al., in preparation).

Context Factors

The factors that differentiated the contexts of surviving and nonsurviving programs reflected the importance of congruence between the values and goals of the general educational community and those expressed in certain (egalitarian) perspectives on social integration. The authors found that communities that had a clearly articulated philosophy emphasizing acceptance of diversity among children, and that emphasized the importance of designing early childhood programs to support and accommodate variance in the learning characteristics of young children (Bredekamp, 1987) were more likely to maintain integrated programs (the extracts throughout the remainder of the chapter are from the authors' own research):

> We wanted to make sure that it was not an academic philosophy, that it was a developmental philosophy and an understanding of how kids learn—that there's plenty of things that the kids can do to work on the prewriting task rather than just sitting down and writing. (early childhood special education administrator)

> We have always believed that it doesn't matter whether kids learn to read in kindergarten or second grade—when they get in the sixth grade they're all about the same, so let's let them be kids a little while longer. (school district superintendent)

Conversely, communities whose programs were not grounded in a common philosophy had more difficulty in maintaining integrated programs:

> There was a little bit of a problem with some of the curriculum for the special ed kids being very academic in nature in terms of their IEPs, I mean, really working on writing their name or making a circle . . . at the co-op preschool that's just not our philosophy about early childhood education. (preschool teacher)

> . . . it was just not working. The philosophies were different, the teacher training was different . . . it was just not a workable situation, so it was in the best in-

terests of both parties that we asked them to move somewhere else. It was said in a nice polite way. (special education teacher)

A closely related factor that differentiated surviving and nonsurviving programs was the degree of cooperation, collaboration, and mutual respect between child development and special education staff in these communities. Nonsurviving programs were often characterized by acrimonious professional relationships, differentiation of professional "status," and intra- and inter-organizational competition for "ownership" and control of programs and children:

> . . . the Children's Center had a head teacher who was in charge of that entire program . . . and the special education teacher didn't feel she should be subjected to that type of structuring. She wanted to have more control of her own program. She didn't feel like the head teacher was qualified to be over her. (classroom aide)

> There seemed to be some reluctance on the part of the school district in believing that what we saw as valid child development theories and valid curriculum for early childhood, were [valid]. (preschool teacher)

While the point here is that the quality of professional relationships, and particularly the amount of mutual respect expressed across disciplines, was an important antecedent condition for successful integration, it was also found that if these conditions were not present initially, relationships often worsened during the integration process (see "Outcomes" below).

Process Factors

Two process factors strongly differentiated surviving and nonsurviving programs. First, the breadth and degree of collaboration and participation in designing the program and in making operating decisions for the program appeared to greatly affect its chances for survival. Several of the nonsurviving programs were essentially planned and implemented by ad-

ministrators or special education staff alone, without the substantive involvement of many of the other professionals, or of parents. In contrast, each of the surviving programs was the result of highly collaborative planning and decisionmaking processes involving both child development and special education professionals. Two of the surviving programs had also involved parents and community members in extensive dialogue and in planning sessions, leading to broadly held agreements regarding the values and goals underlying their efforts to develop an integrated program. Accounts of the history of the surviving programs included several explicit references to the importance of the community support generated through this type of program development process. For example:

> There is another school district near here and they chose to do it (develop an integrated preschool program) without the parent involvement. And because of that they haven't had the strong support, the ties to the community that our program has. There's not a group of people over there protecting the preschool like there is here. (district administrator)

The second process factor that differentiated surviving and nonsurviving programs was the compatibility between the design of special education instruction and the routines and practices of the child development setting in which these were to be implemented. Surviving programs involved more add-on instruction (e.g., before and after school, additional days) or naturalistic instruction that was embedded into typical preschool activities (Bricker & Cripe, 1992; Peck, Killen, & Baumgart, 1989). Nonsurviving programs were more likely to have relied on traditional special education instruction, using one-to-one massed trial direct instruction formats and pull-out services. The difficulty of implementing specialized, intensive instruction (using the traditional approaches) was one of the most frequent complaints about integration voiced by special education professionals in nonsurviving programs.

Outcomes

Outcomes were also very different in surviving and nonsurviving programs, with one important exception. The authors did *not* find evidence that outcomes for children were demonstrably different in surviving and nonsurviving programs. Changes in children were consistently described as being positive in both types of programs. Table 1 compares comments about child outcomes drawn from both surviving and nonsurviving programs.

The failure to detect differences in cognitive or affective outcomes for children across those programs should not be interpreted as conclusive evidence that such differences did not exist. The authors' interpretation of the interview data, however, is that child outcomes were not a factor contributing to the nonsurvival of integrated programs. Several of the professionals who were interviewed expressed similar views. For example, one special education teacher from a nonsurviving program stated:

> Overall I think it has always been a real success, even despite some teacher conflicts amongst ourselves. I think on the day-to-day basis of the classroom setting it really worked . . . it really worked well for the kids.

In contrast, increased conflict and dissatisfaction were common outcomes for adults involved in the nonsurviving programs. The focal points of conflict were philosophical differences between special

Table 1. Outcome descriptions from surviving and nonsurviving programs

Surviving programs	Nonsurviving programs
The parents and my preschool board have been 100% behind it. They found it was a benefit for their children as well as for the handicapped child.	We had about, at the end of the year we were running about 25 kids and we had quite an extensive waiting list of people wanting to put their (nonhandicapped) kids in the program.
We were going to do it because it was just the appropriate thing to do, not really thinking that the child would even really be aware of what was going on but what in fact we found was that three of our kids that are very severely involved both mentally and physically, all of a sudden they were smiling, which they haven't smiled in 2 or 3 years. And doing things that were just amazing to all of us. And we saw a lot of good from that happening for all the kids not just the handicapped kids.	Nobody ever got picked on, if anything they were protected.
	I had reams of paper to show the progress these kids had made. We were chopping off IEP goals left and right.
	. . . from the day it came in to today it has been a very positive experience with the growth and development of the kids.
We were real happy with the things that were happening especially for the handicapped child in the program. I mean her gains were phenomenal. They didn't show up real great on standardized testing because she was so low but, I mean, the parents saw her growth and the kinds, the parents of the regular ed. kids in the pre-school, they got so excited about seeing the handicapped child's progress.	I think on the day-to-day basis of the classroom it really worked . . . It really worked well for the kids. I think the positive outweighed the negative by far.
	And the other thing is that I see things happening with the more severely handicapped kids who definitely model after the peers.
We've had almost, no, I can't think of any, parent complaints about it at all.	I guess what I'll say is the integration of the children was very successful; the integration of the staff was not.

Extracts are from the authors' research.

educators and child development professionals, which typically led to struggles over control of time, activities, and programs for individual children. In five out of the seven nonsurviving programs studied, these conflicts led special educators to advocate withdrawal from the integrated program, citing their concerns about maintaining the quality of special education services. Of the other two programs, one was disbanded when grant funds ended and district special education administrators chose to pull children back into (segregated) district programs, and the other was disbanded because of administrative conflicts over classroom space. Some of the professionals from nonsurviving programs described their attitudes toward integration as becoming more negative as a result of their experiences in trying to implement an integrated program.

In surviving programs, adult relationships were highly, although not uniformly, positive. Professionals reported the experiences of collaborating and working in teams to be rewarding. While differences in opinion also arose in these programs, basic philosophical agreement and the use of relatively clear problemsolving strategies facilitated the negotiation of these difficulties. The professionals participating in these programs reported that their commitment to mainstreaming and social integration had increased greatly over the course of their involvement in the integrated program. One person put it clearly: "We would never go back" (to separate programs).

Summarizing the findings of this study, the authors hypothesized that context, process, and outcome factors all contributed significantly to the survival of integrated programs. None of the factors appeared to have a determinant effect on survival—there were no cases where a single context, process, or outcome variable exclusively predicted survival or nonsurvival. Rather, the authors conceptualized the nature of causal relationships between these factors as transactional, in the sense that they acted upon one another in a mutual and co-evolutionary fashion (Peck, 1989b). For example, the development (or nondevelopment) of a consensus program philosophy affected the likelihood that child development and special education professionals would adopt active and collegial problemsolving strategies when program difficulties arose. The effectiveness of problemsolving efforts in turn affected the participants' attitudes toward and beliefs about integration, either strengthening or weakening their commitment to the goals of the program. Although no data on this point were collected, the authors speculate that these changes in attitudes and beliefs affect subsequent efforts to change the local educational system—contributing to the new context in which innovation and experimentation must occur.

An important finding of this study was that most of the problems in nonsurviving programs were with relationships among professionals, rather than outcomes for children. This interpretation is highly consistent with the findings of the authors' earlier work, which suggested the centrality of sociopolitical factors to the problems encountered in program development efforts (Peck, Hayden, et al., 1989). This perspective underscores the importance of social processes, such as dialogue and negotiation, to the success of integration efforts. The suggestion here is not that the technical aspects of integration are unimportant, but that achieving implementation of any technology necessitates a more substantive study of local sociopolitical factors than has been reflected in the special education literature to date.

Ideological Perspectives

A final issue arising from the findings in this study concerns the sources of profound tension and conflict that recurred so often in the opinions expressed by professionals in nonsurviving programs. The concerns of special educators in these programs focused on the difficulties they experienced in implementing intensive, individually focused instruction; in maintaining control of curriculum decisions; and in maintaining accountability during the instructional process. It was clear that many of these concerns derived from the belief that children would not learn without the program practices advocated by special educators. However, in other cases these practices were insisted upon for reasons that were not clearly related to child outcomes:

> I felt at the time that it [integration] really began to take away from the children's program . . . Our IEP process became quite diluted, which was a concern of mine from the legal standpoint. We were doing some nice things for children, but we really weren't following the goals and objectives. (special education director)

The authors' analysis of this situation is that special education practice in these programs was largely determined by legalistic interpretations of appropriate process, which implicitly required a highly prescriptive approach to learning and development (Ballard-Campbell & Semmel, 1981). For example, the accountability constraints of the IEP process were commonly interpreted by special educators to mean that the only instructional processes that were acceptable were those that could be operationalized prescriptively and for which specific outcomes could be predicted and measured. While this principle of accountability appears, on one level, to be highly desirable, its implementation within the de facto context of scarcity of technical and fiscal resources often constrained definitions of appropriate instructional process. That is, while some special educators acknowledged that "nice things" were happening for children in integrated programs, they were often unable to document them, either because of limited resources or a lack of technical skills (particularly those related to nonprescriptive observation and data collection in relatively unstructured settings). This apparently led them to concentrate on instructional practices that could be more easily documented, in order to meet the accountability demands of the IEP process.

These constraints on the interpretation of appropriate practice existed in the context of a relatively narrow conceptualization of the role and function of special education (Mehan et al., 1986). This does not imply that special educators were not concerned with the broader welfare of children, but that they viewed their role in promoting children's growth and development in terms of a specific set of values, beliefs, and priorities—an ideology. This ideology limits the duty of the special educator to the identification of child deficits, and the prescriptive design and implementation of remedies for these deficits (Dunst, 1985; Fulcher, 1989; Peck, 1989b; Turnbull & Turnbull, 1986). For example, many of the special educators interviewed spoke of their role with children in terms that highlighted their priority of "working on" some problematic aspect of child behavior or development. One teacher explained:

> Our play time is at most 45 minutes. The rest is working on table activities or flash cards . . . If I don't give them that extra structure then I don't feel like I'm getting a lot of their goals met.

Consistent with this ideology, special educators in nonsurviving programs tended to see the instructional benefits of having normal peer models as being the rationale for integrated programs, and they weighed these benefits against their loss of control over other instructional variables that they considered important to the integrity of the special education program. One special education teacher expressed this dilemma clearly:

> I had written goals and objectives I had to meet. If nothing else, I just felt that if I didn't have them (the nonhandicapped children) there I could have been meeting more needs.

The ideology and practice of special education were a source of concern to many child development professionals. In many cases these individuals expressed an alternative ideology—one that reduced the "deficit" emphasis evident in the special education children's programs:

> We seem to think that these kids are behind, so let's really drill them . . . to bring them up to level. I'm just really concerned about that drill or that academic focus with kids who are already experiencing lack of success in those areas. (preschool teacher)

> He liked the sand table and water and worms and sensory kinds of things . . . but he was a behavior problem when he was forced to sit down and tower blocks or draw a circle—but it was mandatory performance because the IEP had stated that he needed those kinds of things. (parent co-op teacher).

A different ideology was evident in the surviving programs that were studied. Individuals in these programs talked about integration in terms that placed more emphasis on the inherent value of belonging to and participating in a community, and on the social acceptance of human diversity:

> Everybody's not the same, and these differences make everyone unique. And that's one of the things that makes me excited about working with these kids is that maybe ten years down the line they're not going to be calling the wheelchair bus the "MR bus," they're going to be saying "there's my friend Susie." (special education teacher)

> We don't segregate because we feel kids are kids first, and everything else is secondary." (special education administrator)

From this ideological perspective, the value of integration did not depend on peer modeling processes alone, but also on the social benefits of inclusion, and on the positive value of accepting and supporting diversity in all of the children involved.

The authors' hypothesis about the importance of this latter ideology is that it enabled special educators to see themselves as functioning effectively and appropriately in a wider variety of professional roles and activities. The fact that children's participation and inclusion in typical educational settings was seen as a valued goal in itself suggested that remediation of child deficits was not the only important objective for special education. In this ideological context, special educators did not have to maintain such direct control over the activities of children with disabilities in order to carry out their perceived role effectively. The authors hypothesized that this made it much easier for special educators to integrate *themselves* into integrated preschool programs.

The research on the implementation of changes in policy and practice reviewed above carries some clear implications for program development efforts related to integration.

IMPLICATIONS FOR PROGRAM DEVELOPMENT AND SOCIAL ACTION

Clearly the most important lesson to be learned from the research on implementation efforts is that the outcomes of *any* approach to program development and change are mediated by local context factors. This principle implies that any program development or change effort must be conceptualized as a general strategy, and not as a procedure or model to be generally prescribed and followed in a lock-step fashion (O'Brien, 1987; Peck, Richarz, et al., 1989).

The literature reviewed in this chapter

suggests that there is little reason to believe that integrated programs can be developed and maintained successfully by relying primarily on policy mandates and other top-down approaches. To simply mandate this type of fundamental change in the organization of educational programs invites the co-option and token compliance described so richly in ethnographic accounts of the implementation process (Mehan et al., 1986; Peterson, 1990). This does not imply that effective action for building integrated programs cannot be initiated from the outside, but that such actions must begin with a careful appraisal of the contexts in which integration is transformed from rhetoric to reality—and these contexts are always local. The authors also do not argue that legislative and administrative coercion have no place in the change process—on the contrary, it seems likely that widespread change cannot be achieved without some modicum of coercion (Huberman & Miles, 1986). Rather, the point is that successful programs, ones that survive, can best be developed through strategies that are responsive to the substantive dilemmas of implementation in the local context.

This review suggests some specific aspects of the local context that are important to consider when planning change efforts.

The Ideological Context

Change efforts must be informed by an understanding of the values and beliefs held by individuals about what is important in children's lives, about how children learn, and about the appropriate forms of educational practice. Identifying common ground between the goals of social integration and broader community values and beliefs should be one of the most important and fundamental goals of a program

development effort. In many cases community attitudes are based on mistaken assumptions about the needs and characteristics of people with disabilities. A process of discussion of and critical reflection on these assumptions, when juxtaposed with personal values concerning the importance of belonging, inclusion, and social acceptance, can lead to great changes in people's points of view about integration. Open and thorough discussions about integration that clarify its relevance to the needs of children with disabilities, as well as to the needs of typical children (Peck, Carlson, & Helmstetter, 1992) should be a priority in program development efforts. While substantial conflicts in ideology may surface in discussions about integration, ignoring these, or failing to resolve them through some consensus-forming process, is likely to set the stage for conflict in any program that is subsequently developed.

The traditional remedial ideology of special education is likely to be a source of ongoing difficulty in integrated programs. In contrast, the emerging *support* ideology within human services (Smull & Bellamy, 1991) seems to offer special educators a wider and more flexible set of roles and functions that are more congruent with the demands of integrated settings. Collegial discussion, critical reflection, and negotiation that leads to reconsideration of ideological perspectives on special education and child development are thus an important part of strategies for implementing integrated programs.

The Political Context

Addressing the political dimension is an important part of any effort to implement integrated programs. The term "political" is not used in any derogotory sense here, but as an acknowledgment that any extant programmatic arrangement represents the results of active, if largely informal, negotiations (and sometimes struggles) among parents, teachers, administrators, and other community members. The interests that are represented in the existing program arrangements must be acknowledged in the (re)design of programs, or these stakeholders may be expected to resist the implementation of change. This does not imply that all interests must be accommodated, but only that any stakeholders who are expected to support the implementation of an integrated program must have their interests explicitly represented in negotiations of change. Thus, one important aspect of change efforts is understanding why existing programs are structured as they are, and which stakeholders have shaped these programs.

The Technical Context

Technical aspects of the local context are the educational practices that are employed in local programs, including those used for assessment, curriculum development, delivery of instruction, and evaluation. Although the authors have focused in the present chapter on the sociopolitical aspects of integration, these affect, and are affected by, technical aspects. One set of technical issues that was particularly salient in the data on surviving and nonsurviving programs was the extent to which the implementation of special education instruction could be accomplished without disrupting the curriculum organization and instructional routines of the basic child development program (Guralnick, 1981). Currently emerging technologies that are based on the utilization of typical preschool activities and other natural social routines as contexts for assessment, instruction, and evalua-

tion (e.g., Bricker & Cripe, 1992; Peck, Killen, et al., 1989; Warren & Kaiser, 1988) should be more easily implemented in integrated settings than traditional special education instructions. Evaluating the extent to which these technical skills are present in local programs is an important step in program development efforts.

The Change Process

A final set of recommendations is offered for local change processes. A more detailed set of process recommendations is described by Peck, Richarz, et al. (1989). Based on the work reviewed above, several specific strategies for designing change processes seem valuable.

The change process should be broadly participatory. The value of directly involving individuals who represent various groups is threefold. First, these individuals are uniquely able to express the needs and concerns of key segments of the community. Their input is critical in linking change efforts with local needs and concerns. Second, the change process itself can and should be highly educative—it can deeply affect the attitudes and beliefs of the individuals involved. Third, the motivational and political investment of participants is likely to increase proportionately to the extent to which the change process is based on their own values and ideas of how an integrated program should be designed to meet needs of the local community.

The change process should be structured to enable individuals to frankly express and explore their concerns about integration through dialogue and discussion. The study of local change processes suggests that it is not necessarily easy to get individuals to express their concerns, particularly if these concerns are not directly linked to the needs of children (see Peck,

Richarz, et al., 1989, for a fuller discussion of this issue). One strategy that may facilitate this process is to use the concerns expressed by parents, teachers, and administrators in other communities as a starting point for discussion (Peck, Hayden, et al., 1989). Investing time in thorough discussion and dialogue is sometimes viewed with impatience by busy administrators and professionals. However, the value of this process for fostering philosophical agreement about the values and goals underlying development of an integrated program should not be underestimated.

Agreements negotiated through the change process should be made public. Efforts should be made to communicate the substance of agreements made by any planning group to the wider constituencies that they represent. Written documents recording philosophical agreements, policy statements, and action plans should be distributed to local parents, teachers, and administrators, and their responses and concerns should be actively solicited. This aspect of the change process should support the expression of concerns and disagreements and should lead to explicit dialogue on such matters. Failure to discuss problematic issues perceived by participants at this stage of the change process could later lead to resistance, co-option, and nonimplementation.

Finally, the change process should include ongoing opportunities for communication, dialogue, and planning as new issues and concerns about integration emerge. One of the things the authors have observed in their own program development efforts is that the individuals involved in the initial change process eventually leave the program, as is most obviously true of parents. Some of the concerns, issues, and difficulties involved in initiating integrated programs are likely to recur as new participants arrive. Failing to maintain active involvement by and dialogue among constituants regarding the rationale and goals of integration makes program survival less likely when key administrators, parents or teachers leave the program.

SUMMARY

Analysis suggests that integration poses substantial ideological and political, as well as technical, challenges to implementation. Efforts to implement policy enactments, as well as technologies and best practices developed in model demonstration programs, proceed within local contexts that have powerful and dynamic effects on actual practice. The authors' review of the research literature on the implementation of change in organizational contexts suggests that neither policy changes nor technical innovations can be expected to override local context. Consequently, implementation processes must be designed to be responsive to local conditions, and to proceed in a fashion that both respects and, when appropriate, challenges the values, beliefs, and power of local participants.

The tasks of implementation clearly go beyond the analyses of child behavior and classroom practice that have been the focus of the research and demonstration work on integration over the past 2 decades. These broader tasks include creating structural and procedural changes in human services agencies, as well as fundamental changes in the values and beliefs that are held in many communities (Sarason & Doris, 1979). In the authors' work on implementation of integrated programs they have encountered numerous professionals who have expressed reluctance to engage in the "politics" of organizational and societal change. The authors' conclusion, however, is that such engagement is essential if more than a rhetorical celebration of integration as public policy is to be achieved.

REFERENCES

Baer, D. (1986). Exemplary service to what outcome? [Review of *Education of learners with severe handicaps: Exemplary service strategies.*] *Journal of The Association for Persons with Severe Handicaps, 11,* 145–147.

Ballard-Campbell, M., & Semmel, M.I. (1981). Policy research and special education: Research issues affecting policy formation and implementation. *Exceptional Education Quarterly, 2*(2), 59–68.

Barber, K., Barber, M., & Clark, H.B. (1983). Establishing a community-oriented group home and ensuring its survival: A case study of failure. *Analysis and Intervention in Developmental Disabilities, 3,* 227–238.

Berman, P., & McLaughlin, M.W. (1976). Implementation of educational innovation. *Educational Forum, 15*(3), 345–370.

Berman, P., & McLaughlin, M.W. (1978). *Federal programs supporting educational change: Vol. VIII. Implementing and sustaining innovations.* Santa Monica, CA: Rand Corporation.

Bredekamp, S. (1987). (Ed.). *Developmentally appropriate practice in early childhood programs serving children from birth through age 8.* Washington, DC: National Association for the Education of Young Children.

Bricker, D.D., & Cripe, J.J.W. (1992). *An activity-based approach to early intervention.* Baltimore: Paul H. Brookes Publishing Co.

Bronfenbrenner, U. (1979). *The ecology of human development.* Cambridge, MA: Harvard University Press.

Clarke, M.A. (1987). Don't blame the system: Constraints on "whole language" reform. *Language Arts, 64*(4), 384–396.

Cohen, D.K., & Ball, D.L. (1990). Policy and practice: An overview. *Educational Evaluation and Policy Analysis, 12*(3), 347–353.

Danielson, L.C., & Bellamy, G.T. (1989). State variation in placement of children with handicaps in segregated environments. *Exceptional Children, 55,* 448–455.

Darling-Hammond, L. (1990). Instructional policy into practice: "The power of bottom over the top." *Educational Evaluation and Policy Analysis, 12*(3), 233–241.

Dunst, C.J. (1985). Rethinking early intervention. *Analysis and intervention in developmental disabilities, 5,* 165–201.

Education for All Handicapped Children Act of 1975, PL 94-142. (August 23, 1977). Title 20, U.S.C. 1401 et seq: *U.S. Statutes at Large, 89,* 773–796.

Education of the Handicapped Act Amendments of 1986, PL 99-457. (October 8, 1986). Title 20, U.S.C. 1400 et seq: *U.S. Statutes at Large, 100,* 1145–1177.

Firestone, W.A., & Corbett, H.D. (1987). Planned organizational change. In N. Bogan (Ed.), *Handbook of research on educational administration* (pp. 321–340). New York: Longman.

Fulcher, G. (1989). *Disabling policies? A comparative approach to education policy and disability.* New York: Falmer Press.

Guralnick, M.J. (1978). (Ed.). *Early Intervention and the integration of handicapped and nonhandicapped children.* Baltimore: University Park Press.

Guralnick, M.J. (1981). Programmatic factors affecting child-child social interactions in mainstreamed preschool programs. *Exceptional Education Quarterly, 1*(4), 71–91.

Guralnick, M.J. (1990). Major accomplishments and future directions in early childhood mainstreaming. *Topics in Early Childhood Special Education, 10*(2), 1–17.

Huberman, A.M., & Miles, M.B. (1984). *Innovation up close: How school improvement works.* New York: Plenum.

Huberman, A.M., & Miles, M.B. (1986). Rethinking the quest for school improvement: Some findings from the DESSI study. In A. Lieberman (Ed), *Rethinking school improvement: Research, craft and concept* (pp. 61–81) New York: Teachers College Press.

Lieberman, A., & Miller, L. (1986). School improvement: Themes and variations. In A. Lieberman (Ed.), *Rethinking school improvement:*

Research, craft, and concept (pp. 96–111). New York: Teachers College Press.

Mehan, H., Hertweck, A., & Meihls, J.L. (1986). *Handicapping the handicapped: Decision making in students' educational careers.* Stanford, CA: Stanford University Press.

Miles, M.B., & Huberman, A.M. (1984). *Qualitative data analysis: A sourcebook of new methods.* Beverly Hills, CA: Sage Publications.

O'Brien, J. (1987). Embracing ignorance, error, and fallibility: Competencies for leadership of effective services. In S.J. Taylor, D. Biklen, & J. Knoll (Eds.), *Community integration for people with severe disabilities.* New York: Teachers College Press.

Odom, S.L., Bender, M.K., Stein, M.L., Doran, L.P., Houden, P.M., McInnes, M., Gilberg, M.M., DeKlyen, M., Speltz, M.L., & Jenkins, J.R. (1988). *The integrated preschool curriculum: Procedures for socially integrating handicapped and nonhandicapped children.* Seattle: University of Washington Press.

Odom, S.L., & McEvoy, M.A. (1988). Integration of young children with handicaps and normally developing children. In S.L. Odom & M.B. Karnes (Eds.), *Early intervention for infants and children with handicaps: An empirical base* (pp. 241–268). Baltimore: Paul H. Brookes Publishing Co.

Peck, C.A. (1989, October). *Qualitative inquiry into mainstreaming at the early childhood level: Two case studies of organizational factors affecting implementation.* Paper presented at the annual meeting of the Division for Early Childhood Council for Exceptional Children, Minneapolis, MN.

Peck, C.A. (1989b). Assessment of social/communicative competence: Evaluating effects of environments. *Seminars in Speech and Language, 10,* 1–15.

Peck, C.A., Carlson, P., & Helmstetter, E. (1992). Parent and teacher perceptions of outcomes for nonhandicapped children enrolled in integrated early childhood programs: A statewide study. *Journal of Early Intervention, 16,* 53–63.

Peck, C.A., & Cooke, T.P. (1983). Benefits of mainstreaming at the early childhood level: How much can we expect? *Analysis and Intervention in Developmental Disabilities, 3,* 1–22.

Peck, C.A., & Furman, G.C. (1992). Qualitative research in special education: An illustrative review. In R. Gaylord-Ross (Ed.), *Research is-*

sues in special education (Vol. II). New York: Teacher's College Press.

Peck, C.A., Furman, G.C., Helmstetter, E., & Reed, D.B. (in preparation). *Factors affecting the survival of early childhood mainstreaming programs: A qualitative study of ten programs.* Vancouver: Washington State University.

Peck, C.A., Hayden, L., Wandschneider, M., Peterson, K., & Richarz, S.A. (1989). Development of integrated preschools: A qualitative inquiry into sources of concern by parents, teachers, and administrators. *Journal of Early Intervention, 13,* 353–364.

Peck, C.A., Killen, C., & Baumgart, D. (1989). Increasing implementation of special education instruction in mainstream preschools: Direct and generalized effects of nondirective instruction. *Journal of Applied Behavior Analysis, 22,* 197–210.

Peck, C.A., Richarz, S.A., Peterson, K., Hayden, L., Mineur, L., & Wandschneider, M. (1989). An ecological process model for implementing the LRE mandate. In R. Gaylord-Ross (Ed.), *Integration strategies for students with handicaps* (pp. 281–299). Baltimore: Paul H. Brookes Publishing Co.

Peterson, P.L. (1990). Doing more in the same amount of time: Cathy Swift. *Educational Evaluation and Policy Analysis, 12*(3), 277–296.

Reed, D.B. (1986, April). *School specialists: Their work and the organizational factors which condition their work.* Paper presented at the annual meeting of the American Educational Research Association, San Francisco, CA.

Richardson, V., Casanova, U., Placier, P., & Guilfoyle, K. (1989). *School children at risk.* New York: The Falmer Press.

Sarason, S.B., & Doris, J. (1979). *Educational handicap, public policy, and social history.* New York: Free Press.

Smith, M.L. (1982). *How educators decide who is learning disabled.* Springfield, IL: Charles C Thomas.

Smull, M.W., & Bellamy, G.T. (1991). Community services for adults with disabilities: Policy challenges in the emerging support paradigm. In L.H. Meyer, C.A. Peck, & L. Brown (Eds.), *Critical issues in the lives of people with severe disabilities* (pp. 527–537). Baltimore: Paul H. Brookes Publishing Co.

Strain, P.S. (1991). (Ed.). *Annual report of the Research Institute on Preschool Mainstream-*

ing (Year I). Pittsburgh, PA: Allegheny-Singer Research Institute.

Strain, P.S., & Odom, S.L. (1986). Peer social imitations: Effective intervention for social skills development of exceptional children. *Exceptional Children, 52,* 543–551.

Strauss, A., Schatzman, L., Ehrlich, D., Bucher, R., & Sabshin, M. (1963). The hospital and its negotiated order. In E. Friedson (Ed.), *The hospital in modern society.* New York: The Free Press.

Turnbull, A.P., & Turnbull, H.R. (1986). Stepping back from early intervention: An ethical perspective. *Journal of the Division for Early Childhood, 10,* 106–117.

Warren, S.F., & Kaiser, A.P. (1988). Research in early language intervention. In S.L. Odom & M.B. Karnes (Eds.), *Early intervention for infants and children with handicaps: An empirical base* (pp. 89–109). Baltimore: Paul H. Brookes Publishing Co.

Weatherley, R.A. (1979). *Reforming special education: Policy implementation from state-level to street-level.* Cambridge, MA: The MIT Press.

Weatherley, R., & Lipsky, M. (1977). Street-level bureaucrats and institutional innovation: Implementing special education reform. *Harvard Educational Review, 47,* 171–197.

Wilson, S.M. (1990). A conflict of interests: The case of Mark Black. *Educational Evaluation and Policy Analysis, 12*(3), 309–326.

Winton, P.J. (1990). A systematic approach for planning inservice training related to Public Law 99-457. *Infants and Young Children, 3*(1), 51–60.

VALUES, ATTITUDES, AND SOCIAL POLICY

Social values, beliefs, and attitudes toward disability, human services, and related issues shape perceptions and actions at every level of analysis, from face-to-face interactions between children and teachers to policy decisions creating and governing complex social organizations. In this final section of the book, a broader perspective on the ecology of integrated programs is adopted in order to clarify some ways in which community values, federal and local education policy, and other factors affect the implementation of integrated programs. In this section Strain and Smith (Chapter 11) explore some of the economic, political, and bureaucratic barriers to achieving widespread implementation of integration as social policy. In Chapter 12, Stoneman reviews research on adult and peer attitudes toward young children with disabilities, and toward integration at the early childhood level, and offers a number of recommendations for efforts to change attitudes. Bricker and Lamorey (Chapter 13) analyze research on outcomes of integration for young children, and suggest some implications of this empirical work for researchers and policymakers. Finally, we conclude this section, and the volume, by summarizing some of the major themes that emerge across chapters at each of the levels of analysis (Bricker, Odom, & Peck, Chapter 14).

Chapter 11

COMPREHENSIVE EDUCATIONAL, SOCIAL, AND POLICY FORCES THAT AFFECT PRESCHOOL INTEGRATION

*Phillip S. Strain
and Barbara J. Smith*

The integration of children, particularly young children, with disabilities has often been characterized by controversy, acrimony, and a less than ideal translation of policy into best practice. This history may well be attributable to the sheer magnitude of structural and functional change that a move toward integration requires (Strain, 1990).

As many of the chapters in this volume illustrate, good, sometimes spectacular progress is being made on the mechanics of integration. For example, much is known about instructional and social integration, about personnel needs and competencies, about the formation and purposeful development of positive attitudes toward integration, and about family roles in the process. By comparison, far less is known about the broad educational and social contexts within which integration takes place, or about policy barriers and conflicts that may ultimately dictate whether integration is a fad or a permanent change (Smith, 1991).

The purpose of this chapter is to highlight some of the educational and social contexts, as well as the policy issues, that demand professional attention and study. Two primary data sources are referred to in this chapter. First, the authors and their colleagues have spent the last 3 years working intensively with 26 school districts across the Commonwealth of Pennsylvania in their efforts to integrate young children with disabilities into daycare, preschool, and kindergarten settings. This experience has provided an opportunity to see first hand how many of the global educational and social forces affecting public education today may influence the development of integrated placement options. These global forces include: 1) the movement toward educational reform as a means for achieving an improved competitive edge in the world market place, 2) the unionization of educational professionals and the resulting increase in protectionism, 3) the trend toward site-based management, 4) the expanded role of parents in schooling, and 5) the unprecedented number of states and municipalities facing severe fiscal difficulties.

The second data source that is used is an ongoing study of public policy at the national, state, and local levels and its impact on integration practices (Research Institute on Preschool Mainstreaming, 1990). This ongoing effort has uncovered policy-related issues pertinent to: 1) accountability and program quality, 2) personnel certification and competency, and 3) conflicting values and attitudes.

COMPREHENSIVE EDUCATIONAL AND SOCIAL INFLUENCES ON INTEGRATION

Most of the professional literature on preschool integration would lead the naive reader to believe that this movement is occurring in a social and educational vacuum, but nothing could be further from the truth. The expansion of integrated service options shares the stage with a myriad of other educational and social trends, many of which directly impinge upon the ultimate success of integrated service delivery. As the authors have worked over the last 3 years with local agencies throughout the Commonwealth of Pennsylvania to expand integrated services, these national trends have taken on a clear and present reality.

Educational Reform and the Need To Compete in World Markets

The political and educational climate in this country has been characterized by a ground swell of complaint during the 1980s. That Americans are growing illiterate, unskilled, and noncompetitive with other industrialized countries is a sentiment voiced by representatives of business and industry, parents, civic leaders, some school officials, and, belatedly, by politicians. The response to this criticism has been broad, ranging from the trivial (e.g., assertions about being the "Education President") to the profound (e.g., changes in curricula, parental choice options for schooling, outcome-driven school districts).

Many current efforts at educational reform are philosophically and operationally intolerant of integration at any level of schooling. At the philosophical level, the negative dimension of the reform movement is best illustrated by the words of those actually involved in implementation:

> Urban District Teacher: "These kids have to learn the material; they have to learn it in the set order; they have to all make the grade."

> Urban District Superintendent: "We are accountable now. I know all my teachers are on the same material on the same day."

> Urban District Parent: "We drill at home. We have to. If he gets behind there is no chance to catch up."

Together, these comments reflect a national trend toward a philosophy of regular education characterized by rigidity in method and a blatant denial of individual differences. Consider the following remarks also:

> Rural District Teacher: "We've cut all our extracurricular services. All the money is going to math and science."

> Rural District Superintendent: "We can't have clowns in class and good achievement too. We use in-school suspension, and now the teachers can teach."

> Rural District Parent: "My older kids have dropped out, they went to school for sports, I guess. They're a big help on the farm."

The comments above reflect another constellation of values and philosophy that may be summarized as follows: Good *academic* outcomes must be achieved at almost any price, including the placement of children in tracks. Obviously, these motives fly in the face of an inclusive philosophy of education.

Many of our national efforts to "toughen-up" curricula, teachers, and schools also call into question whether a typical class can be considered as an educationally or socially viable environment for children with disabilities. Is it a good outcome to be integrated in a "reformed" class where competition is encouraged, where lock-step instruction is acknowledged and valued, and where human variance is seen as a weakness in the economic struggle with Japan and Germany? These comments are not meant to suggest that reform is not necessary. Yet, when reform takes the path toward: 1) a narrow outcome focus, 2) systematic removal of students who may negatively influence overall test scores, and 3) a single curricular sequence for all students, then the well-being of children both with and without special needs must be questioned.

Unionization and Protectionism of Educational Professionals

It can be argued that unionization in the teaching profession has been, overall, a force for positive change (Johnson, 1984). But in regards to integration, the balance sheet seems tipped in the opposite direction, although this negative influence may be an unintended consequence. How does unionization and its protection of constituent interests affect integration practices? Again, consider the words of those most intimately involved:

Special Education Supervisor: "We have some serious problems with this plan to train our staff to consult with preschool and kindergarten teachers. The union prohibits any outside-the-school-day time

requirement and the new contract also prohibits the observation of tenured teachers for evaluation purposes. They will see this as evaluation."

Building Principal: "We don't do mainstreaming in this school because the union representative is against it."

Regular Class Teacher: "The contract says I only have to have three special eds. in my class."

These statements reflect a number of very troubling issues concerning integration, or any other innovation for that matter. For example, union contracts may present barriers to the intensive, job-embedded, competency-based inservice training that is necessary to achieve significant change in practice (Guskey, 1986). Also, with their threats of grievance filing, union members and representatives may short circuit any change in schooling that they do not support. Another obstruction to integration is found in union contracts that have specifically limited the access of children with disabilities to the educational mainstream. Parenthetically, quota systems, like that alluded to in the teacher comment above, lead to limited community-based schooling, expensive transportation costs, and an image of children with disabilities as being detrimental to typical school programs.

At the other extreme, union activity may be highly supportive of integration. Consider these remarks from an adjacent school district:

Union Representative: "We try our best to accommodate everyone's needs in our negotiations. It is very important for us to be in step with new trends and concerns. If we are too far out in front or lag behind, everyone loses. Mainstreaming is a good example. We have really worked to get our teachers the training they need initially and the support they will continue to require."

Superintendent: "Our aim is to work cooperatively on the issues we value as a community. Our relationship with the union is primarily a hand-in-hand proposition. Together, we have built the necessary structures to increase professional development, mainstreaming, and curricular adaptations for students who are not best served by our standard practices. In a district as diverse as ours, we have to be diverse ourselves.

Obviously, unionization, in and of itself, has neither a positive nor a negative influence on integration options. However, unionization will probably always make the integration process more complex by bringing another powerful voice to the debate.

The Preference for Site-Based Management

One of the more common elements of school reform is the preference for site-based management (Elmore, 1991). The notion and motivation behind site-based management are quite simple. Top-down management and regulations are seen as inhibiting good educational practice. As power and decisionmaking is shifted closer and closer to the building level, superior educational practices will emerge. There can be no doubt that many school systems are plagued and stagnated by endless bureaucracy and dysfunctional regulatory practices. The question of import for the purposes of this chapter is whether PL 94-142 procedural guidelines, for example, are seen as part and parcel of the regulatory baggage that site-based management may try to discard. Or will site-based management, in fact, offer an avenue to expanded integration options? Consider the following statements from very different site-based managed schools:

School One Principal: "We've dealt with our conduct problems where the district could not. Our parents and our teachers know what we need for learning. We've removed the bad apples."

School Two Principal: "We value all the kids in this school, like we value all the staff. Everyone can make a contribution when they have the chance to be included. We've decided that integration is what we want as a school and it is working."

School One Teacher: "My friends at Lincoln school are very envious; they can't control what comes in their class and they can't remove those kids who won't learn."

School Two Teacher: "We were all very nervous about the site-based system, but we've really been given the choices we needed. We're most proud of our integration program; it's totally different from the other district schools."

The comments from these two site-based managed schools suggest the range of outcomes that this innovation can lead to for integration. In school one, site-based management is synonymous with a pre-PL 94-142 approach to due process and to the continuum of service delivery. In school two, site-based management has led to integration options that far exceed those provided for in regulatory mandates. If, indeed, site-based management becomes a prevailing trend, then professionals must be prepared to closely monitor the wide range of integration practices that will surely follow. Site-based management also increases the need for early interventionists to expand their efforts to influence all personnel involved in the educational process.

Expanded Role of Parents in Schooling

Early intervention is by no means the only educational arena in which parents are being provided with far greater access to schools and to decisionmaking. The expanded role of parents in the regular educational establishment ranges from the controversial choice-of-school and tax credit options, to home/school collaborative teaching projects, to parental majorities on individual school building voting bodies (Kearns & Doyle, 1988). As with site-based management, the increased role and power of parents may be a double-edged sword vis-à-vis integration. The comments below represent the range of outcomes that might be expected:

> Parent on School Board: "These handicapped kids are wasting our resources, our money, our teachers' time, and our kids'. We need retarded classes just like we need advanced English classes."

> Parent on School Board: "The teachers don't want these kids. If they don't want them then what good will it do to put them in these classes? What do we have special education for anyway?"

> Parent on School Board: "Who wants to be isolated? Not me, not my kids. Don't these parents pay taxes too? I say integration is the only fair thing to do. And I know the rest of you would want it for yourself."

Not only will an expanded role for parents in educational decisionmaking likely increase the range and number of voices speaking and deciding about integration at a local policy level, but so should parents' increased decisionmaking during the early childhood years. Herein lies a troublesome dilemma and potential conflict. That is, suppose one strongly advocates the following: 1) parents should have maximum choice and decisionmaking power in the early intervention program, and 2) full-time integration is best for all children. While there is no hard data on the matter, the authors' strong hunch is that most professionals in the field hold these convictions. But suppose that a family chooses other than an integrated option. Is the professional to relent, argue, or change his or her own values to eliminate the dilemma? Trouble seems to arise most often when the values specific to parental empowerment and integration have been stated in absolute terms, as they usually are. One should not underestimate the psychological costs to parents when values are stated in the extreme by professionals. Consider these comments from parents whose children are now functioning within normal developmental limits after early

intervention (and an integrated early intervention program at that):

> Parent One: "Where can _____ get the attention I want him to have except in a special class. He can test right for placement with some luck. I've been to see the kindergarten where he would go, it's awful."

> Parent Two: "I feel embarrassed because I know what being around normal kids has done for _____. But this class is small, look at all the teachers you have. My Catholic school is an option, but it's so expensive."

> Parent Three: "My husband and I go back and forth. We think he needs extra attention. He needs his peers too. We've been thinking about starting our own school, I don't know what else would work."

Unprecedented Fiscal Problems

The 1980s have seen a growing fiscal calamity in public education. Tax payer revolts, mandatory layoffs, and zero-growth budgets are the rule, rather than the exception, across the country. And in 1992, a recession is exacerbating these financial woes. It is within this shrinking market that all innovations, integration included, must compete for attention and for dollars. On the surface, the fiscal equation is not favorable. The following comments nicely summarize the negative valences:

> School Board Member: "With special education we have the few taking the greatest proportion of resources. The least we can do is see that capable kids are not held back by mainstreaming."

> Superintendent: "We're asked to pick up more and more of the burden for special education. Our regular program is obviously hurt by this. Parents are just not going to stand for this, and they sure don't want anything to do with mainstreaming."

> Preschool Supervisor: "It is really unrealistic for us to look at any kind of significant change in our system. We cannot afford inservice, reduced class size, or new materials. My staff is depressed, they hardly want to hear any new ideas."

These comments are typical of the "circle the wagons" mentality that seems to prevail in any large bureaucracy when difficult times are at hand. The instinctive desire to preserve the status quo is understandable, and it is arguably prudent as well. What is dysfunctional and damaging to integration options is the parallel tendency to shoot criticism inward once the wagons are circled. Notice that the comments above lay blame, directly or indirectly, on children eligible for special education. Not only is this mean spirited, but it is economically and politically naive. At a cost of a billion dollars per day, Desert Storm showed that resources are not scarce, that the root problem is really a lack of concern for education in general, and for children with special needs in particular.

SOME CORRECTIVE IDEAS

When considered against a background of educational reform, fiscal uncertainty, site-based management, increased parent involvement, and other related forces, the integration of young children with disabilities takes on a complex and troublesome character. Yet, this complexity affords professionals the opportunity to alter any of the many variables that affect integration. The following ideas are offered for critical reflection and possible action.

Experimental Analysis of Integration Ecologies

When one examines the factors that affect integration, it becomes obvious that ignorance is the most damaging. The "data" on the topics discussed above, however persuasive, are anecdotal only. If those in the field are serious about nationwide integration, then both energy and dollars must be applied to researching integration from other than a technocratic perspective. Those in the field must understand the sociology, politics, and economics of integration. Some initial work on these subjects

has been done by Peck and his colleagues (Peck, chap. 10, this volume), but there are still far too many unknowns that demand further study. A brief list of important questions might include the following: 1) What political, economic, social, and reform forces affect the expansion of integrated options? 2) When faced with system opposition, what steps can ensure the eventual adoption of integrated programs? and 3) Once integration options have been adopted, what factors determine success?

Synchronizing Rhetoric and Practice

The match between words and deeds is poor in the area of integration. There are many reasons for this disparity: 1) It is easy for individuals to speak in favor of integration, but then do nothing when they encounter predictable barriers. These individuals often refer to themselves as realists or pragmatists, or as being "trapped in an unworkable system." 2) Various regulations (e.g., PL 94-142) require service systems to certify that they do practice some form of integration. But certification is in writing only; seldom is there any direct scrutiny of the system. Put simply, when it comes to integration, service systems receive dollars for saying, not doing. 3) As highlighted in the discussion on parental involvement, integration sometimes conflicts with other elements of service delivery (e.g., parental choice, delivery of maximally intensive services).

How can these reasons for forestalling integration be overcome? The rationalization that integration is unrealistic or nonpragmatic must be dealt with directly; those in the field must acknowledge publicly and often that integration is not an easy, quick-fix option. The personnel, fiscal, and political barriers are real, and not simply lies perpetrated by those who advocate the status quo (Strain, 1990). Simply arguing for integration is not enough; the rhetoric of those in the field must acknowledge what it will actually take to operate quality integrated programs. The practice of tying funding to verbal testimony about integration practices is essentially a resource-allocation issue. Until practices are monitored directly, and programs are directly rewarded for performance, the gap between rhetoric and practice will remain. This monitoring must take place at all administrative levels—federal, state and local. The monitoring need not have a punitive intent, it need only find out the truth and differentially reward genuine attempts to develop integrated service options.

Finally, professionals must acknowledge and publicly discuss the potential value conflicts concerning integration and early intervention service delivery. Most professionals want parents to be decision-makers, and some parents may not wish to place their child in an integrated program. And some integrated programs may offer fewer services than segregated programs do. What are the important factors to consider, given the very real concerns about the quality and intensity of service in both integrated and segregated programs?

Making Integration a Priority

If widespread integration is to occur in the United States, the issue must not be treated as an afterthought to the educational and social forces mentioned earlier; school reform cannot be allowed to proceed without bringing children with special needs into the equation. Notably, Elmore's (1991) seminal work on school reform makes no mention of children with special needs or integration. The job of focusing attention on integration belongs to those in the field. Importantly, they face this challenge with more than an open and empty hand, they have an excellent, but seldom used, entreé to the educational reform movement. Specifically, the intervention procedures developed in early intervention and special education can offer huge dividends to schools interested in improving home–school collaboration, school survival skills, and a host of developmental outcomes for children. Purposeful efforts to help translate and transfer the validated technology of special education and early intervention instruction to regular education will also make typical settings more responsive to the learning requirements of children with special needs.

Those in the field must also bring the concerns of children with special needs and the subject of integration to the world of teachers' unions and contract negotiations. While few may rush with glee to the challenge, this step can no longer be avoided. Unions may operate without any awareness of the integration needs of young children with disabilities, and they fall outside of the legitimate boundaries of regulation and monitoring. Therefore, special educators will have to inform union members and officials of such factors as: 1) potential education law–union conflicts; 2) integration as a valued outcome; 3) data on the effectiveness of integration at the early childhood level; and 4) comments by supportive parents, teachers, and administrators.

POLICY BARRIERS AND POSSIBLE OPTIONS

While best practice encourages mainstream placement, public policies often present disincentives for school personnel to institute such practices. Indeed, given the widespread lack of public school preschool programs for typical children (except kindergarten), school administrators ask, "How can we mainstream preschoolers with disabilities when we do not have programs for their typical peers?" Sykes (1988) explains the dilemma by pointing out that special educational placement options have historically been driven by the "least restrictive environment" (LRE) policy of PL 94-142. This LRE policy requires that " . . . removal of handicapped children from the regular education environment occurs only when the nature or severity of the handicap is such that education in regular classes with the use of supplementary aids and services cannot be achieved satisfactorily" (Sec. 612(5)(B)). This policy is clear when applied to decisions about placement options for school-age children, but less so when placing preschool-age children. For example, what is the relevance of "removal . . . from the regular educational environment" or "regular classes" when the school does not provide educational programming to typical preschoolers? Thus, in attempting to meet the federal requirements in PL 99-457 of full services by 1991–1992, and to follow best practice by providing the most inclusive environment, schools find themselves in an uncertain policy and legal position.

To what extent have mainstreaming practices been implemented? What federal, state, and local policies are standing in the way of preschool mainstreaming? How have these policy barriers been addressed? The Policy Analysis division of the Research Institute on Preschool Mainstreaming has been funded for 5 years by the United States Office of Special Education Programs to answer these questions. The Policy Analysis division has conducted a nationwide survey, asking respondents to identify policy barriers to preschool mainstreaming. Surveys were sent to all state education agency (SEA) special education directors and state education agency preschool coordinators; interagency coordinating councils with a birth–5 focus; Head Start Resource Access Professionals; a sample of parents, childcare workers and Head Start professionals; and local education agency (LEA) directors of special education in 10 geographically distributed states (total survey respondents = 278). Definitions were provided for the following: preschool children with disabilities (3-, 4-, and 5-year-old children with mild to moderate disabilities who are eligible for special education), policies (e.g., written public policies including laws, regulations, fiscal or contracting procedures), and mainstream settings (settings where typical children are found).

Survey respondents were asked if the following specific policy areas were acting as disincentives to mainstreaming in their state and communities:

Public school accountability for program standards and supervision
Fiscal and contracting procedures
Transportation policies
Use of private or non–public school agencies
Conflicting policies (e.g., eligibility, due process)
Personnel policies
Curricula or methods requirements
Values or attitudes

Respondents were asked to answer the following questions: 1) Are there policies related to the issue that are disincentives to mainstreaming? 2) If so, are they local, state, or federal policies? 3) What is the degree of the problem? and 4) Has anyone solved the problem as yet?

The overall survey return rate was 53%. For local directors, state special education directors, and state special education preschool (Sec. 619) coordinators, the response rates were 55%, 60% and 71%, respectively. Following the survey, case studies were conducted to investigate how state and local education agencies have succeeded in changing these policy disincentives.

What Are the Policy Barriers?

Survey respondents most often cited two policy barriers to placing preschool children with disabilities into mainstream settings for special education: 1) policies for fulfilling the PL 94-142 requirement that services meet state special education standards, especially personnel requirements (59.1%) and the related requirement of supervision by the education agency (33.1%); and 2) fiscal policies and procedures governing the use, and particularly the co-mingling, of funds (46.5%).

The state and local respondents reported that because of federal requirements schools are reluctant to place children in community mainstream settings such as childcare or Head Start because these settings do not meet state standards governing quality and are not under the direct supervision of the school. Section 300.4 of the federal regulations governing PL 94-142 (Part B, IDEA) states that a free, appropriate, public education to which children with disabilities are entitled: 1) must be "provided at public expense, under public supervision and direction and without charge"; and 2) "meet the standards of the state education agency." Thus, state approval procedures were developed for placing school-age children into a *more* restrictive setting, and are not applicable to placing preschool children in nonpublic school programs for purposes of achieving the LRE.

Furthermore, personnel standards are also acting as a barrier. Federal, and in some cases state, policies require that personnel providing special education and related services meet state standards. Section 300.12 of the Part B regulations defines a qualified professional as one who "has met state education agency approval or recognized certification, licensing, registration, or other comparable requirements which apply to the area in which he or she is providing special education or related services." Since most community-based early childhood settings do not employ certified teachers and therapists, many sites have been denied approval for the placement of preschool children with disabilities. Respondents also reported that school personnel are reluctant to use community-based early childhood programs because of the assumption that these programs and personnel are not appropriate for children with disabilities. Often, respondents said that attitudes, as much as policies, were serving as barriers (57.9%).

Numerous fiscal policies were also cited as barriers to mainstreaming. In addition to reports of a lack of funding for mainstreaming, policies on the use of funds were also cited as problems. Some respondents said that their district or state had interpreted federal and/or state prohibitions on the use of public resources to benefit religious institutions as disallowing government funding of childcare or Head Start programs located in religious facilities. For instance, the U.S. Education Department General Administrative Regulations (EDGAR) provides that:

(a) no state or subgrantee may use its grant or subgrant to pay for any of the following: 1) religious worship, instruction, or prosy; and 2) equipment or supplies to be used for any of the activities specified in paragraph (a) (1) above . . . and prohibitions on use of federal funds for construction, repair maintenance, etc., of facilities used for activities in (a)(1) (above) or an activity in a divinity school or department. (Sec. 76.532)

A second frequently cited barrier was the tendency to avoid the use of program funds targeted for one population in conjunction with programs for other populations. Specifically, blending funds and resources from special education, at-risk programs, or Chapter 1 (ECIA-Disadvantaged) allocations in order to have an integrated program that combines a variety of teachers, resources, and groups of children was reported as being prohibited either by policy or past practice. Another barrier cited was the inability to contract funds; schools were often prohibited from paying for services in a non–school district program. Also, there was often no policy for determining how to contract and how much time to contract for (half-day, full-day, etc.). Rate-setting policies that provided too low a reimbursement to make it worthwhile for the community-based program were also reported as disincentives. Fiscal policies on the manner in which funds are allocated were also reported as barriers, including child-count policies (i.e., who gets to count the child for funding—the school or the mainstream program). Funding formulas that allocate money to specialized classrooms, rather than to personnel or for contracting, regardless of setting, were also seen as barriers. Also reported were inflexible fiscal and contracting policies, such as those that provide funding for instruction only, resulting in the family's being charged to leave the child at the program during lunch and nap time before the afternoon session begins.

Other policies, mentioned by less than 30% of the respondents, included those related to eligibility criteria, transportation, and cooperative efforts. Eligibility policies were reported as problems particularly related to Head Start. Head Start's disability categories differ from federal and state special education categories and Head Start's income eligibility restricts the number of children who can be placed by schools. Income standards in other public early childhood programs have also posed problems for the same reasons. Less frequently mentioned were other childcare requirements, such as toileting behaviors, that have had a negative impact on mainstreaming. However, some integration options within schools are limited by eligibility criteria such as Chapter 1 (disadvantaged) criteria, and pre-kindergarten and kindergarten readiness criteria. Transportation policies that do not allow for flexible scheduling (to match the hours of the community-based program), convenient routes (to nonschool sites), or out-of-district routes (because of the scarcity of community-based programs) were barriers to using non–school-based mainstream programs. Finally, prohibitive policies or a lack of policies on the coordination of special and regular education programs and resources were also cited.

In many instances, the respondents reported that it was not the policy itself that served as a barrier to preschool mainstreaming, but an interpretation of the policy. In nearly every case the interpretation was unwritten, but widely held as fact. Examples of the most common instances included: 1) interpretation of the "church/state" prohibition as forbidding the provision of government-funded special education in preschool, Head Start, or childcare programs located in religious facilities, regardless of whether these programs include religious activities or instruction; and 2) interpretation of the federal (and often, state) requirement that special education and related services personnel meet state standards as meaning that the regular education staff of the mainstream setting must also meet state special education standards (e.g., certification) in order to mainstream children.

How Can These Barriers Be Overcome?

In order to gain a better understanding of the disincentives and discover possible remedies, case studies were conducted. There were a total of 21 case studies: 6 at the state level (state special education preschool coordinators) and 15 at the local level (local public school administrators or preschool coordinators). State and local dyads were selected in 6 states in order to study the interplay between state and local policies and experiences. Case-study subjects were selected because they met one or more of the following criteria: 1) their responses to the survey were extensive and indicated experience with several of the policy areas, 2) they were named by another survey or case-study respondent as someone who had solved a policy disincentive, or 3) they were known by project staff to have an exemplary early childhood mainstream program. All potential subjects were contacted by telephone and agreed to participate. The case studies consisted of in-depth telephone interviews. Copies of policies that were named as disincentives to mainstreaming and policies that were developed as remedies were obtained for analysis. The interviews and policy analysis provided an in-depth study of each policy area and helped the researchers learn whether the disincentives were a result of the policy itself, or of an interpretation of the policy. The effects of the policy on mainstreaming and the remedies to the disincentives were also explored during the interviews with each respondent.

With the help of the case-study information, several integration options, some of which are described below, are already being implemented in a number of states and locales.

Ensuring General Supervision and Program Standards Initially, schools interpreted the federal requirements related to supervision and program standards (Part B, Sec. 300.4) as meaning that only state or local education agency programs could be used for placement. However, because of the need to address the LRE requirements of Part B, schools have developed options for meeting the supervision and standards requirements as well as the LRE requirements. Options have included:

Developing standards and non–public school program approval procedures that are specific to preschool environments (e.g., using the approval mechanisms of other state agencies that govern preschool programs, including the accreditation procedures of the National Association for the Education of Young Children)

Providing special education and related services in programs where parents have placed children, which alleviates many of the approval responsibilities that normally fall on professionals

Ensuring that special education is implemented under the supervision of special education staff, who may be provided by the local education agency

Requiring contracting agencies to sign assurances like those required by the SEA and LEA under PL 94-142

Ensuring Personnel Qualifications As noted earlier, policy on this subject has been interpreted, in some cases, to mean that all personnel in the mainstream setting must meet the SEA personnel certification requirements for special educators. Strategies that are being implemented include:

Developing state education personnel standards that create new credentials, or rework existing early childhood certification procedures, such as those for the Child Development Associate

Ensuring that the special education and related services in the program are only provided by personnel with credentials recognized by the SEA—by itinerant teachers and related services personnel provided by the education agency, or by program personnel provided in lieu of funding or tuition payments

Providing Fiscal and Contracting Options   Several states have gone so far as to change special or general education statutory provisions in order to eliminate the fiscal barriers to mainstreaming. Others have needed only to change local procedures. Specific options include:

Establishing a local tax base to provide for special education programs, including preschool special education. This helps to maintain an adequate level of funding for all preschool special education, including mainstream efforts

Establishing state special education funding formulas that provide for combining fractions of units to equal one full-time educator, who could act as an itinerant, serving many different children (units) at different sites

Developing funding procedures across programs (special education, at-risk, childcare, etc.) that allow for combinations of various funding streams to be used in one integrated program

Allowing for the actual payment of tuition in mainstream sites and the provision of services such as personnel, parent training, transportation, and related services, in lieu of tuition payments

Developing policies or clarifications regarding the use of programs located in

religious facilities that prohibit such use only if the curriculum or instruction includes religious messages, or if the program is administered by the religious institution or its board. When, for instance, the mainstream program has a separate administration or board of directors, and there is no religious message in the curriculum [which are the actual provisions of Sec. 76.532 of EDGAR], then the U.S. Office of Special Education Programs, which administers federal special education dollars, has ruled that court decisions prohibiting placement in programs located in religious facilities does not apply to those children benefiting from funds that their office allocates.

Redefining Eligibility   Without federal action, there are limited solutions to the problems caused by the discrepancy among federal eligibility requirements for programs such as Part B of IDEA (PL 101-476), Head Start, and Chapter 1 of ECIA (disadvantaged program). Even so, several localities have implemented creative remedies, including:

Allowing schools and Head Start programs to cooperate in the identification of children with special needs, so that those who meet LEA eligibility criteria and are placed in Head Start have their costs paid by the LEA, and those who meet Head Start's eligibility criteria have their service paid for by Head Start (Sometimes, children who meet LEA eligibility requirements are dually enrolled, or LEA and Head Start programs are co-located, so they can be, in effect, combined, while still retaining separate staff and administration.)

Co-locating with Chapter 1 programs and combining children, but retaining separate staff and administration, or team-teaching in integrated Chapter 1 programs with a combination of regular and special education staff

Providing Adequate Transportation
Transportation is an expensive part of any education program, and there are particular policy barriers related to preschool mainstreaming that professionals must address. Options include:

Providing for flexible schedules and routes that coincide with the schedules and locations of mainstream community programs (Head Start, childcare, etc.), including allowing for routes that cross school district lines in order to reach needed programs

Providing for reimbursement to families who arrange for transportation themselves

Facilitating Coordination School officials frequently cited coordination across funding streams and across programs as being keys to the success of mainstream programs. Specific policy options include:

At the state level, SEA early childhood staff (general and special education) engage in cooperative planning and activities, and are sometimes organizationally housed together in an Early Childhood Unit in order to encourage cooperation. Program policies are planned cooperatively across federal programs as well as state programs (educational at-risk preschool programs, school-based childcare programs, as well as other agency programs for such things as childcare licensing, etc.).

At the local level, school-district or regional early childhood staff (general and special education) engage in cooperative efforts and are also sometimes housed together in a district-level Early

Childhood administrative unit to increase cooperation. Local district early childhood staff engage in cooperative activities with the staff of community-based programs, including community coordinating and planning bodies, and district early childhood staff plan activities, such as cooperative training, that help to address the needs of community-based program staff, or staff share related services or parent programs.

SUMMARY

The integration of young children with disabilities is a multifaceted enterprise. It demands simultaneous attention to issues of assessment and curriculum, teacher preparation, friendship formation and social skills, parental concerns, policy barriers, and the global educational context within which this innovation has evolved. Integration proves the adage that complex problems require complex solutions.

As this chapter shows, widespread integration in this country will likely not be possible without a massive, new, coordinated effort to understand and alter many of the fundamental features of the educational practices and policies that are followed today. To assume that integration efforts will grow and blossom regardless of the state of finances, unionization, site-based school management, educational reform, parental concerns, and policy disincentives is naive.

Actions that may reduce the influence of these barriers include:

Training—from the survey and case-study data mentioned earlier, it is clear that professionals at the decisionmaking level condone integrated service options to the extent to which they feel comfortable with the expertise and support available in regular settings. Moreover, the survey respondents insisted that training on integration practices should include regular and special educators at all levels, from teachers to state administrators.

Coordination—in addition to training, professionals who participated in the policy analysis research repeatedly recounted integration success stories that resulted from efforts at the state and local levels to share resources, plan common training experiences, promote a system-wide consensus on target outcomes for all children, and participate in other coordination activities.

Dissemination—by and large, professional efforts in this regard are reminiscent of preaching to the choir. The school reform movement should put special educators on the alert, however, that their insularity is dysfunctional. Local school boards, governors (individually and collectively), chief school officers at the state level, and the general public must be informed of the needs of exceptional children and the efficacy of integrated early intervention.

Advocacy—currently, the education reform movement, and the potential integration barriers that accompany it, are being played out on a political and professional field void of any advocates of children with special needs. The consequences of this could be disastrous, not just for integration, but also for the basic rights of children with special needs guaranteed in PL 94-142. Professionals in the field must insist on being active members in the discussion. They must also insist that any reforms that emerge at the very least do not violate the rights of young children with disabilities and their families.

When facing so large a task, it is tempting to ask if the potential benefits are worth the cost. But is quantitative analysis really appropriate when dealing with issues of equality, respect, and basic human dignity? The authors think not.

REFERENCES

Education for All Handicapped Children Act of 1975, PL 94-142. (August 23, 1977). Title 20, U.S.C. 1401 et seq: *U.S. Statutes at Large, 89,* 773–796.

Education of the Handicapped Act Amendments of 1986, PL 99-457. (October 8, 1986). Title 20, U.S.C. 1400 et seq: *U.S. Statutes at Large, 100,* 1145–1177.

Elmore, R.F. (1991). *Restructuring schools.* San Francisco: Jossey-Bass.

Guskey, T.R. (1986). Staff development and the process of teacher change. *Educational Researcher, 15,* 5–12.

Johnson, S.M. (1984). *Teacher unions in schools.* Philadelphia: Temple University Press.

Kearns, D.T., & Doyle, D.P. (1988). *Winning the brain race.* San Francisco: Institute for Contemporary Studies Press.

Research Institute on Preschool Mainstreaming. (1990). *First year annual report.* Pitts-

burgh: Allegheny-Singer Research Institute.

Smith, B.J. (1991). *Policy option white paper #3.* Allegheny-Singer Research Institute, Research Institute on Preschool Mainstreaming, Pittsburgh, PA.

Strain, P.S. (1990). LRE for preschool children with handicaps: What we know, what we should be doing. *Journal of Early Intervention, 14,* 291–296.

Sykes, D. (1988). *Statutory and regulatory issues in the implementation of the Least Restrictive Environment (LRE) of P.L. 94-142 for the 3–5 population.* Paper presented at the Planners' Conference on Integration and the Least Restrictive Environment for Young Children, GLARRC, Chicago.

U.S. Education Department General Administrative Regulations. (1990). *Use of funds for religion prohibited* (sec. 76.532).

Chapter 12

THE EFFECTS OF ATTITUDE
ON PRESCHOOL INTEGRATION

Zolinda Stoneman

The more homogeneous in appearance the
people a child has seen, the more deviance the
child will note.
(Richardson, 1970, p. 212)

It has become common to hear advocates and others speak about the "attitudinal barriers" that individuals with disabilities encounter as they seek to become more fully integrated into community life. Just as architectural barriers block persons with physical disabilities from entering certain buildings, attitudinal barriers may block persons with a range of disabilities from full participation in schools and communities. Attitudes are learned (Allport, 1954; Fishbein & Ajzen, 1975; Triandis, 1971, Triandis, Adamopoulos, & Brinberg, 1984) and, frequently, they are formed on the basis of minimum evidence. Allport (1954) suggested that the majority of attitudes held by a person are acquired from talking with family and friends. Of-

ten, all that people know about the subject of an attitude is what parents and others told them when they were children (Triandis, 1984). This may be particularly true for attitudes about people with disabilities, since, until recently, segregated programs and living environments have largely kept these people from public view and from the mainstream of school and community life.

The purpose of this chapter is to examine attitudinal barriers as they relate to integrating young children with disabilities into community preschool and daycare settings. In addressing attitudinal barriers to preschool integration, it is important to take a systemic view, focusing not only on the teachers and staff in those

Partial support for preparation of this chapter was provided by Grant No. 04-DD-000-58 from the Administration on Developmental Disabilities, U.S. Department of Health and Human Services.

programs, but also on the attitudes held by parents, young children, early interventionists, early childhood special educators, policymakers, and administrators. Specifically, the chapter will: 1) provide an overview of the theoretical and conceptual issues underlying the research on attitudes about preschool integration, 2) review and critique the relevant research, and 3) offer recommendations for practice.

CONCEPTUAL ISSUES RELATED TO RESEARCH ON ATTITUDES

Research on attitudes has a long and illustrious history. One could fill a small library with this work, so no attempt will be made here to provide a complete summary or review of this large body of literature. However, the conceptual scheme developed by Triandis (1971) is used to organize information concerning attitudes and preschool mainstreaming. Triandis (1971), building on the work of other attitude researchers, suggested that attitudes have three components: the *cognitive, affective,* and *behavioral*. The cognitive component is the idea or knowledge that the person holding an attitude has about its referent. In the words of Triandis et al. (1984), it is a "network of thoughts about categories of people" (p. 22). In the case of young children with disabilities, the cognitive component can include knowledge about disabilities and beliefs about their causes and consequences, as well as beliefs about how behaviors and traits co-vary. Triandis (1971) suggests that it is a human characteristic to *type* other people and groups, and that once a category is formed, there is a tendency to associate members of that category with specific traits, characteristics, and behaviors.

People also have what Schneider (1973) has termed *implicit personality theories,* which include preconceived ideas about what traits or characteristics tend to co-exist in the same person. A person might believe, for example, that children with Down syndrome are happy, compliant children who have trouble learning. The person in this example has a cognitive scheme linking Down syndrome, happiness, compliance, and difficulty in learning, and that scheme then forms the basis for the person's affective and behavioral response to these children, as well as the person's belief as to whether a child with Down syndrome should be mainstreamed. A full cognitive representation of the referent is a minimal condition for having an attitude (Triandis, 1971); if a young child does not perceive that a classmate has a disability, then from a research perspective, that child's attitudes toward the classmate are irrelevant.

As mentioned above, the cognitive component of attitudes includes a person's beliefs about the causes of behavior. This concept is drawn from a literature not commonly associated with the study of attitudes, namely, the body of research inspired by attribution theory (Heider, 1958; Kelley, 1971). Maas, Marecek, and Travers (1978) define social attribution as "the process by which people impute situational, emotional, motivational, and dispositional causes to the behavior of others" (p. 146). Individuals also make attributions concerning their own behavior (Weiner, 1974). Because people are motivated to understand why events occur, these perceived causes affect their behavior and reactions (Heider, 1958). Attribution theorists (e.g., Weiner, 1974) suggest that affective responses to success that is believed to be caused by internal and controllable factors, such as personal effort and hard work, are likely to be more positive than affective responses to success that is believed to be the result of external factors such as luck, chance, or the efforts of others. In addition, affective responses would be more sympathetic when failure is attributed to an uncontrollable cause than when it is attributed to factors controllable by the individual, such as laziness or lack of effort. Similarly, Katz (1981) suggested that stigma, including stigma associated with disabilities, differ to the extent to which the person who is affected is held responsible for his or her own deviance. These attributional differences among disabilities would be expected to have important consequences for the way that children with these various disabilities are treated. As literature is presented in this chapter, the author draws on attribution research in describing the cognitive aspects of attitudes.

The affective component of Triandis's model (1971), is the emotional reaction elicited by the referent. A young child with physical signs of a disability may elicit discomfort, anxiety, and even revulsion in an observer, while another child may elicit pity. Some affective responses make people want to help and get to know specific children; other responses underlie the desire for segregation and social distancing. Thinking about integrating a child with a disability into an established preschool program can make some staff and parents angry or fearful, but may fill others with a sense of enthusiasm and excitement.

The third component of an attitude, behavioral intent, is a predisposition to act in a certain manner, to either seek or avoid contact (Triandis, 1971). In addition to determining desired social distance, attitudes may predetermine certain role relationships between people (Triandis et al., 1984), giving some a tendency to assume superordinate roles (teaching, helping, directing) and others, submissive roles (complying, accepting help). However, there is not always a direct relationship between attitudes and behavior; "attitudes are related to behaviors in complex ways" (Triandis, 1971, p. 24).

Triandis (1971, Triandis et al., 1984) describes the problem as follows: when attitudes are measured, information is usually obtained about a single, narrow class of people or objects, defined by a single characteristic) (e.g., children with disabilities). The judgments that guide behavior, however, are responses to a unique attitude object, which may have multiple attributes that could potentially influence behavior. A young child with Down syndrome may also be a girl who is blond, fair-skinned, in pigtails, frequently wears a Muppets shirt, and has a missing front tooth and a charming smile; she may be the daughter of a local businessman who lives in a prestigious neighborhood and attends the Methodist church. A person's attitudes and behavior toward this child will be determined, in part, by an amalgamation of the attitudes that he or she holds toward each of these characteristics. This complex interplay of attitudes is not likely to be captured using an attitude scale measuring the person's "attitudes toward disability" or "attitudes toward mainstreaming."

The following sections provide an overview of the research on the attitudes held by young children, their parents, teachers, and other key personnel who could potentially become involved in preschool mainstreaming. When research on a given topic is sparse, an attempt is made to draw upon related literatures that prove informative. As much as possible, the presentation is organized around Triandis's (1971) three-component model of attitudes.

RESEARCH

Attitudes of Young Children Toward Peers with Disabilities

Bricker (1978) suggested that one important rationale for preschool integration is the potential positive impact of early exposure to children with disabilities on the values and attitudes of young nondisabled peers. Similarly, parents of children attending integrated preschool programs perceive one of the greatest benefits of these programs to be children's development of a sensitivity to individual differences that comes from sharing the school day with children with disabilities (Blacher & Turnbull, 1982; Green & Stoneman, 1989; Turnbull, Winton, Blacher, & Salkind, 1983). It is likely that attitudes are most malleable during the early childhood period (Horne, 1985; Weinberg, 1978), leading to the possibility that societal attitudes about persons with disabilities could be positively influenced by the experiences of young children and their families (Bricker, 1978).

Although there is a great deal of literature on children's attitudes toward peers with disabilities (see Chiba, 1984; Gottlieb, Corman, & Curci, 1984; Horne, 1985; Reid, 1984; Siller, 1984; Siperstein & Bak, 1986, for reviews), only a limited number of attitudinal studies have focused on preschool children. This omission is not necessarily a result of disinterest in young children. Rather, it stems, in large part, from the substantial methodological challenges that confront the researcher who seeks to assess young children's attitudes. Most existing research has focused on preschool children's attitudes toward peers

with physical disabilities. Adaptive equipment associated with these disabilities (e.g., wheelchairs, braces, crutches) can be depicted effectively in pictorial stimuli that preschool children will easily recognize. Less visible disabilities, such as mental retardation, present a greater challenge for the attitude researcher, and, as a result, have received less research attention.

Two questions have been particularly influential in guiding research on preschool children's attitudes about disability: "Do children notice the presence of disabilities in other children?" and "Do children prefer to be with nondisabled children, rather than children with disabilities?" These questions correspond to the components of Triandis's model of an attitude (1971). The cognitive component is implied in the first question; noticing a disability in a peer is a cognitive prerequisite for the formation of an attitude about that peer's disability. The second and third attitudinal components, affectivity and behavioral intent, are inherent in research focusing on the second question.

Children's Beliefs and Attributions: The Cognitive Component   One of the first studies to examine whether or not young children are aware of disabilities in other children was conducted by Jones and Sisk (1970), who asked 200 children, ages 2–6, to respond to drawings of children with and without a leg brace. By age 4, children consistently perceived the leg brace and related it to the presence of a physical disability. Gerber (1977) investigated the ability of 3- to 5-year-old children in a mainstreamed program to recognize differences in their classmates with disabilities. Results of an open-ended measure (Tell me about . . .) indicated that the children were generally aware of their peers' disabilities. Among the children's classmates, an autistic-hyperactive boy was the most frequently mentioned; a child in a body brace and a child with mild cerebral palsy were mentioned somewhat less often.

Weinberg (1978) showed 101 3- to 5-year-old children pictures of same-sex children sitting either in a regular chair or a wheelchair (half the children were shown each type of picture). No differences emerged in measures of perceived ability of the children in the pictures (yes/no questions asking whether the child could color, sing, or run). Children viewing the picture of a child in a wheelchair were also asked a series of open-ended questions to probe whether or not the children understood why the child in the picture was in a wheelchair. Knowledge that the child was disabled increased with age (17% of 3-year-olds; 71% of 4-year-olds; 75% of 5-year-olds). The lack of differentiation as to whether the children in the pictures could run suggests that the preschool child's understanding of physical disability is still quite immature.

Further evidence for this cognitive immaturity was found in a study by Popp and Fu (1981; Popp, Fu, & Warrell, 1981). In their study, 121 3- to 6-year-old children were read a set of six statements ("I like cookies," "I can have fun playing," "I can listen to stories," "I can ride a trike," "I can throw a ball," "I can hop") and asked which of two children depicted in slides had made each statement. Some of the children pictured were in a wheelchair, had braces, were without arms, were standing, or were sitting. Children noticed both the wheelchair and leg braces and were generally aware that physical disabilities posed certain limitations, but tended to overgeneralize to include limitations unrelated to the specific disability. Children with physical disabilities, for example, were perceived as being less likely than other children to like cookies and to have fun playing. Younger children saw the disabilities as being less restrictive than did the older children. The younger group was also less aware of restrictions placed on activities by specific disabilities. The study subjects were not in integrated programs. The researchers speculated that the children's lack of understanding of the effects of physical disabilities could have resulted from pre-operational thinking or from a lack of exposure to children with disabilities.

Sigelman, Miller, and Whitworth (1986) studied children of from 4 years of age through third grade. The children were presented with drawings of seven types of children, including a child in a wheelchair. Each child was asked to "Tell me about" the child in each picture. In addition, children were shown all seven pictures and asked to identify children who "can/can't do things real well," "are smart/dumb," "do good/bad work in school," "are nice/bad," "do nice/bad things," and "are good looking/ugly," "cute/not cute." In response to the open-ended question asking the child to describe each stimulus picture, most children, including approximately 70% of both 4-year-olds and kindergarten children, mentioned the wheelchair. Few children, however, spontaneously voiced negative evaluations of the child in the wheelchair. Preschool and kindergarten children were more likely than older children to select more negative than positive attributes for the child with a physical disability, and boys offered more negative attributes than girls.

The researchers (Sigelman et al., 1986) concluded that by the time they reach preschool, children seem to have acquired a "schema of normality or similarity to self" (p. 30), which they then apply in evaluating a wide range of deviations from that standard. Few distinctions among nontypical children were made by subjects not yet in first grade. The earliest distinction made by children seems to be "like me" or "not like me." As children mature, "not like me" becomes differentiated. A similar conclusion was reached by Coie and Pennington (1976), who studied children as young as 7 years. Younger children did not seem to make comparisons among children from a normative base, but, rather, identified children whose behavior they particularly disliked or who differed in some way from themselves. This developmental pattern is consistent with the observation made by Triandis (1971), that as attitudes develop, "cognitions become more differentiated, integrated and organized" (p. 25).

There has been little research on young children's beliefs and attributions concerning peers with mental retardation. Given the limited research, it is helpful to briefly examine two related literatures, namely, research on young children's beliefs about intelligence and research on older children's beliefs and attributions about mental retardation. When Leahy and Hunt (1983) studied beliefs about intelligence held by 6-year-old children, they found the children tended to perceive a lack of intelligence as defiance of authority; half believed that parents should respond to unintelligent children with the use of punishment, requests for compliance, or insistence that the child attend school. The children thought that a lack of intelligence could be remedied by listening to others, asking more questions, or watching less television. Studying first-grade children, Yussen and Kane (1983) reported similar findings.

In a related study, Goodman (1989) found that although third-grade children may define intelligence functionally—as

skill or performance, and explained in terms of personal effort or contextual factors—mental retardation is recognized by these children as being different from a lack of intelligence. Unlike a lack of intelligence, mental retardation is recognized as an internalized trait, constitutionally caused, beyond personal control, and irreversible. Interestingly, most third-grade children in Goodman's (1989) study believed it was possible to be both mentally retarded and smart, further suggesting the unconventional distinction between these two constructs made by elementary school children.

Similar findings emerged in a small study of 6- to 7-year old children participating in a mainstreamed program (Lewis & Lewis, 1987). Children in the sample attributed a "lack of cleverness" in classmates to internal causes, under the control of the children, and potentially changeable. Severe learning difficulties in classmates, however, were seen as having physical causes that were beyond the control of the children, and therefore, as being permanent. These findings suggest that the cognitive distinctions between "mental retardation" and "lack of intelligence" made by third-grade children in Goodman's (1989) study may also be present in younger children. Furthermore, Lewis and Lewis (1987) found that nondisabled children thought of peers with severe learning difficulties as being chronologically younger than they actually were.

Elementary school children have low expectations for the performance of peers with mental retardation, even after intervention, and see it as unlikely that these children will attend school alongside themselves in regular education classrooms (Goodman, 1989). Children with lower intelligence, however, are more likely to be seen as potential classmates.

These beliefs, of course, may be quite different in schools practicing full inclusion, where all children are educated together in the same classrooms. Goodman (1989) suggested that children's beliefs about mental retardation being an irreversible condition, beyond the control of the affected child, may form the foundation for the *patronization effect* described by Gibbons, Sawin, and Gibbons (1979), in which individuals with mental retardation receive decreased blame for failure and less credit for success than nondisabled persons. These patronizing attributions have social consequences. When children do not perceive peers with mental retardation as being accountable for their behavior, the nondisabled children tend to be sympathetic (or even pitying) toward the children with mental retardation and engage in increased social distancing.

In addition to finding confusion among elementary school children about the relationship between mental retardation and intelligence, Goodman (1989) also found a lack of distinction between mental retardation and physical disability (and the signs that accompany it). When asked to draw a picture of a child with mental retardation, children tended to draw a child with a bodily impairment. Similarly, when asked to identify children with mental retardation from a series of photographs, children focused on the presence of facial characteristics and on physical disabilities in making this differentiation. Given the confusion of elementary school children concerning the characteristics of children with mental retardation, it seems safe to assume that preschool children also do not have a clear understanding of mental retardation or of the characteristics of peers so labeled.

Attitudes toward children with challenging behaviors have also received only limited research attention. After reviewing the relevant literature, Chiba (1984) concluded that children who exhibit aggressive behavior are targets for negative attention by peers, including young children. Maas et al. (1978) asked subjects as young as 7 years attribution questions about 3 children described in a series of vignettes read to the subjects by the experimenter. Stimulus children in the vignettes included those with withdrawn, self-punitive, and antisocial, aggressive behavior. Young children tended to perceive disordered behavior as being a result of the affected child's lack of efforts to change. In particular, the child with aggressive behavior was seen as wanting to behave as he or she did. The behavior of the withdrawn child, however, was seen as a product of internal, constitutional factors.

There have been no studies of preschool children's beliefs or attributions about peers with sensory disabilities. In a study of older children, Goodman (1989) found that blindness was believed to be environmentally caused, the result of an accident, rather than of constitutional factors or personal effort. Blindness was viewed as being even less curable than mental retardation, and as being unaffected by personal effort. Amelioration, if it occurred, was perceived to be the result of others' efforts.

As discussed earlier, social attribution (Heider, 1958; Kelley, 1971) occurs when children assign causes in order to explain the behavior of others. These attributions are important because they shape behavioral responses. Maas et al. (1978), for example, suggest that children's beliefs about the causes of other children's behavior influence their own social responses and patterns of interaction. Research by Sigelman and Shorokey (1986) that focused on the implications of making it known to peers that hyperactive classmates were being treated by different methods illustrates the importance of attributions. Children of 5–6 years valued efforts at improvement made by a child with hyperactivity, even when those efforts failed. A child being treated with drugs, who also failed to improve, was evaluated less positively. The children seemed to reason that children with hyperactivity could be proud of themselves as long as they tried hard, while being passively treated by adults was less worthy of praise.

Only one study has focused on the attitudes of young children who themselves have disabilities. Dunn, McCartan, and Fuqua (1988) studied 30 children, age 36–83 months, all of whom had physical disabilities. Informal data from parents suggested that siblings or typical peers in mainstreamed settings may serve as stimuli for the child's questions about his or her own disability, as well as for self-awareness of being different from other children. About half of the children in the study believed their disability was permanent. When asked "How are you different from other kids your age?" 22 of the 30 children gave scoreable responses. Of those, seven mentioned their physical disability as a difference; the other 15 named other physical differences, such as hair color. The development of attitudes and self-awareness of young children about their own disabilities, and the effect of mainstreamed preschool programs on these processes, are important, but neglected, areas of study.

Children's Beliefs and Attributions: Affect and Behavioral Intent   Studies of the preferences of nondisabled preschool children for peers with and without disabilities closely correspond to Triandis's (1971) attitudinal components of affectivity and behavioral intent. In the earliest of these studies, Weinberg (1978) found no differences between two stimulus pictures of children, one in a wheelchair and the other in a regular chair, in measures of 3- to 5-year-old children's desire to play with or share a toy with the pictured child. Different findings emerged, however, when children were presented with a forced choice between the two aforementioned pictures; most children preferred the child seated in the regular chair (64% of 3-year-olds; 71% of 4-year-olds; 90% of 5-year-olds). Popp and Fu (1981; Popp et al., 1981) also employed a forced-choice selection between pairs of pictures and pairs of videotaped depictions of children, and found that 3- to 6-year-old children prefer to interact with nondisabled children, even if they perceive a child with a disability as being capable of participating in a given activity.

Richardson (1970) found that by 5 or 6 years of age, a clear preference for nondisabled children had emerged. Sigelman et al. (1986) found that children as young as 4 years of age, when asked to select the best-liked child from pairs of pictures, preferred a nondisabled child over a child seated in a wheelchair. In both studies (Richardson, 1970; Sigelman et al., 1986), girls were more positive than boys toward a child in a wheelchair. Boys, however, were more positive than girls toward children with facial disfigurements or obesity. These gender-related patterns were explained by both authors as reflecting sex-role socialization in which physical ability is more salient to boys, while appearance is more salient to girls.

There is little information on the affective and behavioral components of the attitudes of young children toward peers with mental retardation and other non-physical disabilities (Gottlieb et al., 1984). In the only study the author could locate that focused on younger children, Graffi and Minnes (1988) showed 80 kindergarten subjects a videotape of a child who was presented either as having Down syndrome or not, and as being either mentally retarded or not. The meaning of mental retardation was also described to the subjects, and they were asked to pick one of a set of "happy faces" to indicate how they felt toward the child, to select among a set of positive and negative adjectives to describe the child, and to indicate their behavioral intentions toward the child using a social distance scale. The subjects expressed less positive attitudes and beliefs toward the child labeled as mentally retarded, and, in addition, demonstrated fewer behavioral inclinations to interact with such a child. Whether or not the child specifically had Down syndrome, however, did not influence the subjects' responses.

Although not directly related to disability, a series of studies on young children's preferences for attractive versus unattractive children also proves informative. At as young as 3 years of age, children select pictures of attractive children as desired friends (Dion, 1972); attractive children are expected by preschool peers to be helpful, self-sufficient, and independent, while less attractive children are expected to be aggressive and antisocial (Dion, 1972; Dion & Berscheid, 1974). Kleck, Richardson, and Ronald (1974) found general peer acceptance to be correlated to attractiveness. These findings reinforce those from studies of young children's response to peers with disabilities in that both suggest that preschool children notice physical differences and have already learned cultural stereotypes of valued and less-valued attributes. In addition, the attractiveness research suggests that children

associate certain physical characteristics with patterns of prosocial or negative behavior. These "implicit theories of personality," described by Schneider (1973, p. 294), develop early.

Methodological Issues in the Study of Children's Attitudes As mentioned at the opening of this discussion, researchers wishing to study the attitudes of preschool children are confronted with substantial methodological challenges. When studying adults, attitudes are inferred from what a person says about a referent, from the feelings the person describes, and from the way the person says that he or she will behave in the future (Triandis, 1971). Imagine sitting in front of a 3-year-old child with the task of eliciting this information. This image makes the measurement challenge immediately clear.

Methodological challenges have been met with varying degrees of success in the research reported here. Unfortunately, few studies report data on the reliability or validity of their instrumentation, making evaluation of the soundness of measurement impossible. Several authors (Inderbitzen & Best, 1986; Popp & Fu, 1981; Sigelman et al., 1986) note the differences in the results obtained by using different response options (open-ended, forced-choice, yes/no questions) and response formats (one picture, multiple pictures, adjective checklists). Different measurement strategies yield different findings on young children's attitudes about disability. An additional problem arises when researchers attempt to study the development of attitudes across an age span: simply put, it is impossible to ascertain whether age-related differences in attitudes are due to developmental patterns or to differential reliability of the measurement instrument across the ages studied. Richardson (1970) suggests that the latter may be the case. Obviously, much work remains to be done in order to meet the challenges of conducting valid, reliable research on the attitudes of preschool children.

Socialization of Young Children's Attitudes by Parents and Other Adults

Parents play an important role in their child's attitude development and in providing opportunities for their child to establish contact and develop friendships with children with disabilities (Rosenbaum, Armstrong, & King, 1987). Parents are the primary teachers of prosocial behavior; they inform their children about acceptable behavior; teach values such as helpfulness, sensitivity, generosity, and kindness; stimulate role taking and empathy, and teach children about the consequences that their behavior has on the feelings and well-being of others (Eisenberg & Mussen, 1989). Eisenberg and Mussen (1989) suggest that children encode this learning as rules or norms that are then recalled and applied later, in other situations, keeping the child within the bounds of acceptable social behavior. Attitudes are acquired as a part of this learning process. Triandis (1971) suggested that rejecting an attitude learned from parents is "a little like rejecting them" (p. 104).

Rugg and Stoneman (March, 1988) suggested that one mechanism for the transfer of attitudes from parent to child occurs as parents answer children's questions about children they encounter who have disabilities. Fifty-six parents (33 mothers, 23 fathers) of nondisabled children attending a mainstreamed preschool responded to a series of questions that might be asked by young children seeking information about peers with disabilities. Questions focused on children with mental re-

tardation, cerebral palsy, and aggressive and hyperactive behavior. Responses were coded using an attributional framework.

A majority of the parents listed internal causal attributions for the behavior of aggressive and hyperactive children (e.g., unhappy, want attention, have extra energy); almost a quarter of the parents, however, attributed aggressive behavior to external causes, primarily to bad parenting. Organic/medical causes were mentioned most frequently for children with cerebral palsy. Relatively few parents provided their children with causative information concerning mental retardation; when causative information on mental retardation was provided, it was divided almost evenly between external and organic/medical causal attributions.

Mothers were more likely to include information about the peer's strengths and capabilities in their answers to children's questions than were fathers. Strengths were most frequently mentioned for children with mental retardation; over 80% of mothers mentioned positive characteristics of children with mental retardation. Information provided by parents concerning children with cerebral palsy and hyperactive or aggressive behaviors, however, focused primarily on negative or limiting aspects of their disabilities.

Mothers were also more likely than fathers to teach their child positive values about disability (e.g., people should be accepting of differences, children with disabilities have feelings, and want to be liked). Again, positive values were most frequently mentioned in reference to children with mental retardation. Similarly, parents were most likely to encourage prosocial behavior (e.g., be a friend, play together) in response to questions about children with mental retardation. Parents tended to teach negative values (i.e., child is bad or spoiled, acts like a baby, is not nice) in responses to questions about children with aggressive behavior. Rather than encouraging play or social interaction with these children, mothers frequently recommended that their offspring cope with the behavior of aggressive children by avoiding them. In addition, a majority of children were cautioned by their parents not to model the aggressive behavior of these peers.

In addition to teaching attitudes by answering children's questions about disability, parents may also convey important information in their structuring of children's out-of-school peer contacts. In a mainstreamed preschool program with multiple interventions to increase social play between preschool children with and without disabilities, a parent survey revealed that only one out of over a hundred nondisabled children attending the program had ever invited one of the twelve classmates with disabilities to their home to play, or had ever visited the home of one of the children with disabilities (Rugg & Stoneman, 1988, June). Most nondisabled children, however, had visited the homes of four to five of their classmates and had invited a similar number of school friends over to their own homes to play.

When compared with the social networks of nondisabled preschool children, the social networks of preschool children with disabilities have been found to disproportionately comprise adults and relatives, with only limited contact with peers (Lewis, Feiring, & Brooks-Gunn, 1988). Other research on preschool and elementary school children with mental retardation also shows very low rates of peer involvement for these children after the school day ends (Stoneman, Brody, Davis, & Crapps, 1988, 1991). It is not clear whether these patterns of social isolation during nonschool portions of the day result from the attitudes of parents of nondisabled children, of parents of children with disabilities, of the children themselves, or from an interaction of these factors. The latter explanation would appear the most plausible. Given the important role of parents in structuring the peer contacts of preschool children, the attitudes indirectly transmitted to children by parents' failure to facilitate social contact between children with and without disabilities deserves further research attention.

In a related literature, researchers studying attractiveness have provided data suggesting that stereotyped beauty-is-good attitudes are transmitted to children from parents and other adults (Adams & Crane, 1980). Dion (1972) found that unattractive children were perceived by adults as being dishonest, unpleasant, and antisocial, as compared to attractive children. Preschool and young elementary school children have the same stereotypes based on appearance as do adults, preferring attractive peers as potential friends (Dion, 1974; Kleck et al., 1974; Langlois & Stephan, 1977). Langlois and Downs (1979) found peer-directed aggressiveness in unattractive children at age 5, but not at age 3, and suggested that expectations held by peers, parents, teachers, and others for attractive and unattractive children may create a self-fulfilling prophecy: over time these children internalize the stereotypes associated with attractiveness (or the lack thereof) and behave accordingly. It is logical to suggest that similar processes may operate as parents and adults transmit to the next generation stereotyped attitudes and beliefs about children with disabilities.

Attitudes of Parents
of Young Children with
and without Disabilities

When considering parental attitudes, it is important to differentiate between attitudes held toward young children with disabilities and attitudes held toward preschool integration. It is quite plausible that a parent might hold positive attitudes toward children with disabilities but have substantial concerns about mainstreaming as best educational practice. Conversely, another parent might harbor serious misconceptions about children with disabilities and pity these children, but believe that mainstreaming is a good idea.

In general, the complexity of parental attitudes has not been reflected in the existing research. Typically, researchers have been interested in identifying parents' perceptions of the benefits and drawbacks of integration, and in ascertaining whether or not various groups of parents believe preschool integration to be a good idea. Little information is available on parent attitudes about young children with disabilities. Sobol, Ashbourne, Earn, and Cunningham (1989) studied attributions for compliance in parents of young children with attention deficit hyperactivity disorder (ADHD). Mothers of children with ADHD perceived that compliance was unstable and uncontrollable, caused by factors external to themselves and independent of their parenting efforts. Unfortunately, only minimal research has been conducted on parental attributions concerning the behavior and characteristics of children with disabilities.

Rosenbaum et al. (1987) developed a parent attitude assessment, based on Triandis's (1971) three-component model, to measure the attitudes of parents of non-disabled children toward children with disabilities. When responses of parents of children in the later elementary school grades were factor analyzed, affective and behavioral intent items aggregated together and cognitive statements aggregated separately. The authors concluded that affect is probably closely linked with behavioral predispositions, whereas knowledge represents a separate dimension of a parent's mental set. Although this instrument was not developed for parents of young children, it seems to hold promise as a tool that might assist researchers in reorienting their efforts away from an exclusive focus on parent attitudes about preschool mainstreaming, and toward a more general examination of parental attitudes and beliefs about young children with disabilities.

There is reasonable agreement on parents' attitudes toward integration in the research literature. Parents of preschool children with and without disabilities have been found to have similar views (Reichart et al., 1989). Both groups of parents are in favor of integration (Bailey & Winton, 1987; Blacher & Turnbull, 1982; Reichart et al., 1989; Peck, Carlson, and Helmstetter, 1992; Turnbull et al., 1983) but share reservations as to whether teachers are adequately trained to implement successful integrated programs, and as to whether children would receive adequate instruction and attention in these programs (Bailey & Winton, 1987; Green & Stoneman, 1989; Peck, Hayden, Wandschneider, Peterson, & Richarz, 1989; Turnbull et al., 1983). These findings tend to hold true across different types of integrated settings, including Head Start and First Chance Programs (Blacher & Turnbull, 1982), public school kindergartens (Turnbull et al., 1983), university-based model programs (Bailey & Winton, 1987), community daycare (Green & Stoneman, 1989; Peck et al., 1989) and even among parents of children not attending integrated programs (Green & Stoneman, 1989; Reichart et al., 1989).

There is considerable variability, however, in parents' attitudes toward implementation of an integrated preschool program (Bailey & Winton, 1987). What gives rise to these varying attitudes? One explanation, the *contact hypothesis* (Gottlieb et al., 1984), proposes that parents' mainstreaming attitudes are related to their previous experiences with people with disabilities. Green and Stoneman (1989), in a study of 204 parents (117 mothers, 87 fathers) of nondisabled children between the ages of 18 months and 6 years, found that for mothers, but not fathers, perceived positiveness (but not amount) of previous contact with persons with disabilities corresponded to current attitudes toward mainstreaming. Additionally, although parents who had at least one child in an integrated setting generally had more positive attitudes than did parents with no such experience, parents who negatively evaluated their child's experience were less supportive of mainstreaming. Thus, the most important variable affecting mainstreaming attitudes appeared to be the quality, rather than quantity, of experience with people with disabilities and with integrated settings.

Although less important than personal experience, demographic factors also seem to play a role in the development of attitudes about mainstreaming, particularly for mothers. Mothers in families with higher incomes were less positive about preschool integration than were less affluent mothers (Green & Stoneman, 1989), while parental education had no effect on attitudes about mainstreaming. Younger mothers had more positive attitudes toward integration than older mothers, and were more likely to see benefits that might come to their children through participation in an integrated program. Mothers of older preschool children were more likely to believe that their children would develop a sense of empathy and acceptance as a result of their participation in a mainstreamed program. Fathers of older children, however, were more concerned about disruptive behavior by children with disabilities. Parents of older preschool children were less supportive of integrating children with severe disabilities (e.g., emotional disturbance and severe mental retardation), than were parents of younger children. These findings suggest that parents' attitudes toward integration change over time.

There were also considerable differences between mothers and fathers. Maternal attitudes corresponded to several factors, including the positiveness of past experiences with people with disabilities, family income, parent age, education, and age of the child (Green & Stoneman, 1989). But these factors held almost no predictive power for fathers. The primary predictor of fathers' attitudes was, in fact, the attitudes of their wives. Green and Stoneman (1989) suggested that this pattern may reflect a family system in which mothers set the tone for family attitudes toward mainstreaming based on their own experiences, while fathers, who tend to be less involved in the day-to-day aspects of childcare, adopt the views held by their wives.

Perceived benefits and drawbacks of preschool integration are quite similar across studies and among parents of children both with and without disabilities. The most consistently reported benefit, cited by over 90% of parents across studies, is the anticipation that children will develop sensitivity and become accepting of differences (Bailey & Winton, 1987; Green & Stoneman, 1989; Reichart et al., 1989; Turnbull et al., 1983). Providing exposure to the "real world" for children with disabilities (Bailey & Winton, 1987; Turnbull et al., 1983) and promotion of positive social contact (Reichart et al., 1989) are also frequently cited benefits.

One cause for concern is the consistency across studies that use different samples and different methodological approaches (Bailey & Winton, 1987; Green & Stoneman, 1989; Turnbull et al., 1983) to study what parents perceive to be the drawbacks of integration. Parents consistently express strong discomfort with the level of training and preparation of preschool teachers and daycare staff in skills related to integration. Although parents in each of these studies were generally supportive of mainstreaming, perceptions of inadequate preparation of early childhood educators may be compromising those positive attitudes. Other drawbacks perceived by parents included possible social rejection or teasing of children with disabilities (Bailey & Winton, 1987; Turnbull et al., 1983); inadequate staff–child ratios (Peck et al., 1989); concerns about children with disabilities receiving adequate help, therapeutic services, and individualized instruction (Green & Stoneman, 1979; Peck et al., 1989; Turnbull et al., 1983); lack of teacher attention to nondisabled children (Green & Stoneman, 1989); and the ability of parents to effectively deal with issues arising in integrated programs (Turnbull et al., 1983). Families of children with disabilities also express the concern that mainstreamed settings may encourage comparisons among children, potentially highlighting differences between their own children and normally developing children (Bailey & Winton, 1987; Reichart et al., 1989).

In one of the few longitudinal studies on this subject, Bailey and Winton (1987) assessed the attitudes of parents of children with and without disabilities, ages 6 weeks to 5 years, before and 9 months after the initiation of a university-based mainstreaming program. The attitudes of parents of nondisabled children did not change over time. Some concerns decreased during the program period, such as the belief of parents of children with disabilities that it might be upsetting for them to see the differences between their child and normally developing children. Other issues, such as the concern that children might be teased or rejected, remained high for the full period of the study. Bailey and Winton (1987) concluded that some parental concerns are resolved simply by the passage of time, while others may require individualized interventions.

Examination of the attitudes of parents of nondisabled children toward integrating preschool children with disabilities revealed wide differences dependent on the particular type of disabilities (Green & Stoneman, 1989). Children with physical and sensory disabilities caused the least concern, while the thought of integrating children with mental retardation, emotional disturbance, and behavior problems made parents the most uncomfortable. The more severe the child's mental retardation, the more concerned parents of nondisabled children were about integrating that child. This hierarchy of concern was similar to that reported in the literature on teachers contemplating the mainstreaming of older children (see Horne, 1985).

Teachers, Administrators, and Early Intervention Personnel

Although there is a great deal of research literature on teacher attitudes toward mainstreaming at the elementary and secondary levels (see Horne, 1985; Jamieson, 1984; Salvia & Munson, 1986, for reviews), there is little information on the attitudes that teachers and other personnel have toward preschool mainstreaming. And the existing literature is sparse and scattered across topics. Unlike the situation for older students, where teachers and administrators are key to the implementation of mainstreaming, there is a large and complex network of professionals and paraprofessionals whose attitudes may influence decisions about and opportunities for integration at the preschool level. Mainstreamed or integrated preschool programs can be offered by a myriad of providers, including public schools, private schools, Head Start and other federally supported programs, family care providers, proprietary daycare, churches, hospitals, not-for-profit daycare, parent cooperatives, and businesses and industry. In addition, key personnel, such as early childhood special educators, early interventionists, psychologists, social workers, and related-services professionals can influence whether or not an integrated placement is recommended and cultivated for a given child. It is important to understand how the attitudes of various people in this service network may influence programmatic decisions about integration.

In one of the few studies to directly address these issues, Blacher and Turnbull (1982) sent parents and teachers in Head Start and Handicapped Children's Early Education Programs (now called First Chance programs) questionnaires assessing mainstreaming attitudes. Both parents and teachers were very positive about mainstreaming. The authors noted that teachers in these programs receive training directly related to integration. Peck et al. (1989), utilizing qualitative methods, interviewed 10 teachers and 10 administrators to ascertain the barriers encountered in the development of integrated preschool programs. Concerns clustered into three categories: adequacy of staff preparation, adequacy of resources, and fear of conflicts. Teacher training was of great concern to both groups. Teacher's concerns included release time for planning, sufficient space and materials, and coordination with other professionals. Administrators' concerns included funding, space, transportation, liability, and conflicts among personnel. In a subsequent study (Peck et al., 1992), teachers of mainstreamed preschool classes were found to have positive attitudes about inclusion, believing that integrated programs taught typically developing children to be more aware of the needs of others and more accepting of differences. These teachers did not perceive that nondisabled children in the classroom received less attention because of the presence of children with disabilities.

Larravee and Cook (1979) gave a mainstreaming attitude scale to teachers, including kindergarten teachers. Perception of past success in dealing with children with disabilities was the single most important factor affecting teachers' mainstreaming attitudes. Similarly, regular educators who felt that they had a high degree of competence initiated fewer child referrals for special services and expressed less concern over problem behaviors (Meijer & Foster, 1988).

As with studies on parent attitudes, the research on the attitudes of professionals has focused specifically on integration, to the neglect of attitudes on other subjects relevant to working with young children with disabilities. Once again, it is helpful to examine findings from a parallel body of literature, which focuses on attractiveness.

Teachers rate attractive children as

having greater academic ability, better social adjustment, and as being more likely to have success in life than unattractive children (Clifford & Walster, 1973; Lerner & Lerner, 1977). Elovitz and Salvia (1982) found that school psychologists linked unattractiveness with mental retardation, considering a diagnosis of mental retardation as being more acceptable for unattractive children than for those considered attractive. These same psychologists had high expectations of success for the mainstreaming of physically attractive students, but were more pessimistic about mainstreaming as a programmatic option for less attractive children. These findings suggest that professionals' attitudes toward young children with disabilities may be a fertile area for research.

Attribution theorists (Heider, 1958; Kelly, 1971) would suggest that the manner in which teachers respond to the behavior of young children is, in part, a function of the attributions that these teachers make as to the causes of that behavior. Suppose, for example, that while coloring, a child with mental retardation grabs another child's paper and crumples it. A teacher perceiving this as a deliberate misbehavior would reprimand and possibly punish the child. But a teacher who believed that the child did not have the social or cognitive skills to understand his or her actions might take the opportunity to teach these skills. A teacher who believed that children with mental retardation are too cognitively limited to learn appropriate behavior in such situations might give the offended child a new sheet of paper and ignore the behavior of the offender. The teacher's causal attribution and the resulting response would be expected to either increase or decrease the probability that this socially inappropriate behavior would recur, thereby either facilitating or hindering the ultimate success of the child's mainstream placement. Thus, the cognitive component of teachers' attitudes can directly influence important factors in potential mainstreaming success.

Although the phenomenon has not been studied at the preschool level, there is also evidence that the social misbehaviors of older children with mental retardation are perceived to be less serious than similar behavior in nondisabled peers (Campbell, Dobson, & Bost, 1985). In addition, children with mental retardation are punished less and are held less accountable for misbehavior than are nondisabled children (Propst & Nagle, 1981).

Bar-Tal (1982) found that children learn to make attributions for success and failure from teachers. The optimal pattern is for the child to attribute success to internal, stable, and controllable causes, while attributing failure to internal, unstable, controllable causes. This pattern encourages children to tackle difficult tasks and to rely on effort and hard work to succeed. Unfortunately, as shown above, this is not the pattern of attributions that teachers hold toward children with disabilities, a situation that may compromise a child's motivation to try hard to succeed and negatively influence the reactions of peers to the child's success or failure.

In a disturbing paper, Feldman, Gerstein, and Feldman (1989) reported that both special and regular educators, including kindergarten teachers, were found to hold relatively negative beliefs about the parents of students with disabilities. When contrasted with the beliefs that the teachers held about parents of nondisabled students, fewer parents of children with disabilities were perceived as having trust in the teachers, as being competent parents, or as undertaking instructional efforts at home. This suggests that in addition to studying teachers' attitudes toward preschool integration and toward children with disabilities, it may also be important to better understand teachers' attitudes and beliefs about the parents of these children, and to develop successful strategies for changing unproductive attitudes.

RECOMMENDATIONS FOR PRACTICE

Strategies for Positively Affecting the Attitudes of Young Children

> Why are we so keen on filling children's heads with platitudes? Why do we tell them that "those kids" are just like you and me? In the face of so many dramatically obvious contradictions, do we really expect them to believe that? Do we really believe it ourselves? (Brightman, 1977, p. 64)

Integrated preschool programs provide an opportunity to foster positive attitudes toward children with disabilities (Horne, 1985), but the development of such attitudes is far from certain. As Siperstein and Bak (1980) note, there is no assurance that mere contact with children with disabilities will increase understanding or improve attitudes. Much depends on the quality of the experience and the transfer of information and attitudes to young children by parents, teachers, and other adults.

It seems quite clear from the literature reviewed earlier in this chapter that preschool children notice disabilities in other children. Although most research has focused on physical disabilities, the few studies that examine children's awareness of mental retardation and other disabilities suggest that these conditions are noticed as well. Thus, the first element in the formation of an attitude, awareness of disability (Triandis, 1971), is present even in very young children. Although they have a general awareness of disability,

young children's cognitive understanding of the subject is immature and confused.

It is naive and incorrect to assume that if teachers and other adults simply ignore a child's disability, refusing to discuss, or even acknowledge it, then other children will not notice it. It is possible that this may actually intensify the salience of the disability to other children, placing it in the realm of things that are taboo, so negative that they are unspeakable. Without a free exchange of information between adult and child, the young child has no alternative but to base attitudes on his or her own immature cognitive understanding.

Adults, including teachers and parents, play an important role when they openly assist young children in understanding the meaning of disability. The importance of directly addressing differences and teaching about diversity has been stressed by a number of authors (Blacher-Dixon, Leonard, & Turnbull, 1981; Horne, 1985; Ronald, 1977; Thurman & Lewis, 1979). Millspaugh and Segelman (1977) provide an interesting framework for understanding these issues. They suggest that preschool children easily accept information about disability because all young children are virtually disabled in an adult-designed environment: "Society systematically handicaps all small children by making drinking fountains too high to manage, stairs too steep to climb, and toilet paper dispensers too far [away] to reach" (p. 206). It is quite straightforward to teach children that each person, whether disabled or not, is different from every other person. An additional point should follow: although differences exist, all people are valued members of society (and of the preschool classroom) and are more alike than different.

Integrated preschool programs may stimulate children to ask why some of their peers seem to be so different from themselves (Brightman, 1977). These questions may be posed to the preschool teacher, or to parents after the child returns home. These are legitimate questions that deserve honest, clear answers. Ronald (1977) suggests that the young child's reaction to disability is generally one of curiosity and exploration. When this awakened interest is met by embarrassed parents and teachers who silence questions and avoid discussion, the child is done a disservice, and an opportunity for teaching positive attitudes is lost.

Ronald (1977) found that the most frequent question that children wanted answered about disability was, "How did it happen?" Children want adults to provide a causal attribution for the disability. Unfortunately, adults' communication with children regarding disability can have negative effects, perpetuating cultural stereotypes and increasing social distancing. So, not only do children need to have information about disabilities provided in concrete terms, but that information should also be presented in a form that yields positive attributions and attitudes (Sigelman & Shorokey, 1986).

The findings of Rugg and Stoneman (March, 1988), discussed earlier, suggest that, in addition to information concerning the cause of the disability, parents' answers to questions about disabilities also provide young children with information about values, child strengths, child limitations, and coping strategies. Parents and other adults were sometimes found to be inadvertently teaching negative attitudes when answering these questions. This was particularly true for answers to children's questions concerning peers with aggressive behavior. These children were frequently blamed for misbehaving, and parents were often held accountable for their children's aggressive behavior. Young nondisabled children were advised by their parents to avoid these peers and warned not to model their behavior.

Less obvious negative messages about disability can also be transmitted to young children by adults. Ebert (1977) warned that the ultimate effect of integrated programs may be that nondisabled children learn to gain a feeling of satisfaction about themselves for being "nice" for playing with "poor, unfortunate" children with disabilities. She suggests that this attitude is a child's version of *noblesse oblige*: "I am nice to you because one is nice to people like you" (p. 79). Attitudes based on these patronizing beliefs are potentially as harmful as blatantly negative attitudes, if not more so.

It would seem important to monitor the effects that social interventions may have on the attitudes and attributions of nondisabled peers. Friendships are rooted in equalitarian role relationships (Hartup, 1979). The relationship between children's attitudes and their friendships has not been explored, but it is likely that friendships among children depend on positive attitudes based on social equality. When some children are taught to serve as teachers or helpers to others, the ensuing relationships among children is hierarchical, rather than equalitarian, and may contribute to the attitude of *noblesse oblige* described by Ebert (1977).

To date, most researchers have focused on interventions that decrease the social isolation that some children with disabilities experience in integrated programs. Few of these researchers, however, have examined the impact of their interventions on children's cognitions or attitudes. It would seem plausible that in some instances interventionists may be increasing the level of social interactions among children, but making no real gains toward the development of either positive attitudes or long-lasting, equalitarian friendships.

The media are a source of social influence that cannot be overlooked in trying to understand the development of children's attitudes about disability. Popular programs such as Sesame Street and Mr. Roger's Neighborhood have included children with disabilities in segments and have provided young viewers with information about specific disabling conditions. Other suggestions for developing positive attitudes through children's media include incorporating children with disabilities into film segments on other topics; showing these children participating in everyday activities, without calling special attention to their disability (Sequin, 1977); and showing persons with obvious disabilities in background scenes and in plots in which their disability is not the focus of attention (Blatt, 1977). Providing models of children with and without disabilities playing together, taking turns, and cooperating (Berstein, Hayes, & Shauble, 1977) has also been suggested as a positive strategy.

There are numerous resources, including popular media, books, and curricula that can, their proponents claim, positively influence children's attitudes about disability (i.e., Litton, Banbury, & Harris, 1980). Most of these materials, however, have never been empirically validated. Attempts to influence preschool children's attitudes toward peers with disabilities have met with mixed success (Esposito & Peach, 1983; Vandell, Anderson, Ehrhardt, & Wilson, 1982). Much remains unknown about the development of young children's attitudes toward disability and about effective strategies for influencing these attitudes. Additionally, research is needed on the development of the attitudes and self-concepts of young children with disabilities and about effective strategies for facilitating positive attitudes toward the self and others in these children.

Strategies for Positively Affecting the Attitudes of Parents

Teacher training and staff development programs must take priority if parents are to be fully supportive of preschool integration. Parents have been quite clear in their concerns about the ability of preschool teachers to provide optimal classroom environments that include children with disabilities, particularly severe disabilities. As mentioned above an important variable affecting parents' attitudes appears to be the quality of their past experiences with integrated settings (Green & Stoneman, 1989). It follows that poor-quality integrated programs may actually do harm, making parents of nondisabled children less accepting of future integration efforts.

This suggests a vital need for the training of administrative and direct service personnel who are responsible for successful implementation of these programs. If ith the rapid proliferation of preschool mainstreaming programs, these programs are implemented without trained staff or adequate resources, the resulting low-quality ervices may shut the door to future development of effective, high-quality programs. A commitment to the full inclusion of young children with disabilities into integrated preschool settings requires a commitment to extensive personnel training, provision of adequate resources and support, and high-quality service delivery for all children.

Turnbull et al. (1983) found that almost all parents in their study wanted more information about mainstreaming, and most preferred to get this information from printed materials. Clear, relevant, and readable materials addressing parents' concerns and questions about preschool integration are needed for parents of children both with and without disabilities. Parents of both groups also need to be involved in planning for new integrated programs, and in decisionmaking throughout the period of program implementation (Reichart et al., 1989; Winton, 1986).

The lack of social contact between children with and without disabilities during the hours after school (Rugg & Stoneman, June, 1988; Stoneman et al., 1988, 1991) is another cause for concern. It is of little value to facilitate interactions in the classroom if children with disabilities spend the rest of their time socially isolated in their homes or neighborhoods. Because parents are important mediators of young children's opportunities for play and social contact with peers, it is important that parental attitudes toward friendships between children with and without disabilities receive more research attention. Early intervention and preschool parent groups provide an excellent opportunity to focus parents' attention on the importance of the development of friendships and social competencies during nonschool hours.

Strategies for Positively Affecting the Attitudes of Service Providers

It is quite striking that across studies the most salient concern about preschool integration is the inadequate preparation and training of teachers. Strategies and skills necessary for integration must be incorporated into preservice early childhood teacher education programs, and into programs training generic child development personnel (Turnbull et al., 1983). Because

integrated preschool programs are diverse, and are administered by a variety of agencies and groups, many personnel in these programs are paraprofessionals or persons with college degrees in areas unrelated to working with young children. These personnel need to be reached through a variety of training mechanisms, including inservice and staff development training experiences.

Powers (1983) stresses the importance of implementing inservice programs before beginning integration, and of continuing those programs during implementation. It is important to note, however, that there is only a minimal correlation between teachers' knowledge and their attitudes toward mainstreaming (Green, Rock, & Weisenstein, 1983); training programs that simply increase knowledge may have no effect on attitudes (Green et al., 1983; Siperstein & Bak, 1980). A good example is the introductory course on disabilities mandated as a component of many teacher education curricula. Evidence suggests that this course has little or no impact on attitudes (Horne, 1985), that, in fact, students may be more negative toward mainstreaming after concluding such a course than they were when they enrolled (Buttery, 1981).

There is still much to learn about effective methods for changing teacher attitudes (Horne, 1985). One promising approach at the preservice level is course infusion, in which information and experiences related to young children with disabilities are dispersed across the curriculum, added to generic early childhood education and child development courses (Rugg & Stoneman, 1990). In this approach, all aspects of the early childhood preservice curriculum, from introductory courses through student teaching, are designed to positively influence the student's skills and attitudes relevant to preschool integration.

The attitudes of teachers and staff can make the difference between success and failure of integration at numerous points during implementation. Attitudinal barriers can block integration from ever being seriously considered, either for a particular child or for an entire class of children with disabilities, and can cause premature termination of an integrated placement when problems arise. Siperstein and Bak (1980) suggested that if teachers exhibit unfavorable attitudes toward a child with a disability, nondisabled children will develop similar attitudes and behave accordingly. Thus, even if attitudinal barriers are not so strong as to preclude the mainstreamed placement, they can still hinder successful social integration once placement has occurred. Peck et al. (1989) stressed the importance of allowing teachers and program staff to have input into decisionmaking and program planning concerning integration.

Teacher attitudes toward integration are, in part, a function of the availability of support services and resources (Powers, 1983). Administrators communicate their attitudes toward integration to staff through their allocation of resources (Powers, 1983). Although there is little information on the attitudes of administrators toward preschool mainstreaming, it seems reasonable that attitudes would differ across types of programs. Administrators of for-profit daycare must consider financial issues, such as the tuition loss that would result if parents opposed to integration withdrew their children, and the additional cost if a mainstreamed child requires extra staff time or resources. Conversely, administrators in federally funded programs such as Head Start operate under mandates that require mainstreaming, making financial and attitudinal issues a less important factor in decisionmaking.

There is almost no information on the attitudes of early childhood special educators and interventionists. These persons are in key roles for initiating integrated placements, and their attitudes, although overlooked in the literature, are important. Additionally, the attitudes of related services personnel, health professionals, and others who provide services for young children with disabilities (and advice to their parents) have yet to receive research attention. Without a research database on these issues, making appropriate recommendations for practice is impossible.

SUMMARY

Many professionals in the field have operated with the hope that placing young children together in integrated preschool programs would result in friendships, play, and the development of social sensitivity and positive attitudes among all involved. Unfortunately, this is not always the case. There is nothing magical about integrated service settings; what is important is the quality of service that is provided in those settings (Landesman & Butterfield, 1987).

A large proportion of the research on mainstreaming and integrated programs has been conducted in model demonstration programs, directed by faculty with graduate degrees and implemented by well-trained staff with access to ample resources. Unfortunately, findings on these programs shed little light on critical issues relevant to the realities of integrating children with disabilities into existing community-based care. The American childcare system is an intricate, complex network of programs that includes competing interests and various perspectives. Much has yet to be learned about the attitudes of those working in the system, and of those served by it. This knowledge, once gained, will greatly improve the chances of success for preschool integration efforts.

There is also a need for further research on the factors that influence childrens' attitudes, including the effectiveness of programs and materials designed to positively affect young childrens' knowledge and attitudes about disability, the relationship between children's attributions about peers and the quality of their friendships with those peers, the attitudinal factors underlying the social isolation of young children with disabilities in their homes and neighborhoods, the factors that influence the development of attitudes in young children who themselves have a disability, and the processes through which the attitudes of parents and teachers are transmitted to young children. Other important areas in need of research include identifying effective ways of positively affecting the attitudes about integration held by the myriad of service providers and administrators involved in preschool programs and examining the relationship between the attributions that these service providers make about children with various disabilities and the interventions and services that they implement for those children. And finally, longitudinal research is needed to discover the ways in which attitudes toward disability learned in early childhood forecast future attitudes and behavior.

REFERENCES

Adams, G.R., & Crane, P. (1980). An assessment of parents' and teachers' expectations of preschool children's social preference for attractive or unattractive children and adults. *Child Development, 51,* 224–231.

Allport, G.W. (1954). *The nature of prejudice.* Reading, MA: Addison-Wesley.

Bailey, D.B., & Winton, P.J. (1987). Stability and change in parents' expectations about mainstreaming. *Topics in Early Childhood Special Education, 7,* 73–88.

Bar-Tal, D. (1982). The effects of teachers' behavior on pupils' attributions: A review. In C. Antaki & C. Brewin (Eds.), *Attributions and psychological change* (pp. 177–194). New York: Academic Press.

Berstein, L., Hayes, L., & Shauble, L. (1977). Experimenting with "Sesame Street" for mentally retarded children. In M. Harmonay (Ed.), *Promise and performance: Children with special needs* (pp. 65–77). Cambridge: Ballinger.

Blacher, J., & Turnbull, A.P. (1982). Teacher and parent perspectives on selected social aspects of preschool mainstreaming. *The Exceptional Child, 29,* 191–199.

Blacher-Dixon, J., Leonard, J., & Turnbull, A.P. (1981). Mainstreaming at the early childhood level: Current and future perspectives. *Mental Retardation, 5,* 235–241.

Blatt, J. (1977). Small changes and real difference. In M. Harmonay (Ed.), *Promise and performance: Children with special needs* (pp. 11–22). Cambridge: Ballinger.

Bricker, D.D. (1978). A rationale for the integration of handicapped and nonhandicapped preschool children. In M.J. Guralnick (Ed.), *Early intervention and the integration of handicapped and nonhandicapped children* (pp. 3–26). Baltimore: University Park Press.

Brightman, A.J. (1977). "But their brain is broken": Young children's conceptions of retardation. In M. Harmonay (Ed.), *Promise and performance: Children with special needs* (pp. 59–67). Cambridge: Ballinger.

Buttery, T.J. (1981). Pre-service teachers' affective perceptions on mainstreamed children. *College Student Journal, 15,* 74–78.

Campbell, N.J., Dobson, J.E., & Bost, J.M. (1985). Educator perceptions of behavior problems of mainstreamed students. *Exceptional Children, 51,* 298–303.

Chiba, C. (1984). Children's attitudes toward

emotionally disturbed peers. In R. L. Jones (Ed.), *Attitudes and attitude change in special education: Theory and practice* (pp. 171–183). Reston, VA: Council for Exceptional Children.

Clifford, M.M., & Walster, E. (1973). The effects of physical attractiveness on teacher expectations. *Sociology of Education, 46*, 248–258.

Coie, J.D., & Pennington, B.F. (1976). Children's perceptions of deviance and disorder. *Child Development, 47*, 407–413.

Dion, K. (1972). Young children's stereotyping of facial attractiveness. *Developmental Psychology, 9*, 183–188.

Dion, K. (1974). Physical attractiveness and evaluation of children's transgressions. *Journal of Personality and Social Psychology, 24*, 285–290.

Dion, K., & Berscheid, E. (1974). Physical attractiveness and peer perception. *Sociometry, 37*, 1–12.

Dunn, N.L., McCartan, K.W., & Fuqua, R.W. (1988). Young children with orthopedic handicaps: Self-knowledge about their disability. *Exceptional Children, 55*, 249–252.

Ebert, S. (1977). Paying deference to differences: A child's version of *Noblesse Oblige*? In M. Harmonay (Ed.), *Promise and performance: Children with special needs* (pp. 78–80). Cambridge: Ballinger.

Eisenberg, N., & Mussen, P.H. (1989). *The roots of prosocial behavior in children*. New York: Cambridge University Press.

Elovitz, G.P., & Salvia, J. (1982). Attractiveness as a biasing factor in the judgments of school psychologists. *Journal of School Psychology, 20*, 339–345.

Esposito, B.C., & Peach, W.J. (1983). Changing attitudes of preschool children toward handicapped persons. *Exceptional Children, 49*, 361–363.

Feldman, D., Gerstein, L.H., & Feldman, B. (1989). Teachers' beliefs about administrators and parents of handicapped and nonhandicapped students. *Journal of Experimental Education, 58*, 43–54.

Fishbein, M., & Ajzen, I. (1975) *Belief, attitude, intention, and behavior: An introduction to theory and research*. Reading, MA: Addison-Wesley.

Gerber, P.J. (1977). Awareness of handicapping conditions and sociometric status in an integrated preschool setting. *Mental Retardation, 15*, 24–25.

Gibbons, F.X., Sawin, L.G., & Gibbons, B.N. (1979). Evaluations of mentally retarded persons: "Sympathy" or patronization? *American Journal of Mental Deficiency, 84*, 124–131.

Goodman, J.F. (1989). Does retardation mean dumb? Children's perceptions of the nature, cause, and course of mental retardation. *The Journal of Special Education, 23*, 313–329.

Gottlieb, J., Corman, L., & Curci, R. (1984). Attitudes toward mentally retarded children. In R. L. Jones (Ed.), *Attitudes and attitude change in special education: Theory and practice* (pp. 143–156). Reston, VA: Council for Exceptional Children.

Graffi, S., & Minnes, P.M. (1988). Attitudes of primary school children toward the physical appearance and labels associated with Down syndrome. *American Journal on Mental Retardation, 93*, 28–35.

Green, A.L., & Stoneman, Z. (1989). Attitudes of mothers and fathers of nonhandicapped children. *Journal of Early Intervention, 13*, 292–304.

Green, K., Rock, D.L., & Weisenstein, G.R. (1983). Validity and reliability of a scale assessing attitudes toward mainstreaming. *Exceptional Children, 50*, 182–183.

Hartup, W.W. (1979). The social worlds of childhood. *American Psychologist, 34*, 944–950.

Heider, F. (1958). *The psychology of interpersonal relations*. New York: John Wiley & Sons.

Horne, M. D. (1985). *Attitudes toward handicapped students: Professional, peer and parent reactions*. Hillsdale, NJ: Lawrence Erlbaum Associates.

Inderbitzen, H.M., & Best, D.L. (1986). Children's attitudes toward physically handicapped peers. *Journal of Applied Developmental Psychology, 7*, 417–428.

Jamieson, J.D. (1984). Attitudes of educators toward the handicapped. In R. L. Jones (Ed.), *Attitudes and attitude change in special education: Theory and practice* (pp. 206–222). Reston, VA: Council for Exceptional Children.

Jones, R.L., & Sisk, D. (1970). Early perceptions of orthopedic disability: A developmental study. *Rehabilitation Literature, 31*, 34–38.

Katz, I. (1981). *Stigma: A social psychological analysis*. Hillsdale, NJ: Lawrence Erlbaum Associates.

Kelly, H.H. (1971). *Attribution in social interaction*. Morristown, NJ: General Learning.

Kleck, R.E., Richardson, S.A., & Ronald, L.

(1974). Physical appearance cues and interpersonal attraction in children. *Child Development, 50*, 305–310.

Landesman, S., & Butterfield, E. (1987). Normalization and deinstitutionalization of mentally retarded individuals: Controversy and facts. *American Psychologist, 42*, 809–816.

Langlois, J.H., & Downs, A.C. (1979). Peer relations as a function of physical attractiveness: The eye of the beholder or behavioral reality? *Child Development, 50*, 409–418.

Langlois, J.H., & Stephan, C. (1977). The effects of physical attractiveness and ethnicity on children's behavioral attributions and peer preferences. *Child Development, 48*, 1694–1698.

Larravee, B., & Cook, L. (1979). Mainstreaming: A study of the variables affecting teacher attitude. *Journal of Special Education, 13*, 315–324.

Leahy, R.L., & Hunt, T.M. (1983). A cognitive-developmental approach to the development of conceptions of intelligence. In R.L. Leahy (Ed.), *The child's construction of social inequality* (pp. 135–160). New York: Academic Press.

Lerner, R.M., & Lerner, J.V. (1977). Effects of age, sex, and physical attractiveness on child–peer relations, academic performance, and elementary school adjustment. *Developmental Psychology, 13*, 585–590.

Lewis, A., & Lewis, V. (1987). The attitudes of young children toward peers with severe learning difficulties. *British Journal of Developmental Psychology, 5*, 287–292.

Lewis, M., Feiring, C., & Brooks-Gunn, J. (1988). Young children's social networks as a function of age and dysfunction. *Infant Mental Health Journal, 9*, 142–157.

Litton, F.W., Banbury, M.M., & Harris, K. (1980). Materials for educating nonhandicapped students about their handicapped peers. *Teaching Exceptional Children, 13*, 39–43.

Maas, E., Marecek, J., & Travers, J. (1978). Children's conceptions of disordered behavior. *Child Development, 49*, 146–154.

Meijer, C.J.W., & Foster, S.F. (1988). The effect of teacher self-efficacy on referral chance. *The Journal of Special Education, 22*, 378–385.

Millspaugh, F., & Segelman, M. (1977). Neither fear nor pity: Public-service announcements about differences. In M. Harmonay (Ed.), *Promise and performance: Children with special needs* (pp. 205–211). Cambridge: Ballinger.

Peck, C.A., Carlson, P., & Helmstetter, E. (1992). Parent and teacher perceptions of outcomes for typically developing children enrolled in integrated early childhood programs: A statewide survey. *Journal of Early Intervention, 16*, 53–63.

Peck, C.A., Hayden, L., Wandschneider, M., Peterson, K., & Richarz, S. (1989). Development of integrated preschools: A qualitative inquiry into sources of resistance among parents, administrators, and teachers. *Journal of Early Intervention, 13*, 353–364.

Popp, R.A., & Fu, V.R. (1981). Preschool children's understanding of children with orthopedic disabilities and their expectations. *The Journal of Psychology, 107*, 77–85.

Popp, R.A., Fu, V.R., & Warrell, S.E. (1981). Preschool children's recognition and acceptance of three physical disabilities. *Child Study Journal, 11*, 99–114.

Powers, D.A. (1983). Mainstreaming and the inservice education of teachers. *Exceptional Children, 49*, 432–439.

Propst, L.B., & Nagle, R.J. (1981). Effects of labeling and a child's reaction to punishment on subsequent disciplinary practices of adults and peers. *American Journal of Mental Deficiency, 86*, 287–294.

Raupp, C. (1985). Approaching special needs children's social competence from the perspective of early friendships. *Topics in Early Childhood Special Education, 4*, 32–46.

Reichart, D.C., Lynch, E.C., Anderson, B.C., Svobodny, L.A., DiCola, J.M., & Mercury, M.G. (1989). Parental perspectives on integrated preschool opportunities for children with handicaps and children without handicaps. *Journal of Early Intervention, 13*, 6–13.

Reid, B.W. (1984). Attitudes toward the learning disabled in school and home. In R.L. Jones (Ed.), *Attitudes and attitude change in special education: Theory and practice* (pp. 157–170). Reston, VA: Council for Exceptional Children.

Richardson, S.A. (1970). Age and sex differences in values toward physical handicaps. *Journal of Health and Social Behavior, 11*, 207–214.

Ronald, L. (1977). "How did it happen?": Children's reactions to physical differences.

In M. Harmonay (Ed.), *Promise and performance: Children with special needs* (pp. 23–34). Cambridge: Ballinger.

Rosenbaum, P.L., Armstrong, R.W., & King, S.M. (1987). Parental attitudes toward children with handicaps: New perspectives with a new measure. *Developmental and Behavioral Pediatrics, 8,* 327–334.

Rugg, M., & Stoneman, Z. (March, 1988). *Parental responses to young children's questions about special needs: An analysis of content across handicaps.* Paper presented at the Conference on Human Development, Charleston, SC.

Rugg, M., & Stoneman, Z. (June, 1988). *Project CEEI: A demonstration program for mainstreaming special needs young children.* Paper presented at the Gulf Coast Conference on Early Intervention, Point Clear, AL.

Rugg, M., & Stoneman, Z. (1990). *A model for course infusion in child and family development.* The University of Georgia: Georgia University Affiliated Program for Persons With Developmental Disabilities, Athens.

Salvia, J., & Munson, S. (1986). Attitudes of regular education teachers toward mainstreaming mildly handicapped students. In C.J. Meisel (Ed.), *Mainstreaming handicapped children: Outcomes, controversies, and new directions* (pp. 111–128). Hillsdale, NJ: Lawrence Erlbaum Associates.

Schneider, D.J. (1973). Implicit personality theory: A review. *Psychological Bulletin, 79,* 294–309.

Sequin, J.A. (1977). Beyond handicaps: TV portrayal of talents, dreams, and strengths. In M. Harmonay (Ed.), *Promise and performance: Children with special needs* (pp. 35–43). Cambridge: Ballinger.

Sigelman, C.K., Miller, T.E., & Whitworth, L.A. (1986). The early development of stigmatizing reactions to physical differences. *Journal of Applied Developmental Psychology, 7,* 17–32.

Sigelman, C.K., & Shorokey, J.J. (1986). Effects of treatments and their outcomes on peer perceptions of a hyperactive child. *Journal of Abnormal Child Psychology, 14,* 397–410.

Siller, J. (1984). Attitudes toward the physically disabled. In R.L. Jones (Ed.), *Attitudes and attitude change in special education: Theory and practice* (pp. 184–205). Reston, VA: Council for Exceptional Children.

Siperstein, G.N., & Bak, J.J. (1980). Students' and teachers' perceptions of the mentally retarded child. In J. Gottlieb (Ed.), *Educating mentally retarded persons* (pp. 207–230). Baltimore: University Park Press.

Siperstein, G.N., & Bak, J.J. (1986). Understanding factors that affect children's attitudes toward mentally retarded peers. In C.J. Meisel (Ed.), *Mainstreaming handicapped children: Outcomes, controversies, and new directions* (pp. 55–76). Hillsdale, NJ: Lawrence Erlbaum Associations.

Sobol, M.P., Ashbourne, D.T., Earn, B.M., & Cunningham, C.E. (1989). Parents' attributions for achieving compliance from attention-deficit-disordered children. *Journal of Abnormal Child Psychology, 17,* 359–369.

Stoneman, Z., Brody, G.H., Davis, C.H., & Crapps, J.M. (1988). Childcare responsibilities, peer relations, and sibling conflict: Older siblings of mentally retarded children. *American Journal of Mental Retardation, 93,* 174–183.

Stoneman, Z., Brody, G.H., Davis, C.H., & Crapps, J.M. (1991). Ascribed role relations between children with mental retardation and their younger siblings. *American Journal of Mental Retardation, 95,* 537–550.

Thurman, S.K., & Lewis, M. (1979). Children's response to differences: Some possible implications for mainstreaming. *Exceptional Children, 45,* 468–470.

Triandis, H.C. (1971). *Attitude and attitude change.* New York: John Wiley & Sons.

Triandis, H.C., Adamopoulos, J., & Brinberg, D. (1984). Perspectives and issues in the study of attitudes. In R. L. Jones (Ed.), *Attitudes and attitude change in special education: Theory and practice* (pp. 21–40). Reston, VA: Council for Exceptional Children.

Turnbull, A., & Winton, P. (1983). A comparison of specialized and mainstreamed preschools from the perspectives of mothers of handicapped children. *Journal of Pediatric Psychology, 8,* 57–71.

Turnbull, A.P., Winton, P.J., Blacher, J., & Salkind, N. (1983). Mainstreaming in the kindergarten classroom: Perspectives of parents of handicapped and nonhandicapped children. *Journal of the Division for Early Childhood, 6,* 14–20.

Vandell, D.L., Anderson, L.C., Ehrhardt, G., & Wilson, K.S. (1982). Integrating hearing and deaf preschoolers: An attempt to enhance hearing children's interactions with deaf peers. *Child Development, 53*, 1354–1363.

Weinberg, N. (1978). Preschool children's perceptions of orthopedic disability. *Rehabilitation Counseling Bulletin, 21*, 183–189.

Weiner, B. (1974). *Achievement motivation and attribution theory*. Morristown, NJ: General Learning Press.

Winton, P. (1986). The consequences of mainstreaming for families of young handicapped children. In C.J. Meisel (Ed.), *Mainstreaming handicapped children: Outcomes, controversies, and new directions* (pp. 129–148). Hillsdale, NJ: Lawrence Erlbaum Associates.

Yussen, S.R., & Kane, P.T. (1983). Children's ideas about intellectual ability. In R.L. Leahy (Ed.), *The child's construction of social inequality* (pp. 109–133). New York: Academic Press.

Chapter 13

INTEGRATED PROGRAMS
Effects on Young Children
and Their Parents

Suzanne Lamorey
and Diane D. Bricker

The previous chapters in this volume examine a wide range of issues and topics relating to the integration of young children with disabilities into community-based programs that were originally developed and operated for nondisabled children. The consensus that emerges in these chapters is that the full participation of children who are disabled should be willingly supported and accommodated by neighborhood and community programs. The various authors also make clear that the goal is full participation in community-based programs; simply placing children with disabilities side by side with nondisabled children is not sufficient. Rather, the challenge is to foster meaningful interactions that benefit children both with and without disabilities and their families, as well as the larger community. This position has evolved from professional and parental commitment, as well as from a legislative basis (Bricker, 1978).

One would expect that the overwhelming support provided by early intervention professionals, most parents, informed legislators, and legal personnel would assure that the majority of young children with disabilities are placed in community-based programs that also serve children who are nondisabled. Clearly this is not the case. Given such a large consensus, why has the integration of children with disabilities into community-based programs not yet become a reality? The purpose of this chapter is, in part, to try to answer this important question.

The authors have been unable to find a study or report that has examined the percentage of infants, toddlers, and preschool children with disabilities who participate in integrated programs. According to the Twelfth Report of Congress on the Implementation of the Education of the Handicapped Act (1990), states are still in the process of building data systems that will

Preparation of this chapter was supported, in part, by Office of Special Education Programs Grant No. HD29090110 and Grant No. G008715567 to the Center on Human Development, University of Oregon.

produce an accurate count of infants and young children with disabilities who are being served by early intervention. However, based on a sampling of counties in Oregon, the authors estimate that less than one third of young children eligible for early intervention services are receiving those services in integrated settings.

Why then, given the philosophical and legislative support for the integration of young children with disabilities into community-based programs, has progress toward this goal been so slow? A qualitative investigation by Peck, Hayden, Wandschneider, Peterson, and Richarz (1989) discovered some sources of resistance among parents, teachers, and administrators. Peck and his colleagues suggested that the resistance to integrated preschool programs might be based less on ideology or pedagogy than on sociopolitical factors such as the fear of loss of control over decisions and resources, and the disruption of the negotiated order among community groups. Resistance to systems change in the context of integration efforts discourages program innovation and implementation. However, if professionals urge, or perhaps demand, that parents, teachers, and administrators embrace the major sociopolitical change processes that Peck et al. have suggested, it is subsequently the responsibility of those in the field to organize and understand the intervention research that is relevant to the preschool integration movement.

One major goal of this chapter is to systematically examine the effects of integration on young children and their parents. Specifically, the authors' intent is to review, organize, and explain the literature published between 1988 and 1992 on preschool integration efforts and outcomes. On the basis of this work, and in conjunction with previous reviews, the major

trends of the 1970s, 1980s, and 1990s are discussed. Finally, a summary of the major trends is offered as a basis for future work that may further enhance the research base on integration.

REVIEW OF THE LITERATURE

In 1978, Guralnick edited one of the first major multicontributor works on preschool integration. In that early volume, Apolloni and Cooke (1978) identified several areas in need of further research, including: 1) normative data on the interactions of preschool children in classroom settings; 2) the effects of systematic changes in setting variables; 3) the effects of integration on specific developmental outcomes such as those in the language, motor, and social domains; 4) the effectiveness of specific social interaction programming efforts; 5) the effects of integration on children without disabilities; 6) the use of single-subject as well as group models in research designs; and 7) the effectiveness of teaching procedures when used with diverse groups of children. Much of the empirical work on integration that was done in the 1980s focused on these areas, but they continue to warrant further study in the 1990s.

Ten years after Guralnick's volume appeared, Odom and McEvoy (1988) published a review chapter addressing research findings on the integration of young children with and without disabilities. This comprehensive chapter also raised a number of pertinent questions concerning legal and legislative considerations, educational issues, and ethical concerns. The review included summaries in the following areas: 1) patterns of social interaction between young children with and without disabilities, 2) friendship patterns between young children with and without disabilities, 3) the use of direct intervention to promote imitation, 4) the use of environmental arrangements to facilitate learning, 5) the use of direct intervention to promote social integration, 6) developmental and behavioral outcomes of integration, and 7) parent and teacher attitudes toward early integration.

These past comprehensive and perceptive analyses provide a springboard for the present chapter. What has been learned about preschool integration in the past 15 years? More importantly, where is the field currently headed amidst the challenges posed by PL 99-457 and the controversies ignited by the Regular Education Initiative? What are the major trends according to the empirical work that has focused on the diverse integration efforts underway? What liabilities recur in the field's empirical base, and how can they be transcended, or used as a basis for new hypotheses, better methodologies, or more appropriate outcome measures?

Rather than address studies that have been discussed elsewhere, the authors have chosen to review work that has appeared in the literature since Odom and McEvoy's review in 1988. The 16 studies that are included were chosen on the basis of the following criteria: 1) publication in a peer-refereed journal, 2) inclusion of results of either quantitative outcome measures or qualitative methodology, and 3) a focus on children under the age of 6. The authors have also compiled three tables (Tables 1, 2, and 3) that categorize and briefly describe the studies that met these criteria and are included in this review. These tables, considered in tandem with those developed by Odom and McEvoy (1988) and Esposito (1987), provide the reader with a comprehensive overview of the published empirical and evaluative work on integration.

Analysis of the recent literature suggests three major areas into which investigations can be categorized based on the effects of integration: 1) children's social interactions, 2) children's developmental outcomes, and 3) parents' attitudes and perceptions. In the following 3 sections, the 16 selected integration studies are reviewed and analyzed in some depth. Specific attention is given to the design of the studies—descriptions of variables such as setting, materials, types and degrees of disabilities, and intervention procedures, interpretations, and recommendations. For an in-depth assessment of the design and methodology of research on preschool integration, the reader is referred to the work of Buysse and Bailey (1991).

CHILDREN'S SOCIAL INTERACTIONS

DeKlyen and Odom (1989) examined the influence of teacher-structured activities on children's social interactions. In this study, teacher-imposed structure was defined as "the degree to which the theme of play, roles of participants, and other rules governing play" were stipulated by the teachers (p. 343). Thirty-six children were randomly assigned to three classes (two integrated and one nonintegrated). Twenty-eight of the children had mild or moderate disabilities (mean chronological age [CA] = 51 months; mean mental age [MA] = 50 months), and 8 of the children were nondisabled (mean age CA = 51 months; mean MA = 62 months). In each class, the children were grouped and assigned to one of three play activities that varied in the degree of teacher-imposed structure. These groupings were developmentally integrated in that each group in the integrated and nonintegrared classrooms contained children whose social

Table 1.   Selected information from social interaction studies meeting review criteria

Authors	Subjects/setting	Method of data collection	Results
DeKlyen and Odom (1989)	28 mild-mod DC, 8 NDC; randomly assigned to 2 integ. and 1 seg. class	Observed social interaction between children and amount of teacher-imposed structure	Increased structure yielded increased interaction for both DC and NDC.
Lefebvre and Strain (1989)	3 autistic children, 6 NDC confederates; integ. class	Single-subject analysis of observed social exchanges	Peer confederate training judged successful, group reinforcement maintained DC and NDC interactions even with decreased teacher prompts.
Guralnick and Groom (1988a)	8 integ. playgroups, each with 3 NDC 4-yr.-olds, 3 NDC 3-yr.-olds, & 2 mild DC, and 1 seg classroom with 11 mild DC	Observed social participation and level of cognitive play	Twice as much social interaction and higher levels of play occurred in integrated setting.
Guralnick and Groom (1988b)	8 playgroups, each with 3 NDC 4-yr-olds, 3 NDC 3-yr-olds, & 2 mild DC	Social behavior coding scale used to rate 14 categories of interaction indicating unilateral and reciprocal friendships. Also coded social participation and cognitive play	All children preferred older NDC children. Older NDC preferred same-age mates. Children with physical disabilities were not preferred by either group and were socially separate.
McEvoy, Nordquist, Twardosz, Heckaman, Wehby, and Denny (1988)	3 autistic children, 6 NDC "targets"; integ. setting	Multiple baseline measuring peer interaction, response initiation, and reciprocal interactions as influenced by affection activities	Autistic children increased and maintained reciprocal interactions and initiations.
Honig and McCarron (1988)	4 autistic preschoolers, 10 NDC; integ. setting	Prosocial behaviors coded by activity and level of prompt	Free play setting increased prosocial behaviors while teacher-dominated activity decreased prosocial behavior. There were no differences in initiation patterns between groups.
Peck, Palyo, Bettencourt, Cooke, and Appoloni (1988)	2 DC preschoolers in play group on part-time basis with 15–20 NDC	Direct observation of social and imitative responses during semi-structured play sessions	DC were neither initiators nor recipients of positive social interactions compared to NDC. There were no differences between DC and NDC in negative interactions or imitations.

DC = children with disabilities, NDC = children without disabilities.

Table 2. Selected information from developmental outcomes studies meeting review criteria

Authors	Subjects/setting	Method of data collection	Results
Jenkins, Odom, and Speltz (1989)	56 mild-mod DC matched and randomly assigned to integ. or seg. setting	Compared setting and curriculum using Uniform Performance Assessment System, Peabody Dev. Motor Scale, Preschool Language Scale, California Preschool Social Competence Scale, and social participation	Social curriculum yielded more interactive play and higher language scores in both settings. Structured interactions in integ. class yielded enhanced social competency. Integ. without social curriculum yielded minimal effects.
Esposito and Koorland (1989)	2 severely hearing impaired preschool children in integ. and seg. settings	Multi-element baselines design was used to compare social and cognitive play in both settings	Higher levels of social play occurred in integ. setting for both children. Cognitive play was not affected by setting.
Malone and Stoneman (1990)	12 DC in integ. setting and at home	Play was observed at school and at home, and coded for categories and sequences	More sophisticated, complex, and lengthy play at home. Peak play levels similar.
Harris, Handleman, Kristoff, Bass, and Gordon (1990)	5 autistic children in integ., 5 autistic children in seg., 4 NDC peers	Setting and curriculum compared using Preschool Language Scale for rate of gain and developmental age	All children benefit from lang. intervention.
Cole, Mills, Dale, and Jenkins (1991)	100 mild-mod DC and 24 NDC, randomly assigned to integ. and seg. classrooms	Pretest-posttest design using McCarthy, Peabody Picture Vocabulary Test-Rev., Test of Early Language Development, and Test of Early Reading Ability	There were no significant differences between children in seg. and integ. setting; however, gains were different according to degree of disability.

DC = children with disabilities, NDC = children without disabilities.

competence ranged across a continuum. Groups rotated through the activities daily. The dependent variable was the amount of social interaction between children. Data were collected on social interactions using a social interaction scan method to examine peer interactions and teacher interactions. Using momentary time-sampling procedures, each child was observed each day for 2 months while participating in at least 2 different activities. In addition, observers rated activities for the amount of teacher-imposed structure.

The researchers discovered a strong relationship between teacher-imposed structure and the amount of overall peer interaction for children with and without disabilities. For each class, and for children with and without disabilities, the least amount of structure was associated with the lowest number of overall peer interactions. Although the mean proportion of specifically *social* interactions between children with and without disabilities was the same across all levels of structure, there was a significant increase in the overall number of interactions (e.g., teacher-assigned roles and directives, as well as social interactions) between children with and without disabilities at the higher levels of teacher-imposed structure. An analysis of the nine least socially competent children

Table 3. Selected information from parent attitudes and perceptions studies meeting review criteria

Authors	Subjects	Method of data collection	Results
Green and Stoneman (1989)	117 mothers and 87 fathers of NDC, with/without prior integration experience	Parental Attitudes Toward Mainstreaming Scale, demographics, history of contact w/DC, benefits and obstacles to integration, satisfaction w/prior integration, comfort with various DC in child's classroom	Parents had positive attitudes. Mothers' past integ. experience predicted attitudes and comfort. Increased income and mothers' education related to less positive attitudes. Mothers of older kids had positive attitudes, fathers concerned w/behavior problems. Mat./pat. attitudes correlated. Benefits included sensitivity, acceptance, knowledge; obstacles included teacher training and less teacher attention for NDC.
Reichart, Lynch, Anderson, Svobodny, DiCola, and Mercury (1989)	51 parents of DC and NDC, prior to integration program	Parent Perceptions of Integration survey	Parents of DC and NDC had similar attitudes toward socio-emotional issues, teacher–parent issues, classroom issues, and philosophical issues. Parents of DC were more concerned with child comparisons and some preferred seg. setting.
Bailey and Winton (1989)	31 parents of NDC and 9 parents of DC, all involved in integrated program	Sociometric measure of friendship and acquaintance patterns of parents over time	Parents of DC were more likely to be friends with other parents of DC and less likely to be friends of parents of NDC. Parents of DC were not satisfied with friendships among other families.
Peck, Carlson, and Helmstetter (1992)	125 parents of NDC attending integrated early childhood programs	Survey of parent perceptions	Parents of NDC perceived positive integrated outcomes for their children in areas of social cognition, prosocial personal characteristics, and acceptance of human diversity.

DC = children with disabilities, NDC = children without disabilities.

revealed that they were involved in seven times more peer interactions at the highest level of teacher-imposed structure.

Lefebvre and Strain (1989) examined the effects of combined peer training and group reinforcement procedures on the social interaction skills of three children with confirmed diagnosis of autism in an integrated classroom (their CAs were 53, 72, and 82 months). Six typical children in the class served as confederates. Two independent variables were introduced: social interaction training for peer confederates, and the use of group contingencies.

Peer confederate training consisted of 9 sessions of 10–15 minutes each, during which teachers demonstrated and rehearsed interaction strategies. Teachers were required to follow a set of roles developed to encourage them to reinforce correct responses by the peer confederates using a modified sequential withdrawal design. Following training, the children were rewarded with tokens for each appropriate use of a target strategy. The accumulation of a certain number of tokens resulted in a reward for the entire class.

Data on social exchanges among the children with autism, peers, and teachers were recorded using an observational system. Single-subject analyses across baseline, intervention, reversals, and reinstatement were conducted. The results indicated that teacher prompts and consequences dropped during peer training, with no change in peer confederate behavior. When group reinforcement was introduced, an increase in peer responses was noted. Withdrawal produced a decrease, but reinstatement produced a positive acceleration. This study found that: 1) group reinforcement can maintain peer social behavior toward disabled peers, 2) peer confederate training can be effective and nondisruptive to classroom procedures, and 3) a reduction in teacher prompts does not necessarily alter the level of peer interaction.

Guralnick and Groom (1988a) compared the social interactions of children with mild developmental delays in segregated and integrated settings. Eleven children with disabilities (mean CA = 54 months;

mean MA = 44 months) participated in the segregated intervention program. Two observers coded live observations of the children with disabilities in the segregated setting. The integrated component included 8 play groups composed of 3 nondisabled 3-year-old boys, 3 nondisabled 4-year-old boys, and 2 4-year-old boys with disabilities. These age configurations provided both age-appropriate and developmentally appropriate peers for the children with mild developmental delays. The children in integrated settings were videotaped in their play groups, which met 5 days per week for 2 hours a day over a 4-week period.

Each child was observed for 100 minutes. Two dependent measures were recorded: the quality of social participation and the level of cognitive play. Results indicated that more cognitively sophisticated play occurred in the integrated groups, and that the rates of positive social interaction for children with disabilities were twice as high as in the segregated play groups.

Guralnick and Groom (1988b) also investigated the friendship patterns of the preschoolers in the integrated play groups described above. Measures for this study included an individual social behavior coding scale consisting of 14 categories of social interactions. The coding included criteria for determining unilateral, as well as reciprocal, friendships between children. Categories of social participation and cognitive play were also coded.

Results indicated that most of the children demonstrated preferences for specific peers soon after entering the integrated play groups. Normally developing older children strongly preferred other normally developing older children for interactions, unilateral friendships, and reciprocal friendships. Most of the normally developing 3-year-olds, and children with mild developmental delays, also preferred the normally developing older children, but these relationships were not reciprocal. The normally developing younger children who were able to develop reciprocal relationships usually selected other normally developing age-mates. Overall, the interactions of normally developing older and younger children revealed a lack of preference for children with mild delays for either unilateral or reciprocal friendships.

Guralnick and Groom concluded that the children with mild developmental delays were socially separate from other children in the same play group; they tended to be isolated, and did not sustain the interactions necessary for group play. On the basis of these findings, the researchers emphasized the need to investigate the cognitive, language, and social components involved in the development of preschool friendships. The results of this study strongly support previous findings that indicate that the physical integration of children with disabilities into integrated settings does not automatically ensure that interactions will occur and friendships develop.

McEvoy et al. (1988) attempted to assess the effects of *affection activities* on interactions between nondisabled children and children with disabilities. This study moved beyond the physical placement of children in the same environment to active environmental manipulation aimed at producing a desired outcome (e.g., increased social initiations and reciprocal interactions). Using a multiple-baseline design, three children with autism, ranging in age from 4 to 7 years, were observed across baseline, intervention, and follow-up conditions. The dependent measures were peer interactions, response initiations, and reciprocal interactions. The independent variables were affection activities (e.g., hug your neighbor, pat your friend) through which children were encouraged and reinforced for social interactions. Observations and data collection were conducted in a kindergarten class of 27 students. Six of these children were selected as the target nondisabled peers to be present during the baseline and intervention conditions. All the children were present during the follow-up.

All of the children with autism dramatically increased their reciprocal peer interactions and their initiations to peers during training, and maintained response levels above baseline during follow-up. Reciprocal interactions also increased noticeably for two of the children with autism, and to a lesser degree for the third, who was the youngest and by description exhibited the most inappropriate behavior. These outcomes suggest that placement of children with disabilities into integrated settings, in conjunction with attempts to encourage and support social initiations and interactions, can have desirable effects. However, these data also indicate that younger children with more serious disabilities may need longer, more intense training and follow-up.

Honig and McCarron (1988) conducted an observational study of social interaction between 10 nondisabled preschoolers and 4 preschoolers with autism (mean CA = 4.4 years) who participated in an integrated program. Children were observed for 20 minutes in each of 4 activity settings (freeplay, circle time, structured play, and gym). Six prosocial initiation behaviors were coded: sharing, helping, nurturing, cooperating, sympathizing, and praising. In addition, observers noted whether an initiation was spontaneous or teacher-directed. A total of 261 prosocial behaviors were recorded.

Results indicated that the setting significantly influenced the occurrence of prosocial behaviors, with the highest frequency of prosocial behaviors occurring during freeplay, and the lowest during teacher-dominated circle time. Sharing, helping, and cooperating behaviors occurred frequently, while supporting, nurturing, and praising did not. In all settings, more initiations were spontaneous than were teacher-directed. There were no differences in initiation patterns between groups.

Using a different approach, Peck, Palyo, Bettencourt, Cooke, and Apolloni (1988) focused on the outcomes of a preschool partial-integration program conducted in a public school facility. Peck et al. examined the effects of the part-time presence of 2 preschoolers with disabilities on interactions during a daily free play session in a regular preschool classroom of 15–20 nondisabled children. The two preschoolers with disabilities regularly attended a segregated special education class, and were integrated with the typical children only during the play sessions. No special teaching procedures were employed during the semistructured play sessions, which lasted 30 minutes per day over a 6-week period. The social and imitative responses of the children were coded and analyzed.

Results indicated that nondisabled children demonstrated a significantly greater number of positive social interactions with other nondisabled children during the free play sessions, while children with disabilities were neither initiators nor recipients of such social interaction. There were no significant differences between groups in the rates of negative interactions or of imitation. Anticipated cross-group social interaction did not occur, in spite of a 4 week warm-up period, which was included prior to the study in order to introduce the children to the integrated experience. In addition to recording the dismal results of this part-time integration effort, Peck et al. noted that most preschool integration studies described in the literature have been conducted in university-affiliated settings with a wealth of resources. The authors suggest that findings from resource-rich studies may not be applicable to typical community preschool settings.

Summary

This group of seven studies reports a number of interesting outcomes that are consistent with much of the past work on social interactions between children with and without disabilities. Perhaps most important is the consistent finding that structured or organized interventions can increase positive outcomes (e.g., interactions, play, affection responses). A second important finding is that teacher behavior affects the level of interaction; in some settings the level of teacher-directed intervention can either reduce or increase the number of opportunities for responses by children, which, in turn, can affect peer interactions. Perhaps the most serious criticism of this work is the lack of research on the generalization of findings across populations and settings.

CHILDREN'S DEVELOPMENTAL OUTCOMES

Jenkins, Odom, and Speltz (1989) examined the effects of preschool integration on children with and without disabilities using four experimental sets of conditions. Fifty-six children with mild to moderate disabilities were randomly assigned to an integrated program designed to promote social interaction, a segregated program designed to promote social interaction, an integrated program designed to promote child-directed activities, or a seg-regated program designed to promote child-directed activities. This design allowed the researchers to determine if child change was due to integration or to the particular curriculum.

Class size was the same in each set of conditions, as was the time allowed for activities, the physical space, and the children's access to materials. Children were assessed before and after intervention using the Uniform Performance Assessment System (White, Haring, & Edgar, 1978), the Peabody Developmental Motor Scales (Folio & Fewell, 1983), the Preschool Language Scale (Zimmerman, Steiner, & Pond, 1979), and the California Preschool Social Competency Scale (Levine, Elzey, & Lewis, 1969). The social interaction intervention included daily structured play situations based on the Integrated Preschool Curriculum (Odom et al., 1988), with direct social skills intervention for the most socially isolated children. The control was a child-directed play model adapted from the High/Scope Preschool Cognitive Curriculum (Hohmann, Banet, & Weikart, 1979). Research assistants monitored the implementation of both curricula across settings.

The children's play was observed using categories derived from Parten's (1932) scales of social participation, including isolated or unoccupied state, proximity to other children, interactive involvement, negative (i.e., hostile or aggressive) interactions, and teacher-oriented interactions. An instantaneous probe system of observation was used to collect a minimum of 150 observations per child over a minimum of 3 weeks.

Results indicated that the social interaction intervention yielded significantly more interactive involvement in both the integrated and segregated settings, and produced significantly more social integration of the groups of children in the integrated classroom. Integration alone had little effect on fine motor, language, preacademic, and social competencies. Children participating in the social interaction interventions in both the integrated and segregated classrooms scored significantly higher on postexperiment language tests. Children who participated in the structured play intervention in the integrated setting scored higher on the social competency scale than did children in any of the other conditions. These results support the hypothesis that teachers in both integrated and segregated preschools need to provide structured experiences in order for social integration to occur. In addition, this study points out the limited, or perhaps just elusive, effects of integration on developmental outcomes other than enhanced social competency.

Esposito and Koorland (1989) compared the social and cognitive play of two children with hearing impairment (3.5 and 5 years of age) in integrated and segregated settings. Both children had severe binaural hearing impairment and attended a segregated class for children with hearing impairment in the mornings and an integrated daycare center in the afternoons. A multi-element baseline design was used to compare the children's play behaviors in the two settings. Percent interval data were collected for categories of play behavior based on Parten's (1932) social play categories and Smilansky's (1968) cognitive play categories.

Both children were observed for 2 10-minute sessions daily for 4 days during a 2-week period, yielding 4 observation sessions for each child in each setting. To determine the stability of the findings, a second set of observations was made 4 months later. In addition, three normally hearing children were also observed at the daycare center during the morning and afternoon sessions in order to eliminate the possibility of time-of-day confounds.

Results indicated that for both children, nonsocial parallel play occurred more often in the segregated setting, while social associative play occurred more often in the integrated setting. The social play behavior of both children was within the range of normative peer behavior in the integrated setting, but generally outside of the normative range in the segregated setting. In addition, the younger, less competent child engaged in a higher percentage of overall play (versus nonplay) in the integrated setting, while the older child engaged in fairly equal amounts of overall play in both settings. Cognitive play (i.e., levels of manipulative, functional, and pretend play) was not consistently influenced by the setting for either child.

These results suggest that, for young children with hearing impairment, integration has important implications for social play development. Esposito and Koorland (1989) noted that, compared to normally hearing children, children with hearing impairments exhibited social play less often, and of less complexity. In the case of these two children with hearing impairments, integration proved to be a powerful intervention for the enhancement of social play.

Malone and Stoneman (1990) compared the cognitive play of children with mental retardation in a group-play classroom setting to that in an independent-play situation in the home. The subjects were 12 boys with mild cognitive impairment (mean CA = 55 months, mean MA = 48 months) who attended an integrated preschool program. For each child, play was observed and videotaped during 2 30-minute visits in the child's home, and dur-

ing 2 30-minute free-play periods at the child's school.

An interval-coding procedure was used to code play categories using a play scale developed by the researchers. Play sequences were also coded according to the number of play schemes and the organization of play. Dependent variables included total proportion of play, proportion of play by categories, global play sophistication, peak level of play, proportion of time spent sequencing, average sequence length, and proportion of each level of play sequencing.

Results indicated that the children played more in the independent home situation than in the integrated classroom. Play at home was also proportionally more sophisticated than play in the classroom, and play sequences were more complex, and maintained longer, at home. There were no differences in optimal play levels between home and school settings. These results were contrary to the expectations of the researchers, because the integrated school setting had been expected to provide the children with disabilities an opportunity for exposure to more sophisticated nondisabled peer models. The researchers subsequently hypothesized that the classroom setting may have distracted the children with disabilities, while the home situation may have given those children an opportunity to consolidate and strengthen their play competencies.

Harris, Handleman, Kristoff, Bass, and Gordon (1990) used a quasi-experimental design to study the effects of integration, as well as the effects of an intensive language curriculum, on the language development of 10 preschool children with autism. Five children with autism (mean CA = 58 months, mean IQ = 62.6) were assigned to a segregated classroom setting, while a second group of 5 children with autism (CA = 55.8 months, mean IQ = 69) were placed in an integrated preschool classroom. These assignments were not random, but were based on the severity of the children's behavioral problems. Children with more difficult behaviors were placed in the segregated class in order to avoid the disruption that was anticipated in the integrated setting. Four normal peers (mean CA = 45.25 months, mean IQ = 108.5) participated in the integrated classroom.

The curriculum for both classrooms was based on the same goals and objectives, with an emphasis on language, cognition, fine motor, gross motor, socialization, and adaptive skills. In particular, all children were exposed to formally structured group language instruction. Instruction took place within the context of incidental as well as structured learning through individualized programs, small groups, and class lessons. More individualized instruction was used in the segregated setting, which had an adult–child ratio of 3:5, compared to the integrated class's ratio of 3:10. The Preschool Language Scale (Zimmerman et al., 1979) was administered to each child as a pre- and post-intervention measure. Rate of development and a measure of developmental age were recorded for each child prior to and after intervention.

Children with autism in integrated and segregated settings benefited significantly from the language intervention, as did the normally developing children who attended the integrated program. A comparison of developmental age outcomes also indicated that both the typical children and the children with autism in the integrated class were functioning at a significantly higher level after intervention. The children with autism in the segregated setting also showed a trend in this direction, although the change was not statistically significant. Comparing rates

of development, all children in both settings progressed at a more rapid rate after intervention, particularly the children with autism in the segregated setting and the typical peers in the integrated setting.

The researchers concluded that the language stimulation treatment was successful for normally developing children as well as children with autism. The contribution of the presence of the normally developing children to the language development of the children with autism was questioned, as the language rate gains made by children with autism in both integrated and segregated conditions were impressive. The researchers noted the necessity of continuing to explore the possible contribution of typical peers to the language development of children with autism.

The final study reviewed in this section was conducted by Cole, Mills, Dale, and Jenkins (1991) to determine the effects of integration and segregation on children with mild to moderate disabilities, with a focus on the extent to which the initial level of development affected the gains achieved in the two settings. Data for this study were collected over a 4-year period involving 2 classes per year, one integrated and the other segregated. During the 4 years, a total of 100 children with disabilities and 24 children without disabilities were randomly assigned to the integrated and segregated classes in a special education preschool program.

All children were administered a variety of measures using a pretest-posttest design. The measures included were the McCarthy Scales of Children's Abilities (McCarthy, 1972), the Peabody Picture Vocabulary Test—Revised (Dunn & Dunn, 1981), the Test of Early Language Development (Hresko, Reid, & Hammill, 1981), and the Test of Early Reading Ability (Reid, Hresko, & Hammill, 1981). Each class was staffed by a head teacher, an assistant, and a variety of professional and student helpers. Teachers used a formal curriculum, but were not given specific instructions regarding the deployment of the nondisabled children to foster development in the less able children.

When comparing performances on the pre- and post-test measures, no differences were found between children in the segregated and integrated classes. However, an aptitude-by-treatment analysis indicated that students with mild disabilities gained more from the integrated setting, whereas students with more moderate degrees of disability benefited more from the segregated classes. Although an interesting finding, the investigators cautioned against using these results as a reason for placing less able children in segregated settings. Rather, Cole et al., (1991) suggest that this outcome simply indicates that the effects of integration on children with different behavioral repertoires are complex and interactive. The researchers also emphasize the need for additional investigation in this area to focus on critical intervening variables and their effects on children.

Summary

For children with disabilities, the effects of integration were generally significant in the areas of social competence and social play. However, there were no significant effects found in the preacademic, motor, cognitive play, or language domains. These results seem to support the findings reported in quasi-experimental integration studies conducted during the early-to-mid 1980s, which indicated that integration contributed to the children's social skills, and only negligibly affected other developmental domains.

PARENTAL ATTITUDES AND PERCEPTIONS

Green and Stoneman (1989) examined maternal and paternal attitudes toward preschool integration of parents who had experience with an integrated preschool program, as well as for parents who had not had experience with integration. A total of 117 mothers and 87 fathers of non-disabled children of ages 18–72 months participated in the study. The majority of the parents were white, middle class, and well-educated.

Parents completed a 32-item Parental Attitudes Toward Mainstreaming Scale, developed by the researchers, which addressed general attitudes toward the integration, academics and classroom procedures, behavior problems in the classroom, the impact of integration on the nondisabled child, and the impact of integration on the child with disabilities. In addition, the parents provided demographic information, a history of contact with persons with disabilities, the perceived benefits of integration, the perceived drawbacks of integration, and their satisfaction with any prior experiences involving preschool integration. Parents were also asked to rate their feelings (referred to as a *comfort score*) regarding the presence of children with various disabilities in their child's classroom.

In general, parents held moderately positive attitudes toward integration. For mothers, but not fathers, positive past experiences with persons with disabilities predicted positive scores on the integration attitude questionnaire, as well as higher comfort scores. In addition, parents who had prior experiences with preschool integration had significantly higher comfort scores, as well as more positive scores on the integration questionnaire.

Ratings of satisfaction with integration were strongly correlated to overall attitudes toward integration for experienced parents. Higher income mothers and mothers with more education were less comfortable with integration and held less positive views toward integration. Mothers of older preschool children were more likely to see the benefits of integration; however, fathers of older children were more likely to be concerned with behavior problems that might be displayed by children with disabilities in an integrated setting. Benefits frequently cited included typical children's increased sensitivity, acceptance of differences, and increased knowledge of disabilities, while perceived drawbacks included inadequate teacher training and reduced teacher attention to nondisabled children in the integrated setting.

Reichart et al. (1989) described how parents of nondisabled preschoolers and parents of preschoolers with disabilities perceived the issues surrounding preschool integration prior to the actual implementation of an integrated program model. Subjects included 51 parents who either had preschool children with disabilities attending a segregated model program or had nondisabled preschool children attending a traditional daycare program. All participating parents completed a 17-item Parent Perspective on Integration Survey developed by the researchers, which focused on parental concerns regarding the integration of their child and on parental perspectives on successful integration factors. Survey items were categorized into socio-emotional issues, structural and organizational issues, parent and teacher issues, and philosophical issues. The authors reported the mean percentage of parent responses for each group and each category.

In terms of socio-emotional issues, mean results indicated that both groups of parents agreed that integrated settings promote social contact and improve children's self-concepts. Both groups of parents felt that integration would not result in increased behavior problems, inadequate emotional and physical protection for young children, or immature behavior on the part of nondisabled children due to the presence of peers with disabilities. On structural and organizational issues, both groups of parents indicated that integration could meet all children's needs, allowing children to work at their own pace. However, parents of children with disabilities indicated concern that integrated settings might result in negative comparisons being made among children more often.

Parent responses to the category of parent and teacher issues also yielded similarities between both groups of parents. Both groups indicated that they would feel comfortable together, and that they did not feel that their children would receive less attention from teachers. Both groups of parents agreed that teachers need training in working with children who have disabilities, and that the staff should display accepting attitudes toward all children.

Finally, in terms of philosophical issues, both groups of parents disagreed with the notion that nondisabled children and children with disabilities had little in common and agreed that children can develop an acceptance of differences. Interestingly, parents of children with disabilities were split on the issue of whether their children would best be educated in segregated classrooms, while most parents of nondisabled children disagreed with the importance of segregated classrooms. The researchers suggested that these responses may offer hope for future integration planners, in that a high percentage of parents of nondisabled preschoolers and parents of preschoolers with disabilities responded similarly and favorably to major issues involved in the implementation of integrated preschool programs.

Bailey and Winton (1989) investigated the friendship and acquaintance patterns of families whose children attended an integrated daycare program. Thirty-one parents with nondisabled children and nine parents of children with disabilities participated in the study. The integrated day care program offered full-time services for children, including occasional center-wide parent meetings. Children were organized into *family groups* composed of a caregiver, five nondisabled children, and one child with disabilities. All family groups were mixed in terms of age. All children were exposed to an active learning curriculum derived from a variety of sources.

A sociometric measure was developed and used to evaluate four dependent variables: 1) how well parents of children with disabilities knew other parents of children with disabilities from the daycare program, 2) how well parents of children with disabilities knew parents whose typical children were in their own child's family group at the daycare program, 3) how well parents of children with disabilities knew parents whose typical children were not in their own child's family group at the daycare program, and 4) how satisfied the parents were with how well they knew other families from the daycare center. The sociometric measure was administered prior to a child's enrollment in the daycare program and again 9 months later. Each dependent measure was analyzed as a function of group membership and of time.

The results indicated that parents of children with disabilities were more likely to know and be friends with other parents

of children with disabilities, and that this trend grew stronger over time. Parents of children with and without disabilities were more likely to know the families of typical children who were in the same family group as their own child. Parents of children with disabilities were less likely to know parents whose typical children were not in the same family group as their own child. In terms of parent satisfaction, there was a significant indication that parents of children with disabilities were less satisfied with their acquaintances and friendships with other families than were parents of typical children.

According to the researchers, these data confirm previous suggestions that parents who have children with disabilities attending integrated programs may not themselves be integrated in terms of parent–parent interactions. As has been suggested in the preschool integration literature, the mere presence of children with disabilities (or in this case their parents) in an integrated setting does not automatically result in interactions with nondisabled children (or their parents). As methods of promoting child–child social interactions are investigated, so too may methods of promoting parent–parent interactions.

Peck, Carlson, and Helmstetter (1992) investigated the specific benefits of integration according to the perceptions of parents of nondisabled children attending integrated early childhood education programs across the state of Washington. Using past qualitative inquiries on parent issues as well as issues raised in research reports, a survey was developed to capture parents' perceptions of specific changes that occur for nondisabled children in integrated settings. Surveys were then completed by 125 parents whose nondisabled children were participating in 44 integrated early childhood programs. These programs represented a range of both rural and urban populations in Washington State.

Results indicated that parents perceived that their child's overall experience in the integrated programs was positive. Parents reported that their child showed more acceptance of human difference, more awareness of other children's needs, less discomfort with people with disabilities, less prejudice about people who look or behave differently, and more responsiveness to other children. Parents did not feel that their child received less teacher attention because of the presence of children with disabilities or that their child had learned undesirable behaviors from children with disabilities. Overall, parents strongly agreed that they would not prefer that their child be educated in an environment with only other nondisabled children.

Peck et al. (1992) noted that according to these parents, the perceived benefits to nondisabled children were in areas such as social cognition, prosocial personal characteristics, and acceptance of human diversity. These are areas that are rarely addressed in formal program evaluation studies. According to these researchers, the inclusion of a broader and more diverse array of social outcomes is necessary in studies of integrated programs. The traditionally narrow view of child outcomes, which focuses on cognitive and academic benefits, may not allow researchers to assess significant types of changes experienced by children with disabilities, as well as children without disabilities, in integrated programs.

Summary

Overall, parents of children with and without disabilities generally have positive attitudes toward integration. As parents accumulate more experience with integration, they report greater comfort and more positive attitudes about those experiences. Both groups of parents perceive more benefits than drawbacks in participating in integration efforts with their children. Parents of children with disabilities seem to have more reservations about their children's needs being met, and may also have some questions about their own adult friendship needs being met by parents of children without disabilities. It appears that much intervention research is yet to be done in the realm of parent-to-parent interactions.

TRENDS

The results of this review of current literature have been synthesized into a list of trends that are presented below. Comparisons between these trends and those derived from previous studies are included as well. But before discussing the noted trends, two general comments are in order.

First, it should be emphasized that there is considerable heterogeneity in populations, settings, approaches, designs, methodologies, and outcomes in the studies that are reviewed here and elsewhere (see, e.g., Buysse & Bailey, 1991). This heterogeneity accurately reflects the integration efforts taking place in the field, and should not be seen as the result of poorly controlled investigations. However, this heterogeneity also makes the definition of valid trends difficult, and exceptions can be found to many of the trends listed below.

A second general comment is that most of the outcomes reported tend to be positive or supportive of integration efforts. Perhaps the most consistent negative finding over the years is that interaction between children who are disabled and nondisabled will not occur without careful, consistent, and structured efforts. The literature contains few reports of negative effects (e.g., reduction in developmental gains or development of inappropriate behavior) occurring for typical children who participate in integrated programs.

Below are described 10 major trends drawn from the empirical work on integration. Table 4 summarizes these 10 trends, and includes projections for changes that the authors believe may occur in the future.

Trend 1:   There have been increased efforts to place a range of children who are disabled into community-based programs developed primarily for nondisabled children.

Trend 2:   There have been increased efforts to study the effects of integration on children and families using more sci-

entifically defensible approaches than have been employed in earlier studies. These approaches include the use of comparison groups of children, monitored curriculum implementation, and, in some cases, the use of random assignments to different programs.

Trend 3:   There has been a move from examining more general effects toward examining more specific outcomes. Early work (Bricker & Bricker, 1971) focused on general group or subgroup outcomes, using gross indices such as mental age. Contemporary studies are more inclined to examine specific outcomes, such as changes in social behavior or language development.

Trend 4:   Much of the early work used group designs, while current work frequently makes use of a single-subject

Table 4.   The ten major trends in integration research, and their status in 1970, 1990, and 2010

Trend	Decade		
	1970	1990	2010
1. Frequency of placement in integrated settings	Rare	Occasional	Frequent
2. Study approach	Clinical	Empirical	Empirical
3. Outcomes	Global	Specific	Specific
4. Design	Group	Single-subject	Mixed
5. Methodology	Quantitative	Qualitative	Mixed
6. Subjects	Disabled child and parents	Disabled and nondisabled child and parents	Disabled and nondisabled infant, toddler, child, and parents
7. Parent effects	Satisfaction	Attitudes	Behaviors
8. Environmental manipulation	Little	Some	Considerable
9. Measures	Standardized, focused on cognitive behavior	Observational, focused on social behavior	Observations, sociometrics, questionnaires, affection and interactional measures
10. Setting	Demonstration programs	Demonstration and community programs	Community programs

approach. Increasingly, much of the more methodologically defensible work is using time-series designs.

Trend 5:   The early work used almost exclusively quantitative methodologies. The use of qualitative methodologies is expected to grow in the future. These studies may produce information and perspectives that are difficult to obtain using quantitative methods.

Trend 6:   There has been a move from focusing primarily upon the effects of integration on children with disabilities to examining the effects on nondisabled children and on the families involved in integration.

Trend 7:   There is an increased effort to examine more closely the various effects of integration on the parents of preschool children. Initially, the focus was on parent satisfaction, but the current trend is to examine parent attitudes and specific issue-related perceptions toward the effects of integration upon children.

Trend 8:   There is a trend toward manipulating the physical and social environment in order to produce specific outcomes. Examples of this trend include the studies that focus on shaping the behavior of peer confederates to produce change in those children as well as in the children with disabilities. In the realm of environmental manipulation, a significant aspect of the contemporary trend is the focus on specific and discrete outcomes, and on the relationship between these outcomes. For example, reports from current studies indicate that there is a relationship between the amounts and types of adult intervention and children's peer interactions.

Trend 9:   There is a movement to redefine the areas deemed worthy of intervention. For example, the early work focused on measuring change in general cognitive and language skills as determined by standardized test scores. More recently, investigators are interested in measuring changes in social interaction, affective responses, social cognition, and prosocial personal characteristics using observational approaches.

Trend 10:   Importantly, there is a shift in the settings in which integrated programs are conducted. The early work was conducted primarily in the context of specialized university demonstration programs. Current work is expanding to settings that include community-based, daycare, and recreational programs.

RECOMMENDATIONS

This chapter begins with a question. The authors asked why the integration of young children with disabilities into community-based programs has not yet become a reality, in spite of strong support by parents and professionals, as well as the legislators who represent the citizens of this country. The studies reviewed in this chapter have not yielded any answers, but some of the outcomes, in conjunction with information from other sources, as well as the authors' own nonempirical hunches, offer insights that may be helpful.

First, more recent studies reaffirm the conclusion that merely placing children with disabilities into programs with nondisabled children is not likely to yield developmental outcomes any better than those achieved through segregated early intervention programs and social interaction. Effective integration requires additional resources, especially personnel who are trained to develop and execute sound programs. Most community-based programs do not currently have the necessary resources or personnel to implement effective integration efforts, and without major readjustments in the service delivery system, these programs are not likely to receive the support they need. Until community-based programs are able to include trained personnel who can orchestrate effective integration programs that satisfy all constituencies (e.g., parents, professionals, and taxpayers), progress in this area will continue to be slow.

Second, studies have indicated little carryover of social integration for children once they leave the environments specifically designed to encourage reciprocity between nondisabled children and children with disabilities. It is clear that social interaction between these groups can be increased using sound principles of reinforcement and programming. It is equally clear that such interactional patterns are not maintained outside the training environment. This remains a major challenge.

A final insight is that many variables external to the direct intervention occurring in integrated programs can account for programs' successes. Initiation and continued maintenance of integrated programs are dependent on community attitudes, the commitment of personnel, parental understanding, preparation, and feelings of control. These are all important factors that account for successfully integrated community-based programs.

The research on integration has produced a variety of outcomes and insights that are fundamental to the current level of understanding. Investigations are difficult to conduct, and most are methodologically flawed, but nonetheless, as a group they contribute substantially to the understanding of how to successfully integrate children with disabilities into community-based programs. Great challenges remain and can be most easily met by building upon previous empirical work.

Based on the work reviewed here and elsewhere, the authors are proposing the following recommendations for future research. First, investigators and interventionists need to carefully select goals for integration efforts, as the structure and content of each intervention effort is likely to have a significant effect on outcomes. For example, if social interactions between peers are the target, then the intervention must be specifically designed to promote those interactions between peers, with precautions taken to ensure that other factors, such as teacher behavior, do not interfere with the stated goals (see Odom & Brown, chap. 3, this volume).

Second, methodological problems, particularly heterogeneity of disabilities, inclusion of low-incidence populations, control subjects, random assignment, and control of relevant variables (e.g., teacher, setting, and parents) should be addressed. Single-subject analysis may be the most appropriate approach in many cases. Qualitative methods may also offer an approach that will yield significant information on integration.

Third, investigators should acknowledge and control, when possible, factors such as setting effects, group membership effects, gender effects, socioeconomic status effects and interventionist variables that can affect outcomes. This recommendation takes on added difficulty with the recognition that much of the future research should be conducted in community-based programs and not in demonstration sites, which may differ significantly in personnel and resources.

Fourth, the use of informal observational measures can present a major obstacle to program replication and interpretation of data. It seems that each investigative effort yields yet another observational system. A few standard observational systems should be adopted in order to increase validity and enhance comparisons.

Fifth, the majority of investigations have focused on integration efforts for the population of preschool-age children. Future work should be expanded to assess the effects and outcomes of integration for populations of infants and toddlers. This is most likely to occur in daycare settings.

Sixth, there is a strong need to recognize and acknowledge the concerns of parents, teachers, and administrators involved in the implementation and maintenance of integrated programs. Investigators need to spread their net to address organizational issues, "ownership" issues, and funding issues.

The authors believe that attention to this set of recommendations will help guide future empirical work toward rich and productive areas, and that this work will, in turn, help to ensure the improvement of integration efforts for young children with disabilities and their families.

SUMMARY

As states across the nation struggle with the implementation of PL 99-457, the practice of integration, and along with it thousands of very young children, will move from university and model demonstration settings to neighborhood, community-based programs. In urban and rural settings, in church basements, in family daycare homes, and in preschools operated by national franchise chains, very young children with and without disabilities will be spending their days together, growing up together. Future research efforts can do much to ensure that these experiences are satisfying and productive for all children.

In this chapter, the authors have reviewed in some detail 16 investigations focused on the effects of integration. Using this and past reviews, the major trends in the area of integration have been identified. The authors have also provided a list of research recommendations for the future. This has been a small, but the authors hope, significant, effort toward meeting the monumental challenge of achieving the successful integration of children with disabilities. When a sequel to this chapter is written, its merits will be better evaluated. However, more important than evaluating the impact of this chapter will be the evaluation that future chapters will offer of our children, our communities, and our best investigative efforts to actualize a law, a policy, and a social value called integration.

REFERENCES

Apolloni, T., & Cooke, T.P. (1978). Integrated programming at the infant, toddler, and preschool levels. In M. Guralnick (Ed.), *Early intervention and the integration of handicapped and nonhandicapped children* (pp. 147–166). Baltimore: University Park Press.

Bailey, D.B., & Winton, P.W. (1989). Friendship and acquaintance among families in a mainstreamed day care center. *Education and Training of the Mentally Retarded, 24*, 107–113.

Bricker, D.D. (1978). A rationale for the integration of handicapped and nonhandicapped preschool children. In M. Guralnick (Ed.), *Early intervention and the integration of handicapped and nonhandicapped children* (pp. 3–26). Baltimore: University Park Press.

Bricker, D.D., & Bricker, W.A. (1971). *Toddler Research and Intervention Project Report-Year 1.* (IMRID Behavioral Science Monograph No. 20). Nashville, TN: Institute on Mental Retardation and Intellectual Development.

Buysse, V., & Bailey, D. (1991). *Mainstreamed versus special settings: Behavioral and developmental effects on young children with handicaps*. Unpublished manuscript, University of North Carolina at Chapel Hill, Frank Porter Graham Child Development Center.

Cole, K., Mills, P., Dale, P., & Jenkins, J. (1991). Effects of preschool integration for children with disabilities. *Exceptional Children, 58,* 36–45.

DeKlyen, M., & Odom, S.L. (1989). Activity structure and social interactions with peers in developmentally integrated play groups. *Journal of Early Intervention, 13,* 342–352.

Dunn, L., & Dunn, L. (1981). *Peabody Picture Vocabulary Test-Revised*. Circle Pines, MN: American Guidance Service.

Education of the Handicapped Act Amendments of 1986, PL 99-457. (October 8, 1986). Title 20, U.S.C. 1400 et seq: *U.S. Statutues at Large, 100,* 1145–1177.

Esposito, B.G. (1987). The effects of preschool integration on the development of nonhandicapped children. *Journal of the Division for Early Childhood, 12,* 31–46.

Esposito, B.G., & Koorland, M.A. (1989). Play behavior of hearing impaired children: Integrated and segregated settings. *Exceptional Children, 55,* 412–419.

Folio, M.R., & Fewell, R.R. (1983). *Peabody Developmental Motor Scales*. Allen, TX: DLM Teaching Resources.

Green, A.L., & Stoneman, Z. (1989). Attitudes of mothers and fathers of nonhandicapped children. *Journal of Early Interventions, 13,* 292–304.

Guralnick, M.J. (Ed.). (1978). *Early intervention and the integration of handicapped and nonhandicapped children*. Baltimore: University Park Press.

Guralnick, M.J., & Groom, J.M. (1988a). Peer interactions in mainstreamed and specialized classrooms: A comparative analysis. *Exceptional Children, 54,* 415–425.

Guralnick, M.J., & Groom, J.M. (1988b). Friendships of preschool children in mainstreamed classrooms. *Developmental Psychology, 24,* 595–604.

Harris, S.L., Handleman, J.S., Kristoff, B., Bass, L., & Gordon, R. (1990). Changes in language development among autistic and peer children in segregated and integrated preschool stttings. *Journal of Autism and Developmental Disability, 20,* 23–31.

Hohmann, M., Banet, B., & Weikart, D.P. (1979). *Young children in action: A manual for preschool educators*. Ypsilanti, MI: High/Scope Press.

Honig, A.S., & McCarron, P.A. (1988). Prosocial behaviors of handicapped and typical peers in an integrated preschool. *Early Child Development and Care, 33,* 113–125.

Hresko, W., Reid, D., & Hammill, D. (1981). *Test of Early Language Development*. Austin, TX: PRO-ED

Jenkins, J.R., Odom, S.L., & Speltz, M.L. (1989). Effects of social integration on preschool children with handicaps. *Exceptional Children, 55,* 420–428.

Lefebvre, D., & Strain, P.S. (1989). Effects of a group contingency on the frequency of social interactions among autistic and nonhandicapped preschool children: Making LRE efficacious. *Journal of Early Intervention, 13,* 329–341.

Levine, S., Elzey, F.F., & Lewis, M. (1969). *California Preschool Social Competence Scale*. Palo Alto, CA: Consulting Psychological Press.

Malone, D.M., & Stoneman, Z. (1990). Cognitive play of mentally retarded preschoolers: Observation in the home and school. *American Journal on Mental Retardation, 94,* 475–487.

McCarthy, D. (1972). *McCarthy Scales of Children's Abilities*. New York: The Psychological Corporation.

McEvoy, M.A., Nordquist, V.M., Twardosz, S., Heckaman, K., Wehby, J.H., & Denny, R.K. (1988). Promoting autistic children's peer interaction in an integrated setting using affection activities. *Journal of Applied Behavior Analysis, 21,* 193–200.

Odom, S.K., Bender, M., Stein, M., Doran, L., Houden, P., McInnes, M., Gilbert M., DeKlyen, M., Speltz, M., & Jenkins, J. (1988). *Integrated preschool curriculum*. Seattle: University of Washington Press.

Odom, S.L., & McEvoy, M.A. (1988). Integration of young children with handicaps and normally developing children. In S. Odom & M. Karnes (Eds.), *Early intervention for infants and children with handicaps: An empirical base* (pp. 241–268). Baltimore: Paul H. Brookes Publishing Co.

Parten, M.B. (1932). Social participation among preschool children. *Journal of Abnor-*

mal and Social Psychology, 27, 243–369.

Peck, C., Carlson, P., & Helmstetter, E. (1992). Parent and teacher perceptions of outcomes for typically developing children enrolled in integrated early childhood programs: A statewide survey. *Journal of Early Intervention, 16,* 53–63.

Peck, C.A., Hayden, L., Wandschneider, M., Peterson, K., & Richarz, S. (1989). Development of integrated preschools: A qualitative inquiry into sources of resistance among parents, administrators and teachers. *Journal of Early Intervention, 13,* 353–364.

Peck, C.A., Palyo, W.P., Bettencourt, B., Cooke, T.P., & Apolloni, T. (1988). An observational study of partial integration of handicapped students in a regular preschool. *Journal of Research and Development in Education, 21,* 1–4.

Reid, D., Hresko, W., & Hammill, D. (1981). *Test of early reading ability.* Austin, TX: PRO-ED

Reichart, D.C., Lynch, E.C., Anderson, B.C., Svobodny, L.A., DiCola, J.M., & Mercury, M.G. (1989). Parental perspectives on integrated preschool opportunities for children with handicaps and children without handicaps. *Journal of Early Intervention, 13,* 6–13.

Smilansky, S. (1968). *The effects of sociodramatic play on disadvantaged preschool children.* New York: John Wiley & Sons.

United States Department of Education. (1990). *Twelfth annual report to Congress on the implementation of the Education of the Handicapped Act.* Washington, DC: U.S. Government Printing Office.

White, O.R., Haring, N.G., & Edgar, E. (1978). *Uniform Performance Assessment System (UPAS).* Seattle: Experimental Education Unit, Child Development and Mental Retardation Center, University of Washington.

Zimmerman, I.L., Steiner, V.G., & Pond, R.E. (1979). *Preschool Language Scale.* Columbus, OH: Charles E. Merrill.

Chapter 14

INTEGRATION
Campaign for the New Century

Diane D. Bricker,
Charles A. Peck,
and Samuel L. Odom

The purpose of this book is to review research on the programmatic integration of young children with and without disabilities and their families. Specifically, the contributors focus on analyzing the field's progress since 1978, the year of publication of Guralnick's seminal work, *Early Intervention and the Integration of Handicapped and Nonhandicapped Children.*

The book's contributors meet this purpose, and what remains is to synthesize their individual conclusions into what the editors believe is a solid campaign platform for future work. Our review of the work contained in this volume has led to the identification of three major dilemmas or barriers: 1) competing values, 2) implementation, and 3) critical context variables. We shall use this chapter to discuss these barriers, as well as what we believe will be the most satisfactory resolution of these dilemmas from the perspective of those wishing to enhance integration efforts.

COMPETING VALUES

Several contributors describe dilemmas caused by competing values or agendas. For example, Wolery and Fleming (chap. 6, this volume) and Richarz (chap. 5, this volume) compare the different curricular approaches employed in early childhood education and special education. These authors emphasize the difficult but necessary task of overcoming theoretical and philosophical differences in order to provide appropriate, individualized, and effective programs for children. Similarly, Odom and Brown (chap. 3, this volume) and Notari and Cole (chap. 2, this volume) discuss the programmatic differences across early childhood education curricular approaches and special education intervention techniques for promoting social and communication skills. All of these authors stress the difficult but necessary task of balancing the need to provide individualized educational programs for children with disabilities with the need for the integration of children with disabilities into regular early childhood education settings.

Not all parents, interventionists, administrators, legislators, or tax payers support the integration of children with disabilities into community-based programs. Some individuals are opposed to integration at the conceptual level (e.g., they may feel that children who are developmentally delayed should be protected from unfair comparisons and competition, or from the unthinking social snubs of other children). Other individuals may support integration philosophically but resist it because of real or perceived practical problems (e.g., they may fear that children with disabilities will not receive adequate attention from trained personnel).

Given the reality of philosophical and practical differences, can the field of early intervention offer integrated programs as the only option for children, families, and professionals? Some advocates of integration appear to want to limit options by saying that all placements for children with disabilities must be in regular early childhood education environments or settings (Salisbury, 1991). Although strong supporters of integration, we believe that such a singular position violates two important principles.

First, this country is dedicated to allowing each individual freedom of choice whenever possible. There may be parents, caregivers, and professionals who sincerely believe that attending specialized programs is in a child's best interest. It may well be that until the quality of care and instruction in integrated community settings is improved, this judgment will remain common. Second, the passage of PL 99-457, and its recent reauthorization in PL 102-119, strongly support the involvement of parents in the assessment and treatment of their children with disabilities. Genuine parental involvement requires participation in decisionmaking concerning their child. If professionals support the concept of parents as partners, then parents must be allowed to weigh the options and decide which is the best course of action for their child and family. After examining options and information, some parents may choose participation in a segregated program for their child. Professionals must respect such decisions.

These two principles, freedom of choice and parental decisionmaking, demand that, at least for now, community programs should offer several alternatives for children with disabilities. Parents and professionals, in partnership, should be permitted to determine the program option that they believe is best suited to the child's needs and the family's goals and values. In many communities that may mean that integrated programs will have to be made available for the first time.

As heartily as we endorse integrated programs, we more strongly support parent and professional choice. No single program or approach is appropriate or functional for *all* children, parents, and professionals who hold an array of different values and perspectives. We also strongly suggest that the program development and research conducted on the topic of integration during the decade of the 1990s will become increasingly persuasive as to the benefits of integration to all involved. We predict that, given choice and the opportunity to explore options, the majority of professionals and parents in the 21st century will choose to become participants in quality early intervention programs that serve children with and without disabilities together, and equally well.

IMPLEMENTATION

Implementation is a theme addressed repeatedly throughout this volume, with emphasis placed on moving from research findings to application. A review of the wide array of investigations discussed in this volume leads us to the conclusions that the emphasis in research on integration is shifting and that there is increased sophistication in the empirical work.

The initial focus of research on integration was primarily directed at determining its effectiveness. Investigators and consumers first wanted to know if children with and without disabilities could be successfully served in the same program. The early work (e.g., Bricker & Bricker, 1971) reflected the common concern that young normal children might be negatively affected (e.g., develop bizarre behavior, experience slower developmental progress) by their association with children with disabilities. There was also concern about the effects of integration on the child with disabilities. Was the overall progress of these children accelerated, or were the effects negative?

At this point, researchers seem to have tentative answers to both of these questions. Several studies have shown that typically developing children tend to make developmental progress that is equivalent to that of peers who are enrolled in high-quality early childhood special education programs (Bricker, Bruder, & Bailey, 1982; Hoyson, Jamieson, & Strain, 1984; Odom, DeKlyen, & Jenkins, 1984); integrated placements do not seem to harm or limit the development of nondisabled children. For children with disabilities, it appears

that, at a minimum, they tend to make developmental progress that is equivalent to children with disabilities in special education settings (Lamorey & Bricker, chap. 13, this volume; Odom & McEvoy, 1988), and in some cases their developmental progress may exceed expected rates (Hoyson et al., 1984). However, there is enough contrary evidence (Cole, Mills, Dale, & Jenkins, 1991; Cooke, Ruskus, Apolloni, & Peck, 1981; Fewell & Oelwin, 1990) to suggest that the developmental progress of children with disabilities in mainstreamed settings should be closely monitored.

Currently, most of the helpful contemporary investigative work is not focused on examining the effects of integration, but rather on discovering ways to make integrated programs more beneficial for children with and without disabilities and their families. Federal and state regulations advocate most inclusive placement for children with disabilities, and this governmental position, in large measure, makes the effectiveness controversy irrelevant. To move forward, professionals need to concentrate on discovering how to make integration more beneficial.

A second trend in the investigative work on integration is the increasing degree of sophistication of the research. Again, the more helpful work has moved from pre–post evaluations to single-subject analysis (e.g., Peck, Killen, & Baumgart, 1989), comparative designs in which children are carefully matched (e.g., Jenkins, Odom, & Speltz, 1989), and the use of different methodologies (e.g., Peck, Hayden, Wandschneider, Peterson, & Richarz, 1989).

The shift in the types of questions being posed and the increased sophistication with which answers to those questions are being sought should yield important new findings. These new outcomes will not only direct research for the new century but will also do much to frame intervention efforts into more palatable and productive outcomes for children and families.

CRITICAL CONTEXT VARIABLES

The third set of issues or dilemmas identified in the contributors' analysis of research outcomes centers on the general need to refocus the research on integration efforts. Bronfenbrenner's (1977) and other similar models that explain the interactive effects between children and their physical and social environments illustrate the critical need to observe behavioral phenomena in the situations and under the conditions in which they usually occur. Dividing complex interactive variables into fragments for analysis often yields incomplete, and sometimes misleading, results. For example, evaluating the effects of an integrated program on children's IQ scores may reveal little of the dynamics and effects that may reverberate throughout the entire program (e.g., among parents, staff, community, and children, to mention but a few).

Few scientists or practitioners would argue with the point raised above, and yet there are at least three problems that arise when attempting to conduct research and program evaluation that includes all potentially relevant variables. First, all the potentially relevant variables are seldom identified. For example, there may be variables within the family, such as siblings' reactions to the program, that affect a child's success in mainstreamed settings (Winton, chap. 4, this volume) without the knowledge of the researchers. The quality of the early childhood education setting undoubtedly affects children with disabilities, but the nature of the eco-behavioral relationships within those set-

tings is largely unknown. These and other potentially relevant variables may need to be identified, described, and observed.

A second problem is that the importance or relevance of specific variables may be differentially effected by various other factors. Observing a sibling's reactions to the program may be important for some families, but not for others. The development of social skills may be critical if children do not have such skills, but may be unimportant if children possess the skills but simply do not use them. In the latter case, the environment would need to be arranged to simply elicit, rather than teach, the skills.

A third problem is related to cost of conducting multifaceted and multivariate research. Assessing, observing, tracking, and evaluating an array of contextual variables (e.g., child change in several developmental areas, parent and family reactions, professionals' comfort and satisfaction) require large subject pools and are expensive endeavors. The current funding levels for research projects do not allow for such comprehensive examinations of the effects of mainstreamed programs. The clear exception to this point is the funding provided by the U.S. Department of Education for Early Childhood Research Institutes, one of which is devoted to mainstreaming and integration.

What can we hope for in the next century? Reality requires limits, but the field of early intervention, and researchers in particular, should make two changes. First, professionals need to undertake investigations that are more comprehensive. It is clearly not possible to track all potentially relevant variables but researchers should be able to expand their vision beyond studying outcomes on one variable. In addition, systems for examining potentially important context variables should be developed. A second important step is to work toward agreement on which variables will yield the most useful information. For example, investigators and interventionists may be able to agree that the social interactions between children in integrated settings is an important target that should be included as a dependent measure in most studies. There may be a range of other variables that should be included in order to expand the knowledge and common data base of the field. Such agreements may not solve the dilemma of measuring all potentially important variables, but it may lead toward the identification of the most critical contextual variables.

SUMMARY

As we move toward the 21st century, early intervention personnel have many issues to address and problems to solve if quality services are to be delivered to eligible children and their families. One of the major issues, addressed in this book, is the integration of children with disabilities into community-based programs.

How well are we doing? One's conclusion depends on the benchmark chosen to measure progress. If one compares the information presented in this volume with that presented in the 1978 Guralnick volume, the answer is that we are doing well. If, however, the benchmark is the provision of high-quality services to all children with disabilities in integrated community-based programs, the answer is that there is still far to go.

Without doubt, a volume will appear at the beginning of the 21st century that will analyze the progress made toward the integration of young children with disabilities into community programs during the 1990s. If we are sensible and learn from our past, the analysis should record considerable positive progress. But if we fail to address the issues surrounding the dilemmas of competing values, implementation, and the complexity of the integration effort, we may find a 21st century analysis to be disappointing. Such a disappointment would be a serious blow to children with disabilities and their families, as well as to larger community efforts to develop tolerance and understanding for all persons.

REFERENCES

Bricker, D.D., Bruder, M.B., & Bailey, E. (1982). Developmental integration of preschool children. *Analysis and Intervention in Developmental Disabilities, 2,* 207–222.

Bricker, W., & Bricker, D. (1971). Toddler research and intervention project report: Year 1. Nashville: *IMRID Behavioral Science Monographs,* No. 20. Institute on Mental Retardation and Intellectual Development, George Peabody College.

Bronfenbrenner, U. (1977). Toward an experimental ecology of human development. *American Psychologist, 32,* 513–536.

Cole, K.N., Mills, P.E., Dale, P.S., & Jenkins, J.R. (1991). Effects of preschool integration

for children with disabilities. *Exceptional Children, 58,* 36–46.

Cooke, T.P., Ruskus, J.A., Apolloni, T., & Peck, C.A. (1981). Handicapped preschool children in the mainstream: Background, outcomes, and clinical suggestions. *Topics in Early Childhood Special Education 1*(1), 73–83.

Education of the Handicapped Act Amendments of 1986, PL 99-457. (October 8, 1986). Title 20, U.S.C. 1400 et seq: *U.S. Statutes at Large, 100,* 1145–1177.

Fewell, R.F., & Oelwin, P.L. (1990). The relationship between time in integrated environments and developmental gains in young children with special needs. *Topics in Early*

Childhood Special Education, 10(2), 104–116.

Guralnick, M. (Ed.). (1978). *Early intervention and the integration of handicapped and non-handicapped children.* Baltimore: University Park Press.

Hoyson, M., Jamieson, B., & Strain, P.S. (1984). Individualized group instruction for normally developing and autistic-like children: The LEAP curriculum. *Journal of the Division for Early Childhood, 8,* 157–172.

Individuals with Disabilities Education Act Amendments of 1991, PL 102-119. (October 7, 1991). Title 20, U.S.C. 1400 et seq: *U.S. Statutes at Large, 105,* 587–608.

Jenkins, J.R., Odom, S.L., & Speltz, M.L. (1989). Effects of social integration of preschool children with handicaps. *Exceptional Children, 55,* 420–428.

Odom, S.L., DeKlyen, M., & Jenkins, J.R. (1984). Integrating handicapped and non-handicapped preschoolers: Developmental impact on the nonhandicapped children. *Exceptional Children, 51,* 41–49.

Odom, S.L., & McEvoy, M.A. (1988). Integration of young children with handicaps and normally developing children. In S.L. Odom & M.B. Karnes (Eds.), *Early intervention for infants and children with handicaps: An empirical base* (pp. 241–267). Baltimore: Paul H. Brookes Publishing Co.

Peck, C., Hayden, L., Wandschneider, M., Peterson, K., & Richarz, S. (1989). Development of integrated preschools: A qualitative inquiry into sources of resistance by parents, teachers, and administrators. *Journal of Early Intervention, 13,* 353–364.

Peck, C.A., Killen, C.C., & Baumgart, D. (1989). Increasing implementation of special instruction in mainstreamed preschools: Direct and generalized effects of nondirective consultation. *Journal of Applied Behavior Analysis, 22,* 197–210.

Salisbury, C.L. (1991). Mainstreaming during the early childhood years. *Exceptional Children, 58,* 146–155.

INDEX